CAMBRIDGE TE
HISTORY OF POLITI

ANTONIO GRAMSCI
Pre-Prison Writings

CAMBRIDGE TEXTS IN THE
HISTORY OF POLITICAL THOUGHT

Series editors
RAYMOND GEUSS
Lecturer in Social and Political Sciences, University of Cambridge
QUENTIN SKINNER
Professor of Political Science in the University of Cambridge

Cambridge Texts in the History of Political Thought is now firmly established as the major student textbook series in political theory. It aims to make available to students all the most important texts in the history of western political thought, from ancient Greece to the early twentieth century. All the familiar classic texts will be included but the series does at the same time seek to enlarge the conventional canon by incorporating an extensive range of less well-known works, many of them never before available in a modern English edition. Wherever possible, texts are published in complete and unabridged form, and translations are specially commissioned for the series. Each volume contains a critical introduction together with chronologies, biographical sketches, a guide to further reading and any necessary glossaries and textual apparatus. When completed, the series will aim to offer an outline of the entire evolution of western political thought.

For a list of titles published in the series, please see end of book.

ANTONIO GRAMSCI

Pre-Prison Writings

EDITED BY
RICHARD BELLAMY
Professor of Politics, University of East Anglia

TRANSLATED BY
VIRGINIA COX
Lecturer in Italian, University of Cambridge

CAMBRIDGE
UNIVERSITY PRESS

Published by the Press Syndicate of the University of Cambridge
The Pitt Building, Trumpington Street, Cambridge CB2 1RP
40 West 20th Street, New York, NY 10011–4211, USA
10 Stamford Road, Oakleigh, Melbourne 3166, Australia

First published 1994

Printed in Great Britain at the University Press, Cambridge

A catalogue record for this book is available from the British Library

Library of Congress cataloguing in publication data
Gramsci, Antonio, 1891–1937
[Selections. English. 1993]
Antonio Gramsci: pre-prison writings / edited by Richard Bellamy
: translated by Virginia Cox.
p.   cm. – (Cambridge texts in the history of political
thought)
Translated from Italian.
Includes bibliographical references and index.
ISBN 0 521 41143 2. – ISBN 0 521 42307 4 (pbk.)
1. Communism – Italy.   2. Communism.   3. Fascism – Italy.   4. Italy –
Politics and government – 1914–1945.   I. Bellamy, Richard (Richard
Paul)   II. Cox, Virginia.   III. Title.   IV. Series.
HX288.G69213   1993
335.43 – dc20   92–47069   CIP

ISBN 0 521 41143 2 hardback
ISBN 0 521 42307 4 paperback

WV

Contents

Contents

Contents

Acknowledgements

The editor would like to thank Virginia Cox for her good humour and tenacity in coping with Gramsci's prose and editorial deadlines and revisions, and David Forgacs, Stephen Gundle, Quentin Hoare and Mario Piccinini for supplying various bits of arcane information about Gramsci's life, times and occasionally obscure terminology. Darrow Schecter offered invaluable advice on the selection of articles and Martin Clark was exceedingly generous in letting me walk off with his vast Gramsci library for over a year and in putting up with incessant questioning about the minutiae of the Italian labour movement in the meantime. Finally, I am grateful to the series editors for their helpful comments on the introduction and editorial apparatus. Needless to say, the responsibility for all errors and remaining lacunae is mine.

Introduction

Gramsci's status as a canonical figure within the tradition of Western Marxism often has led to an overly schematic reading of his work. Gramsci has been credited with the formulation of a strategy for communist parties operating within the developed States of the West that was both revolutionary and democratic. As such, his ideas have appeared to offer a radical alternative to social democracy on the one hand and the autocratic party bureaucracies of the countries of 'actually existing socialism' on the other. This view drew support from and provided legitimacy for the Eurocommunist movement of the 1970s and early 1980s, especially its chief protagonist – the Italian Communist Party (PCI). The largest communist party outside the Soviet bloc, its historic links with Gramsci, who was promoted throughout this period as the PCI's chief ideological inspiration, greatly strengthened the credibility and prestige of the Euro-Gramscian thesis. However, in the aftermath of the collapse of Communism in Eastern Europe and the former Soviet Union, this thesis has lost its allure. Many if not most of the main proponents of Euro-communism have ended up disavowing Marxism altogether, with even the PCI abandoning its Communist past and transforming itself into the Party of the Democratic Left. Thus, paradoxically this attempt to stress Gramsci's relevance has ended up by seeming to deprive him of any contemporary interest at all.

Fortunately, this negative judgement need apply only to one school of interpretation of his thought. Whilst the Eurocommunist view of Gramsci contained a kernel of truth, it also distorted central aspects of his thinking. In spite of Gramsci's deep commitment to the unity

ix

of theory and practice, this reading of his writings divorced the first from the second and applied his ideas to events and movements which he neither knew nor could have anticipated. The original context of the crisis of liberal democracies at the end of the First World War, the Russian Revolution and the rise of Fascism was exchanged for the very different world that emerged from the Second World War. Above all, the distinctively Italian dimension of his ideas became lost from sight. There was always a certain incongruity about the fact that the supposed champion of a revised Marxism suited to the advanced economies and political systems of the West came from a peripheral region of one of the West's least industrialized nations and most fragile liberal democracies. One of the advantages of approaching Gramsci through the pre-prison writings rather than the *Prison Note-books* is that the original intent and frame of reference of his ideas are harder to avoid. For most of the key concepts of the *Notebooks* can be found in the early texts, as this collection amply demonstrates. In particular, the emphasis on what Gramsci came to call 'hegemony' or ideological power, which forms the most distinctive feature of his Marxism, figures implicitly throughout his analysis of the contemporary Italian State and his views on the organization of the fledgling Communist Party of Italy (PCd'I), as it was then known. Seen within this Italian context, however, such characteristic Gramscian themes as the relative autonomy of political from economic struggle, and the role of will and education in the formation of a revolutionary consciousness, take on a rather different significance from that attributed to them by much of the traditional scholarship. Instead of providing the basis for a Marxist strategy suited to advanced capitalism, they can be seen to refer to the rather different problems posed by a somewhat earlier stage of development of the modern nation State.

Born in Ales, Sardinia on 22 January 1891, Gramsci was able to reflect on the failings of the Italian State from an early age. Owing to its peripheral status, Sardinia shared the lot of southern Italy as an economically and politically marginalized region. Throughout his writings, Gramsci displayed a mixture of profound affection for the traditions and culture of his native region mixed with outrage against the injustices and chronic poverty that characterized the life of the majority of its inhabitants. However, Gramsci never fell into the sentimentalism that frequently marks provincial nationalism. A hunchback, probably as a result of contracting Pott's disease, he suffered from the local superstition towards any one or thing that was different, and often felt rejected as a consequence. He appreciated at first hand, therefore, the narrowmindedness that sometimes characterizes folk cultures. His political education began early when his father, a local government official, fell victim to the endemic corruption of Italian political life. Having aligned himself with the losing faction in the 1897 election, Francesco Gramsci was suspended from his post in the registrary office and subsequently charged with embezzling electoral funds and sentenced to five years' imprisonment. The financial difficulties this caused the Gramsci family forced the eleven-year-old Antonio temporarily to suspend his school studies and work in an office until, three years later, his parents could afford to send him to secondary school in the Sardinian capital of Cagliari. Here he lived with his elder brother Gennaro, who was an active member of the Italian Socialist Party (PSI) and introduced Antonio to socialist literature and circles. At this time, however, Sardinianism was more important to him than socialism and the most significant influences on him were the writers grouped around the Florentine journal *La Voce*.

The editor of this remarkable review, Giuseppe Prezzolini, had gathered together a highly diverse set of contributors linked largely by a common dissatisfaction with contemporary Italy. They felt Italian unification had been doubly incomplete. First, there were the cultural and economic divisions existing between both the different regions of the peninsula, particularly the developing north and the underdeveloped south, and the educated classes and the unschooled masses. Second, and largely as a result of these differences, there was the tension between 'legal' Italy, the set of liberal institutions resulting from political unification, and 'real' Italy, the fragmented social reality of divergent regional traditions, economic attainment and polarized classes. Both these problems were epitomized in the 'southern question', to which (as Gramsci later recalled) *La Voce* devoted a special issue on 16 March 1911. Unification was held to have subordinated the south politically, economically and culturally to the needs of the north in ways that had merely served to exacerbate the region's relative backwardness and suppress its distinctiveness. In particular, they argued that the centralized political system of the new State had given rise to a 'transformist' politics based on patronage and compromise between local elites and clienteles. These groups effectively blocked any reform of the social and economic inequities from which they derived their power and hindered the involvement of the masses in political life, who vented their frustration in widespread lawlessness and brigandage.

The chief goal of the *vociani* was to integrate Italy socially and culturally as well as politically in ways that built upon rather than suffocated the nation's regional strengths and popular energies. Their views of this common aspiration differed widely, however. Although Prezzolini had recently come under the influence of the Italian idealist philosopher Benedetto Croce, who also helped the journal financially, the contributors were an eclectic bunch, ranging from the elitist proto-futurism of Giovanni Papini to the democratic positivism and free trade arguments of the southern specialist Gaetano Salvemini. Much of this eclecticism fed into Gramsci's later Marxism and is particularly in evidence in the articles in the first section of this selection. He took from Prezzolini an appreciation of the political and educative role of culture, from Croce a concern with the role of human will in the fashioning of history, from Papini a certain iconoclasm, and from Salvemini a respect for the detailed empirical analysis of problems and a profound understanding of the links between the transformist political system, the import tariffs protecting certain landed and industrial interests, and the social and economic decline of the south. From the movement as a whole, he took the desire to build a new State commanding the active allegiance of all sections of Italian society.

Although Gramsci was sympathetic to socialism, it took some time before he incorporated these Vocean elements into a distinctively Marxist and socialist perspective. In 1911 he won a scholarship to the University of Turin. At first he was alienated by this proletarian city, identifying it with the industrial north's subjugation of the predominantly agrarian south. Angelo Tasca and his fellow Sardinian Palmiro Togliatti, who were also students in Turin and through whose friendship he became active in the PSI, both described him as still being more of a Sardinian nationalist than a socialist at this time. His Sardinianism even carried into his studies, as Gramsci became interested in the prospect of working on Sard dialects with the pioneering socio-linguist Matteo Bartoli. Significantly, he overcame this slight antipathy to socialism only when, returning to Sardinia for the elections of 1913, he began to see how socialist politics was capable of linking the concerns of northern workers and southern peasants. In the first elections held under near universal franchise, the local landowners had been unable to secure their vote without the collaboration of the mainland power brokers. Gramsci quickly appreciated that the socialists offered the most effective counter to this strategy and participated actively in the PSI campaign, signing the pro-south anti-protectionist petition that they supported and that was later published in *La Voce*. On returning to Turin, he joined the Party.

His newly acquired socialist principles mixed with rather than replaced his earlier Vocean allegiances. Moreover, the two were not entirely compatible. For example, one of his first initiatives within the local Party was to sponsor the adoption of Gaetano Salvemini, a frequent critic of the PSI, as a parliamentary candidate for one of the Turin electoral districts as an act of solidarity between the northern proletariat and the southern peasants. Salvemini turned down the offer, so the plan was never attempted, but it would almost certainly have generated a conflict with the national Party had it been implemented. The potential tension between Gramsci's Voceanism and his socialism is similarly evident in the first article he published in a national newspaper, on 'An Active and Functional Neutrality'. The PSI had been one of the few socialist parties successfully to maintain the Second International's opposition to worker participation in an 'imperialist' war after the outbreak of hostilities in 1914. Gramsci's piece developed out of an editorial in the Party journal *Avanti!* by Mussolini, then a leader of the maximalist wing of the PSI, who had cast the case for intervention in a new revolutionary light. Responding to the rebuttal of this argument by his comrade Angelo Tasca, Gramsci contended that 'absolute neutrality' risked degenerating into mere passivity. Such an attitude could not satisfy 'revolutionaries who conceive of history as the creation of their own spirit made up of an uninterrupted series of lightning raids on the other active and passive forces in society, in an attempt to create the most favourable conditions possible for the final raid (the revolution)' (p. 5). Now that the war was engaged, the Party had to be ready to exploit the revolutionary possibilities that might present themselves in this new situation. Like Mussolini, Gramsci shrewdly recognized the weakening of the liberal State and opportunities for mass mobilization likely to arise from intervention.

A number of points of Gramsci's analysis are worth underlining, for they reveal how early on some of the key themes of his thought emerged. First, the article illustrates Gramsci's independence of mind. 'Interventionism' was one of the major heresies of the PSI, particularly amongst those on the left of the Party, and Mussolini was ultimately expelled for this reason. It was characteristic of Gramsci that he did not falter from holding unpopular positions. Second, equally heretical was his emphasis on the role of ideas and the human will – a view that led to him being accused of 'voluntarism' at the 1917 PSI conference in Florence. The revolutionary wing of the Party typically adopted a more 'orthodox' Marxism that stressed the internal dynamics of the historical process and the necessary collapse of capitalism under its own contradictions. Gramsci, in contrast, argued that such vulgar versions of historical materialism encouraged an attitude of submission to the prevailing economic and political system, noting that reformists also generally embraced a vulgar positivism. Third, and as a corollary of his more idealist Marxism, he stressed the need to educate and organize the collective will of the masses, preparing them for the coming revolution through the dissemination of new values that gave them a critical purchase on their current situation and galvanized them to action. Fourth, he linked the achievement of the revolutionary goal with the creation of a new type of State. Indeed, he described the Party as 'a State *in potentia* which is gradually maturing; a rival to the bourgeois State, which is seeking, through its daily struggle with this enemy, and through the development of its own internal dialectic, to create the organs it needs to overcome and absorb its opponent' (p. 4). Even at this early stage, Gramsci had begun to formulate what was to become one of his most distinctive doctrines – the strategy of preparing for the revolutionary seizure of power by building a counter-State within the structures of civil society via a plethora of Party run organizations. Finally, although Gramsci embraced the cause of international socialism, he insisted that the PSI must remain at present relatively 'autonomous'. In the medium term, the Party had to concentrate on those special circumstances of the Italian situation that determined its '*particular, national* characteristics' and committed the Party 'to assuming a specific function, a particular responsibility in Italian life' (p. 4). This insistence on the 'Italian road to socialism' followed on from his undogmatic Marxism, which rejected the schematic generalizations of orthodox Marxists and allowed him to comprehend the peculiarities of the

Italian State. Gramsci elaborated all these points as his thought matured.

Ill-health and growing political commitments led Gramsci to break off his studies in 1915, and he began to devote himself full time to journalism for the socialist press – one of the traditional routes to advancement within the PSI. His writing was incredibly varied, ranging from drama and general cultural criticism to commentary on daily local, national and international events. The outbreak of the Russian revolution in February 1917 gave a tremendous stimulus to his thinking. He regarded it as confirming his anti-deterministic interpretation of Marxism, revealing the 'real and undying Marxist thought' to be that which 'continues the tradition of German and Italian idealism' and was uncontaminated 'by positivist and naturalist incrustations' that often sullied Marx's own writings. For it was 'a revolution against Karl Marx's *Capital*', that showed 'the canons of historical materialism are not as iron-clad as . . . it has been thought' (p. 40). Far from occurring as part of the natural process of social evolution, as the positivist interpreters of Marx claimed it would, he argued that the revolution had sprung from the organization of the people's will and social consciousness to a sufficient level to be able to take advantage of the revolutionary opportunity when it had arisen. It is important to note that Gramsci's position was not quite so voluntarist as it first appears. He was not denying that revolution could occur only under the right structural conditions, merely that these in themselves were insufficient to bring about social and political change. For revolution to occur, it was necessary both to know these conditions and to have the capacity to exploit their potential. Economic facts constrained but did not mechanically determine politics; it was necessary for people 'to understand . . . and to assess them, and to control them with their will, until this collective will becomes the driving force of the economy, the force which shapes reality itself' (p. 40).

The education and cultural preparation of the proletariat played a correspondingly central role in Gramsci's thinking. As he put it in a famous article on 'Socialism and Culture', 'every revolution has been preceded by a long process of intense critical activity, of new cultural insight and the spread of ideas through groups of men initially resistant to them' (p. 10). The State education system served the mass of people extremely badly, with Italy having some of the highest illiteracy rates in Europe – rising to as much as 70 per cent in parts of the south. However, Gramsci was not greatly impressed by the attempts of the labour movement to remedy this through organizations such as the Popular Universities. He believed that these bodies failed to relate the knowledge they imparted to the needs and practical concerns of the workers. Culture, in Gramsci's view, entailed much more than the mere acquisition of esoteric information. It involved self-knowledge and with it self-mastery: 'the attainment of a higher awareness, through which we can come to understand our value and place within history, our proper function in life, our rights and duties' (pp. 9–10). In accord with his reinterpretation of Marxism, Gramsci saw education as enabling the masses to take conscious control of the forces moulding their lives and to make the most of the emancipatory potential of existing material conditions. Once again, however, the superficially voluntarist and libertarian nature of this argument needs qualifying. For Gramsci firmly believed the Marxian thesis that the liberation of the individual could come about only with the emancipation of the proletariat and with it the whole of humanity through the overthrow of capitalism and the creation of a communist society. Thus, he insisted that revolution would be achieved only by the individual's overcoming his or her rebelliousness and joining the collective will of the mass movement of the proletariat. Hence, he stressed discipline as being the necessary complement to freedom, going so far in his later writings as to treat the Party line as a moral imperative that all workers had a categorical duty to follow.

In spite of these authoritarian implications, Gramsci's linking of education to *self*-emancipation sought to guard against the intellectual and political elitism into which even the socialist intelligentsia had a tendency to fall. Intellectuals had to avoid adopting a 'traditional' paternalistic attitude and seek to act 'organically' and aid the ordinary person's self-awareness of his or her situation by teaching people to teach themselves. He even regarded attempts to popularize ideas by expressing them in a simplified form as condescending. In the article on 'Why We Need a Cultural Association' and the letter to Lombardo Radice about his short-lived 'Club of Moral Life', Gramsci outlined the sort of educational organization he had in mind. History played a vital role in his programme, since he maintained that an understanding of the cultural and social influences that form us was at the heart of the self-understanding necessary for our gaining control over our lives. The historicist idealism of Croce and the 'actualist' doctrine of Gentile, whose pedagogical theories were particularly well developed, greatly influenced Gramsci's ideas in this respect, and he urged his comrades to study their writings and those of their followers. Although he had an interest in certain aspects of the contemporary *avant-garde*, being an early enthusiast for the plays and stories of the Sicilian writer Pirandello and sympathizing with some of the experimental elements of the Soviet *Prolekult* movement, many of his favourite authors and not a few of his views – such as his emphasis on the 'classics' and the benefits of 'sweating at' grammar – would be considered traditionalist now. However, it needs to be remembered that the writers he admired, such as the great literary historian and philosopher respectively of the late nineteenth century, Franceso De Sanctis and Bertrando Spaventa, and their contemporary followers and continuers, Croce and Gentile, were in the process of *constructing* a cultural tradition, rather than merely defending an existing canon. Although Croce later joined the liberal and Gentile the Fascist establishment, at this time they were outspoken critics of the low level of contemporary Italian cultural life, which they, like the *vociani*, related to the corruption of the Italian political system. Gramsci shared their contempt, merely radicalizing their analysis.

Vocean themes continued to shape his socialism after the war and the Russian revolution. The pieces on 'Cocaine' and 'Football and Scopone', for example, not only show his skill as a journalist in drawing out the wider significance of everyday occurrences and practices, but also a Vocean desire to *épater les bourgeois* manifested in his almost puritanical loathing for what he regarded as the degeneracy of the Italian bourgeoisie and the society they had created. His more detailed discussions of Italian politics, such as 'Class Intransigence and Italian History', 'Three Principles and Three Kinds of Political Order' and 'Men, Ideas, Newspapers and Money', show the influence of Salvemini in particular, with Gramsci even espousing the arguments of free market economists such as Luigi Einaudi and Vilfredo Pareto who saw protectionism as the chief source of the nation's failure to evolve into a fully fledged parliamentary democracy. Like them, he believed the Italian State reflected an admixture of capitalist and quasi-feudal social and economic relations, the dire effects of which were summed up in the south's economic dependence on the north and the political dependence of northern elites on the southern clienteles. To a large extent, therefore, Gramsci still saw himself as participating in the general project of the anti-Giolittian intellectuals of renewing Italy via a new cultural identity suited to its present social and political conditions, and as broadening that enterprise to include and promote the interests and aspirations of the working class. However, unlike them, he believed that only socialism could provide this new culture, for it was 'the one ideal which unites the Italian people'. Moreover, as 'the tangible representation of this unity, of this new consciousness, of this new world', the task of building this new order fell to the Socialist Party and its supporters (p. 29).

The weekly journal *L'Ordine Nuovo* that Gramsci founded with Umberto Terracini, Tasca and Togliatti in May 1919 was initially a continuation of this policy of cultural politics, similar in style to an earlier attempt of Gramsci's to create a socialist *La Voce* in the single issue *La Città Futura*. However, it soon became something far more important in Gramsci's eyes, namely the intellectual voice of a revolutionary movement – the Factory Councils that grew up in Turin over the next few months. The councils evolved out of the 'internal commissions' that had emerged within a number of engineering and metal-working factories around 1906 and become widespread during the war. Although function and composition varied, they were essentially a small elected body of workers designed to handle everyday problems of discipline and arbitration and to implement national wage agreements at a local level. At this stage, they were seen as part of the national union machinery, and in an agreement between the metal-workers' union FIOM and the employers' federation in Turin, they became incorporated into the official labour relations mechanism there in April 1919. However, the Russian revolution led many to interpret them in a different light, seeing them as an Italian equivalent of the soviets. Although in practice Lenin's position on the soviets was ambiguous, given that they were often dominated by the Bolsheviks' rivals, the Socialist-Revolutionaries and Mensheviks, he hailed them in *State and Revolution* and other writings as a model of the new socialist politics and as contemporary equivalents to the form of democratic organization Marx had praised in his analysis of the Paris Commune. As a result, Gramsci, in common with most other foreign sympathizers, saw the soviets as the most distinctive feature of the Russian revolution. They were the means whereby the Bolsheviks had not merely seized power but altered its nature by creating a new type of political organization. In Gramsci's eyes, the soviets, or rather their native counterparts – the Factory Councils – offered a model for the reconstruction of the Italian State.

As he related in the article 'The Programme of *L'Ordine Nuovo*', the paper switched from being 'a review of abstract culture' to become 'the journal of the Factory Councils' in June 1919, following 'an editorial *coup d'état*' in which Togliatti and Gramsci ousted Tasca (p. 181). The need for this *coup* resulted in large part from Tasca's close links to the trade unions, which had put up most of the original finance. For reasons explained below, the unions regarded the development of the Councils into semi-autonomous bodies with some ambivalence. Gramsci, in contrast, viewed this movement away from the traditional labour organizations as marking a significant departure on the part of the workers from reformist to revolutionary action. He therefore aimed to encourage it. Drawing on his theory of the role of education and culture, he argued that rather than seeking to hand down 'cold, intellectual artefacts', the educational and cultural task of the journal must now be to help the workers articulate and build on their 'feelings, desires and passions', revealing the dramatic events in which they were engaged 'as moments in a process of inner liberation and self-expression on the part of the working class' (p. 181).

Initially, Gramsci enjoyed great success. The 'two red years' of 1919–20 resulting from the economic crisis and political upheaval after the First World War, together with the expectations aroused by the Russian revolution, created an environment in which it was widely felt that revolution was just around the corner. By the end of 1919 his ideas had been adopted by the Turin branch of FIOM and the local section of the PSI and the circulation of *L'Ordine Nuovo* had reached 6,000 copies. The formation of Factory Councils frightened the employers into a lock-out in March 1920, provoking a general strike in April which explicitly aimed at political control of industry and involved over 200,000 workers. Ultimately a failure due to concerted action by employers and the government, the strike nevertheless heightened the prestige of the *L'Ordine Nuovo* group – particularly as the PSI and CGL refused to back it. In September 1920 a breakdown in negotiations over a new national wage in the engineering industry led to the occupation of factories throughout Northern Italy. The Prime Minister, Giolitti, decided to play a waiting game and did not intervene. Meanwhile, the factories carried on production as the workers began an experiment in self-management based around the Councils. Gramsci's theory of workers' democracy was part response and part attempt to shape these events.

Gramsci looked on the Councils not only as a means for workers' control of industry, but as the basic unit of a totally new form of democratic State that reflected the interests and activities of the true producers of economic wealth, the proletariat. Linking his account in characteristic fashion to the unification of Italy, he argued that the industrial system of Turin and Piedmont would act as the model and agent of the proletarian revolution in much the same way as it had for the bourgeois Risorgimento (p. 138). Ultimately, however, the Councils would serve to unify humanity as a whole. In Gramsci's eyes, the Councils overcame the divisions of the bourgeois State between capital and labour, giving the workers the responsibility and self-discipline to work with each other for the benefit of all rather than just for themselves. He believed participation within them would have an educative function, making the worker aware of his or her station and its duties within the organization of production as a whole. He envisaged the Councils as forming part of a whole network of similar bodies feeding into territorially based ward, urban and regional Councils including delegates from all crafts and workplaces and connecting up with a parallel system for peasants and other rural workers. In this way, every stage of the production process would be connected within a single global political and economic system. 'English *coal* will merge with Russian *oil*, Siberian *grain* with Sicilian *sulphur*, *rice* from Vercelli with *wood* from Styria . . . in a single organism, governed by an international administration which supervises the wealth of the whole world in the name of the whole of humanity.' For Gramsci, therefore, the Factory Council constituted merely 'the first step in a historical process which will culminate in the Communist International, no longer as a political organization of the revolutionary proletariat but as a reorganization of the world economy and the whole human community, both on a national and a world level' (p. 167).

The role of the Party and the unions within this set-up was far from clear. Gramsci argued that they had both 'grown up on the terrain of bourgeois democracy', and although they led the working class within this system 'they do not supersede the bourgeois State' (p. 164). The Councils, in contrast, had developed on the revolution-

ary terrain of the factories where class struggle was engaged in earnest
and where, as we have seen, Gramsci believed a new form of proletarian State was in the process of formation. The Councils would
revolutionize the Party and unions rather than the other way around,
therefore, the latter being necessary only in the transitional phase
when the Councils were still operating within the bourgeois system.
Consequently, he maintained that the Party and unions 'should not
project themselves as tutors or as ready-made structures for this new
institution'. Instead, 'they should project themselves as the conscious
agents of its liberation from the constraining forces concentrated in
the bourgeois State. They should set themselves the task of organizing the general (political) external conditions in which the process of
the revolution can move forward at the maximum possible rate and
the liberated productive forces extend themselves to the full' (p. 167).
Needless to say, neither the reformists in the CGL, nor the absten-
tionists or the maximalists in the PSI gathered around Bordiga and
Serrati respectively, were very pleased with the subordinate position
Gramsci had allotted them. Once again he found himself accused of
syndicalism, although he strongly denied the charge.

Gramsci's somewhat utopian vision of the new order involved a
number of tensions. A radical model of bottom-up democracy, it was
nevertheless hierarchically organized and the relationship between
the different levels was never fully clarified. Gramsci implied, for
example, that the Councils and their derivative structures could be
organs both of worker self-management and a mechanism for admin-
istering a unified economic plan, but he did not explain how they
could effectively be both at the same time. A similar difficulty arose
in his view of the relationship between the Party and the Councils.
On the one hand, he thought the Councils had to feed into the Party
in an almost spontaneous fashion. He criticized the German SPD,
for example, for creating tame Councils 'from above'. On the other
hand, he regarded the existence of a strongly disciplined Communist
Party as indispensable during the transitional period of the 'dictatorship of the proletariat', although he believed the Party had to
win control over the Councils by its 'prestige' rather than by seeking
directly to supplant them. Even the proletarian army, necessary for
the final seizure of power, was to emerge fully formed out of the
Councils, with every factory supplying 'one or more regiments ...
with its own NCOs, its own liaison services, its own officer corps

and general staff' (p. 99). Here too, he appears to have believed that the mere fact of delegation resolved the tension between liberty and control within his theory, removing any authoritarian element from the discipline of the officers.

The coherence of Gramsci's position rested largely on the holistic ontology that underpins most 'organic' theories of the State. He assumed, in other words, that within communist society the different activities of the productive process, which he came close to identifying with the entire life of the community, would be inherently complementary and harmonious. Whilst Gramsci derived much of this view from Marxist sources, particularly Lenin's ideas on 'dual power' and Rosa Luxemburg's conciliar communism, his organicism was also influenced by the 'ethical State' tradition of the Italian neo-Hegelians, especially Gentile, and by the Italian syndicalists, both of which ultimately fed into Fascist corporatist doctrines. The prime inspiration for Gramsci's doctrine, however, was the new forms of factory organization. The Fiat works had introduced the innovatory 'scientific' management techniques and assembly line production methods pioneered by F. W. Taylor and Henry Ford in the United States. Gramsci never unequivocally endorsed these procedures, but he was clearly fascinated by them and published a series of articles supportive of 'Taylorism' in *L'Ordine Nuovo*. Like many other Marxists of the period, he saw them as maximizing and simplifying industrial production and disciplining the workforce in ways which made the system largely self-regulating, thereby paving the way for workers' control of industry. Unlike the young Lukacs or later Hegelian Marxists, he remained relatively oblivious to the alienating and reifying aspects of modern technology. He seems to have been more concerned with overcoming anomie by having the worker assimilate the norms he believed, in quasi-Durkheimian fashion, to be inherent to the integrated work processes of industrial production.

As Gramsci insisted in the *Prison Notebooks*, his organicism was 'progressive' in conception rather than 'regressive', like the Fascist versions, because he saw little need to impose this order from without. The Party and intellectuals were merely to facilitate its emergence. This liberal interpretation of his theory proves plausible, however, only if we accept Gramsci's contention that the new order would generate its own objective morality, and that this ethic would be capable of rationally co-ordinating the self-realization of individuals in a mutually enhancing way. Unfortunately, the empirical evidence suggests otherwise. Some human activities, such as playing in an orchestra or team games, do possess these characteristics, but not all. The economic focus of Gramsci's theory led him to pigeon-hole the individual according to his or her role within the productive process, with no account given of its relation to other aspects of human life. Yet, co-operative production based on an increased division of labour is more likely to diminish than to enhance human fulfilment, except in a very restricted sense. Gramsci tended to ignore this problem by associating the growth of freedom with greater productive efficiency. However, an increase in collective productivity does not necessarily entail any increase in the opportunities or autonomy of individual workers – a boring repetitive job remains such under any circumstances. Once outside the economic sphere, Gramsci's organic thesis runs into these sorts of difficulties even more frequently, since clashes between competing goals are likely to occur more often. Within a society of any complexity, allowing for a fair degree of individual diversity, the hypothesis that all human activities will prove naturally and rationally assimilable to a single moral framework becomes correspondingly less and less plausible. However, without this optimistic assumption Gramsci's Council theory risks requiring the totalitarian social engineering of which organic conceptions of the State are traditionally accused.

Unlike Lenin, Gramsci was saved the embarrassment of having to face up to these theoretical limitations of his scheme by never having to implement it. Giolitti wilily sought to defuse the tension brought about by the occupation by setting up a committee to study the problem and promising a Parliamentary bill on industrial democracy. These measures gave support to the reformists, whilst the various revolutionary factions remained in any case ambivalent about a movement they had neither initiated nor controlled. At a meeting in Milan held from 9 to 11 September, the CGL and PSI voted by 591,245 to 409,569 with 93,623 abstentions to restrict the action to gaining official recognition of union control in the plants. In spite of resistance to this policy by FIOM and the *L'Ordine Nuovo* group, the workers finally vacated the factories on 25–30 September and returned to working for their employers on the 4 October. Although Gramsci had come to realize that the restriction of the movement to Turin and the North rendered it too isolated to achieve the revolution, he was bitterly disappointed by the defeat and placed the blame squarely on the incapacity of the Party to take the initiative. He now shelved discussion of the future society for the more pressing task of organizing the revolutionary forces in the increasingly hostile atmosphere created by the rise of Fascism.

In retrospect, 1919–20 marked the highpoint of the revolutionary situation in Italy and was soon followed by the reactionary backlash, culminating in the Fascist seizure of power in 1922. In accounting for this setback, Gramsci was led to develop a far more complex account of the nature of the bourgeois State than many of his Marxist colleagues. The orthodox position, represented by Bordiga, regarded Fascism as a straightforward expression of the ruling capitalist class. Since bourgeois democracy was merely a fig leaf for capitalist oppression of the working class, its suppression and replacement by a Fascist regime simply signified an intensification of the class struggle brought on by the imminent collapse of capitalism. Gramsci, in contrast, sought to relate Fascism much more specifically to certain distinctive characteristics of the class structure, economy and political system of Italy. On this analysis, of which 'A Study of the Italian Situation' provides the most developed statement, Fascism was associated with States belonging to the capitalist periphery, such as Spain, Portugal and Italy. Such countries had relatively undeveloped and weak economies, and had therefore been disproportionately affected by the inter-war depression. They also possessed far fewer political resources than advanced capitalist nations such as Britain. Here 'the State apparatus is far more resistant than it is often possible to believe; and, at moments of crisis, it is far more capable of organizing forces loyal to the regime than the depth of the crisis might lead one to suppose' (p. 297). In typical peripheral nations, however, the political forces are less efficient, so that economic crises tended to lead immediately to a crisis of the State. Finally, he linked this weakness of peripheral State structures to the existence of 'a broad band of intermediate classes', composed of white-collar workers, small shop-keepers, small landowners etc., located 'between the proletariat and capitalism' (p. 298), itself a consequence of the low level of industrial development.

In Italy, these factors had been exacerbated by the regional concentration of what industry there was in the north and the failure of the bourgeoisie either to recruit mass support for liberalism or to achieve an ascendency over the rural landowners. The resulting politics of compromises and economic protectionism for vested industrial and agrarian interests, typified by Giolitti, had gradually disillusioned the petite bourgeoisie. Squeezed between large-scale capitalism and the proletariat, they had felt increasingly marginalized. Fascism was the expression of their frustration. As such, it was not as easily assimilable to the interests of the bourgeoisie as many Marxist analysts had supposed. So long as the fear of creeping proletarianization that motivated many of those in the Fascist movement vented itself in attacks on labour organizations, it was compatible with the interests of the large financial, industrial and landed groups. However, the petit bourgeois mass base of the Fascist movement felt equally threatened by these major groups, since it became clear that capitalist stabilization could only be achieved by policies, such as the concentration of capital, that were as inimical to them as they were to the workers. Thus, far from seeking to secure the bourgeois State, as some liberals initially hoped, Fascism aimed to replace it with a quite different kind of regime and to oust the established ruling class. There were 'two Fascisms', therefore, that of the movement itself and that of the big capitalists and landowners who sought to exploit it for their own ends. In the articles on Fascism translated in section three, Gramsci charts the unfolding tensions between these two aspects of Fascism as Mussolini was obliged to purge the Fascist Party of its original cadres and merge it with the existing structures and personnel of bourgeois class power in order to consolidate his regime. Gramsci came to believe that a prime task of the Communist Party had to be the exploitation of this tension in order to win the non-proletarian masses to the revolution.

Gramsci's views on the composition and function of the Communist Party evolved along with his understanding of Fascism. The Communist Party of Italy resulted from the secession from the PSI, at its Seventeenth Congress in Livorno in January 1921, of certain left-wing maximalists and the communist factions gathered around Bordiga and the *Ordine Nuovo* group. The split resulted from the growing disillusionment of these groups with the PSI's tepid support for revolutionary action and its failure to expel the reformists and implement the '21 points' required by the Comintern. However, it divided the Italian labour movement at a crucial time, considerably weakening its ability to respond to the rise of Fascism. By December 1921 the

Comintern was putting pressure on the PCd'I and PSI to patch up their differences and form a 'united front' at trade union and party level. Bordiga, the leader of the Party, found any collaboration with the Socialists anathema, and was supported in this stance by most of the membership, including Gramsci. Bordiga argued that the Fascist movement was a symptom of the crisis of capitalism and hence brought the revolutionary confrontation nearer. In this circumstance, the working class required decisive leadership from a vanguard party. He considered co-operation with a reformist PSI would inevitably sap the PCd'I's ability to provide such direction. Bordiga's position remained PCd'I policy until 1923, gaining official endorsement at the Party's Second Congress in Rome in March 1922, where his Rome Theses were passed by a large majority.

As we have seen, however, Gramsci came to adopt a subtler view of Fascism, and a new leading group, far more open to the Comintern united front policy, began to form around him and Togliatti. His stance was further strengthened by his period in Moscow as the PCd'I representative from June 1922 to December 1923, although he opposed the Comintern's tendency to dictate to the member parties without consideration of their particular national situation and refused moves to make him General Secretary instead of Bordiga. Nonetheless, on returning to Italy in 1924 after election as a deputy, he quickly assumed the Party leadership. He saw the crisis precipitated by the murder of the Socialist deputy Giacomo Matteotti in June as the culmination of the tension between the 'two Fascisms' and an opportunity that the Party had to exploit, if need be by joining with other opposition parties. He maintained that it was vital that the Party claim the peasants and the petite bourgeoisie from the Catholic Popular Party (PPI) and the Fascists, respectively. Drawing on Soviet discussions of the 'agrarian question' and the Comintern's call for the 'Bolshevization' of communist parties through the building up of cells, Gramsci sought to reorientate the PCd'I organization around the formation of 'worker and peasant committees' which would form the basis of a future network of Councils. Gramsci also continued to emphasize the importance of education. He advocated the creation of a Party School and insisted on the need for 'democratic intellectuals' to break the ideological hold of figures such as Giuseppe Fortunato and Croce. Although Gramsci was committed to a centralized Party structure, he considered it important to obtain the active consent of the membership through mass democratic organization. Consequently, he was alarmed by the increasingly bureaucratic imposition of Party discipline within the Soviet Union, voicing his doubts in the letter to Togliatti of October 1926. He steadily consolidated his own control of the PCd'I, however, and the Third Congress of the PCd'I of January 1926 approved the 'Lyons Theses' drawn up with Togliatti by 90.8 per cent, decisively defeating the Bordiga faction.

Essential to Gramsci's discussion of both Fascism and the Party was his recognition of the relative autonomy of the political and ideological power of the State from the economic structure. Although he would only explore the full implications of this thesis with the elaboration of his conception of hegemony in the *Prison Notebooks*, many of its main features are already present in his early journalism, and occasionally he even uses the term. In particular, he had already begun to distinguish the revolutionary strategies required in the developed States of advanced industrial Western countries, from those suited to the less complex States of peripheral Western nations such as Italy. He had also begun to contrast both with the tactics Lenin had been able to adopt in the even more fragile State system of Russia.

In this regard, it is important to note that the concept of hegemony or *gegemoniya* had a long history in the Russian labour movement going back to the writings of Plekhanov. Within this tradition it had been used to refer to the need to form a revolutionary awareness and political will amongst the proletariat that went beyond their narrow corporate interests, but it did not have the additional meaning Gramsci gave it to describe the mechanisms of ideological consensus within a developed political system. Lenin had adopted the term from the Russian Social-Democrats and it was employed in the external documents of the Third Communist International, from which source Gramsci almost certainly picked it up. However, the term also has an Italian lineage in the writings of the nineteenth-century philosopher Vincenzo Gioberti, who used it in an analogous manner to signify the 'moral primacy' one province within a national grouping might exert over others, a thesis he related to the unification of Italy by Piedmont. Moreover, the essential features of the concept were clearly present in Gramsci's early writings on the role of education and culture in the organization of a socialist consciousness. Characteristically, Gramsci assimilated the Russian–Comintern usage to the

Italian. Although he had yet to employ Vincenzo Cuoco's notion of 'passive revolution' to describe how the Italian bourgeoisie had come to rule Italy without gaining the consensual adherence of the population that only came through establishing a cultural and hegemonic ascendency, this thesis was implicit within his analysis of the contemporary Italian State. He believed that it was imperative that the proletariat did not repeat the liberals' mistakes. In promoting a second and truly revolutionary Risorgimento, it was necessary for the Communist Party to gather to it all the oppositional forces within the country. To achieve this goal, Bolshevik means had to be incorporated within the Giobertian end of achieving a national moral supremacy over the Italian people. Developing his argument in the essay 'Some Aspects of the Southern Question', he insisted that 'for the proletariat to become the ruling, the dominant class, it must succeed in creating a system of class alliances that allow it to mobilize the majority of the working population against capitalism and the bourgeois State' (p. 316). This entailed getting the allegiance of the peasants and petite bourgeoisie and counteracting the intellectual influence of the Church and liberal thinkers such as Croce.

On the evening of 8 November 1926 Gramsci was arrested in defiance of his immunity as an elected deputy. The prosecutor at his trial in May 1928 called for his imprisonment on the grounds that 'We must stop this brain from functioning for twenty years.' The phrase was to prove ironic. In the tradition of his hero Machiavelli, withdrawal from politics forced him to engage in continuous reflection upon it. Like Machiavelli, however, he was no abstract system builder and the thirty-three exercise books that make up the *Prison Notebooks* are the fruit of a decade as one of the principal actors in the political life of his country and the socialist movement. The prime virtue of this collection, therefore, lies in providing the appropriate practical and theoretical context for understanding his work. What emerges from these early writings is a Gramsci as much concerned with the creation of a modern nation State as with its overthrow, and who was particularly preoccupied with explaining the peculiarly illiberal and fragile nature of the bourgeois regime in Italy. As Eastern Europe attempts to rebuild itself in the aftermath of the fall of communism, it will be his analysis of peripheral capitalist states rather than his attempts to build a Communist Party that will continue to absorb our attention.

Bibliographical Note

Primary Works

Italian Editions of Gramsci's Pre-Prison Writings

A first edition of these writings was published in five volumes by Einaudi of Turin from 1954 to 1971. They appeared in the following order: *L'Ordine Nuovo: 1919–20* (1954); *Scritti giovanili: 1914–18* (1958); *Sotto la Mole: 1916–20* (1960); *Socialismo e fascismo. L'Ordine Nuovo: 1921–22* (1966); *La costruzione del Partito communista: 1923–26* (1971).

These volumes were later supplemented by new attributions and discoveries, many of which were included in an important selection *2000 pagine di Gramsci*, Vol. I *Nel tempo della lotta (1914–16)*, Vol. II *Lettere edite e inedite (1912–37)*, ed. G. Ferrata and Niccolo Gallo (Milan: Il Saggitore, 1964). A critical edition, also published by Einaudi and incorporating all the new material, is now in the process of being compiled. The following five volumes have appeared to date: *Cronache torinese: 1913–17*, ed. Sergio Caprioglio (1980); *La Città Futura: 1917–18*, ed. Sergio Caprioglio (1982); *Il nostro Marx: 1918–20*, ed. Sergio Caprioglio (1984); *L'Ordine Nuovo: 1919–20*, ed. Valentino Gerratana and Antonio Santucci (1987); *Lettere: 1908–26*, ed. Antonio Santucci (1992).

English Translations of Gramsci's Pre-Prison Writings

The most important selections can be found in two volumes published by Lawrence and Wishart of London, *Selections from Political*

Writings: 1910–20, ed. Q. Hoare, trans. J. Mathews (1977) and *Selections from Political Writings: 1921–6*, ed. and trans. Q. Hoare (1978). Another selection is *History, Philosophy and Culture in the Young Gramsci*, ed. P. Calvalcanti and P. Piccone (St Louis: Telos Press, 1975). A number of pre-prison pieces are also included in *The Modern Prince and other Writings*, ed. and trans. L. Marks (London: Lawrence and Wishart, 1957) and *An Antonio Gramsci Reader*, ed. D. Forgacs (London: Lawrence and Wishart, 1988). The present collection overlaps in some respects with all of these, but also includes material not found in any of them.

Secondary Works

Biographies

There are two biographical studies available in English: G. Fiori, *Antonio Gramsci: Life of a Revolutionary*, trans. T. Nairn (London: New Left Books, 1977), which gives a highly readable account of his life, and A. Davidson, *Antonio Gramsci: Towards an Intellectual Biography* (London: Merlin Press, 1977), which sketches in the intellectual and political background and also provides brief accounts of his major writings.

General

Most general accounts focus mainly on the *Prison Notebooks*, but include a briefer section dealing with the earlier writings. J. Joll, *Gramsci* (London: Fontana, 1977) provides a basic introduction to his ideas and political activity; W. Adamson, *Hegemony and Revolution: A Study of Antonio Gramsci's Political and Cultural Theory* (Berkeley: University of California Press, 1980) is good on the intellectual context; A. S. Sassoon, *Gramsci's Politics*, 2nd edn (London: Hutchinson, 1987) offers a useful if uncritical exegesis, especially of Gramsci's conception of the Party; D. Germino, *Antonio Gramsci: Architect of a New Politics* (Baton Rouge: Louisiana State University Press, 1990) verges at times on the hagiographical, but gives a detailed and up to date account of the pre-prison period. J. Femia, *Gramsci's Political Thought: Hegemony, Consciousness and the Revolutionary Process* (Oxford: Clarendon Press, 1981), although concerned with an analysis of the *Prison Notebooks*, frequently refers back to some of the earlier writings and is particularly valuable on the role of consciousness in Gramsci's theory; C. Buci-Glucksmann, *Gramsci and the State*, trans. D. Fernbach (London: Lawrence and Wishart, 1980) is a provocative and thorough if occasionally impenetrable study, somewhat dated by the anti-Althusserian polemics in which it is engaged.

More Specialist Studies

a Books

The following three collections of articles all contain some pieces relating to the early writings: J. A. Davis (ed.), *Gramsci and Italy's Passive Revolution* (London: Croom Helm, 1979), is a collection of historical essays exploring Gramsci's interpretation of Italian history; C. Mouffe (ed.), *Gramsci and Marxist Theory* (London: Routledge, 1979) contains a selection of French and Italian articles from the early 1970s; A. S. Sassoon (ed.), *Approaches to Gramsci* (London: Writers and Readers, 1982), is a selection of general and more specialized pieces on various aspects of Gramsci's life and works.

R. Bellamy, *Modern Italian Social Theory: Ideology and Politics from Pareto to the Present* (Cambridge: Polity, 1987), traces the Italian tradition of social theory and (in chapter 6) situates Gramsci's writings within it; R. Bellamy and D. Schecter, *Gramsci and the Italian State* (Manchester: Manchester University Press, 1993) offers a detailed analysis of the whole Gramscian corpus and its relationship to the Italian political tradition.

J. M. Cammett, *Antonio Gramsci and the Origins of Italian Communism* (Stanford; Stanford University Press, 1967) is a good historical account of Gramsci's activities in the labour movement before, during and after World War One, although now occasionally superseded by later research; P. Spriano, *The Occupation of the Factories*, trans. G. Williams (London: Pluto Press, 1975), is a narrative history of the movement; G. Williams, *Proletarian Order: Antonio Gramsci, Factory Councils and the Origins of Communism in Italy 1911–1921* (London: Pluto Press, 1975) is a more narrowly Marxist analysis of the same events; M. Clark, *Antonio Gramsci and the Revolution that Failed* (New Haven and London: Yale University Press, 1977), together with the University of London PhD on which it is based, is the classic historical study of the *biennio rosso* in Turin, which is especially interesting in its use of more recent sociological literature to discuss the issue of workers' control; D. Schecter, *Gramsci and the Theory of Industrial Democracy* (Aldershot: Avebury, 1991) offers a detailed analysis of the theoretical arguments Gramsci evolved out of the Factory Councils.

b   Articles

A. Davidson, 'The Varying Seasons of Gramsci Studies', *Political Studies*, XX (1972); J. Femia, 'The Gramsci Phenomenon: Some Reflections', *Political Studies*, XXVII (1979); C. Mouffe and A. S. Sassoon, 'Gramsci in France and Italy – A Review of the Literature', *Economy and Society*, VI (1977); and G. Eley, 'Reading Gramsci in English: Observations on the Reception of Gramsci in the English-Speaking World 1957–82', *European History Quarterly*, 14 (1984), offer reviews of the debates of the late 60s and the 70s.

P. Anderson, 'The Antinomies of Antonio Gramsci', *New Left Review*, 100 (1976–7) is a classic critique of Gramsci's views of State power and political strategy, which also contains useful information on the pre-history of the concept of hegemony in Russia; B. Lumely, 'Gramsci's Writings on the State and Hegemony', Occasional Paper No. 51, Centre for Contemporary Cultural Studies, University of Birmingham, 1977 is a partial response to Anderson, which usefully traces continuities in Gramsci's thought between the early and the later writings; R. Bellamy, 'Gramsci, Croce and the Italian Political Tradition', *History of Political Thought*, XI (1990) and D. Schecter, 'Gramsci, Gentile and the Theory of the Ethical State in Italy', *History of Political Thought*, IX (1990) develop themes touched on in the introduction; A. Davidson, 'Gramsci and Lenin 1917–22', *Socialist Register* 1974 (London: Merlin Press) and D. Schecter 'Two Views of the Revolution: Gramsci and Sorel, 1916–20', *History of European Ideas*, XII (1990) examine Gramsci's debts to Lenin and Sorel respectively.

Chronology

26 July. *L'Ordine Nuovo* publishes 'The Programme of the Communist Faction', which first appeared in Bordiga's *Il Soviet* as the manifesto of his communist abstentionist grouping.

November–December. Factory Council movement develops in Turin.

1920   13–24 April. General strike in Turin.

July–August. Breaks with Tasca over the function and autonomy of the Factory Councils *vis-à-vis* the unions. In a report on the Turin council movement sent to the Communist International (Comintern), advocates 'factory communist groups' as the base of a future Communist Party. The Second Congress of the Comintern sets conditions (the '21 points') for membership and the PSI is invited to expel its reformists. Lenin praises Gramsci's motion calling 'For a Renewal of the Socialist Party' against the objections of the Italian delegation.

September. The occupation of the factories occurs.

November. Participates at PSI congress in Imola, where the communist fraction is formed. The Turin edition of *Avanti!* assumes the masthead of *L'Ordine Nuovo*, which is transformed into a daily under Gramsci's direction.

1921   January. Gramsci and others found the Institute of Proletarian Culture, affiliated to the Soviet Prolekult. At the Seventeenth Congress of the PSI held in Livorno the communist fraction secedes and on 21 January creates the Communist Party of Italy (PCd'I).

December. Comintern launches its 'united front' policy for collaboration between Communists and Socialists at both Party and union level. Policy opposed by PCd'I.

1922   March. At Second Congress of PCd'I 'Rome Theses' criticizing the 'united front' passed by large majority. Gramsci designated PCd'I representative to Comintern and departs for the Soviet Union, not returning to Italy for two years. Taken ill in Moscow and spends several months in a sanatorium, where he meets his future wife Julia Schuct.

28 October. Mussolini seizes power with the 'March on Rome'.

November–December. Fourth Congress of Comintern deals with the 'Italian question' and recommends the fusion of PCd'I and PSI. Majority of PCd'I against this resolution but accept it out of discipline. However, the fusion never takes place.

1923 February. The Italian police arrest a number of the executive committee of the PCd'I.

April–June. Bordiga sends an appeal to Party comrades from prison criticizing the Comintern's decisions. Originally accepted by Togliatti and others, Gramsci refuses to sign. A new executive is chosen for the PCd'I by the Comintern and Bordiga resigns from the Central Committee. Gramsci communicates the Comintern's decision to publish a new workers' newspaper to PCd'I executive. Gramsci proposes the name *L'Unità*, and for the first time develops his thesis of the need for an alliance between the Northern proletariat and the Southern peasants.

November. The Comintern transfers him to Vienna to maintain links between PCd'I and other European Communist parties.

1924 February. Publication begins of *L'Unità* and a new fortnightly series of *L'Ordine Nuovo*. Writing from Vienna, Gramsci outlines to Togliatti and Terracini the need to create a new Party leadership around the positions of the Comintern.

April. Elected as deputy.

May. Protected by parliamentary immunity, he returns to Italy. He joins the executive of the PCd'I.

June. Following Matteotti's assassination by the Fascists, Gramsci participates in the meetings of the Aventine Secessionists.

August–September. Made General Secretary of PCd'I. Son Delio born. Comintern calls for 'Bolshevization' of Communist Parties, application of 'united front' policy, restructuration of Party on basis of cells, adoption of slogan 'workers' and peasants' government'.

November. Frustrated by the 'legalistic' position of the Aventine opposition, Gramsci leads PCd'I back to Parliament for new session.

1925   March. Returns to Moscow for meeting of Comintern Executive.

16 May. Speaks in Parliament for first and only time, against Fascist legislation aimed at outlawing secret societies.

June–August. Sets in train the 'Bolshevization' of the Party desired by the Comintern and negotiates the dissolution of the 'Committee of Agreement Between Components of the Left' gathered around Bordiga.

1926   January. Third Congress of the PCd'I held at Lyons. The new leadership wins overwhelming support with 90.8 per cent of the vote compared to 9.2 per cent for Bordiga's faction. Prepares with Togliatti the 'Lyons Theses' outlining the general political situation in Italy.

14 October. Sends a letter on behalf of the political office of the PCd'I to the Central Committee of the Soviet Communist Party expressing disquiet at the factional disputes between Stalin and Bukharin on the one side and Trotsky, Zinoviev and Kamenev on the other. In Moscow, Togliatti holds on to the letter, regarding it as imprudent, but conveys its contents to Bukharin.

November. The Fascist regime passes exceptional measures taking away parliamentary immunity. Gramsci together with other Communist deputies is arrested and on the 18th under laws pertaining to public security is sentenced to five years in police custody.

1928   May 28. Trial begins against Gramsci and other PCd'I leaders before the Special Tribunal for Defence of the State. He is sentenced to 20 years, 4 months and 5 days of prison.

1937   April. Granted freedom after international campaign, but on 25th he suffers a cerebral haemorrhage and dies on 27th.

Glossary of Terms

Corporatism   A form of sociopolitical organization based around occupational groupings rather than territorial units, which supposedly offers an institutional alternative to the putatively individualistic liberal-democratic parliamentary system. Championed in Italy, albeit with very different emphases, by Catholic social theorists, syndicalists and nationalists, it was adopted by Fascism after 1924, when Mussolini was seeking an alternative to the liberal State. In spite of a number of reforms from 1926 to 1939 creating a corporatist State structure, it was always more ideology than reality and continued to mean very different things to the various wings of the Fascist movement.

Hegemony   Gramsci probably acquired the term from the Comintern debates of 1923–6 and the writings of the Italian philosopher Vincenzo Gioberti. He employed the term in two ways. The first usage goes back to the Russian Social Democrats and came to refer to the leadership the proletariat must seek to exert over other potentially allied classes, such as the peasants, by getting them to identify with its interests through political and ideological means and by not pursuing a narrowly self-interested policy. The second usage refers more broadly to the organization of the cultural, moral and ideological consent of the population to the prevailing political and economic system through the institutions of civil society, such as schools, churches, parties etc. This usage, which is less well-defined in the pre-prison writings, was refined by Gramsci in the *Prison Notebooks* drawing on Benedetto Croce's concept of the 'ethico-political'.

Although related to the realm of politics and relatively autonomous from the economic sphere, Gramsci insisted that true hegemony could only be exercised by a class that was dominant economically.

Interventionist   One who campaigned for Italian intervention in the First World War during the period of Italy's neutrality in 1914–15. Later extended in socialist circles to mean a warmonger etc.

Jacobinism   In his pre-prison writings, Gramsci used this term in a pejorative manner to suggest a sectarian, mystical, abstract or elitist attitude on the part of certain sections of the left. Benedetto Croce employed the term in a similar way, and possibly influenced Gramsci in this respect. In the *Prison Notebooks*, however, he 'revalued' the term and gave it a positive sense to mean leadership of a national–popular alliance bringing together countryside and city, peasants and workers. This new usage has been attributed by some to his reading of Lenin's *Two Tactics of Social Democracy* (1905).

Labourite   A derogatory term of the revolutionary left referring to those who adopted an essentially reformist stance of working through bourgeois parliamentary institutions and confining union activity to negotiating better wages and conditions with employers – a position that was associated with that of the British Labour Party.

Maximalist   Term initially used to denote the radical factions of the PSI which affirmed its maximum revolutionary programme against reformist or other deviations. After the First World War, it came to acquire a more precise meaning as a commitment to socialist revolution, the Third International, the Soviet system and an unwillingness to co-operate with bourgeois parliamentary politics in any shape or form. In this sense, it was often equated with Bolshevik, translated as 'majoritarian' or 'maximal'. In practice, however, many sections of the PSI and trade union leadership never went beyond the rhetoric of maximalism and so for many of the communists the term gradually took on pejorative connotations to refer to the Serrati unitarian wing of the Party, who formally adhered to the Third International but opposed expelling the reformists or changing the PSI's name to the PCd'I.

Risorgimento   Meaning 'Resurrection', it is the term usually applied to the nineteenth-century movement for national unification.

It had the following four phases:

i   1815–47, the period of intellectual preparation
ii 1848–9, when there were a number of abortive republican revolutions and disillusionment with the liberal papacy
iii 1850–61, the period of Cavour and political unification under Piedmont and the House of Savoy, and the liberation of the South by Garibaldi
iv 1861–70, the final phase of consolidation, with the acquisition of Venetia in 1866 and the occupation of Rome in 1870.

Nationalists regarded the movement incomplete until Italy obtained the Trentino in 1919. Since all the hopes and aspirations of the first phase remained unfulfilled, both Fascists and resistance fighters frequently spoke of a 'second Risorgimento' of moral regeneration to complete the political settlement obtained by the first.

Southern Question   The annexation of the Kingdom of the Two Sicilies into the new Italian State in 1860–1 proved fraught with difficulties, more Piedmontese soldiers dying putting down the outbreak of brigandage that followed than were killed expelling the Austrians from the north. The extent of the social, economic and political problems besetting the region were brought to light by the pioneering sociological investigations of Leopoldo Franchetti and Sidney Sonnino in the 1870s. Their work was followed up by later champions of the south, known as *meridionalisti*, such as Giustino Fortunato, Gaetano Salvemini and Pasquale Villari. They claimed that government policies since 1860 had served to increase the corruption and social and economic degradation of the area rather than to reduce it, and special legislation was passed after 1900 to combat malaria, provide public works, promote industry and reduce taxation etc., with varying degrees of efficacy. Both problems and solutions continue to multiply.

Syndicalism   The syndicalist movement promoted the ideal of a self-governing federation of communities based around local trade unions or *syndicats*. Associated with the anarcho-communist ideas of Georges Sorel and Ferdinand Pelloutier in France, its main Italian exponents were the Neapolitans Arturo Labriola and Enrico Leone, who linked its ideas to the rectification of the problems of the south of Italy. Initially a part of the Socialist Party, the syndicalists split from the PSI in 1908. The syndicalists were opposed to the state and other forms of centralized organization and urged workers to ignore political parties and concentrate instead on the struggle in the work place. They put forward the idea of a 'general strike' as a necessary 'myth' for galvanizing revolutionary action. By 1917, however, Italian syndicalism had largely lost its revolutionary fervour, concentrating instead on its anti-political vision of a society of producers participating directly in public life through organizations based on economic function. Many of its leaders sided with Mussolini and played a role in the development of his corporatist doctrine. NB There is a problem in Italian that *sindacato* and its derivatives *sindacalismo* and *sindacalista* are used for both trade union, trade unionism and trade unionist and syndicalism and syndicalist. Editor and translator have therefore had to decide which translation is most appropriate given the context.

Transformism   The term initially was used to describe the coalitions between factions of the historical Left and Right parties of the post-Risorgimento era after 1876. Later on it came to be extended to describe the more general process whereby liberal politicians kept themselves in power by 'transforming' erstwhile opponents into allies by the use or abuse of government patronage, legislative concessions and compromises.

Glossary of Political, Labour and Other Organizations

Avanti!   The official organ of the PSI, editorship of which was often more important than formal leadership of the Party itself. It was edited by Leonida Bissolati from its founding in 1896 until 1903, and then underwent six editorial changes before the First World War under respectively Enrico Ferri, Oddini Morgari, Bissolati again, Claudio Treves, Giovanni Bacci and finally Mussolini. After the war it came under concerted Fascist attack, squads burning down the Milan HQ in 1919 and the Rome offices in 1920. After the split with the communists editorial control passed first to Giacinto Serrati and then to Pietro Nenni, the latter strongly opposed to any deal with the PCd'I. It was outlawed by the Fascists in 1926, but revived in 1943 and continues to be the official daily of the Italian Socialist Party.

Camere del Lavoro   Literally Chambers of Labour, they were the focus of local unions and other workers' organizations, such as co-operatives and savings banks, within a given commune or district.

CGL: Confederazione Generale del Lavoro   General Confederation of Labour, composed of trade unions and *camere*. Allied to the PSI, its leaders were generally reformists concerned with 'economic' as opposed to 'political' agitation and improvements.

CIL: Confederazione Italiana del Lavoro   Italian Confederation of Labour, a Catholic union federation that grew rapidly after recognition by the Papacy in 1918, reaching over a million members.

Corriere della Sera   Milan newspaper founded in 1876. Under Luigi Albertini, who joined the staff in 1896, it became a powerful organ of conservative liberal opinion, opposed to Giolitti's reforms and supporting the nationalist case for imperialism and intervention in the First World War. Generally supportive of Fascism until 1923, it then moved into the opposition until Mussolini forced the Albertini brothers from ownership and the paper into upholding the regime in 1925.

FIOM: Federazione Italiana Operai Metallurgici   Italian Federation of Metal-Mechanical Workers, founded in 1901 and based in Turin. Reformist socialist trade union, affiliated to the CGL.

PCd'I: Partito Communista d'Italia   Communist Party of Italy (later renamed the Partito Communista Italiano or Italian Communist Party (PCI)). Founded 21 January 1921 at Livorno.

PPI: Partito Popolare Italiano   Italian Popular Party, a Catholic but 'non-confessional' interclass party founded in 1919 by the Sicilian priest Luigi Don Sturzo and others. The chief elements of its programme were proportional representation, corporatism, agrarian reform, female suffrage, political decentralization, independence for the Church and social reform. Allied with CIL, it won 100 seats in the 1919 elections doing particularly well in rural areas. Fascists frequently attacked its premises in 1922, although some populists joined Mussolini's first cabinet in the hope of taming him. Violence against the party continued, however, and it ultimately joined the anti-Fascist parliamentary boycott, the Aventine Secession of 1924–6, when it was suspended by Mussolini along with all other opposition parties. It was reborn after 1943 as the Christian Democratic Party.

PSI: Partito Socialista Italiano   Italian Socialist Party. Originating from the Party of Italian Workers founded in 1891, it adopted the name Socialist in 1893. Having a complicated federal structure, organizational and ideological unity was difficult to maintain and it contained numerous contesting factions. It became the largest party in the 1919 elections, winning 156 seats, but was soon beset with numerous rifts as first the communists and then the reformists split off to form separate parties.

La Stampa   Turin newspaper founded in 1867 as the *Gazzetta Pie-*

montese and renamed in 1895. After 1900 first Luigi Roux and then Alfredo Frassati turned it into a genuinely national daily, loyal to Giolitti. Giovanni Agnelli, the owner of Fiat, acquired a third of the shares and joined the board in 1920. Agnelli acquired control when Frassati sold his interests in October 1926 and the paper went over to the Fascist cause.

UIL: Unione Italiana del Lavoro Italian Union of Labour, a small 'interventionist' 'syndicalist' body formed in part by a breakaway from the USI. Based on Parma and rather small, it supplied recruits to Fascism.

USI: Unione Sindacale Italiana Italian Syndical Union, founded by militant anarcho-syndicalists in 1912 and strong in areas such as Liguria, Emilia and the Marches. Scorned parties and sought to build an anti-state within the industrial unions that would take over control via a revolutionary 'general strike'. Grew rapidly after the war, claiming 800,000 members in 1920.

L'Unità The title was first used by Gaetano Salvemini for a weekly newspaper he founded and edited between 1911 and 1920. It was intended as a radical independent voice devoted to the causes close to Salvemini's heart, particularly the reform of the south, the attack on protectionism and the corruption of the parties and politicians, particularly Giolitti, and of the political system more generally. It had a tremendous appeal to the younger generation of Italian socialists, especially Antonio Gramsci who in 1924 adopted it as the title for the official organ of the PCd'I. It continues to be the daily newspaper of the renamed Communist Party, the Party of the Democratic Left (Partito Democratico della Sinistra or PDS).

Biographical Outlines

Amendola, Giovanni (1882–1926)   Philosopher and politician, he became a leader of the constitutional opposition to Fascism 1923–6, founding the Unione Democratica Nazionale in 1924 and the National Union of Liberal and Democratic Forces in 1925. His outspoken denunciations of Fascism resulted in him receiving two savage beatings, the second, sustained on 20 July 1925, contributing to his premature death at Cannes the following year.

Baldesi, Gino (1879–1934)   Syndicalist leader and member of PSI, he was made assistant secretary of the CGL in 1918. Elected a deputy in 1921, he attended the Livorno Congress and voted with the reformists, subsequently adhering to the Partito Socialista Unitario. Attempted unsuccessfully to create an apolitical syndicalist movement with the Fascists, and in 1922 signed the Pacification Pact. By 1924 moved into anti-Fascist opposition, joining the Aventine Secession until ousted from Parliament in 1926. Thereafter politically inactive.

Bonomi, Ivanoe (1873–1951)   Initially a leading member of the reformist wing of the PSI, he was expelled from the party in 1912 for his support of the invasion of Libya after which he founded the Reformist Socialist party with other defecting Socialist deputies. He was a minister in successive liberal governments between 1916 and 1921, in June of which year he succeeded Giolitti as Prime Minister serving until February 1922. Like so many others of the liberal political class, his attitude to Fascist violence was ambivalent and tempered by a greater antagonism to the communists and other sections of the radical left. He withdrew from public life during the

Fascist period, emerging after Mussolini's fall to lead the short-lived coalition grouping hastily formed in 1944 following the liberation of Rome.

Bordiga, Amadeo (1889–1970)   Became prominent nationally in 1910 when he argued against the purely 'cultural' role of the Italian Socialist Youth Federation (FGSI). Fiercely against the First World War, he became prominent in the 'intransigent' fraction of the PSI. After war founded and led the abstentionist communist fraction, who proposed 'abstaining' from any involvement with bourgeois institutions. This group, gathered around his journal *Il Soviet*, opposed both the reformists and Gramsci and the *Ordine Nuovo* group, which they felt understressed the role of the elite party. His followers formed the core of the original Communist Party of Italy, of which he was the first leader 1921–3. After 1922 he was increasingly out of step with Comintern, refusing to fuse with the PSI or engage in anti-Fascist alliances – views codified in the 'Rome Theses' passed at the Second Congress of the PCd'I in March 1922. Arrested and imprisoned February–October 1923, he was displaced from the leadership of PCd'I by Gramsci in 1924. Much attacked within the Party for support of the Left-wing 'committee of agreement' in 1925, he became increasingly isolated mustering only 10 per cent of the vote at the Lyons Congress of 1926. Suffered Fascist imprisonment and deportation 1926–30, expelled from the Communist Party in 1930 but remained active in small Bordigist groups that came to form the International Communist Party.

Corradini, Enrico (1865–1931)   Started up the nationalist journal *Il Regno* (1903–6) and was leader of the Italian Nationalist Association from its founding in 1910 until its fusion with Fascism in 1923. A populist-conservative, he advocated colonial expansion in Africa as an alternative to Italian emigration and the creation of a 'proletarian nation' based around a corporate society of producers.

Croce, Benedetto (1866–1952)   Born at Peccasseroli in Apulia, Croce was the major Italian philosopher of his day. Together with Gentile, he spearheaded the revival of the native idealist tradition. His copious writings on aesthetics, literature, history and ethics were intended to constitute a complete humanist philosophy, which he championed through his cultural journal *La Critica* and his influence over the Laterza publishing house. He became a senator in 1910 and a Minister of Education under Giolitti 1920–1. A conservative liberal, he did not immediately oppose Mussolini. However, he ultimately became one of the major intellectual critics of the Fascist regime and the figurehead of the liberal opposition. Protected by his fame and private fortune, he was not forced out of his Neapolitan home or prevented from publishing until the allied invasion.

D'Annunzio, Gabriele (1863–1938)   Italian poet, novelist, adventurer, and radical nationalist. D'Annunzio enthusiastically supported Italian intervention in the First World War and served in the army from 1915 to 1918. In 1919 he led a mixed band of ex-combatants, anarcho-syndicalists and nationalists and seized Fiume to prevent its going to Yugoslavia. The regime he set up there prefigured many of the more baroque elements of Fascism, such as the Roman salute. His own creed was a bizarre mixture of Nietzsche, syndicalism, populist nationalism and sado-masochism.

Ferri, Enrico (1856–1929)   Ferri was a criminologist in the positivist school of Cesare Lombroso, who linked crime to economic conditions and heredity. His best known book was *Socialismo e scienza positiva. Darwin–Spencer–Marx* (1894). Initially a socialist, he edited *Avanti!* 1900–5, he went over to Fascism in 1922.

Fortunato, Giustino (1848–1932)   Born in Basilicata, he was a leading champion of the Mezzogiorno or Italian south. Elected to the Chamber of Deputies in 1880, where he sat on the Right with the followers of Sonnino, he became a senator in 1909. He was instrumental in overturning the 'myth of the south' as a naturally fertile region, arguing that its problems were economic and geographic as well as social and political. His most important work, expounding his remedies as well as his diagnosis of the south's ills, was *Il Mezzogiorno e lo stato italiano* (1911).

Gentile, Giovanni (1874–1944)   Sicilian philosopher, he played a prominent part with Benedetto Croce in the revival of idealist thought in Italy, collaborating closely on the latter's journal *La Critica* until 1924. Appointed Minister of Education in Mussolini's first administration, he joined the Fascist Party in 1923 and ultimately placed his 'actualist' doctrine at the service of the regime, becoming the official philosopher of Fascism. A supporter of the Fascist Republic of Salò, he was assassinated by partisans in Florence on 5 April 1944.

Gioberti, Vincenzo (1801–52) Born in Turin, he was ordained a priest in 1852. A philosopher, he aimed to rally the Papacy to the nationalist cause. In 1843 he wrote *Del primato morale e civile degli italiani* (Of the Moral and Civil Supremacy of the Italians), which had a great influence on the liberal Catholic, neo-Guelph supporters of Pius IX. His hope that the Church would take an active political stance proved illusory, however. He headed the Piedmontese government from December 1848 to March 1849, when he retired, condemned by the Papacy for his politics and philosophy.

Giolitti, Giovanni (1842–1928) The major Italian statesman of the period, he first entered politics in 1884 as a member of the parliamentary grouping known as the Left. He served as Minister of Finance in 1889, forming his first ministry in 1892. Between 1903 and 1921 he headed four more ministries, lasting eleven years in all, longer than any other elected Italian Prime Minister. He attempted to 'put Marx in the attic' by undermining support for the socialists with a number of social and electoral reforms. He remained nevertheless a conservative liberal and cynics interpreted these measures as manoeuvres to remain in power. This is slightly unfair since he was perceptive enough to oppose colonial expansion and entry into the First World War, which led to his fall from office. His response to Fascism was more one of withdrawal than opposition, a weakness he shared with Italian liberals as a whole.

Gobetti, Piero (1901–26) Son of a Turin grocer, he was an extraordinarily precocious intellect, founding his first review, *Energie Nuovo*, in 1918 at the age of seventeen. Although much influenced by Gramsci and *L'Ordine Nuovo* group, he remained a socialistic liberal rather than a communist. In 1922 he set up a weekly, *La Rivoluzione Liberale*, which took over from *La Voce* as an eclectic meeting point for social and cultural criticism. In 1925 he was forced into exile, dying in Paris of bronchitis and heart failure.

Lenin, Vladimir Ilyich (1870–1924) Marxist theorist, party organizer and first leader of the Soviet state. His main contribution to Marxist thought and practice was his account of the proper organization of a revolutionary party, its relationship to the class system and its role in political mobilization – most importantly in *What is to be Done?* (1902). Although on the eve of the Russian Revolution of October 1917 he developed in *State and Revolution* a utopian vision of the communist future integrating Marx's teaching on the Paris Commune with his own understanding of the soviets, once in power successive crises led him to alter his views and to insist instead on the transitionary importance of a dictatorship of the proletariat. As leader of the Communist International (Comintern) he forced acceptance of Bolshevik organizational notions upon other member parties, causing a split with reformist socialist movements.

Marinetti, Filippo Tommaso (1876–1944) The founder and leader of Italian Futurism, for which he wrote the first manifesto in 1909. Initially a broad cultural movement praising the creativity and dynamism inherent in the industrial world, particularly as found in the speed of cars and aeroplanes, it gradually took on nationalistic overtones. Marinetti participated actively in the interventionist campaign on the eve of the First World War, in which he fought. This brought him into contact with Mussolini, who honoured him though without making Futurism the official art of Fascism as he had hoped. He supported Mussolini's German puppet Republic of Salò, and his death was the occasion of a major state funeral.

Mussolini, Benito (1883–1945) Founder of Fascism and dictator of Italy. Born of modest family in Romagna, Mussolini was initially an active member of the PSI, emerging as a leading protagonist of the revolutionary wing and editing the Party newspaper *Avanti!* from 1912 to 1915. Initially a staunch supporter of the internationalist opposition to the First World War, he came to favour intervention as a revolutionary act and was expelled from the PSI in 1915. At the end of the war he tried to build up a coalition of interventionists and founded the *Fasci di Combattimento* in 1919. Although their programme contained leftist elements, their most distinctive feature was violent anti-Socialist action – especially in rural areas. Through skilful manipulation of the political weaknesses of liberal politicians – their lack of a mass base, fear of socialism and need for parliamentary coalition partners – he was able to force himself into power in the March on Rome of 1922 and to gain legitimacy from much of the liberal establishment. However, following the 1924 elections and his

survival of the Matteotti crisis, when he was implicated in the assassination of a PSU deputy, he went his own way. By 1929, with the
Lateran Pacts establishing an accord with the Vatican and a national
plebiscite demonstrating popular consensus for Fascism, the regime
was fully established. Following the conquest of Ethiopia 1935–6, he
became increasingly preoccupied with Italy's cultural mission and the
role it would play in building a new civilization following the impend-
ing international crisis. Although Mussolini attempted to stay on the
side lines to some extent, increasing involvement with Hitler's Germany cemented by the Pact of Steel of 1938 led to Italy's disastrous
entry into the Second World War on 10 June 1940. Removed from
power in a palace coup on 25 July 1943, he was rescued from jail by
the Nazis and established as the puppet ruler of the Italian Social
Republic of Salò in the north of Italy. He was shot by partisans near
Como on 27 April 1945.

Nitti, Francesco (1868–1953)   Born in Basilicata, he began his
career as a proponent of the South. He entered parliament in 1904
and held the portfolio of agriculture in Giolitti's fourth ministry of
1911–14. During the war he served as treasury minister, but resigned
over the terms of the peace becoming an early critic of the Treaty of
Versailles. From June 1919 to June 1920 he was Prime Minister,
implementing the system of proportional representation and trying to
solve the Fiume crisis. An opponent of Fascism, he was forced to
flee in 1924 and was captured by the Germans in France in 1943.
After the war he became a prominent member of the National Democratic Union Party, and was nominated to the Senate in 1948.

Papini, Giovanni (1881–1956)   Like Prezzolini, he was a self-
taught cultural spokesman of great influence, largely as a result of
his cultural review *Leonardo* (1903–8). Originally a pragmatist with
Nietzschean overtones, his thought consisted of an uneasy mixture
of elitism, nationalism, mysticism and realism. Trying to sustain this
mix led him first into futurism, then, around 1918, to Catholicism
and finally made him a keen Fascist and almost establishment figure,
whose *Life of Christ* (1921) became a massive bestseller.

Prezzolini, Giuseppe (1882–1982)   An autodidact, he had a profound influence on Italian culture before the First World War. He
co-edited the review *Leonardo* (1903–5) with Giovanni Papini, later

founding the influential journal *La Voce* (1908–14). A Crocean with syndicalist sympathies, he succeeded in gathering together a large number of diverse contributors of all points of view. An inveterate non-conformist and critic, his sympathy for Fascism was short-lived and he ultimately went to the United States to teach and write his memoirs. He ended his long life as a self-styled Voltairean figure, writing polemical pieces from his home in Lugano, Switzerland.

Rocco, Alfredo (1875–1935)   The most prominent Nationalist and right Fascist theorist. He viewed the nation as a quasi biological organism, with which the individual could be almost totally identified. He proposed transforming the Italian state via a roughly corporatist system of hierarchically organized socioeconomic groupings which would allow the political elite to control the working masses and organize national production, international economic competition and imperialist war. When the Nationalist Association merged with the Fascist Party in 1923, he quickly rose to prominence becoming the major architect of the Fascist state as Minister of Justice from January 1925 to July 1932.

Salvemini, Gaetano (1873–1957)   Radical politician and historian, he campaigned vigorously for the reform of parliament and the relief of the South. His journal *L'Unità* argued that general equality between north and south remained to be fought for. An outspoken critic of political corruption, his pamphlet *Il governo della malavita* (1913) denounced the Giolitti regime. A deputy from 1919 to 1921, he went into exile in 1925, ultimately becoming professor of history at Harvard University.

Serrati, Giacinto Menotti (1876–1926)   1912–14 a prominent member of the intransigent anti-reformist fraction within the PSI. After Mussolini's defection, became editor of *Avanti!* and virtual leader of the Party. Supported the Third International, but refused to expel reformists or change Party name, leading to polemics with Lenin, Gramsci and Bordiga. Remained leader of PSI after 1921 schism, but tried to effect a reconciliation, finally expelling reformists in October 1922. Attempt to reunite two Parties nonetheless failed, and he and his fraction joined the PCd'I in 1924.

Sonnino, Sidney (1847–1922)   Florentine statesman and financier, together with Leopoldo Franchetti he conducted an exhaustive study

1

of the Italian south which was published in 1877. Elected deputy in 1880, he was Minister of Finance in 1893, Prime Minister 1906–9 and Foreign Minister 1914–19, becoming a Senator in 1920 and largely withdrawing from politics until his death.

Tasca, Angelo (1892–1960)   Son of Turin worker and heavily involved in union movement, he inducted Gramsci into the PSI. A founder member of *L'Ordine Nuovo* in 1919, he broke with Gramsci in 1920. Part of electionist communist fraction July–August 1920 and helped found the PCd'I in 1921. Between Bordiga and Gramsci, he shared leadership of Party with Togliatti after Gramsci's arrest but was expelled as a right-winger in 1929. In exile, became prominent socialist historian.

Terracini, Umberto (1895–1983)   Law student in Turin and colleague of Gramsci and Tasca. Founder member of *L'Ordine Nuovo*, joining directorate of PSI 1920. Part of electionist communist fraction July–August 1920 and entered PCd'I 1921, joining its executive. Although initially a Bordigist, he rallied to Gramsci. Arrested 1926 and jailed by Fascists for many years, he played a prominent part in the Resistance in 1943. Expelled from the Party in 1943, he was readmitted in 1944 and after the war was briefly President of the Constituent Assembly. He was a communist senator from 1948 until his death, and a prominent lawyer.

Togliatti, Palmiro (1893–1964)   Fellow Sard and student with Gramsci at Turin, he joined Tasca's youth section of the PSI in 1914. A supporter of intervention, he fought in the First World War, rejoining the Party in 1919. Co-founder of *L'Ordine Nuovo*, he played an active part in the Factory Council movement along with Gramsci. Initiator of the electionist communist fraction in Turin July–August 1920, he became a founder member of PCd'I. Shared leadership with Tasca after Gramsci's imprisonment, he became leader in 1930. Fought in Spanish Civil War and during Second World War remained in exile in Soviet Union, where he essentially compromised with Stalinist line. However, on returning to Italy in 1944 he began to sketch an independent 'Italian road to socialism', for which he claimed the posthumous support of Gramsci's *Prison Notebooks*.

Treves, Claudio (1869–1933)   A journalist and lawyer, Treves was a major exponent of the reformist socialist position. Born in Turin, he edited the local PSI journal *Il Grido del Popolo* from 1896 to 1898, when he moved to Milan and became a close collaborator of Turati regularly contributing to his journal *Critica Sociale*. He edited the PSI daily *Avanti!* from 1910 to 1912, when the reformist wing was finally overwhelmed by the various maximalist factions. He remained close to Turati, helping him to create the Partito Socialista Unitario (PSU) in 1922 when the reformists were expelled from the PSI. In 1926 he was forced by Fascist repression to escape to France, where he eventually died from a heart attack.

Turati, Filippo (1857–1932)   A founder member of the PSI and leader of the 'gradualist' or 'minimalist' wing of the Party, and editor of the journal *Critica Sociale*. A firm believer in socialist unity, he maintained a precarious hold on the Party until 1904. Thereafter the more radical 'maximalist' wing came to predominate, despite various left-wing successions such as the syndicalists (1908) and the communists (1921). His willingness to join with other parliamentary parties to oppose Fascism led to his expulsion in 1922 and his formation of the Unitary Socialist Party (PSU). Imprisoned by Mussolini, he was spirited away to France in 1926 where he eventually died.

Vico, Giambattista (1688–1744)   Neapolitan philosopher, his great work *La scienza nuova* (1744) with its central doctrine that we can only know fully what we have made was adopted by the Italian idealists Croce and Gentile and made the linchpin of their own historicist philosophies.

Part One
Our *Marx*

An Active and Functional Neutrality[1]

The Concrete Problem

Even in the midst of the extraordinary confusion in which the present European crisis has left individuals and parties, there is one point on which everyone is in agreement. The present historical juncture is one of inexpressible gravity; its consequences could be extremely grave. Because so much blood has been spilt and so much vital energy wasted, we must ensure that an answer is found for as many of the unanswered questions we have inherited from the past as possible, so that humanity can return to its path without finding its way blocked again by such a grim mass of misery and injustice and without finding its future marred, before long, by another catastrophe like this one, demanding the same formidable wastage of human life and activity.

And we, as Italian socialists, must face the question: 'What should be the role of the *Italian* Socialist Party (*not*, I stress, of the *proletariat*, or *socialism* in general), at this moment in *Italian* life?'

Because the Socialist Party to which we dedicate our energies is

---

[1] After the outbreak of the First World War, the PSI adopted a policy of 'absolute neutrality'. On 18 October 1914, Mussolini, the editor of the official PSI daily *Avanti!* challenged this policy in an editorial, 'From Absolute Neutrality to Relative and Functional Neutrality', in which he suggested that under certain conditions Italy should intervene. Mussolini soon found himself isolated amongst the PSI leadership and was forced to resign from his editorship of *Avanti!* On 15 November, he started up his own paper, *Il Popolo d'Italia*, and, on 24 November, he was expelled from the Party.

the *Italian* Socialist Party, which is to say that section of the Socialist International which has taken on the task of winning the Italian nation for the International. This *immediate* task, this day-to-day task, gives the Party *particular, national* characteristics, which commit it to assuming a specific function, a particular responsibility in Italian life. The Party is a State *in potentia*, which is gradually maturing: a rival to the bourgeois State, which is seeking, through its daily struggle with this enemy, and through the development of its own internal dialectic, to create the organs it needs to overcome and absorb its opponent. And, in carrying out this function, the Party is *autonomous*. It depends on the International only for its ultimate aim, and for the essential nature of its struggle, as a struggle between classes.

But as for the form which this struggle should take in various contingencies and the timing of its progress towards the final revolution, the only competent judge of these issues is the PSI itself, which is actually living this struggle and is the only entity which knows its shifting realities.

It is only this consideration that can justify the laughter and scorn which greeted both G. Hervé's insults and the German Socialists' attempts at conciliation, when the PSI launched its formula of 'absolute neutrality' – even though both Hervé and the Germans were speaking on behalf of the International, of which they believed themselves to be official representatives.

The Two Neutralities

Because, let us be clear, it is not the concept of neutrality itself which is at issue (by this we mean, of course, the neutrality of the proletariat), but rather the form this neutrality should take.

The formula 'absolute neutrality' was extremely useful at the outset of the crisis, when we were caught unawares by events, relatively unprepared for their magnitude, because, at that point, only a dogmatically intransigent, uncompromising statement could provide us with a solid, impregnable bulwark against the first wave of passions and individual interests. But now that the elements of confusion have dropped out of that initial, chaotic situation; now that everyone is having to assume responsibility for himself, that formula is only of any use to the reformists, who say that they do not want to place rash bets (even though they let others do so and win). They would rather that the proletariat looked on, as an impartial spectator on events, waiting for those events to create their opportunity for them; while, in the meantime, our opponents get on with creating their own opportunities, and preparing the platform for the class struggle for themselves.

But revolutionaries who conceive of history as the creation of their own spirit, made up of an uninterrupted series of lightning raids on the other active and passive forces in society, in an attempt to create the most favourable conditions possible for the final raid (the revolution), must not content themselves with the initial, temporary formula of 'absolute neutrality', but must transform it into another: 'active and functional neutrality' Which means restoring to national life its original character as a class struggle. The working class, by forcing the class in power to assume its responsibilities, forcing it to carry its premises through to their logical conclusion, to submit to an examination of the way in which it has been preparing for the end which it claims as its own, will constrain it (in our case, in Italy) to admit that it has failed entirely in its aim, because it has led this nation, of which it proclaimed itself the sole representative, into a blind alley, from which the nation cannot escape except by abandoning to their fate all those institutions which are directly responsible for its present, miserable state.

Only in this way can the dualism of the classes be restored, and the Socialist Party slough off all the bourgeois incrustations which fear of the war has piled up on it (never has socialism had so many sympathizers, serious and less serious, as in these last two months). And, having brought home in the clearest terms to the nation (which in Italy is neither wholly proletarian nor wholly bourgeois, given the scant interest the broad mass of the people has always shown in political struggle; and, for this reason, is all the more ripe for conversion by those who show themselves to possess energy and a clear sense of the way ahead) that those who claimed to have its mandate have shown themselves incapable of action in any form, the Party can prepare the proletariat to supplant them, prepare it to put into action that supreme raid on power, which signals the natural passage of civilization from an imperfect form to a more perfect one.

The Mussolini Case

It seems to me, therefore, that 'a.t.'[2] should have shown a little more caution when he wrote about the so-called Mussolini case in the last issue of *Il Grido*. He should have distinguished, in the declarations of the editor of *Avanti!*, between what was coming from Mussolini the man, the *romagnolo* (the relevance of his background has been discussed), and what from Mussolini the socialist, the Italian. He should, that is, have identified what was most original, most vital in Mussolini's stance, and directed his criticism towards that, either in order to annihilate it, or in an attempt to find a means of reconciling the doctrinaire formalism of the remaining Party leadership and the concrete pragmatism of the editor of *Avanti!*

The Myth of the War

But, in any case, the central nucleus of 'a.t.''s argument strikes me as mistaken. When Mussolini says to the Italian bourgeoisie: 'Go where your destiny leads you' – in other words, 'If you believe that it is your duty to make war with Austria, the proletariat will not sabotage your actions' – he is not by any means backtracking on his past attitude to the Libyan War, which led to what 'a.t.' calls the 'negative myth of war'. When he says '*your* destiny', speaking to the bourgeoisie, he is talking about that destiny which, given the historical function of the class, must inevitably lead it to war. War thus retains its character as the irreducible antithesis of the destiny of the proletariat: a character ever more apparent as the proletariat acquires consciousness of this fact.

 ⌈ What Mussolini wants, then, is not a general reconciliation, a fusion of all parties in national unanimity, because then his position would be anti-socialist. What he is hoping for is that the proletariat, having acquired a clear awareness of its might as a class and of its revolutionary potential, but recognizing for the moment that it is not ready to take up the helm of the State [. . .]

[. . .] an ideal discipline, and would allow free rein to the operation

---

[2] Angelo Tasca ('a.t.') had criticized Mussolini's advocacy of intervention in an article entitled 'The Myth of War', in *Il Grido del Popolo*, 24 October 1914. He had maintained that the proletariat did not have the capacity to dominate events and that neutrality was therefore its only course of action.

of those forces which the proletariat feels to be strongest, and which it knows that, for the moment, it is not in a position to supplant.[3] And sabotaging a machine (because absolute neutrality is nothing more than sabotage – a sabotage, apart from anything else, enthusiastically welcomed by the ruling class) certainly does not prove that the machine is not perfect, that it is no use for anything.

Nor does Mussolini's position exclude the possibility (indeed, it presupposes it) that the proletariat might renounce its antagonistic attitude, and that, after a failure or a proven weakness on the part of the ruling class, it might be able to dispose of that class entirely and take up the reins of government – that is, at least, if I have interpreted his rather muddled declarations correctly and if I have developed them in the same direction as he would have done himself.

What Will the Proletariat Say?

I cannot imagine the proletariat as a kind of motor which was started up in July with the switch of absolute neutrality and which now, in October, cannot be stopped without breaking down.

What we are dealing with here, on the contrary, are men who, especially in the past few years, have shown themselves to possess an agility of mind and a freshness of sensibility, of which the amorphous and apathetic bourgeois mass does not have the faintest trace. We are dealing with a mass which has shown itself capable of assimilating and bringing to life the new values which the new, revived Socialist Party has put into circulation. Are we afraid of the work it will involve to make the proletariat assume this new task, which could perhaps signal the beginning of the end of its status as a ward of the bourgeoisie?

In any case, the comfortable position of absolute neutrality must not allow us to forget the gravity of the present situation and to abandon ourselves, even for a moment, to the over-ingenuous option of passive contemplation, of a Buddhistic renunciation of our rights.

Il Grido del Popolo, 31 October 1914

---

[3] [Translator's note] A sentence is missing in the original, at this point, and it is impossible to establish the subject of this sentence.

Socialism and Culture

An article by Enrico Leone recently came to our attention, in which, in that woolly and convoluted manner which all too often characterizes his writing, he rehashes a few commonplaces on culture and intellectualism and their relation to the proletariat, drawing a contrast between culture and *practice*, the *historical fact* of this class preparing its future with its own hands. It would not, we consider, be a useless exercise to return to this question, which has already been aired on previous occasions in 'Il Grido', and, more particularly, in the youth federation's 'Avanguardia', where it received a more rigidly doctrinaire treatment in the polemic between Bordiga from Naples, and our own Tasca.

Let us start by recalling two passages. The first is from a German romantic writer, Novalis (who lived from 1772 to 1801), who said that: 'The supreme problem of culture is that of taking charge of one's transcendental self, of being at the same time oneself and the self of oneself. So we can scarcely be surprised at our lack of empathy with and complete understanding of others. Without a perfect understanding of ourselves, we shall never really be able to know others.'

The second, which we will paraphrase, is from Giambattista Vico, who (in his 'First Corollary concerning Speech by Poetic Characters among the First Nations', in his *The New Science*), gives a political interpretation of the famous saying of Solon's, 'Know thyself', subsequently appropriated for philosophy by Socrates. Vico maintains that, with this phrase, Solon intended to provoke the plebeians, who believed themselves to be *bestial in origin*, while the nobles were *of divine origin*, to reflect on themselves and recognize themselves as being of *the same human nature as the nobles*, and therefore to claim to be made *equal with them in civil rights*. And he then identifies this consciousness of the shared humanity of plebeians and nobles, as the basis and the historical reason for the rise of democracies in antiquity.

We have not brought these fragments together at random. It seems to us that these passages afford some insight, even if it is not fully developed and refined, into the scope and the principles of a true understanding of the conception of culture, and of culture in its relation to socialism.

It is essential to get out of the habit of conceiving of culture as encyclopedic knowledge, and, correspondingly, of man as a receptacle to be crammed with empirical data, with crude, unconnected facts which he must file away in his brain, as though in the columns of a dictionary, in order to be able to respond, on any given occasion, to the different stimuli of the world around him. This form of culture really is harmful, especially to the proletariat. It can only serve to create misfits, people who believe themselves superior to the rest of humanity because they have amassed in their memory a certain quantity of facts and dates, which they trot out at any opportunity, setting up a kind of barrier between themselves and others. This false conception of culture serves to create that feeble and colourless intellectualism so mercilessly flayed by Romain Rolland, which has given birth to a whole swarm of arrogant windbags, more harmful to the life of a society than tuberculosis or syphilis germs are to the health and beauty of the body. The smug little student who knows some Latin and history, the vain little lawyer who has taken advantage of his teachers' laziness and apathy to wrangle himself a threadbare degree – these people think themselves superior to the most skilled of skilled workers, who performs a precise and essential task in his life and who is a hundred times better at his work than they are at theirs. But this is not culture, it is pedantry; it is not intelligence, but intellectualism; and any attack on it is more than justified.

Culture is something quite different. It is the organization, the disciplining of one's inner self; the mastery of one's personality; the attainment of a higher awareness, through which we can come to understand our value and place within history, our proper function

9

in life, our rights and duties. But all this cannot happen through spontaneous evolution, through actions and reactions beyond the control of our will, as occurs in the vegetable and animal worlds, in which each individual entity adapts itself and develops its organs unconsciously, obeying ineluctable laws. Man is primarily a creature of spirit – that is, a creation of history, rather than nature. Otherwise, it would be impossible to explain why it is that, when the exploiters and the exploited have always existed, the creators of wealth and those who greedily consume it, socialism has never yet come into being. The fact is that it is only step by step, stage by stage, that humanity has acquired an awareness of its own value and has won the right to live in independence of the schemes and the privileges of those minorities who happened to come to power at an earlier moment in history. And this awareness has not developed beneath the brutal goad of physiological necessity, but rather through intelligent reflection, first on the part of a few, then of a whole class, on the reasons why certain situations exist and on the best means of transforming what have been opportunities for vassalage into triggers of rebellion and social reconstruction. Which means that every revolution has been preceded by a long process of intense critical activity, of new cultural insight and the spread of ideas through groups of men initially resistant to them, wrapped up in the process of solving their own, immediate economic and political problems, and lacking any bonds of solidarity with others in the same position. The latest example, the closest to us in time and thus the least alien to us, is the French Revolution. The preceding period in culture, known as the Enlightenment, a period which has been so slandered by facile critics of theoretical reason, was in fact not – or at least not entirely – a featherweight gathering of superficial, dilettante intellectuals, discoursing about anything and everything with complacent indifference, believing themselves to be men of their time only when they had read D'Alembert and Diderot's *Encyclopédie*. It was not, that is to say, simply a phenomenon of pedantic, arid intellectualism, like the one we see before our eyes now, exhibited in its full glory in the low-grade popular Universities. The Enlightenment was a magnificent revolution in itself; and, as De Sanctis acutely observed in his *History of Italian Literature* it created a kind of pan-European unified consciousness, a bourgeois International of the spirit, with each part sensitive to the tribulations and misfortunes of the whole, which was the best preparation for the bloody revolution which would subsequently take place in France.

In Italy, in France, in Germany, the same things were being discussed, the same institutions, the same principles. Each new play by Voltaire, each new pamphlet was like a spark running through the wires which already stretched between one state and another, one region and another; and it found the same sympathizers and the same opponents everywhere at the same moment. The bayonets of Napoleon's armies found their way already cleared by an invisible army of books and tracts, which had been swarming out of Paris since the first half of the eighteenth century, preparing men and institutions for their badly needed renovation. Later, when the events in France had welded consciences throughout Europe still more tightly, a popular uprising in Paris could set off others in Milan, in Vienna, even in the smallest towns. To careless observers, all this may seem a natural, spontaneous phenomenon, but, in fact, it would be incomprehensible if we did not take into account the cultural factors which had already primed men's minds so they were ready to explode for what was felt to be a common cause.

The same phenomenon is occurring again today, with socialism. It is through a critique of capitalist civilization that a unified proletarian consciousness has formed or is in the process of formation. And a critique is something cultural; it does not arise through spontaneous natural evolution. A critique involves precisely that discovery of the self which Novalis defined as the aim of culture. Discovery of the self as it measures itself against others, as it differentiates itself from others and, having once created an objective for itself, comes to judge facts and events not only for what they signify in themselves, but also according to whether or not they bring that objective nearer. To know oneself means to be oneself, to be master of oneself, to assert one's own identity, to emerge from chaos and become an agent of order, but of one's own order, one's own disciplined dedication to an ideal. And one cannot achieve this without knowing others, knowing their history, the succession of efforts they have made to be what they are, to create the civilization they have created, and which we are seeking to replace with our own. It means having some notion of nature and its laws, in order to understand the laws which govern the life of the spirit. And it means learning all this without losing sight of the ultimate aim, which is to know oneself better through learning about others, and to know others by learning about oneself.

If it is true that history is a chain of efforts man has made to free himself from privileges, prejudices and idolatry, then there is no reason why the proletariat, as it seeks to add one more link to that chain, should not know how and why and by whom it has been preceded, and how useful that knowledge can prove.

Il Grido del Popolo, 29 January 1916

History

Give up to life your every action, your every ounce of faith. Throw all your best energies, sincerely and disinterestedly, into life. Immerse yourselves, living creatures that you are, in the live, pulsing tide of human existence, until you feel at one with it, until it floods through you, and you feel your individual personality as an atom within a body, a vibrating particle within a whole, a violin-string which receives and echoes all the symphonies of history; of that history which, in this way, you are helping to create. In spite of this utter abandonment of the self to the reality which surrounds it, in spite of this attempt to key your individuality into the complex play of universal causes and effects, you may still, suddenly, feel a sense that something is missing; you may become conscious of vague and indefinable needs, those needs which Schopenhauer termed metaphysical.

You are in the world, but you do not know why you are here. You act, but you do not know why. You are conscious of voids in your life; you desire some justification of your being, of your actions; and it seems to you that human reasons alone do not suffice. Tracing the causal links further and further back, you arrive at a point where, to co-ordinate, to regulate the movement, some supreme reason is necessary, some reason which lies beyond what is known and what is knowable. You are just like a man looking at the sky, who, as he moves further and further back through the space which science has mapped out for us, finds ever greater difficulties in his fantastic wanderings in the infinite until, arriving at the void, and incapable of conceiving of this absolute void, he unconsciously populates it with divine beings, with supernatural entities, to co-ordinate the vertiginous, and yet logical movement of the universe. Religious sentiment is entirely built up from these vague aspirations, these instinctive, inner reasonings, which have no outlet. And some trace, some quiver of this sentiment lurks within the blood of each one of us, even those who have best succeeded in dominating these inferior manifestations of the self – inferior because they are purely instinctive, mere uncontrolled impulses.

But what can conquer them is the force of life itself; historical activity can annul them. They are simply the products of tradition, the instinctual vestiges of millenia of terror and of ignorance of the reality that surrounds us. Their origin can be traced. To explain them is to overcome them. To make them the object of history is to recognize their emptiness. And then one can return to the active life, and experience more authentically the reality of history. By bringing feeling, as well as fact, within the sphere of history, one can finally recognize that it is in history alone that the explanation of our existence lies. What can be historicized cannot be supernatural in origin, the vestige of some divine revelation. If something still remains inexplicable, that is due only to our cognitive deficiencies, to the still imperfect grasp of our intellect. Recognizing this may make us more humble, more modest, but it will not throw us into the arms of religion. Our religion becomes, once again, history. Our faith becomes, once again, man, and man's will and his capacity for action.

We feel an enormous, an irresistible force from our human past. We recognize the good things it brings us, like the energetic certainty that what has been possible will be possible again; all the more so, in that we have become wise through the experience of others. But we also recognize the bad, like these inorganic vestiges of transcended states of mind. And this is why we inevitably feel ourselves to be in conflict with Catholicism; and this is why we call ourselves modern. Because, though we feel the past fuelling our struggle, it is a past that we have tamed; our servant, not our master; a past which illuminates and does not overshadow us.

Avanti!, 29 August 1916

Socialism and Co-operation

The officious economist of Italian Nationalism, Professor Alfredo Rocco, is convinced of having utterly destroyed the collectivist programme of socialism with the following formidable objection. The national wealth of Italy fluctuates between 80 and 100 billion lire. Now, wage-earners are in such a massive majority over capitalists that, if the profits of production were to be shared out collectively, among everyone, the increase in personal well-being for the humble worker would be minimal, and certainly not of an order to justify the crisis which would be provoked by the passage from one system to the other.

The objection is a puerile one, because the aim of socialism is not simply to solve the problem of the distribution of finished products. On the contrary, the moral justification for our struggle, and for the revolution this struggle will bring about, comes from the conviction, acquired by the proletariat through its critique of the existing means of production, that collectivism will serve to accelerate the rhythm of production itself, by eliminating all those artificial factors which limit productivity.

Among these factors, and by no means the last or the least important, is the fortuitous nature of the distribution of wealth among individuals. It is almost always capitalists who become industrialists, whether or not they possess the intelligence and technical competence needed for the social task they are called on to perform. True, the bourgeois system itself has already managed to go some way towards combating this immorality of fortune. Banks and building societies tend to accumulate the capital of the more inert members of society, and put it into the hands of bolder and more active elements. In a more modern development, public companies, which, broadly speaking, are nothing other than industrial co-operatives, formed with the aim of exploiting capital more profitably and using it more effectively, represent the furthest that the bourgeois system can go towards eliminating the capitalist monad, towards separating the *technical* element in production from the provision of *capital*. Public companies are, for this reason, a social experiment of the greatest interest for socialism, because they serve to demonstrate ever more clearly the truth that the capitalist is by no means necessary; that the spirit of initiative, the vital motive force of the economy, is not deadened by the fact that the managers and the technical staff of a firm are mere salaried workers, without a personal interest in the profits, down to the last farthing.

If even these forms of capitalist co-operation can provide confirmation of the claims of socialist propaganda, then how much more can be had from consumers' co-operatives like the Alleanza Torinese, which have acquired a distinct class profile and are closely tied to the development of the proletariat.

Consumption is a relatively neutral field of social activity. It is on the basis of production, rather than consumption, that the populace divides into two classes. Consumption can become an arena for the struggle only for political, rather than economic reasons, in that the State, as the administrative and executive committee of the capitalist bourgeoisie, uses protectionism and customs barriers to match consumption to domestic production. But everyone is a consumer; and the entire populace, excepting those few people who look to retail for their profits, may find itself united in protest against harsh measures and price rises, even though each group will differ in the methods of its protest, and the different political ends that its protest is intended to serve. For this reason – since, in consumption, class boundaries are to some extent blurred – it certainly cannot be claimed that the co-operative movement is socialist in essence, and it would be naive and extremely damaging to suggest that this movement is all there is to the socialist programme.

But, even leaving aside the enormous advantages that the co-operative movement brings to *all* consumers (the advantages described so well by 'o.p.' in a previous issue),[1] co-operatives on the Alleanza model are impressive, large-scale laboratories for refining and purifying the socialist sense of social responsibility. The enthusiastic words which Georges Sorel used to use, in the old days, to praise the reconstructive work of the trade unions could be applied, with still more justification, to co-operatives like this today. Because co-operatives like this are an attempt to make socialist economic ideals a reality. Sadly, they suffer from the inevitable disadvantage of being grafted onto a heterogeneous trunk, to which they must adapt, to some extent, in order to survive and develop, and by which they, then, inevitably, find themselves conditioned. But, nevertheless, they are still bursting with a life of their own, which can barely be contained, and they can still cause irreparable breaches in the system.

Besides, capitalism itself is not, in its historical essence, a bourgeois phenomenon. Rather, it is a bourgeois superstructure; the concrete form taken by economic development at some time after the new class's rise to political power, resulting from its struggle to establish its roots ever more firmly in the world. And just as it was the economic nuclei which had emerged before 1789 – already potentially capitalistic, but suffocated by the remains of feudalism – which made the first breaches in the feudal system; so, equally, the economic nuclei created and nurtured by the proletariat for its own class ends, within the very heart of bourgeois society, may become a powerful lever for breaking that society apart.

From this point of view, even consumers' co-operatives can, if we want them to, take on a revolutionary role. Even in their present form, they are a kind of link, welding the present and the future. Developed, reinforced and multiplied, they will become so many weapons pointed directly against the bourgeois system. Just as the current war differs from previous wars because it entirely absorbs all the nation's activity, so, equally, the proletariat revolution differs from the bourgeois revolution because of the immediate and extraordinarily far-reaching repercussions it will have on international activity.

[1] Ottavio Pastore, 'Il valore socialista della cooperazione', in *L'Alleanza Cooperativa*, x, no. 112, 2 June 1916. Pastore was a leading member of the Turin Co-operative Alliance.

So, the more consumer organizations of this kind that the proletariat can succeed in creating, the more easily it will be able to get over the terrible crisis which will result when it achieves its emancipation.

L'Alleanza Cooperativa, 30 October 1916

Three Principles and Three Kinds of Political Order

'Order' and 'disorder' are the two words which recur most frequently in political disputes. 'The party of order', 'upholders of order', 'the public order' . . . Three phrases which all hinge on the same axis of order: the fixed point around which political phraseology rotates, more or less tightly, depending on the particular forms assumed, at various moments in history, by individuals, the parties and the state. The word 'order' has a healing power; and the preservation of political institutions is entrusted, in great part, to this power. The existing order is presented as harmonious and stable; and the mass of citizens is hesitant and fearful at the thought of a radical change, uncertain of what it might bring. Common sense, fatuous as usual, teaches that it is better to enjoy your egg today than hope for a chicken tomorrow; and common sense is a terrible slave-driver of the spirit. All the more so when, to get the chicken, you need to break the egg. Change conjures up the image of something violently torn apart. No-one visualizes the new order which might replace the old one, better organized than the old and more alive, because it would replace dualism with unity and the static immobility of inertia with the dynamism and energy of life. But no-one looks beyond the violent destruction of the old order, and the terrified mind holds back, fearful of losing everything, of being faced with chaos and ineluctable disorder.

The prophesies of utopians can be seen as an attempt to overcome this fear of change. A utopia envisages a future status quo which is already established and tidy, thus removing any impression of a leap into the darkness. But utopian social constructions have always collapsed, precisely because they were so neat and tidy. If just one detail could be shown to be wrong, the whole edifice collapsed. These kinds of construction had no foundation; they were too analytic, founded as they were on an infinity of details, rather than a single moral principle. Now, the concrete details of a system depend on so many causes that they finish up having no real cause at all, and being entirely unpredictable. And, in order to act, man needs to be able to predict things, at least in part. It is impossible to conceive of the will being directed at something other than a concrete aim. It is impossible to conceive of a collective will which does not have a concrete universal aim. But this aim cannot be a single factual detail, or a series of details. It can only be an idea, or a moral principle. The inherent defect of utopias is this: believing that a vision of the future can be a vision of factual details, whereas it can only be a vision of principles, or of juridical maxims. Legal axioms (law and judgement are morality in action) are creations of the human will. If you want to give a direction to men's wills, you must give them as their aim the only thing that can be their aim; otherwise, after a first rush of enthusiasm, you will see them start drooping and fading away.

The various existing political orders were created out of the desire to translate a juridical principle into practice as fully as possible. The revolutionaries of 1789 did not foresee the capitalist order which would result from their actions. They wanted to translate into practice the principle of the rights of man. They wanted to ensure that certain rights were enjoyed by each member of the community. After the initial shattering of the old shell, these rights became gradually stronger and more concrete; they were transformed into a force which could act on reality and they began to shape and determine affairs. The result was bourgeois civilization: the only form of civilization which could result, as the bourgeoisie was the only effective social force, the only force capable of moulding history. The utopian idealists were defeated then, as ever, because none of their visions was realized in all its detail. But the principle was realized, and from this principle grew the structures and the political order we know today.

Was the principle that the bourgeois revolution translated into history a universal one? Yes, without a doubt. And yet it is often said that if Jean-Jacques Rousseau could see where his preachings had led, he would probably disown them. This paradoxical assertion contains an implicit criticism of liberalism. But it is, precisely, a paradox; that is, it says something fair in an unfair way. Universal does not mean absolute. In history, there is nothing absolute and fixed. The tenets of liberalism are 'ideal standards', which, once they were recognized as rationally necessary, were translated into 'operative ideals'. They were realized in practice in the bourgeois state; they served the purpose of provoking an antithesis to that state, in the form of the proletariat, and they have now worn themselves out. They may be universal for the bourgeoisie, but they are not universal enough for the proletariat. For the bourgeoisie, they were ideals to be aimed at, while for the proletariat they are a starting-point for further developments. And, indeed, the complete liberal programme has become the minimalist programme for the socialist party; the programme, that is, which guides our day-to-day existence, as we wait until the right moment is judged to have come for [. . .].[1]

As an ideal standard, the liberal programme creates the ethical state; that is, a state which, ideally, stands above class conflicts and the endless realignments and clashes between different groupings which constitute the traditional, economic reality of the state. This state is a political aspiration, more than a political reality, existing only as a utopian model. But it is precisely the fact that it is a mirage that strengthens it and makes it into a conservative force. It is the hope that one day, finally, this state will be realized in its full perfection which still moves many people not to reject it and therefore not to attempt to replace it.

Let us take a look at two of these 'model states'; two typical examples, the two examples which are the yardstick for all political theorists. The English state and the German state. Both have become extremely powerful, both have succeeded, by different means, in establishing themselves as solid political and economic organisms. But it has never been possible to confuse these two states. Each has an unmistakable character of its own; a character which, at the present conjuncture, is pitting it against the other.

The idea that has served as the driving force for the internal,

---

[1] [Translator's note] A few words censored.

parallel energies within the two can, in the case of England, be encapsulated in the word '*laissez-faire*'; in the case of Germany, in the words: 'authority informed by reason'.

'*Laissez-faire*' is a formula which subsumes a whole history of struggles, of revolutionary uprisings to win particular freedoms. It is the *forma mentis* which has gradually evolved through these many uprisings. It is the conviction that has gradually taken shape in the minds of the ever greater numbers of citizens who, by means of these struggles, have come to participate in public life, that it is in the free expression of their own beliefs, in the free development of the productive and legislative forces of the country, that the secret of happiness lies. Of happiness understood in a particular sense, of course: a happiness which stems from thinking that whatever goes wrong cannot be blamed on individuals, and that, if a project does not work out, this can be explained away by the fact that its initiators were not yet in a strong enough position to carry their plans through to a successful conclusion.

Where England is concerned, to cite an example, the theory and practice of *laissez-faire* found its champion before the War, in Lloyd George, who, as a Minister of State, in a public address, knowing that his words would be taken as indicating government policy, said this, more or less, to the workers: 'We are not socialists; that is, we are not aiming at an immediate collectivization of production. But we do not have any theoretical objection to socialism. Each to his own task. If our society is still a capitalist society, that must mean that capitalism is still a historical force to be reckoned with. You socialists say that socialism is ripe for action. Prove it. Prove that you are the majority. Prove that you are not just potentially but actually a force capable of governing the nation's fate. And we will happily let you take our place.' We in Italy are accustomed to seeing the Government as something sphinx-like, something completely detached from the nation, and detached from any real polemic about ideas and events. Words like Lloyd George's seem quite incredible to us. But they are not so incredible – and nor are they simply empty rhetoric – if we think that England has conducted its political struggles in the public eye for the past two hundred years, and that the right to the free expression of all political forces is a right which has been fought for, not a natural right, unthinkingly accepted as such. Just recall that the radical government in England deprived the

House of Lords of its right of veto[2] in order to push through Irish independence. Just recall that, before the War, Lloyd George was proposing an Agriculture Bill which, starting from the premise whoever owns land and does not cultivate it properly loses his rights over that land, would have handed over much privately-owned land from its owners to those who would have worked it. The existence of this kind of bourgeois state socialism – unsocialist socialism – meant that the proletariat did not look too unkindly on the state as government. Convinced, rightly or wrongly, that its interests were being looked after, it conducted its class struggle discreetly, without that moral outrage which characterizes the workers' movement.

The German conception of the state is worlds apart from the English, but its effects are the same. The *forma mentis* of the German state is essentially protectionist. Fichte has codified the closed state; that is, the state ruled by reason, the State which must not be left in prey to the free and spontaneous play of human forces, but must, in everything, in its every act, show the mark of a united will, a programme determined in advance and preordained by reason. And for this reason, in Germany, the parliament does not have the same powers as it does elsewhere. It is a mere consultative body, which is retained solely because it would be irrational to claim that the executive powers of the state are entirely infallible, and because parliament and discussion may also contribute to the truth. But the majority has no recognized right to the truth. The final word rests with the Ministry (the Emperor), which arbitrates and makes decisions, and which cannot be replaced except by Imperial decree. But the various classes have the conviction – not an empty conviction, or a spineless one, but one formed through a long experience of good administration, and proven distributive justice – that their basic rights are being taken care of, and that their activity must consist of trying to become the majority, in the case of the socialists, or, in the case of the conservatives, to preserve their majority and thus prove their continuing historical justification. An example: the passing of the measure, in 1913, to allocate a billion marks in increased military spending; a measure approved by the Socialists, as well. The majority of Socialists voted in favour because the billion marks was raised not from taxpayers in general, but by an exceptional expropriation from the very rich (at

---

[2] [Translator's note] 'Voto' (vote) in the original: presumably a misprint.

least, that is how things seemed). It seemed like an experiment in State socialism; it seemed that it was a just principle in itself to place the burden of military expenditure on the capitalists. So the expenditure was approved – to the benefit, as it turned out, of no-one but the bourgeoisie and the Prussian military party.

These two types of constituted order are the basic models for the Italian 'parties of public order'. The Italian Liberals and Nationalists say, or used to say, that they wanted to see in Italy something similar to, respectively, the English state and the German state. The polemic against socialism is all woven around this aspiration to a potential ethical state in Italy. But Italy has missed out completely on that period of gradual development which made possible the England and the Germany of today. So if you carry the reasoning of the Liberals and Nationalists through to its logical conclusion, the formula you will come up with, in the immediate term, is a sacrifice on the part of the proletariat. A sacrifice of its own needs, of its personality, of its will to fight; and all in order to allow things to take their course, to let the wealth of the country accumulate, and its administration to improve its record [. . .].[3] The Nationalists and the Liberals do not go as far as to claim that some kind of order does exist in Italy. What they claim is that order can and will be established, just as long as the socialists do not stand in the way of its inevitable progress.

This state of affairs in Italy is for us a source of greater energy and fighting spirit. Think of how difficult it is to convince a man to do something if he has no immediate reason to do it. How much more difficult it is to convince a mass of people to act; especially where there is not, as there is in Italy, a concerted policy, on the part of the government, of suppressing the aspirations of those people, of taxing their patience and their productivity in every possible way. In countries where there is no fighting in the streets, where the most fundamental laws of the state are not seen to be trampled on, and the will of the few does not carry the day, the class struggle loses its bitterness, the revolutionary spirit loses its urgency and weakens. The so-called law of least effort becomes popular – a law for layabouts, which often simply means doing nothing at all. In countries like this, the revolution is less probable. Where some kind of order exists,

---

[3] [Translator's note] Three lines censored.

it is less likely that the will can be found to replace it with a new order [. . .].[4]

It is not the task of the Socialists to substitute one order for another. They must establish an order where there was none. The juridical maxim that they want to translate into practice is: 'that all citizens should be able to develop their own, human personality to the full'. As this maxim is realized in practice, all privileges will cease. There will the maximum of freedom with the minimum of constraint. Individuals' lives, their roles in society, will be determined solely by their ability and productivity, outside all traditional patterns. Wealth will not be an instrument of slavery, but, belonging to all, impersonally, it will give everyone the means to enjoy the highest possible standard of living. Education will be for all intelligent people, whatever their background, and not the prize for [. . .].[5] From this one maxim stem all the other principles of the full socialist programme. And the socialist programme, I repeat, is not a utopia. It is a concrete universal; it can be realized by the will. It is a principle of order, of socialist order. Of that order which I believe will be realized in Italy, before it is elsewhere [. . .].[6]

La Città futura, 11 February 1917

[4] [Translator's note] A few words censored.
[5] [Translator's note] Four lines censored.
[6] [Translator's note] Five lines censored.

Freedom and Discipline

Joining a movement means taking your share of the responsibility for the events which are in the pipeline; becoming one of the people who are shaping these events. A young man who joins the Socialist youth movement is taking a step towards independence and freedom. By subjecting oneself voluntarily to a discipline, one becomes independent and free. Water is pure, free and itself when it is running between the two banks of a stream or a river, not when it is messily spread on the ground, or when it is released, rarified, into the atmosphere. Anyone who does not follow a political discipline is, precisely, matter in a gaseous state, or contaminated by foreign bodies: that is, useless and harmful. The discipline of politics sloughs off this waste, and refines the pure metal of the spirit. It gives an aim to life; and, without an aim, life is not worth living. Any young proletarian who is conscious of how heavily the burden of class slavery weighs on his shoulders should take his first step towards freedom by joining his local Socialist youth group.

La Città Futura, 11 February 1917

Socialism and Italy

The hunt is on. They are out to get us – to get socialism, to get the socialists. Anyone want to join in, to spit in the faces of the Judases, the traitors? Anyone want to bring along some nails and crucify the Antichrist?

Liberals, conservatives, clerics, radicals, republicans, nationalists, reformists – the beaters are out, the hunt is in full flow. Come on, everyone, after the socialists. Don't be afraid – the State is with you, the government is with you, the army chief of staff is with you. You have a *voice*. Your newspapers can write away, polemicize away, have the last word, the last, triumphal word. They can form a climate of public opinion to absolve you and hymn your praises. That's all you want, after all – the intoxicating feeling of triumph. You want the feeling of being in charge, even if it is only for a moment: the feeling of being in control of 35 million people, the masters of their destinies, the supreme and unchallenged arbiters of their lives.

It will be the triumph of a moment. You have not even thought it through. You say that you are revolutionaries. You identify revolution with Jacobinism. Until yesterday, you were nothing in comparison with Authority, with the state. Now you are *something*; you have managed, for a few, isolated moments, to dictate the direction that Authority has taken. And, because of this, you have convinced yourselves that you have brought about the revolution. You have convinced yourselves that you have become identified with Authority, with the State. In fact, you have only reinforced Authority, reinforced the State. The State has remained exactly as it was, with the same convictions, the same programmes. It has not been transformed; it has been reinforced. It has acquired a greater confidence in itself, in its own organs. It has distanced itself still further from the Italian people, becoming even more alienated from the nation, from the real energies of the nation; from the nation which is coming into being, organizing itself, transforming itself, slowly and with great effort, and acquiring consciousness of its own being, its own becoming.

The history of the Italian people has yet to be written – its secret, its spiritual history.

Fifty years ago there was no such thing as an 'Italian people' – it was just a rhetorical expression. There was no social unity in Italy then; there was only a geographical unity. There were just millions of individuals scattered throughout Italian territory, each leading his own life, each rooted in his own soil, knowing nothing of Italy, speaking only his own local dialect, and believing the whole world to be circumscribed by his parish boundary. He knew the tax collector, he knew the policeman, he knew the magistrate, the Court of Assizes; and that, for him, was Italy. Yet this individual, many of these millions of individuals, have progressed beyond this parochial stage in their development. They have formed a social unity. They have discovered themselves to be citizens, sharing a life which goes beyond their local horizon and stretches across ever vaster tracts of the world, across the entire world. They have come to feel solidarity with other men; they have learned how to judge other men; they have learned to speak Italian, as well as their own dialect. All because a new social organism has come into being in Italy; an organism created by these men themselves, which they feel themselves to be part of, and which has given them access to the life of the world, to the history of the world.

They have realized, at last, what it is to be human. They have transcended their abject, degrading condition; they have discovered within themselves the dignity of man, the creator of life. The beginning of the twentieth century has signalled a new Renaissance for Italy; a plebeian Renaissance, a Renaissance of the humble strata of Italian humanity. It has signalled the entry into civilized life, into the political struggle, into the life of the world, of millions of new citizens: hard-working, sincere and confident of their strength. The Italian people has organized itself and adopted a discipline, because a new feeling and a new idea have emerged in its heart and its mind. Italy has become a political unity, because a part of its populace has united around an idea, a single programme. And socialism, socialism alone, was able to provide this idea and this programme. Socialism has meant that a peasant farmer from Puglia and a worker from Biella have come to speak the same language; that, in spite of the distance that separates them, they have come to express themselves in the same way when confronted by the same problem and to arrive at the same judgement of men and events. What other idea, in Italy, has ever achieved anything like this? Are there any two cities in Italy in which the Liberal Party presents itself with the same ideas and wins with the same policies? The Liberal Party has shattered Italy. It has widened the gulf between north and south with its legislation on customs duties, creating a kind of industrial feudalism, which has broken Italy up into many different zones with opposing interests.

⌈ Socialism has become the one ideal which unites the Italian people.⌉ Socialism has become the consciousness which unites the Italian people. Millions of Italians have become men, have become citizens, because there was an idea – the idea of socialism – which shook them up, and made them think, and taught them to transcend the abject and degrading condition they found themselves in.⌈The Socialist Party⌉is the tangible representation of this unity, of this new consciousness, of this new world. And now they are out to get us, to hunt down the Socialist Party, to hunt down the Socialists. In the name of a moment's shallow, Jacobin triumph, they are proposing to destroy a whole history, to cancel out a whole consciousness, to bulldoze ideas and feelings. They have all pledged themselves to the task. They are all in agreement. They want their moment of triumph. They want the illusion of having the destiny of thirty-five million men in their hands. They want the sadistic pleasure of being the dictators of public opinion. And, to achieve their end, they are willing to destroy, to unhinge, to demolish the history of the Italian people.

The hunt is on. Come on, just try and get us – use all the powers of the State to hunt us down. You will not uproot socialism. All you will do is break one – or two or three – thousand individuals. You will throw humanity into darkness and force thousands of individuals back into their previous degrading condition, when they had just begun to raise their heads and recognize their own dignity. You will shatter the social unity of the Italian proletariat. But you will also, in doing so, enslave yourselves, because the only thing which constrains the State to respect your liberty as citizens is the existence of a force antagonistic to the State. In debasing others, you will debase yourselves, because any liberty there is in Italy is owed to the existence of a strong and united Italian proletariat.

Come on then, just try and get us. Repress, shatter, unhinge. All you will really be doing is cutting yourselves off from the Italian people, from its consciousness, its solidarity. Debase men, make them aware of the huge, implacable weight of authority, and then just try appealing to their feelings, to their hearts.

It is you yourselves you are shackling. It is yourselves you are reducing to slavery. You are alienating yourselves from Italian history – not from the history written in the history books, but from the greater, the richer history which is not written in the books. Because you are cutting off every bond of solidarity between you and the Italian people, even the bond of shared humanity which links one man with another. Because you want to block off the light which millions of Italians see by, the light which illumines the world for them – the only reason they have for feeling themselves to be human and for believing that life is worth living.

Il Grido del Popolo, 22 September 1917

Notes on the Russian Revolution

Why is the Russian Revolution a proletarian revolution?

Reading the papers, and piecing together the confusing selection of news items the censors have allowed to be published, it is not easy to work out what is going on. We know the revolution was the work of proletarians (of workers and soldiers). We know there is a committee of worker-delegates controlling the functioning of the administrative organs which have had to be maintained to deal with everyday affairs. But does the fact that a revolution is the work of proletarians make it a proletarian revolution? War, too, is the work of proletarians, but that fact alone does not make it a proletarian event. For that to be the case, other, spiritual, factors must come into play. The revolution is not simply a matter of power – it must be a revolution in people's behaviour, a moral revolution. The bourgeois newspapers have stressed the question of power, telling us that the forces of autocracy have been replaced by other forces, whose identity is as yet uncertain, but which they hope will prove to be the forces of the bourgeoisie. And they have immediately established a parallel between the Russian revolution and the French Revolution, and they have found the events to be similar. But it is only on the surface that they resemble each other, as one act of violence resembles another act of violence and one act of destruction another.

And yet I am convinced that the Russian Revolution is an act of the proletarian spirit, as well as a historical event, and that it will necessarily result in a socialist regime. With hard, solid information in such short supply, an exhaustive proof is impossible. But there *are* some elements present which justify our drawing this conclusion.

The Russian Revolution has been innocent of any trace of Jacobinism. The point of the revolution was to overthrow autocracy, not to win power through violence. Jacobinism is a purely bourgeois phenomenon: a characteristic of the bourgeois revolution that took place in France. The bourgeoisie had no universal programme when it brought about the revolution. It was serving its own, particular interests, the interests of its own class, and it did so with the mean and petty mentality common to all people who are pursuing their own particular ends. The violence of the bourgeois revolution is a double violence: it is violent in its destruction of the old order, and violent in its imposition of the new. The bourgeoisie imposes its force and its ideas not only on the previous ruling class, but also on the people – the class it is preparing to dominate. It is a case of one authoritarian regime replacing another.

The Russian Revolution has destroyed authoritarianism, and has replaced it with universal suffrage, extending it even to women. Authoritarianism has been replaced by liberty, and the Constitution by the free expression of the conscience of the universal consciousness. Why have the Russian revolutionaries been able to avoid Jacobinism? Why, in other words, have they not replaced the dictatorship of a single man by the dictatorship of a reckless minority, prepared to go to any extent to ensure that its aims are carried through? Because they are pursuing an ideal which, of its nature, cannot be limited to the few. Because they are sure that, when the entire Russian proletariat is called on to make its choice, its answer cannot be in doubt. The answer is already there, in the conscience of the people, and it will become an irrevocable decision just as soon as it can be expressed in a climate of absolute spiritual freedom, when police intervention and the threat of hanging or exile are no longer distorting the vote. The industrial proletariat is already prepared for this step – even culturally prepared – and the agricultural proletariat, which is already familiar with the traditional forms of collective communism, is equally well prepared for the transition of a new form of society. Socialist revolutionaries cannot be Jacobins. Their only task in Russia at the moment is to make sure that the bourgeois organisms (the *duma*, the *zemstva*) do not get up to any

Jacobin tricks to engineer an inconclusive result in the voting, and to twist the violent overthrow to their own interests.

There is a further, revealing happening to which the bourgeois newspapers have not attached any importance. The Russian revolutionaries have released not only political prisoners, but also prisoners serving sentences for common crimes. In one house of detention, the common criminals, when they heard they were free, replied that they did not feel they had the right to accept their freedom, because they should pay for their crimes. In Odessa, prisoners met in the prison courtyard and voluntarily swore an oath to become honest men, and to resolve to live by their own labour. From the point of view of the socialist revolution, this piece of news is as significant, or more significant, than the news of the deposition of the Tsar and the grand-dukes. The Tsar could equally well have been deposed by the bourgeoisie. But, in bourgeois eyes, these prisoners would still have been the enemies of their order; subversives, eating away at their wealth and their peace of mind. To my mind, the liberation of these prisoners has this meaning: the revolution in Russia has created a new way of life. It has not simply replaced one power by another. It has replaced one way of life by another, created a new moral atmosphere, brought in a new freedom of the spirit, above and beyond physical freedom. The revolutionaries have not been afraid to allow back into circulation men whom bourgeois justice had branded with the shame of a criminal record; men whom bourgeois science had classified in the various categories of criminal offenders. Only in an atmosphere of real and passionate social renewal could something like this occur, when the whole way of life and the prevailing mentality have changed. Liberty makes men free. It widens their moral horizons, turning those who were the worst of criminals under an authoritarian regime into martyrs in the cause of duty, and heroes in the cause of right. It says in one newspaper report that these 'criminals' have refused to be freed, and have chosen to be their own warders. Why have they never done this before? Why did their prison have to have massive walls all around it and bars on the windows? The people who went to offer them their freedom must have had very different faces from the magistrates and warders they were used to, and these 'common criminals' must have heard words very different from those they were used to, for such a transformation to take place in their consciences; for them to become so free, suddenly, as to be able to choose segregation over freedom, and to impose a voluntary punishment on themselves. They must have felt that the world had changed – that even they, the dregs of society, had come to count for something; that even they, those the world had rejected, had been given the freedom to choose.

This is the most glorious result that human action has ever achieved. The Russian Revolution has turned man at his most abject – the 'common criminal' – into man as envisaged by Immanuel Kant, the theorist of absolute reason: the man who can say 'beyond me, the vastness of the skies; within me, the imperative of my conscience'. What these little news items reveal to us is no less than a liberation of the human spirit, the initiation of a new moral sense. It is the advent of a new moral order, which coincides with everything the prophets of our movement told us. And once again the light comes from the East and shines over the aged Western world – and the West is so dazed that its only response is the trite and stupid chatter of hacks.

Il Grido del Popolo, 29 April 1917

Why We Need a Cultural Association

On behalf of myself, and of many other people, I should like to express my approval of Comrade Pellegrino's proposal that a Cultural Association should be set up for our comrades here in Turin, both for locals and for comrades from elsewhere who are resident in the city.

I believe that, however unpropitious the moment may seem, this could be done very successfully. Many comrades, wavering in their convictions, and impatient with the day-to-day work which has to be done, have drifted away from our political organizations, lured by the appeal of mere amusements. The Cultural Association would satisfy these people's instinctive need for diversion, and they would find in it a source of relaxation and education which would renew their attachment to the political movement, to our ideal.

And this initiative, to which all comrades will wish to give their support, might also offer a solution to the problem of comrades who belong to Sections in different parts of the country, which has never been resolved precisely because of the difficulty of finding a field of common interest in which they might be active.

Bartolomeo Botto

Avanti! has been very pleased to publish Pellegrino's proposal and the statements of support it has received. In this letter, Botto has made some very interesting points, which we believe deserve to be developed and presented in a systematic form for the attention of all comrades.

There has never been any kind of popular cultural organization in Turin. The Popular University is best ignored – it has never become a real, living presence; never had a function which responded to any real need. It is bourgeois in origin, and it responds to a vague, confused criterion of spiritual humanitarianism. It is about as effective as those charitable institutions which set out with their bowls of soup to provide for the physiological needs of the poor – those wretched creatures who cannot feed themselves, and who move the tender hearts of their masters to pity.

The kind of Cultural Association which the socialists should promote must be one whose scope and aims are defined by class. It must be an institution of the proletariat, directed to precise ends. At a certain point in its development and its history, the proletariat becomes conscious that a vital organ is missing in its complex make-up; and it creates it for itself, with its own energies, its own good will, for its own ends.

In Turin, the proletariat has reached a point of development which is among the highest, if not the highest, in Italy. The Turin Section of the Socialist Party, in its political activity, has achieved a very distinct class identity; the economic organizations are strong and, through co-operation, it has been possible to succeed in creating a powerful institution like the Alleanza Cooperativa. So it is easy to understand why the need to integrate its political and economic activity with an organ of cultural activity should have arisen in Turin, and should be most keenly felt here. This need for integration will arise and assert itself elsewhere in Italy as well. And the proletarian movement will gain from it, becoming stronger and more unified and more determined in its struggle.

One of the most serious deficiencies in our activity is this: that we do not get round to discussing problems and establishing our policies until forced into it by events. And then, constrained as we are by the urgency of the situation, we come up with half-baked solutions – half-baked in the sense that not everyone who participates in the movement has grasped the precise nature of the issues at stake, so that, if they follow the policy which has been established, they do so out of a spirit of discipline and because of the faith they have in their leaders, rather than out of any intimate conviction, any spontaneous, reasoned consent. This is why, at every important historical conjuncture, we start to get splits in the movement, signs of weakening, internal squabbles, disputes between individuals. This lack of true discussion can explain, as well, the phenomenon of leader-worship, which is an inconsistency within our movement, and ends up letting in through the back door the authoritarianism we have driven out of the front.

What the movement lacks is a firm base of conviction at grass-roots level. It has neglected the long-term task of educating and mentally priming its members, which is needed to ensure swift and sure decision-making at any given moment, and guarantee the kind of immediate, effective, deep-rooted consensus which provides a solid foundation for action.

It is for the Cultural Association to take charge of the process of education, to set about creating convictions. The Association could discuss everything which regards the proletarian movement, or which might regard it in future. And it could discuss it disinterestedly, without awaiting the stimulus of events.

Besides, there are problems – philosophical, religious and moral – which underlie political and economic action, but which economic and political organisms are not equipped to discuss or to promote solutions for. These problems are of great importance. It is they which are the cause of the movement's so-called 'spiritual crises' and, every now and then, they throw up some controversial case as a stumbling-block. Socialism is a whole vision of life: it has its own philosophy, its own faith, its own morality. The Association would be an appropriate forum for discussing and clarifying these problems, and opening them to debate.

It would also solve, in great part, the problem of the 'intellectuals'. Intellectuals represent a dead weight within our movement, because they do not have a specific task in it, a task suited to their capacities. They would find it in the Association; and their intellectualism – their real intellectual qualities – would be put to the test.

By setting up this cultural institute, the socialists would deliver a death blow to the dogmatic and intolerant mentality which a Catholic and Jesuitical upbringing has instilled in the Italian people. The Italian people lack the spirit of disinterested solidarity, the love of free discussion, the desire to attain truth by the purely human means offered by intelligence and reason. The socialists would provide a living, working example of this spirit of free enquiry and, in doing so, they would go a very long way towards stimulating a new habit of mind, freer and more daring than the present one, and readier to accept the principles and the ends of socialism. In England and in Germany there existed – there still exist – extremely powerful organizations of proletarian and socialist culture. A particularly well-known example, in England, is the Fabian Society, which was a member of the Socialist International. The task of this Society is that of debating, exhaustively and in depth, all the economic and moral problems which the proletariat has encountered or will encounter in the course of its life. And it has succeeded in recruiting a very significant segment of the English intellectual and academic world to this task of civilization, of liberating minds.

Given the nature of the environment in Turin, and the maturity of its proletariat, it is here that the first nucleus could emerge – and *should* emerge – of a cultural organization with a distinct socialist and proletarian identity, which would become, along with the Party and the Confederazione del Lavoro, the third organ in the Italian working class's drive to assert its rights.

Avanti!, 18 December 1917

The Revolution Against *Capital*

The Bolshevik revolution is now definitively part of the general revolution of the Russian people. Up to two months ago, the maximalists were acting as catalysts, preventing events from stagnating, and the march on the future from slowing up and giving way to some kind of definitive settlement, which would inevitably have been a bourgeois settlement. But now the maximalists have seized power and established their dictatorship; now they are elaborating the socialist framework within which the revolution will finally have to settle, if it is to continue to develop harmoniously and without excessive strife, building on the great conquests which have already been made.

The Bolshevik revolution is made up of ideologies, more than events (and hence, when it comes down to it, it does not matter that we do not know any more about what is happening than we do). It is a revolution against Karl Marx's *Capital*. In Russia, Marx's *Capital* was more the book of the bourgeoisie than of the proletariat. It was a critical demonstration of the necessity that events must take a certain course in Russia: a bourgeoisie had to develop, the capitalistic era had to get under way and civilization on the Western model be introduced, before the proletariat could even start thinking about its own revolt, its own class demands, its own revolution. But events have overtaken ideology. Events have exploded the critical schemas whereby Russian history was meant to develop according to the canons of historical materialism. The Bolsheviks have renounced

Karl Marx and they have shown, with the backing of real actions, actual achievements, that the canons of historical materialism are not as iron-clad as it might be thought, as it *has* been thought.

Yet there is a kind of fatality even in these happenings and, even if the Bolsheviks renounce certain of Marx's assertions in *Capital*, that does not mean that they renounce the deeper message which is its lifeblood. All that it means is that they are not 'Marxists'; they have not used the Master's works to compile a rigid doctrine, made up of dogmatic and unquestionable claims. They are *living out* Marxist thought – the real, undying Marxist thought, which continues the heritage of German and Italian idealism, but which, in Marx, was contaminated by positivist and naturalist incrustations. And this true Marxist thought has always identified as the most important factor in history not crude, economic facts, but rather men themselves, and the societies they create, as they learn to live with one another and understand one another; as, out of these contacts (civilization), they forge a social, collective will; as they come to understand economic facts, and to assess them, and to control them with their will, until this collective will becomes the driving force of the economy, the force which shapes reality itself, so that objective reality becomes a living, breathing force, like a current of molten lava, which can be channelled wherever and however the will directs.

Marx predicted what could be predicted. He could not predict the war in Europe, or rather, he could not predict that it would last so long, or have the effects it had. He could not predict that, in three years of unspeakable suffering and unspeakable hardship, this war would have aroused in Russia the popular collective will it has. *In the normal course of events*, it would have taken a long process of gradual diffusion through society for such a collective will to form; a vast range of class experiences would have been needed. Men are lazy. They need to be organized, first externally, into corporations and leagues; then internally, in their thought, in their will, in an endless continuity and multiplicity of external stimuli. And that is why, *in the normal course of events*, the canons of Marxist historical criticism are successful in grasping reality, snaring it, laying it open to analysis. *In the normal course of events*, it is through a gradually intensifying class struggle that the two classes of the capitalistic world create history. The proletariat is acutely aware of its abject poverty, the unending privations it suffers, and it pressures the bourgeoisie to improve its conditions. It enters into struggle; it forces the bourgeoisie to improve the technology of production, to maximize the efficiency of production to make it possible for it to satisfy at least the most urgent needs of the proletariat. The result is a headlong race for improvement, which accelerates the rhythm of production and continually boosts the output of goods useful to society. It is a race in which many are left behind, and the desire of the remaining contestants becomes still more urgent; in which the masses are continually in a state of turmoil. And, out of this chaos, they develop some order in their thoughts, they become more and more aware of their own potential, their own capacity to assume social responsibility for themselves, to become the arbiters of their own destiny.

All this in the normal course of events. When events are repeated with a certain rhythm. When history is developing through a series of moments, each more complex than the last and richer in meaning and value, but nonetheless similar. But, in Russia, the war has served to galvanize the people's will. As a result of the massed sufferings they have suffered over these three years, their will has very rapidly become as one. Famine was imminent. Hunger, starvation was threatening everyone, threatening to crush millions of men at a stroke. In these circumstances, at first purely mechanically, and then, after the first revolution, actively and consciously, the people's wills became one.

Socialist propaganda has put the Russian people in touch with the experiences of other proletariats. Socialist propaganda brings the whole history of the proletariat to life in one dramatic instant: its struggles against capitalism, the lengthy series of efforts it has had to make in order to free itself, in thought, from the chains of servility which made it so abject, and to become the new conscience of the world and a testimony today to a world yet to come. Socialist propaganda has forged the collective will of the Russian people. Why, then, should the Russian people wait for the history of England to repeat itself in Russia, for a bourgeoisie to form, for the class struggle to be set in motion – all so that class consciousness may be born and the final downfall of the capitalist world brought about? The Russian people has passed through all these experiences in thought, even if only in the thought of a few. It has overtaken these experiences. It is using them now, in order to assert itself, just as it will use the technological experience of Western capitalism in order to bring itself up to the standards of production in the Western world in a short space of time. North America is more advanced than England, as a capitalist society, because the Anglo-Saxon settlers in North America got off to a head start, starting, as they did, from the stage England had reached after a long evolution. The Russian proletariat, with its socialist education, will take as its starting-point the highest level that production has reached in England today, because, since it has to start from scratch, it will start from what has already been perfected elsewhere and, from that advantaged starting-point, it will get the momentum to reach that level of economic maturity which, according to Marx, is a necessary pre-condition for collectivism. The revolutionaries will themselves create the conditions needed to realize their ideal fully and completely. And they will create them in far less time than it would have taken a capitalist system. The criticisms socialists have directed at the bourgeois system, emphasizing its deficiencies and its squandering of resources, will permit the revolutionaries to do better, to avoid this kind of squandering and escape falling into the same traps. At the outset, it will be a collectivism of poverty and suffering. But a bourgeois regime would have inherited the same conditions of poverty and suffering. Capitalism could not achieve any more in Russia than collectivism can, *in the immediate term*. It would achieve a great deal less, *in the immediate term*, because it would have a discontented and frenetic proletariat on its hands, incapable of going through all the suffering and bitterness of economic hardship for the benefit of others. Even from an absolute point of view, from the point of view of humanity, there is a justification for socialism in Russia now, at this moment. The suffering which will be ushered in by the peace will only be bearable at all if the proletarians feel that the power to end this suffering in the shortest time possible lies in their will and their dedication to their work.

One has the impression that at this moment the maximalists have acted as the spontaneous expression of an almost *biological* necessity – that they *had* to be there, to prevent the Russian people from falling into the most horrendous calamity; to protect Russian humanity, now embarking on the colossal task of self-regeneration, from the threat of the ravening wolves outside, and to prevent Russia from becoming a vast killing-field of wild beasts tearing each other to pieces.

Avanti!, 24 December 1917

Critical Criticism

Claudio Treves has written an article in the latest *Critica Sociale*, with the twin aims of preserving for posterity a letter of Leon Martov's, and registering the 'alarming' ignorance of the new generation of Italian socialists.

The 'new generation' has 'adapted the doctrine of Marx in such a way that *determinism* has been replaced by *voluntarism*, the *transforming power* of the labour force by the heroic or hysterical *violence* of individuals or groups. There is a mood of frenetic subjectivism, and the worst distortions of the demagogues are greeted with flattery and applause.'

It is certainly true that the 'new generation' is lamentably ignorant. But, probably, the new generation is no more ignorant than the 'old guard' and, still more probably, its ignorance is not quite the kind of ignorance which Treves makes out. In addition to the Communist Manifesto, for example, the 'new generation' has also read Marx and Engels' pamphlet on 'critical criticism', and has been struck by the fact that the Bauers of this world have not been cured of their liking for scrambling up concepts and facts into fantastic pseudo-philosophical concoctions. It has also read and studied the books which have come out in Europe since the flowering of Positivism, and has discovered (hardly a great discovery) that the sterilization of Marx's doctrines at the hands of the Positivist Socialists was not exactly a mighty cultural advance, and was not accompanied by any great practical advances, either.

43

So, how is it that *Social Criticism* has turned into a latter-day *Critical Criticism*? The reason is that its writers are doing just the same things that Marx found so ridiculous in messrs Bruno Bauer, Faucher and Szeliga, who wrote for *Allgemeine Literaturzeitung*. Because, just like Bruno Bauer with his 'self-consciousness', Treves substitutes abstractions like 'determinism' or 'the transforming forces' for real, living, individual human beings. Because Treves, with that high culture of his, has reduced Marx's doctrine to an abstract scheme, a kind of natural law, operating deterministically, quite outside the sphere of men's wills, of their collective activity, of the social forces developed by this activity. For Treves, this law, in itself, is what comes to determine progress, and is the motive force which generates new forms of production.

In this way, Marx's doctrine became the doctrine of the inertia of the proletariat. Which is not to say that *voluntarism* was denied in practice (the constraints of our language force me to use this word, even though it does not mean much). Voluntarism was simply reserved for the petty skirmishes of the reformists. It became something vulgar. The power of the will became the power to will ministerial compromises, small victories. Better to have your egg today than wait for a chicken tomorrow, even if, as Ruta said, the egg in question is a flea's egg.

The work of proselytizing was dropped (what use were 'individual men'?). The historical action of the proletariat, however effective, could not impinge on the process of development of the capitalist economy. Even from the point of view of the reformists, the role of *Critical Criticism* has been a negative one. With its customary 'flea's egg' approach, it completely ignored the great national problems, which concern the entire Italian proletariat. It should not be forgotten that, in 1913, when the Socialist Party presented itself at the elections with a manifesto in favour of liberalizing trade, *Critical Criticism* published two protectionist articles written by Treves and Turati.

If it were not for Gaetano Salvemini's *Unità*, then, perhaps, Treves would be able to talk about the 'lack of sophistication' of the new generation of socialists. But Salvemini and Mondolfo (and we are talking here about men of the same tendency as Treves) have exposed what the so-called 'sophistication' of *Critical Criticism* is based on so often that even the youngest socialists will not worry too much about 'Very Well''s reproach.

The 'new generation', therefore, refuses to take seriously not the old generation as a whole, but the generation which has found its niche in the columns of *Critical Criticism*.

The socialists of the 'new generation', it seems, want a return to the original doctrine of Marx, for whom the individual man and reality, the instrument of work and the will, are not disjoined, but fused together in the action of history. They believe, then, that the canons of historical materialism are to be used only retrospectively, as an instrument for studying and understanding the events of the past; but that they should not be a burden on the present and the future. They believe, not that the War has destroyed historical materialism, but certainly that the War has modified the conditions of the normal environment for historical action, giving an importance to men's collective will which it would not have under normal conditions. These new conditions are economic factors, just as much as the old were, and they have completely changed the face of the systems of production. The process of educating the proletariat has necessarily had to adjust to this new situation and in Russia, this adjustment has led to dictatorship.

(Lenin's decrees, the butt of Treves' facile irony, are not, in fact, arbitrary and anti-historical. They are the necessary outcome of the new legislative environment which has been gradually emerging and is now consolidating itself. They are certainly a great deal more valid than those worthless little laws and decrees which Treves and his parliamentary group have managed to get passed by the Italian ministers in office in twenty years of activity in Rome. Treves' *Critical Criticism* – which delights in facile ironies and certainly never reaches the level of philosophical dignity of Bruno Bauer's equivalent publication – has pronounced that Lenin's decrees are invalid. To be valid, of course, these decrees should really be countersigned by Giovanni Giolitti, and they should be the result of compromise and manoeuvring in the corridors of power, rather than of the class action of the proletariat, and the momentum of class organization.)

The human will, when it comes down to it, exists for Treves as well; but it is a defensive, rather than an offensive will; a will which lies in ambush, rather than coming out into the open. Even for Treves, culture cannot exist in a vacuum – that precious 'culture' of his, which, if he had listened, would have reminded him that, long before Marx, Giovanni Battista Vico said that belief in divine providence had been a positive force in history, as it had proved a stimulus for conscious action. If even a belief in divine providence can act in this way, then a belief in 'determinism' could have the same effect, for Lenin in Russia, and for others elsewhere.

Il Grido del Popolo, 12 January 1918

Socialism and Economic Organization[1]

We are publishing this piece by a young comrade, because he assures us that it represents the thinking of an important section of the Socialist movement in Turin. We should make it clear, from the start, that we are not going to make any attempt to place it within the history of ideas, or the history of the expression of ideas. We shall examine it in itself, and on its own terms, as a manifestation of convictions which may, indeed, be shared, and which may determine particular attitudes.

While we agree, on a general level, with very many of comrade R.F.'s assertions, we believe him to be in error in certain of his views, and the consequences he derives from them. The split that syndicalist critics perceive between politics and economics, between the organism and its social environment, seems to us nothing but a theoretical abstraction from the empirical, entirely practical necessity of temporarily dividing up the active social unity, in order to study it better, and to understand it better. When we analyse a phenomenon, it is necessary to reduce this phenomenon to what we might call its elements, even though each of these elements is really nothing but the same phenomenon, viewed at one moment rather than another,

---

[1] Gramsci's article was appended to a piece signed R.F. in which the author argued that the 'social organism' and the 'social environment' were distinct forces and that the 'attempt to alter the organism by transforming the environment had revealed itself to be a chimera'.

viewed with an eye to one particular end, rather than another. But society, like man himself, always remains an irreducible historical and ideal entity, which develops by continually contradicting itself and surpassing itself. Politics and the economy, the human environment and the social organism are one and the same thing, and always will be; and it is one of the great merits of Marxism that it has asserted this dialectical unity. What has happened now is that the syndicalists and the reformists, through the same kind of error in their thinking, have specialized in different branches of the empirical language of socialism. The first have arbitrarily extracted one term from the unified whole of social activity – the term 'economy'. The others, equally arbitrarily, have chosen the term 'politics'. The syndicalists have become fossilized in their professional organization: that initial distortion in their thinking has led them to practise bad politics and worse economics. The reformists, meanwhile, have become fossilized into an abstract parliamentary, legislative role and, for the same reason as the syndicalists, they practise bad politics and appalling economics.

Out of these deviations, the chance for, and the need for, revolutionary socialism are born: a socialism which can restore the original unity of all social activity; a socialism which practises politics and economics without adjectives; a socialism which aids the development and the gradual rise to self-consciousness of the spontaneous, untrammelled and historically necessary energies of both capitalism and the proletariat, so that from their antagonism there can arise provisional syntheses, ever more finished and perfect, destined to culminate in the final act, the final event, which subsumes them all, with no trace of privilege and exploitation remaining. This conflictual social activity will not result in a professional State, like that dreamt of by the syndicalist, nor in a State which has monopolized production and distribution, like that dreamt of by the reformists. Instead, there will be an *organization* reflecting the freedom of all and for all, which will not have a stable and pre-determined character, but will be a continual search for new forms, for new relationships, ever more closely attuned to the needs of individuals and groups, so that all initiatives will be respected, as long as they are useful and all freedoms will be jealously guarded, as long as they are not freedoms endowed by privilege. These theoretical considerations are being tested now in the heat of experience, in the Russian Revolution, which, up till now, has consisted in a titanic effort to stop any static conception of socialism from establishing itself definitively, closing down the process of revolution and fatally drawing it back into some kind of bourgeois regime which, if it turned out to be liberal and *laissez-faire* in its sympathies, would finish up by lending historicist credentials to either a professional regime, or a centralized, state-worshipping regime.

It is not correct, then, to assert that socialist political activity may be defined as such simply because it is practised by men who call themselves socialists. It would be just the same as saying of any other activity, that it is what it is said to be, just because the same adjective is given to the men who practise it.

We would do far better to call bad politics by its real name – a racket – and not to let the racketeers wheedle us into renouncing an activity which is an integral and necessary part of our movement. Besides, as Kautsky has acutely observed, political and parliamentary phobias are a petit bourgeois weakness: a weakness of lazy people, who do not want to make the effort of trying to control their own representatives, and of ensuring that they are at one with their deputies, or that their deputies are at one with them.

Il Grido del Popolo, 9 February 1918

Socialism and Actualist Philosophy

Thinkers are all too often carried away, just like everyone else, by the passions aroused by events and, for some time now, the only thing they have had to say about socialism and the workers' movement is that they are theoretically inane and historically invalid. This is not the attitude assumed, however, by a young philosopher, Professor Giuseppe Saitta, in an article entitled, *The Great Victor*.[1] Saitta is one of the most promising disciples of Giovanni Gentile, the Italian philosopher who has produced more than any other in the field of thought in the past few years. His system of philosophy is the latest development in the German Idealist tradition which reached its culmination in Georg Hegel, the master of Karl Marx. It consists of the rejection of any transcendentalism and the identification of philosophy with history, with the act of thinking: an act in which truth and historical fact are united, in a dialectical progression, which is never definitive and complete. Gentile, who has written a volume on Marx's philosophy, used explicitly Marxist concepts, only a few days ago, in a judgement on the League of Nations. What follows is what Professor Saitta writes about socialism: these rapid statements may be taken as a judgment made according to the 'actualist' system of philosophy, and they prompt the hope that these thinkers may decide to enrich the literature of socialism with some good publications, which will serve to revitalize our thinking, to make it more lucid and precise.

Il Grido del Popolo, 9 February 1918

[1] *Il Resto del Corlino*, 5 February 1918.

The Club of Moral Life

Turin, March 1918

Dear Sir,[1]

I write enclosing an article my colleague Andrea Viglongo has written for *Il Grido del Popolo* on your pamphlet, *The Concept of Education*.[2] The occasional discrepancy or inaccuracy in the piece may be explained by the fact that the young man is an autodidact. I know and admire the contribution you have made to the spiritual improvement of Italian youth; that is why I am writing, to tell you about the modest work we Socialists are attempting to carry out in Turin – yes, in this city which is a byword in Italy for proletarian and defeatist barbarity and stupidity. I believe that your goodness and kind-heartedness have preserved you from contagion by the corruption which has become endemic: our difference of opinion over the role the Socialist proletariat should perform in the war cannot cancel out our mutual respect.

We in Turin believe that it is not enough just to exhort people in words to adopt the principles and moral maxims which must necessarily accompany the advent of the new Socialist civilization. We have attempted to organize our exhortation and, in doing so, to provide new (for Italy) models of association. And so a *Club of Moral Life* has

---

[1] The letter is addressed to G. Lombardo Radice, a follower of Giovanni Gentile.
[2] This appeared on 16 March 1916.

recently been set up.[3] Through this club, we intend to accustom the young people who join the Socialist political and economic movement to the disinterested discussion of ethical and social problems. We intend to accustom them to research; to disciplined, systematic reading; to setting out their convictions in a clear and objective manner. The work is divided up as follows. I (who, as the founder of the Association, find myself in the role of *excubitor*) allot the young person an *assignment*, which might be your pamphlet on education, or a chapter from something like Croce's *Culture and Moral Life* or Salvemini's *Social and Educational Problems* or *The French Revolution* or *Culture and Laicality*, again by Salvemini, or maybe a chapter from the *Communist Manifesto*, or a short piece by Croce from *La Critica* – anything that reflects the influence of the current Idealist movement. The student reads, takes notes and then presents the results of his researches and reflection at a meeting. Then someone – a member of the audience, if someone has prepared, or myself – intervenes to make objections, suggest alternative solutions and perhaps explore the broader implications of a given idea or argument. In this way, a discussion opens up, which ideally continues until *all* those present have been enabled to understand and absorb the most important results of this collective work. Beyond this, the Club has among its objectives a full acceptance of reciprocal control by the members over each person's daily activity – family life, work and social interaction. We want each member to have the courage and moral energy to make a public confession and to accept the advice and guidance of his friends. We want to create a reciprocal bond of trust: an intellectual and moral communion, uniting us all.

Viglongo's article is the result of a Club meeting. Viglongo is seventeen years old and works as a clerk. He is educated up to lower-school standard in technical studies. The *Grido del Popolo* has published other pieces by him: a study of Croce's *Faith and Programmes* and another on Croce's *Sensual Nationalism*. Viglongo is currently working on another on the *Southern Question*, taking as his starting-point the writings of Salvemini.

I know you follow all new pedagogical developments with interest and it would give me great pleasure if you would be so good as to send

[3] The *Club di vita morale* was founded by Gramsci with Carlo Boccardo, Attilio Cavena and Andrea Viglongo towards the end of 1917, meeting mainly at the latter's house. It was dissolved in March 1918, when Boccardo, Cavena and Viglongo were called up.

me your opinion of this initiative of ours, which we are struggling to establish and develop against considerable odds. The young people involved are all workers: Turinese Socialism is distinctly working-class in character and the few students we have are away on military service. Although the young people we are working with are intelligent and willing, we are having to start from the simplest and most elementary things: from language itself. Could you help me out with some advice, by sketching out a plan which would fill in the gaps in my proposals? Or by pointing out the errors I may fall into? I would be extremely grateful and your words of help would give my young friends new energy to persevere and redouble their efforts.

Yours faithfully,

Antonio Gramsci
Corso Siccardi, 12-Turin

Our Marx

Are we Marxists? Is there such a thing as a Marxist? Stupidity, thou alone art immortal. The question will probably be taken up again in the next few days, as the centenary of his birth is coming up, and rivers of ink and inanity will flow in answer. Empty chatter and pointless hair-splitting are part of the inalienable heritage of humanity. Marx did not write some neat little doctrine; he is not some Messiah who left us a string of parables laden with categorical imperatives and absolute, unchallengeable norms, lying outside the categories of time and space. His only categorical imperative, his only norm: 'Workers of the world, unite!' Recognizing the duty to organize and propagandizing this duty to organize and join forces should therefore be what distinguishes Marxists from non-Marxists. Too much and too little: who, in this case, would *not* be a Marxist?

And yet that is the way it is: everyone is a bit of a Marxist, without knowing it. Marx was a great man, and his action in the world produced results, not because he invented anything from nothing, not because he conjured up some *original* vision of history, but because he turned what had been fragmentary, incomplete and immature into something mature, systematic and self-conscious. And his own personal consciousness can become the consciousness of everyone: it has already become the consciousness of many. Because of this, Marx is not merely a scholar but a man of action; he is as great, as productive in his action as in his thought; his books have transformed the world, just as they have transformed the way we think.

Marx means the advent of intelligence into human history, into the realm of consciousness.

His work falls into just the period when the great battle was taking place between Thomas Carlyle and Herbert Spencer on the role of man in history.

Carlyle: the hero, the great individual, the mystical synthesis of a spiritual communion, leading the destinies of humanity towards an unknown and evanescent goal, in the chimerical land of perfection and sanctity.

Spencer: nature, evolution, mechanical, inanimate abstraction. Man: an atom within a natural organism, obeying a law which is abstract in itself, but becomes concrete, historically, within individuals: immediate utility.

Marx plants himself squarely in history with the solid stance of a giant: neither a mystic, nor a positivist metaphysician, but a historian, an interpreter of the documents of the past – *all* the documents, not just a selection of them.

This was the intrinsic defect of all histories, all researches into human events: that they examined and took into consideration only a selection of the documents available. And this selection was made not by the will of history, but as a result of partisan prejudice, which was still prejudice even when it was unconscious and involved no bad faith. Historical research had as its end not truth, precision and a complete vision of the past, but rather the highlighting of a particular activity or the confirmation of a pre-established thesis. History was the domain of ideas alone. Man was considered as pure spirit, pure consciousness. Two mistaken consequences derived from this conception: the theses which were being demonstrated were often simply arbitrary and fictitious and the facts which were given importance were anecdote, not history. If history was ever written – history in the true sense of the word – then it was due to the intuitive genius of isolated individuals, rather than to any systematic and conscious scientific activity.

With Marx, history remains the dominion of ideas, of the spirit, of the conscious activity of individuals, whether single or in co-operation. But the ideas, the spirit, take on substance, lose their arbitrary character; they are no longer fictitious religious or sociological abstractions. Their substance lies in economics, in practical activity, in the systems and relations of production and exchange.

History, as event, is entirely composed of practical activity (economic and moral). An idea does not become realized because of its logical consistency with truth in its pure form, humanity in its pure form (which exists only as a project, as man's general ethical end). Ideas are realized when they find their justification – and the means to assert themselves – in economic reality. In order to establish with precision the historical ends of a nation, a society, a social grouping, the most important thing to know is what systems and relations of production and exchange obtain in that nation, that society. Without this knowledge, one can write narrow monographs, dissertations which may be useful for the history of culture; one can identify side-effects and far-flung consequences. But one will not be writing history; and practical activity will not be disclosed in all its compactness and solidity.

The idols are falling from their altars, the gods are watching the clouds of perfumed incense thin out around them. Man is acquiring a new awareness of objective reality; he is mastering the secrets which govern what happens in the world. Man is coming to know himself, to know how much his individual will can be worth and how powerful it can become, if, by bowing to necessity, by disciplining itself to obey necessity, it can come to dominate necessity itself, by identifying necessity with its own ends. Who is it who really knows himself? Not man in general, but the man who submits to the yoke of necessity. The search for the substance of history, the process of identifying that substance within the system and relations of production and exchange, allows us to discover that society is divided into two classes. The class which possesses the instruments of production already, necessarily, knows itself, and has a certain awareness – even if confused and fragmentary – of its power and its mission. It has its individual ends and it realizes them through its own capacity to organize, coldly, objectively, without worrying about whether its path is paved with famine-ravaged bodies or with the dead of battle.

The establishment of the real laws of historical causality takes on the character of a revelation only for the other class; it becomes a principle of order for that vast, shepherdless herd. The herd acquires a consciousness of itself, of the task it must perform now so that this other class may assert itself. It becomes aware that its individual ends will remain purely arbitrary, mere words, an empty, bombastic whim, until it possesses the means to act, until whim has been converted into will.

Voluntarism? The word means nothing, or it is used in the meaning of arbitrary will. Will, in a Marxist sense, means consciousness of ends, which in turn implies having an exact notion of one's own power, and the means to express it in action. So it means, in the first place, that the class must become distinct and individuated; that it must acquire a political life independent from that of the other class and organize its activity in a solid and disciplined manner towards its own, specific ends, without deviations or hesitations. It means cutting a straight and direct path through to the ultimate end, without detours into the green meadows of happy brotherhood, tender with fresh green shoots and mellow declarations of mutual esteem and love.

But the phrase 'in a Marxist sense' is otiose; in fact, it is a phrase which could give rise to misunderstandings and to yet more fatuous outpourings of words. 'Marxists', 'in a Marxist sense' . . . the words are worn as thin as coins which have passed through too many hands.

For us, Karl Marx is a master of moral and spiritual life, not a shepherd wielding a crook. He is a harrier of the mentally lazy, a rouser of good energies which are half-asleep and need to be awakened for the good fight. He is an example of the kind of intense and tenacious work which is needed to achieve that clarity and integrity of ideas, and that solid culture which are necessary if we do not want to talk in a void, about abstractions. He is a monolithic bloc of conscious, thinking humanity: someone who does not watch his tongue when speaking, or put his hand on his heart to feel, but constructs iron-clad syllogisms which encircle reality in its essence, and dominate it; which penetrate people's minds, and break down the accretions of prejudice and fixed ideas and strengthen the moral character.

For us, Karl Marx is not the infant whimpering in his cradle, nor the bearded man who puts the fear of God into sacristans. He is not to be found in any of the anecdotal episodes of his biography, in any gesture, brilliant or crude, of his outward self as a human animal. He is a vast and serene thinking brain; one individual moment in humanity's strenuous, age-old struggle to acquire awareness of what it is and what it is to become, to grasp the mysterious rhythms of history and to disperse the mystery which surrounds it, to become stronger in our thought and in our actions. He is a necessary and integral part of our human spirit, which would not be what it is now, if Marx had not lived and thought and fired off sparks of light from the clash of his passions and ideas, of his misfortunes and ideals.

When it glorifies Karl Marx, at the centenary of his birth, the international proletariat is glorifying itself: its self-conscious power and the dynamism of its conquering spirit which is already undermining the dominion of privilege, as it prepares for the final struggle which will crown all its efforts and sacrifices.

Il Grido del Popolo, 4 May 1918

Class Intransigence and Italian History

La Stampa has just published two more articles on the 'socialist rift'. *La Stampa* insists on the purely 'cultural' and informative character of these features. What remarkable disinterest! What a pure and unworldly desire to inform and educate the Italian nation! But let us not press the point. Let us concentrate on the issues of substance; on the real consequences that the attitudes of the interested parties in the current dispute between intransigents and relativists in our party may have for political affairs and Italian history.

To all intents and purposes, *La Stampa* has come out in support of the parliamentary group. The offensive against the intransigents is being conducted deftly, with all the cunning dexterity that characterizes Giolitti's followers. The articles in *La Stampa* are written by a 'sympathizer': very convenient for making the paper's proletarian readers drop their critical guard. They are written by a man of talent, who has mastered Marxist critical language; a man of high culture, skilled in the fine art of distinguishing and sifting concepts in the light of the most recent advances in idealist philosophy. In the natural logic of things and values, this 'sympathizer' has become theorist to the collaborationists. The three articles published so far have provided a whole torrent of polemical motifs, inferences and logical formulae which will be seized upon in papers, but more particularly in private conversation, as a way of propping up the relativist thesis.

Because of this, we consider it necessary to subject the whole argument to an extremely close critical scrutiny. This will take some time, unfortunately, but those readers who have the goodwill to follow us through to the end will see that it was worth it: that the polemic between the editors of *Avanti!* and the collaborationists is far more than a petty skirmish over parliamentary tactics and party discipline; that it is in fact the prelude to a formidable battle in which the form of the Italian State and the next twenty years of Italian history are at stake.

The nucleus of the dispute (in the words *La Stampa* places in the mouths of the relativists) is this.

> The interventionist parties are gradually taking over all the powers and mechanisms of the State machine, regulating and controlling them both directly and indirectly. *Moreover*, they are taking advantage of this control over State powers, this gradual 'annexation' of State power on the part of their parties – to the point where they identify the organization of the State with their own party organization – in order to weaken, dislocate and finally reduce to impotence the political instrument of the working class: the Socialist Party.

This is how the collaborationists argue and *La Stampa* applauds them. Why? Because the first and only victims of the 'annexationist' phenomenon are Giolitti and his party; because the 'annexationist' phenomenon represents the beginning of a new form of government for Italy: one which presupposes a class State, in the face of which all the bourgeois parties are equal and none has any advantage. It represents the beginning of a democratic era, born not as a result of the goodwill of one party or another, but as a product of the inexorable logic of events. Giolitti's exclusive right to govern has been corroded. Another party has managed to stay in power for longer than expected and is seeking to consolidate its position. In similar cases, the logic of history has led to the following optimal outcome (the history of the parties in England is a case in point): under the pressure of a fierce competition between two equally strong parties, each of which fears the predominance of the other, the State shakes off its burden of encumbering functions, the administration is decentralized, the tyranny of the bureaucracy is attenuated and the seats of power become independent. The State loses its feudal, despotic and militaristic structure and reconstitutes itself in such a way that the dictatorship of a party leader becomes impossible, for there is always the possibility of an alternation in power: whoever represents what is most essential in the political and economic forces of the country succeeds to power. The result for the country is an active encouragement of the natural and spontaneous energies that arise from its economic activity, rather than a morbid expansion of those parasitical sectors of society that eat their way from politics into the field of economic activity and whose sole *raison d'être* is the extraordinary privileges they enjoy.

Class, State, Parties

What does the State represent from a socialist point of view? The State is the economic–political organization of the bourgeois class. The State is the real, concrete expression of the bourgeois class. The bourgeois class is not a unified entity outside the State. As a consequence of the principle and practice of free competition, new groups of capitalist producers are constantly being formed to fulfil the regime's economic capacity. Each of these groups would like to escape from the cruel fray of competition by imposing a monopoly. The State's function is to find a juridical settlement to internal class disputes and the friction between opposing interests; to unify the different groupings and to project the outward image of the whole class. The government, State power, is the locus where the competition between the various groupings is concentrated. The government is the prize for the strongest bourgeois grouping. By virtue of its strength, the latter wins the right to regulate State power, to turn it to any particular end and to manipulate it practically at will, according to its economic and political programmes.

The bourgeois parties and the Socialist Party have completely different attitudes to the State. The bourgeois parties are either spokesmen for certain categories of producers or they are simply a swarm of 'coachman-flies'[1] who make not the slightest impact on the real structure of the State but drone away at their speeches and suck away at the honey of handouts.

The Socialist Party is not a sectional, but a class organization: its

---

[1] [Translator's note] The reference is to La Fontaine's fable, 'Le coche et la mouche' (*Fables*, VII, 8), in which a fly perched on the back of a coach is convinced that it is through its efforts that the vehicle is ascending a hill.

morphology is quite different from that of any other party. It is only in the State, the whole complex of bourgeois class power, that it can recognize an antagonist that is its equal. The Socialist Party cannot enter into competition for the conquest of the State, either directly or indirectly, without destroying itself: without losing its nature and becoming a mere political faction, estranged from the historical activity of the proletariat; without turning into a swarm of coachman-flies hunting for a bowl of blancmange in which to get stuck and die its inglorious death.

The Socialist Party does not conquer the State; it replaces it. It replaces the regime, abolishes party government and replaces free competition by the organization of production and exchange.

Does Italy have a Class State?

In discussions and debates, historical reality is all too often obscured by the words superimposed on it. When speaking of Italy, we use words like 'capitalists', 'proletariat', 'State' or 'parties', as though these words represented social entities that had reached the peak of their historical maturity, or at least a high degree of maturity, as is the case in the economically advanced countries. But in Italy capitalism is in its infancy and the law is in no way adapted to the real situation. The law is a modern excrescence on an ancient edifice. It is not the product of an economic evolution, but of a process of international political mimicry. It is the outcome of the intellectual evolution of jurisprudence, rather than an evolution in the instruments of labour.

Giuseppe Prezzolini drew attention to this recently in connection with the polemic over 'democracy'. Behind a thin facade of democratic institutions, the Italian State has retained the substance and structure of a despotic State (the same can be said of France). There is a bureaucratic, centralist regime, based on the tyrannical Napoleonic system, designed to crush and contain any spontaneous impulse or movement. Foreign affairs are conducted in the utmost secrecy; not only are discussions not public, but even the actual terms of treaties remain a mystery to those affected by them. The army operated on a career basis (at least until the War blew the antiquated system apart); it was not the nation in arms. There is a State religion, financed and aided by the State; there is no separation of Church and State, no equality of all religions. Schools are either completely lacking or rely on teachers chosen out of the limited ranks of the needy (given the paltriness of the wages) and who are not up to the challenge of educating the nation. The suffrage was restricted right up to the last elections and even now it is very far from enabling the nation to express its will. Free competition, the essential principle of the capitalist bourgeoisie, has not yet touched the most important activities of national life. And so we have a position in which political forms are mere arbitrary superstructures, lacking any real muscle and producing no results. The seats of power are still confused and interdependent and there are no large parties organized by the agrarian and industrial bourgeoisies. (Parliament is effectively subject to the executive power; it lacks any capacity for effective control. The deputies are nothing but messenger-boys for the local groups of peasants or the third estate, who go to the capital to ask for particular privileges, just like under an all-out feudal regime, rather than to establish the rule of the law.)

So there does not exist a class State, in which the principle of free enterprise reaches its peak of efficacy, with the alternation in power of great parties representing the vast interests of whole productive categories. What has existed is the dictatorship of one man, a representative of the limited political interests of the Piedmont region, who, in order to keep Italy united, has imposed a centralized and despotic system of colonial domination on the country. The system is falling apart. New bourgeois forces have arisen and consolidated themselves; and they are demanding recognition of their interests in order to be able to assert themselves and develop. Interventionism is a contingent phenomenon, as is passivism – the War will not last for ever. What is threatened with collapse in the future is the despotic Giolittian State and the whole mass of parasitical interests encrusted on this old State. It is the old enfeebled bourgeoisie which feels its entrenched privileges threatened by this ferment of bourgeois youth demanding its place in government and demanding to be part of the free play of political competition. Provided that its evolution is not interrupted by some new event, this new bourgeois current will undoubtedly rejuvenate the State and throw out all the débris of tradition. For a democratic State is not the product of a kind heart or a liberal education; it is a basic necessity of life in a world of large-scale production, intensive exchange and the concentration of the population in modern, capitalist cities.

The Unspoken Promise[2]

The historical situation stands in the following terms. In twenty years of unchecked dictatorship, the Giolittian grouping has made a show of doling out formal freedoms, while in fact consolidating the despotic State dear to the memory of Emanuele Filiberto. The weapon of this grouping's domination, its dictatorship, has now fallen into the hands of the enemy grouping (we do not refer to either as a party since both lack any kind of political or economic structure). This latter has held on to it for longer than was expected and is now making use of it, moulding it to its own ends and turning it back against its former masters. If this struggle remains one between bourgeois groupings of sectoral interests, a new, liberal State will arise from the furious clash between the two sides. The era of party government will begin: great parties will be formed and small discords will disappear, swallowed up by higher interests.

The Giolittians would like to avoid the clash. They have no desire to do battle over vast institutional programmes, which could raise the political temperature of the nation to an uncomfortably high degree. God knows (the god of the bourgeoisie) how little the nation can take another overheating and what effect such a shock could have on the proletariat. The Giolittians would like to avoid the clash and find a parliamentary resolution to the problems that are goading them. In other words, they are keeping up their tradition of minimizing every important problem, excluding the nation from political affairs and avoiding any reference to public opinion. The Giolittians are in a minority. And just look! The Socialist deputies are off hunting butterflies, while the sirens sing their nostalgic airs on freedom, parliamentary control and the need for collaboration if the nation is to move, act and break with inertia.

---

[2] [Author's note] In a fourth article added today (17 May), *La Stampa* explicitly discusses the possibility of a collaboration for peace. *La Stampa* is of the opinion that this discussion should be deferred until the time is ripe. We on the other hand, given the democratic constitution of our party, believe that it is necessary for the party federations and local sections to engage in an exhaustive discussion immediately on the problem of peace, as on other issues, and to issue the party with a firm and resolute political line of intransigent class struggle. We must not allow ourselves to be caught unawares and disunited, because that would allow the parliamentary group to sow confusion in the party and elevate itself into a pseudo-power. There would be the most colossal *marché des dupes* and the party would be liquidized for the next couple of decades, while the 'realistic' parliamentary forces triumphed . . .

And just look, as well, how *La Stampa* comes to their aid with the 'sympathizer''s articles, which place at the service of the wrong cause just that vital, new culture that the proletariat's representatives in Parliament unfortunately lack; lending them a 'realism', a Marxist Hegelianism, that they would not even recognize if they saw it. Just look how the intransigents are presented as mystical dreamers, as vacuous abstractionists – or even as stupid, since their ideas are apparently based purely on the simplistic and gratuitous hypothesis that 'the workers will return from the trenches, after the armistice, with the conscious will and political capacity to achieve socialism'. Intransigence is presented as mental and political inertia; there are allusions to the *improved position* the proletariat could win for itself.

A hidden suggestion pervades this whole argument, imperious and seductive. It is unexpressed and all the more fascinating for it, but it fills the dry, nervous sentences with a swelling sense of hidden meaning. It is being subtly suggested that the war can be resolved, the problem of the peace can be resolved, by stitching up an agreement in parliament. This hidden motif is the dominant theme. The hope is that in this way – especially in this way – a state of intellectual disorientation can be created in the proletariat, a blunting of its critical class sense, that will result in its putting pressure on the party leadership and in this way bringing about, at best, an enthusiastic or at least a resigned consent to an alliance or, at worst, a provisional loosening of the parliamentary group from the obligation of party discipline. What matters is action in parliament: the vote that will take the Giolittians to power. The direct intervention of the proletariat will in this way be exorcized. The example of Russia and the wretched fate of the anti-Tsarist bourgeoisie, swept away by the rising tide of popular fury, terrifies the timid souls of these democratic troglodytes, these parasites used to gnawing away in secret at the treasure-chests of the State and handing out little laws and favours like monks doling out soup to a horde of scabby beggars.

Realism and Empiricism

The point of view that *La Stampa* attributes to the relativists is puerile, when it comes to it, even in theoretical terms. Collaboration cannot be justified either by contingent reasons or by logic-chopping. It is both a historical and a logical error.

Collaborationist realism is pure empiricism. It stands in the same relation to intransigence as a barber-surgeon does to Augusto Murri.[3]

> 'History', according to *La Stampa*, 'demonstrates how the contradiction between two social theses – the class antithesis – has always been resolved in a synthesis, in which a part of *what was* is always alienated and *what will be* is increasingly incorporated, so that, by gradual transformation, utopia becomes reality and expresses in its design a correspondingly new social constitution.

It is true enough that history demonstrates this, but it does not show that the 'synthesis', 'what will be', has been already determined in advance by a contract. Anticipating the historical synthesis is a childish whim. Mortgaging the future by making a contract between classes is just empiricism, not a keen sense of history. We made the same point in simpler terms in last week's *Il Grido del Popolo*:

> Every day, a part of our maximum demands (utopia) is achieved (*what will be*). But this part cannot be determined *a priori* because history is not a mathematical calculation. The part that is achieved is the dialectical outcome of the continuous interplay between social activity and maximum goals. Only if these maximum goals are pursued by the method of intransigence can the dialectic be one of history and not of childish whim: a solid achievement and not a mistake that needs to be undone and corrected.

To put it in even simpler terms, both the intransigent and the relativist are saying that to get a spark, you have to strike the flint against the steel. But when the intransigent is just about to start striking the two together, the relativist says, 'Hang on, I've got the spark in my pocket.' He lights a match and says, 'Here you are – here's the spark that would have come from striking them together, so we don't need to strike them together any more.' And he lights his cigar. But who would take this pathetic conjuring-trick for a Hegelian sense of history or for Marxist thought?

---

[3] Augusto Murri: an eminent contemporary surgeon.

The Function of the Proletariat

Just as the Socialist Party, the organization of the proletarian class, cannot enter into competition for government without losing its intrinsic value and becoming a swarm of coachman-flies, so it cannot collaborate with any organized bourgeois parliamentary grouping without doing mischief: without bringing about pseudo-developments that will need to be undone and corrected. The political chaos that class collaboration brings with it is due to the spasmodic expansion of a bourgeois party that is not satisfied with simply holding on to the State itself, but also wants to make use of the party that is antagonistic to the State. In this way it becomes a ghastly hybrid, a historical monster devoid of will or particular aims, concerned solely with its possession of the State, which it grows on like rust. State activity is reduced to mere legalities, to a settling of disputes at a formal level, without ever touching on the substance. The State becomes a gypsy caravan held together with old bits of wood, teetering like a mastodon on four tiny little wheels.

If it wishes to maintain and consolidate its position as the executive organ of the proletariat, the Socialist Party must itself observe and must make everyone else respect the method of the fiercest intransigence. And the bourgeois parties, if they wish to form a government without any help from outside, will have to evolve, get in touch with the nation, put an end to their sectional squabblings and forge themselves a distinctive political and economic structure. If they do not wish to do this, then, since no party is capable of standing on its own, a permanent and dangerous crisis will arise, in which the stable and united proletariat will be able to accelerate its rise and evolution.

Intransigence is not inertia, because it constrains others to move and act. It is not based on stupid assumptions, as *La Stampa* cleverly insinuates. It is a principled policy, the policy of a proletariat that is conscious of its revolutionary mission as an accelerator of the capitalistic evolution of society: as a reagent, clarifying the chaos of bourgeois production and politics and forcing modern States to pursue their natural mission as dismantlers of the feudal institutions that still survive, even after the shipwreck of the old societies that created them, and that are still standing in the way of history.

Intransigence is the only way in which the class struggle can be expressed. It is the only evidence we have that history is developing and creating solid, substantial values and not 'privileged', arbitrary 'syntheses' cooked up by a mutual accord on the part of a thesis and antithesis which have thrown in their lots together, like the proverbial oil and water.

The supreme law of capitalist society is free competition between all social forces. Merchants compete for markets, bourgeois groupings compete for government and the two classes compete for the State. Merchants seek to create monopolies by means of protectionist laws. Each bourgeois grouping wants to monopolize the government and keep the energies of the class that is outside governmental competition in thrall to its own interests. The intransigents are freetraders. They do not want barons – whether in sugar or steel or in government. The law of freedom must operate without restraint. It is intrinsic to bourgeois activity. It is the chemical reagent that is continually dissolving its cadres and forcing them to improve and perfect themselves. The great Anglo-Saxon bourgeoisies have acquired their present productive capacity through this implacable play of free competition. The British State has evolved and been purged of its noxious elements through the free clash of the bourgeois social forces that eventually constituted the great historic parties, the Liberals and Conservatives. The proletariat has indirectly benefited from this conflict, winning cheap bread and a substantial series of rights guaranteed by law and custom: the right to assemble, the right to strike and a security of the individual which in Italy remains a chimerical myth.

Class struggle is not a childish whim, a voluntaristic act – it is a basic necessity of the regime. To obstruct its clear path, quite arbitrarily, with pre-established syntheses dreamt up by inveterate pipe-dreamers, is a childish error and a dead loss in historical terms. The non-Giolittian parties now in power (apart from the fact of the War, which is contingent and which is already proving too much for the political capacity of the ruling classes of the smaller nations) are unconsciously carrying out the task of dismantling the feudal, militaristic, despotic State that Giovanni Giolitti perpetuated to use as an instrument of dictatorship. The Giolittians can feel their monopoly escaping them. Then let them get moving, for God's sake, let them struggle, let them call on the nation to judge. But no: they want the proletariat to do the moving for them or, better still, they just want to rely on the votes of the Socialist deputies.

So intransigence is inertia, is it? But movement is not simply a physical act; it is intellectual as well. Indeed, before it can be physical, movement must always be intellectual – except in the case of puppets. Take away from the proletariat its class consciousness and what do you have? A load of puppets! And just look at them move!

Il Grido del Popolo, 18 May 1918

Cocaine

Have they allowed the Mogol club to re-open its doors, and to serve customers again? I have had neither the opportunity, nor the curiosity to find out. But it certainly would not surprise me if a tacit concession had been made.

The Mogol was closed on the orders of the Chief of Police: young people used to meet there after hours to get intoxicated on cocaine. Why was the Mogol closed down? Because it admitted customers outside licensing hours, or because these customers used to intoxicate themselves with cocaine there? The names of these poor wretches have not been released by the police, nor has the name of the chemist who used to sell them the poison. Which means that the fact itself does not constitute a crime in the eyes of the authorities, and the names are not the names of criminals, whom it is important to identify publicly, as dangers to the well-being of society. The authorities are worried only about the unauthorized opening hours.

The right-thinking papers have had a brief flight of moralism. One of them has just realized that cocaine addiction is not illegal in Italy, and is concerned about the fact; another has cooked up a little impro-vised sermon, reminding the scoundrels in question that the father-land is at war, that their brothers are suffering in the trenches and other, similar moral spurs which, because of the pomposity and fatuity with which they are expressed, ring as flat as lead pennies.

In Rome and in Bologna, as well as in Turin, lovers of intoxicating drugs have been 'discovered' (!) And everywhere, there is the same mannered phraseology. Tut! Tut! You cannot get rid of vice by making laws against it. Surely, vice is a necessary adjunct of modern civilization! . . .

And indeed it is, of a purely superficial civilization, which has work as its base, but the work of others. It is quite natural that this kind of putrid scum will be produced: people without ends, without morals, without history. What does life consist of for most people? Pure animality, the pleasures of the senses, the mechanical action of nerve and muscle. Why not drug themselves with cocaine? I am amazed that so *few* slip down the slope of destructive pleasures. The reason why vice is not more widespread is not a sense of moral duty, but indifference, sheer animal indifference. They put up with far less, that is all, but the phenomenon is just as serious as if there were half a million morphine addicts, instead of just five hundred.

Certainly the root cause is the lack of moral ends; but can a member of the bourgeoisie have moral ends? If he is a hero, perhaps, but the average is anything but heroic. Work, activity save members of the bourgeoisie from decadence, but a certain number of individuals in this class do not work at all; they would not know how to fill the twenty-four hours of the day usefully. Benedetto Croce must be the only millionaire who spends eight hours a day at his desk; the others prefer the racetrack, or the beach resort, Montecarlo, the novels of Luciano Zuccoli and cocaine. The only thing that can save them is a dullness of the senses or avarice – in other words, falling below the average level of human animality.

Is it possible to construct moral ends, to instil them in tender minds, on school benches? But school is a continuation of society, and life in society is something very different from the life in the little moral tales good old Giannetto used to tell Pinocchio. Work is the only thing that confers moral impulses; it is the crucible in which the spiritual essences that can give a meaning to our lives are volatized. Most moral impulses are immediate; it is only when they are linked together that one gets to something more general. The fatherland, the family, humanity, goodness, justice, if they are to be real, need to be put into practice over and over again in the course of the day, in humdrum activities, which demand hard work and sacrifice, and which give satisfaction and joy. These words have to be transformed into paper to be covered with ink; into weights to be lifted on shoulders; into tools or machines to be started up. Morality consists simply in relating the smallest activity to the greatest end, and this is what makes it so necessary to practise those small, inconsiderable actions, an infinite rosary of these actions to tell every day. Otherwise, all there is is inebriation with cocaine or inebriation with empty words: physical hallucinations or the spiritual hallucination of some hornet-like word beating its wings against the sides of one's skull: a word like fatherland, humanity, the people, justice . . .

Most people do not exist outside some organization, whether it calls itself the Church or the Party, and morality does not exist without some specific, spontaneous organ within which it is realized. The bourgeoisie is a moment of chaos not simply where production is concerned, but also where the spirit is concerned. It has broken down the Church, the organization of an authoritarian moral life, but, in our lands, it has not passed through the phase of puritanism and clubmania. The liberal style of association has produced nothing more than dance-clubs and mandolin societies, and now we are beginning to get little gatherings of the friends of intoxication. Bourgeois associations have pleasure as their end, not duty. Their aim is to excite nerves which are not worn down by work, rather than to find some way to restore the body after work, by balancing it with some intellectual activity.

The use of cocaine is an index of bourgeois progress: capitalism is evolving. It constitutes categories of people who are entirely irresponsible, with no worries about tomorrow, no troubles and no scruples. Are these individuals harmful? No, because society – in which one is all, and all are one – is not a bourgeois thing. They are no harm at all. Their names are not made public, the chemist will be let off with a warning, the Mogol will re-open its rooms. What is the use of kicking against destiny?

Avanti!, 21 May 1918

Football and *Scopone*

Italians are not very keen sportsmen; they prefer *scopone*[1] to sport. Rather than being in the open air, they prefer to be cooped up in some dive of a café. Rather than moving, they prefer to slouch round a table.

Observe a game of football: it is a model of individualistic society. It demands initiative, but an initiative which keeps within the framework of the law. Individuals are hierarchically differentiated, but differentiated on the grounds of their particular abilities, rather than their past careers. There is movement, competition, conflict, but they are regulated by an unwritten rule – the rule of fair play, of which the referee's presence is a constant reminder. The open field – air circulating freely – healthy lungs – strong muscles, always primed for action.

A game of *scopone*. Closeness, smoke, artificial light. Shouting, fists slamming on the table and often in the faces of opponents . . . or partners. Warped brainwork (!) Mutual distrust. Secret diplomacy. Marked cards. Shady strategies involving the legs or toes. The rules? Where are the rules that have to be respected? They vary from one place to another; there are various different traditions: it is a constant source of protests and squabbling.

Games of *scopone* have often been known to end up with corpses

---

[1] A popular Italian card game.

on the floor, fractured skulls. One certainly never reads about games of football ending in that way.

Even in these marginal human activities, we can see a reflection of the economic–political structure of different states. Sport is a popular activity in those societies in which the capitalist regime's economic individualism has transformed the whole way of life, so that economic and political freedom are accompanied by a freedom of the spirit and tolerance of the opposition.

Scopone is the characteristic form of sport of countries which are backward economically, politically and spiritually, where the characteristic forms of civic life are the police spy, the plain-clothes police-man, the anonymous letter, the cult of incompetence and career-mongering (with corresponding pay-offs and favours for the politicians).

Sporting countries carry over the concept of 'fair play' into politics as well.

Scopone produces the kind of gentlemen who get workers sacked because they have dared contradict them in a free discussion.[2]

Avanti!, 27 August 1918

---

[2] This refers to an anecdote recounted in a previous article ('Accident at Work', 24 August), concerning a worker who was engaged in a political discussion by a client in whose house he was working and who was later dismissed at the client's request for having questioned the latter's anti-socialist views.

Cultural and Poetic Mysteries

'. . . And it is in vain that the author casts his net against science, and the glorious school.' In her notes on these lines in a sonnet of hers published in 'Difesa delle Lavoratrici', Comrade Cristina Bacci explains this as a reference to 'one of those writers who supported Léon Daudet in his campaign against the Positivist School, with the aim of leading humanity back into obscurantism'.

Why has comrade Cristina Bacci chosen Léon Daudet, of all people, as the leading champion of the campaign against the 'Positivist School' and in favour of leading humanity back into obscurantism? A cultural mystery. Bacci is evidently not acquainted with Daudet, nor is she well-informed about the ideas of *Action Française*, of which Daudet is co-editor (the other editor is Charles Maurras).

Daudet is a practising Catholic, but at the same time, he is a positivist, as well: the nationalistic and monarchist doctrine propounded by Daudet and Maurras is entirely based on the philosophy, or so-called philosophy, of positivism, as interpreted by the editors of *Action Française*. Indeed, for them, the last great philosopher to be produced by the 'true' national spirit of France is Auguste Comte (they are fiercely hostile to Bergson, and never miss a chance to ridicule him in the various columns of the paper), while the last great historian is Hyppolite Taine – two of the founding fathers of the 'Positivist School'.

How can we explain this phenomenon? Well, there is nothing at

75

all strange about it: positivism, which should have remained a straightforward continuation and logical structuring of the positive, experimental model in science, has decided to turn itself into a doctrine of being and of knowledge. It has betrayed its own nature, becoming a metaphysics, a mystical doctrine. The Catholic dualism between the human spirit and a God who cannot be known – a God who transcends that spirit, but whom the spirit strives towards, purging itself of original sin, to become worthy to ascend to the joys of Paradise and knowledge of the supreme creator – is reborn in positivism, which has constructed an identical scheme. For the positivist, the dualism is between human consciousness and nature; nature, too, transcends consciousness, but consciousness strives towards it, purifying itself of the prejudices and 'obscurantism' by means of the Popular Universities and cut-price popular science. It is easy to understand how a Catholic can be, at the same time, a positivist: with a light dusting of pseudo-science on the traditional doctrines, God can become identified with Nature, without disturbing the original, ideal conception in any very significant way.

The contributors to *Action Française* are Catholic and positivist. The conception they have of history is essentially a positivist one; we shall attempt to give an outline of it, using a metaphor to make our task easier. French society, for Daudet and Maurras, is like a plant, the fleur-de-lys of the centuries-old dynasty of the kings of France. This plant plunges its roots into the soul of the French race and people: a national soul which, even though it branches off into the various regional and individual souls, still preserves a profound unity and a unified thrust of historical evolution. What has happened is that the revolution has interrupted this process of evolution; it has corrupted the national soul. The French revolution was like an ignorant and inexpert gardener, who brutally snapped the flower from the lily plant and grafted a red carnation on to its stem. France has become an aborted plant, a hybrid confusion of ideals. The 'Revolution' is not really French in its origins; it comes from the Protestant Reformation, whose political ideology is liberalism, the origin of all revolutionary ideologies and the direct source of socialism (and this is the reason why certain French monarchists, though sceptical and atheistic in their convictions, are pro-Catholic in their political programmes). The original conception of France is the conception of 'order': an order which rests ultimately on one supreme authority, the monarch, and which takes the form of a precapitalistic social organization, whose hierarchical organs are workers' guilds, small landowners, the clergy, the aristocracy and the traditional hereditary dynasty. *Action Française*'s writers rarely allude to capitalism and never refer to the specific, historical conditions of social organization which capitalism has given rise to.

From this brief summary, it should be clear what the fundamental error of *Action Française*'s contributors is, what their social thinking is, and how it is possible that Catholics like them can also be positivists. It is also clear that there can be nothing in common between positivism and critically informed communism.

For the French monarchists, history is not development, but natural evolution: the pseudo-concepts of race, origin, soul, order, hierarchy, heredity are the principal factors, in their view, in causing and consolidating events. Society, for them, is a natural organism, whose evolution is governed by fixed laws which can be defined and precisely and rigidly formulated by means of the experimental and positive scientific method. Which is fine, except that they find the 'raw data' of experience in arbitrary concepts, which they use as their feelings and passions and the political policies they endorse dictate. According to the 'experimental, positive method', their political policies should spring up spontaneously in the course of their 'disinterested and dispassionate' investigation of historical reality. Instead, in this doctrine, the investigative process is subordinated to political passions and a ready-made policy, and, out of the whole of experience, they choose to take into account only those 'facts' which can help them to demonstrate the validity of their policies.

The critical doctrine of communism has nothing in common with philosophical positivism, with its metaphysics and theology of Evolution and Nature. Marxism is based on philosophical idealism, which is something which has nothing in common with what is generally understood by the word 'idealism' – giving oneself up to dreams and to the treasured illusions of feeling; always having one's head in the clouds, with no concern for the necessities and needs of practical life. Philosophical idealism is a doctrine of being and knowledge, in which these two concepts are unified, and the object of our theoretical knowledge becomes reality, our own self. That Marx should have introduced positivist elements into his work is hardly surprising, and it is easily explained: Marx was not a philosopher by profession, and even he had his off days. What is certain is that, in its essence, his doctrine is dependent on philosophical idealism, and that the more recent developments in this philosophical tradition constitute the ideal current into which the proletarian and socialist movement historically flows. Just think about the way in which socialists use the word 'consciousness', when we talk about 'class consciousness' and 'proletarian and socialist consciousness'. Implicit in this language is the philosophical notion that one 'is' only when one 'knows oneself to be', when one is 'conscious' of one's own being. A worker is only a proletarian when he 'knows' himself to be one, and acts and thinks in accordance with this 'knowledge'.

For critically informed communism, 'natural' concepts like race, blood, heredity, geographical origin, and an intangible, definitive 'order' are puerile expressions, without the least justification: pure word-mongering, pure phrase-making. History is a product of humanity, a humanity which divides up into classes, one of which is dominant, at a given time, and directs society in accordance with its own ends, challenged by the other side, which strives to assert itself and take charge. It is not a question of evolution, but of substitution of one thing for another: something which can only be done by a self-conscious and disciplined use of force.

The experimental, positive method, as a dispassionate and disinterested method of scientific research, is also the method of historical materialism (though it is independent of materialism: it is the method proper to the sciences, and the first man to think it through logically was Galileo Galilei). Historical materialism has demonstrated that historical research should address itself systematically to economic phenomena, as well as other factors; indeed, that it should address itself *particularly* to the study of these phenomena. Otherwise, history is a shell without substance, a lick of gaudy paint on the surface, without dynamic vibrations, without any possibility of development, of progress: a chaos of frenzied phrase-making, rather than a scientific pursuit. Historical materialism has, therefore, incorporated the experimental, positive method, applied to the study of human events and social phenomena. It cannot be confused with this scientific positivism, just as it cannot be confused with philosophical positivism.

So why did comrade Cristina Bacci fall into this error? Because, even if, in her words, she exalts 'positivism', and those who struggle against 'obscurantism', in fact, her information on 'positivism', 'idealism' and the politico-religious doctrines of the monarchists of *Action Française* and Léon Daudet is vague, confused and erroneous. Which is to say that she does not apply to her own intellectual life the canons of the experimental and positive method, according to which one should write only what one knows, and one should be acquainted with all the documentation available on the subject on which one is writing, in order not to let one's judgement be distorted by partisan interests or passions. Certainly, Léon Daudet is a mediocre writer, a polemicist without intellectual integrity and without scruples, capable of using a fragmentary conversation between two hotel porters to reach the peremptory conclusion that an adversary of his is a common rogue and that hanging would be too good for him. He is not a respectable politician, but a contemptible demagogue: in *Action Française*, he takes the role of the fierce mastiff – or the vile hyena, as Paolo Valera picturesquely represents him – who throws himself on individuals within the enemy camp, to destroy the public's respect for them, and to drag them before the executioner. (In the paper, the organic, constitutional conception of French monarchism is the province of Charles Maurras; the conception of international harmony, that of Jacques Bainville; the religious and artistic doctrine is dealt with by Louis Dimier; and small-scale, day-to-day political polemic by Robert Havard. *Action Française* is written almost entirely by these five editors, who stoke its regular columns every day. It is technically very well organized for political activism, but the only elements in French society which it represents are the individual and ideological remnants of the precapitalist era: the landed nobility, the high clergy, and a part of the officer class of the army. Economically, it seeks to speak for the petit bourgeois and corporatist thinking which is still quite widespread in France, where heavy industry is little developed and small-scale production prevails.)

Léon Daudet is all this, but he is also a positivist and, when she writes about him, comrade Cristina Bacci should have made it her duty to know this fact, if she really had the triumph of the 'experimental method' at heart, and if she was really against 'obscurantism'. 'Obscurantism' can also be a lack of education, or an education picked up in a Popular University.

Men, Ideas, Newspapers and Money

Mr Italo Minnuni has left the editorial desk of the *Gazzetta di Torino*, and he is to be replaced by Mr Tomaso Borelli, previously editor of *Il resto del Carlino* and *Il Tempo*. If the lessons we have learned from the economic and political history of other nations, and from certain war-time episodes here, are of any value in helping us pinpoint the social trends which are now maturing, and in logically anticipating what is going to happen in future, then the substitution of Mr Italo Minnuni is something more than just the sacking of an inefficient employee.

The industrial and landed bourgeoisie of our nation is in a state of confusion. The problem of planning the customs policy for the post-war period has left it split; it has created conflicts in its breast which cannot be healed. Where customs policy is concerned, our ruling class divides into three sections: the steel magnates, who need extremely high protective tariffs to protect their business; the farmers of Central and Southern Italy and the islands, for whom, on the contrary, freedom of trade is a necessity of life; and the leaders of the mechanical industry of Turin, who do not know which way to turn. On the one hand, a policy of free trade within the Italian State would be advantageous to them, in that it would help them compete in international markets and would permit greater flexibility on salaries. On the other hand, though, it would not suit them to clash too violently with the steel men, who have enjoyed political dominance until now and have been calling the tune for the whole nation.

The farmers of the south lacked political muscle before the war. The only organ which propounded ideas favourable to their activity was a weekly paper called *L'Unità*, run by Gaetano Salvemini. The Southern farmers had a flaw, which is a fatal one in a capitalist regime: they had very little money at their disposal, they were disorganized, and their activity was archaic and not very profitable. The war has changed these conditions to some extent: it has put money in a lot of pockets, and, what is more, it has stimulated the spirit of initiative and the capitalistic desire to get rich. In addition to *L'Unità* – which has become ever more important in the life of the nation, because of the sympathies its fiery and dogged campaigns have excited in the young and in intellectuals – the farmers now have at their disposal two great daily papers: *Il Tempo*, in Rome and *Il Mezzogiorno*, in Naples, both founded in this last year. The Southern farmers have decided to give battle, and with no holds barred. The statements of their Chambers of Commerce are quite explicit about this, and those from the Chambers of Commerce in Bari and Cagliari will remain in the history of the Italian economy. The Commune of Bari, presided over by Commendatore De Tullio, even went so far as to declare that the farmers will pursue their struggle as far as is necessary, even at the cost of jeopardizing national unity.

And, in reality, the farmers of the South have every reason to assume this kind of attitude. The memory of the recent past is a terrifying spectacle for them. The crisis into which Southern Italy and the islands were pitilessly plunged during the Franco-Italian tariff war was a terrible thing. The export trade in agricultural products and livestock saw its most natural and profitable markets closed off to it. There followed a cut-back in activity which was all the more harmful because the forces of production were already weak and wavering. The big banks which had administered credit for agriculture failed spectacularly, and the savings of thousands and thousands of small landholders, scraped together by blood and sacrifice – the sacrifice of their own children, but particularly of the rural proletariat – all went to ruin. Terrible years, which in Sardinia, for example, have left the same kind of memories as the year 1812, when there were people dying of starvation in the streets, and a bushel of grain would be surreptitiously bargained for the corresponding field of arable land. The inquest on Sardinia by the Honourable Pais is a document which will remain an indelible mark of infamy on Crispi's policy and the economic interests which supported it. The island of Sardinia was literally razed to the ground, as if by a barbaric invasion. The forests were cut down – the forests which had regulated the climate and the average rainfall – in order to provide some readily saleable goods, to scrape some credit together. And to take their place the vultures moved in to corrupt political customs and moral life. When one is crossing the Golfo degli Aranci, to Cagliari, some old shepherd will still point out the bare granite mountains sparkling in the torrid sun, and will remind one that, at one time, they were covered with forests and with flocks. But, since the deforestation, the torrential rains have washed the whole layer of fertile earth down to the plains and the sea. Cagliari Chamber of Commerce is quite right to fight tooth and nail to prevent such a thing ever happening again. What the farmers are fighting for against the metal magnates is their life, nothing less: it is not just a case of competing for ever greater profits.

Last July, in Rome, there was a conference which brought leaders of industry and agriculture together to attempt to agree on a plan which would be advantageous to all parties. There were extremely grave problems to be overcome before the conference could even be held. The leaders of the steel industry were quite unshakeable in their determination to use the State for their own ends, by imposing a customs policy consisting of a double tariff system: a maximum tariff (without any limitations) and a minimum one (giving a protection of 30 per cent of the value of the goods). They also wanted to abandon the system of treaties which have facilitated the export of agricultural products, by easing the protection of domestic production of their goods in certain markets (particularly the Central Empires). The steel men were quite open about the fact that they wanted to go over the heads of the farmers; it was up to the local prefects and policemen to keep these oafish, starving peasants in their place, before they could jeopardize national industry. The leaders of the Turin mechanical engineering industry offered themselves as mediators (Dante Ferraris was the man who cooked up this little deal) and the conference was able to start, but the promotors had to interrupt it before there was a definitive breakdown in relations, and they postponed it until September. In the meantime, *Il Tempo*, passed into the hands of the farmers and *Il Mezzogiorno* was founded. In *Il Tempo*, Dante Ferraris published an interview with himself, defending the interests of the farmers, swinging in the other direction. But the conference was never held, and the agreement has dissolved.

Mr Italo Minnuni, let us recall, came to Turin after working on *L'Idea Nazionale*, followed by *Perseveranza*, the organ of the Marquis Ridolfi, of Iron and Steel. In October, Mr Minnuni, a fanatical protectionist if a superficial writer, was replaced as editor of the *Gazzetta di Torino* by Mr Tomaso Borelli, a young liberal, previously editor of *Il Tempo*. And, just as Mr Minnuni was the outrider for the Marquis Ridolfi, so, today, Mr Borelli is the outrider of Commendatore De Tullio, of Bari Chamber of Commerce. So it seems that the mechanical engineers are taking courage, that they are allying themselves more closely with the Southern farmers, with whom they have so many interests in common. The leaders of the steel industry have lost ground, politically as well. It seems ever more unlikely that their man Giolitti will be returned to power and, even if this were to happen, he would find the conditions under which he held power very different. Just think that the Honourable Salandra was the first Prime Minister there has been from the South of Italy (the Sicilians who have got into power have been more Piedmontese than the Piedmontese – one only has to think of Crispi); and the Honourable Salandra succeeded in creating such a *Pugliese* environment in the House as to reduce Borelli to a pitiful farce and to make the Orlando–Nitti cabinet indispensable – a Sicilian and a Basilisk.[1]

A change in the editorship of the *Gazzetta di Torino* can be an indication of all this. The post-war period in Italy will witness a formidable struggle between the great bourgeois interests in Italy – on one side, the metal industry; on the other, the farmers and engineers – recalling the great struggle in England between industrial and agricultural interests. In our case, however, the roles have been reversed, as a result of the particular conditions in which the unification of the regions took place: in Italy, the farmers are in favour of a policy of *laissez-faire*, while the industrialists are protectionists. But that is perfectly rational. In England, because of the great iron and coal riches, it was industry which needed free trade, in order to expand. In Italy, there is no iron or coal: it is mechanized agriculture which needs to expand, and mechanical engineering, which uses

---

[1] [Translator's note] *Basilisco* means 'a basilisk', but the word is also a punning reference to Nitti's origins (he was born in the Basilicata region).

semi-manufactured metal. The political dictatorship which Piedmont has exercised over its Italian 'colony' has produced artificial fortunes, fortunes without a future; and now the fresh, new capitalistic energies that have grown up in all the privations of the protectionist regime, emboldened by their experience of war production and war prices, are preparing to do battle, to take over the dominance of state powers from the weary and worn-out rackets of the steel barons. If no more radical developments intervene in the meantime, it is certain that Italy will see a revolution in its whole economic structure, which is still essentially patriarchal where agriculture is concerned, and petit bourgeois where manufacturing industry and engineering are concerned – just as the political life of Italy is patriarchal and petit bourgeois: that is, pompous, rhetorical and grandiloquent.

Avanti!, 23 October 1918

Part Two
The New
Order

The Sovereignty of Law

Today, the Italian people should be celebrating the seventy-first anniversary of the establishment of the sovereignty of law. For the last seventy-one years, Italians have no longer been at the mercy of the irresponsible powers of the State. Rule by whim, by arbitrary decree, have disappeared from the social scene: our society has become a society of 'citizens', equal in their rights and duties, which are equally watched over and protected by the founding Charter of the realm. This should be the day of the people, a day consecrated to freedom and progress.

After five years of war, five years of rule by decree, this idea seems an atrocious mockery. All guarantees of freedom have been suppressed and we have lost all sense of the security, the normality of life under the rule of law. The 'State' has once again become the supreme arbiter of our destinies, of our elementary physiological life and our superior life of the spirit. The 'State', which is to say the people in government at the present moment: the President of the Council of Ministers, along with the administrative system which depends on him; the hierarchy of prefects, vice-prefects, questors, vice-questors, delegates, policemen. A policeman today 'ranks' more than a member of Parliament, because the policeman has a stake in power, while the member of Parliament is just a juridical fiction.

Our society has become one enormous barracks, governed by irresponsibility and floundering in disorder and chaos. All civic activity

87

is controlled, riddled, regimented, and ruined by authority. The anti-socialist myth of the 'barracks State' has become a terrible, asphyxiating bourgeois reality, which is forcing society into an abyss of unruliness, frenzy and homicidal chaos. We are imprisoned in a strait-jacket which is driving us into madness and desperation.

All this was part of the destined order of historical events. The Constitution – that juridical fiction of the impartial and superior sovereignty of the law, voted in by the representatives of the people – was, in reality, the beginning of the dictatorship of the propertied classes, their 'legal' conquest of the supreme power of the State. Private property became a fundamental institution of the State, guaranteed and protected against both the arbitrary decisions of the sovereign and the invasions of the rural poor whose land had been expropriated. With the Constitution, the king is stripped of any power to intervene in the regulation of questions concerning private property; on the contrary, the dynasty becomes tied to the fate of individuals' property. Society is cut loose from any kind of collective bonds and reduced to its primordial element of the citizen-individual. And society begins to dissolve, eaten away by the corrosive acids of competition; dragons' teeth are sown amongst men and frenetic passions, unquenchable hatreds, implacable enmities spring up, enormous, amongst them. Every citizen becomes a gladiator, who sees, in other people, enemies to vanquish or to subjugate to one's own interests. All the higher bonds of love and solidarity are dissolved: from the bonds of craftsmen's guilds and social castes, to those of religion and the family. Competition becomes enshrined as the practical foundation of human interaction: citizen-individuals are the atoms which make up the social nebula – unstable, inorganic elements which cannot adhere in any organism. The concept of the sovereignty of the law is based on precisely this social instability and lack of cohesion. It is a purely abstract concept, a covert trick played on the good faith and innocence of the people. It is an anti-social concept, because it envisages the 'citizen' as being locked in an eternal war with the State. It regards human beings as the perpetual and implacable enemies of the State, which is the living, the elastic form of society – which means that it regards human beings as enemies of themselves. The Constitution is a codification of disorder and anti-human chaos.

But, even though the principle of bourgeois society is juridically enshrined as a perpetuity, the era of the proletariat is beginning. The proletariat is born out of a protest on the part of the historical process against anything which attempts to bog down or to strait-jacket the dynamism of social development. The Marxist critique of liberal economics is a critique of the concept of the perpetuity of human economic and political institutions. It is a reduction of all the events of this world to a state of historicity and contingency. It is a lesson in realism for the purveyors of pseudo-scientific abstractions, defenders of the strongrooms.

Bourgeois competition initially benefits proletarians, because it gives them the right to circulate and to get a better deal for their labour. But this 'freedom' immediately turns to the disadvantage of the proletariat: the worker becomes a commodity subjected to all the repercussions of fluctuations in the market, with no guarantees, and no security for his life and for his future. The conditions of the salaried worker become worse than those of the slave or the serf. His hunger, his unemployment, the danger he runs of dying of starvation become just so many stakes in the gamble of bourgeois competition. The safes are brimming with the blood of workers and the splendour of the civilization created by capitalism hides a tragic reality of suffering victims, of barbarity, of unchecked iniquity.

The workers' movement is the spiritual revolt of humanity against the new and pitiless feudal lords of capitalism. It is the reaction of a society which is striving to remake itself as a harmonious organism, living in solidarity, governed by love and compassion. The 'citizen' is displaced by the 'comrade'; social atomism by social organization. The cells of the new order spring up spontaneously; they adhere to one another, and lay the foundations for far greater stratifications of solidarity. The baleful power of 'freedom' is circumscribed and controlled; and limits are placed on the sway of capitalism in the workplace. The worker wins a degree of autonomy for himself, a degree of real, effectual freedom. He is no longer one individual standing against the world: he is a member of collectivities which mesh together into other, ever greater and more powerful collectivities, which cast their dense net over the whole world. Competition starts afresh, from a new foundation and on a gigantic scale; instead of a competition between individuals and classes, an entire class, extending across the whole world, is pitting itself against the exploitative practices of all the bourgeois classes of individual nations, in order to expropriate from them the means of production and trade and the privately and nationally owned property of the soil and what lies under it; of the ports, of the rivers, of the oceans. This formidable assault is shaking to its roots the entire juridical superstructure of capitalism, and accelerating the process of its dissolution and disorder. Every juridical fiction collapses: liberty is suppressed, Parliament closed, individual rights dropped. Everything is confusion and uproar: a chaos without confines. Behind the appearance of the most rigid discipline, which reduces human society to a pestilential barracks, there reigns nothing but government by arbitrary whim and the most shameless bad faith.

And today all those violators of the Constitution – all those 'citizens' who have sworn 'to observe the Constitution and the other laws of the State faithfully, for the inseparable good of king and country', and who, every day, make mincemeat of the freedom of the individual – today they are celebrating the advent of liberty, of the sovereignty of the law, of the 'citizen'. An appalling farce which will not last for very much longer, because 'citizens' will be replaced by 'comrades' and individualistic freedom by social freedom; disorder will be succeeded by organization, and the State of lies and betrayal by the social State of solidarity and work.

Avanti!, 1 June 1919

The Price of History

What does History still require from the Russian proletariat before it can legitimize its conquests and make them permanent? What further toll of blood and sacrifice is demanded by this absolute sovereign of the destinies of men?

The difficulties and the resistance which the proletarian revolution has had to overcome have revealed themselves as vastly superior to those of any other revolution in the past. Past revolutions only tended to modify the form of private and national ownership of the means of production and exchange; they affected only a limited part of the human community. The proletarian revolution is the ultimate revolution: since its aim is to abolish private and national ownership, and to abolish the classes, it involves the whole of mankind, not only a minority. It constrains the whole of mankind to mobilize, to intervene in the struggle, to declare itself, explicitly, for one side or the other. It transforms society at a very fundamental level: from a unicellular organism (made up of citizen-individuals) into a pluricellular one. It establishes as the basis of society nuclei which are already, in themselves, organic segments of society. It forces the whole of society to identify itself in the State; it transforms the whole of mankind into spiritual and historical consciousness. It is because of this that the proletarian revolution is a true revolution of society; it is because of this that it must overcome unprecedented difficulties and unprecedented resistance. It is because of this that History is demanding as the price of its success the kind of monstrous ransom that the Russian people is now being forced to pay.

The Russian revolution has so far triumphed over all the obstacles History has put in its path. It has uncovered for the Russian people an aristocracy of statesmen such as no other nation possesses: a couple of thousand men who have dedicated their whole life to the (scientific) study of politics and economics; men who, in the course of their decades of exile have analysed and dissected all the problems of the revolution; men who, in the course of their struggle, their unequal duel against Tsarism, have forged a character of steel for themselves; men who, living as they have in contact with all the forms of capitalist civilization in Europe, Asia, America, immersing themselves in the world currents of trade and history, have turned their consciousness of their responsibility to precision, honing it as sharp as the swords of the conquerors of empire.

The Russian communists are a first-class ruling elite. As all those who have dealt with him have attested, Lenin has revealed himself as the greatest statesman of contemporary Europe. He is a man who radiates prestige, a man who can enflame and discipline whole populaces; a man whose vast brain can dominate all those social energies, throughout the world, which can be turned to the benefit of the revolution; a man who can check, and even checkmate, the most wily and refined statesmen of the bourgeois political *routine*.

But communist doctrine – and the political party that propagates it and the working class that consciously embodies it – is one thing. The vast Russian people is something quite different: a people disnatured and disorganized, which a long and disastrous war has thrown into a dark abyss of abject poverty, barbarity, anarchy and disintegration. The political stature of the Bolsheviks, their historical masterpiece, consists, precisely, in this: that they have hoisted the fallen giant back into place, recreated (or created) a concrete, dynamic form out of this disorder and chaos. They have succeeded in welding together the communist doctrine and the collective consciousness of the Russian people. They have laid down the solid foundations on which communist society has begun its process of historical development. In a word, they have historically translated the Marxist formula about the dictatorship of the proletariat into the reality of lived experience. A revolution is a genuine revolution and not just empty, swollen rhetorical demagoguery, only when it is embodied in some type of State, only when it becomes an organized system of power. Society can only exist in the form of a State, which is the source and the end of all rights and all duties, and the guarantor of the permanence and success of all social activity. The proletarian revolution only earns that name when it gives rise to and is embodied in a form of State which is typically proletarian in character; which acts as a custodian of the rights of the proletariat and performs its essential function as an expression of the life and power of the proletariat.

The Bolsheviks have created a State out of the historical and social experiences of the Russian proletariat, which are the experiences of the class of workers and peasants everywhere. They have articulated and shaped into a complex, organic whole the proletariat's most intimate life, its tradition, its deepest-felt and most-loved spiritual and social history. They have broken with the past but, at the same time, they have preserved continuity with the past; they have cut off one tradition, but enriched and developed another. They have broken with the past of a history dominated by the propertied class, but they have continued, developed and enriched the vital tradition of the proletarian class, the class of workers and peasants. In this, they have been revolutionary, because they have established a new order, a new discipline. The break is irrevocable, because it touches on what is most essential in history. There is no possibility of any return, because any attempt to change things back would bring an immeasurable disaster crashing down on Russian society. And so a formidable duel had to be waged against all the exigencies of History: all those things, from the most elementary to the most complex, which had to be incorporated in the new proletarian State, dominated by the new State and brought within its bounds.

It was necessary to win over to the new State the loyal majority of the Russian people. It was necessary to reveal to the people of Russia that the new State was *their* State: their life, their spirit, their tradition, the most precious heritage they possessed. The State formed by the Soviets had a leading elite, the Bolshevik Communist Party, and it had the support of a social minority – industrial workers – that represented the consciousness of the entire class; the consciousness of the vital and permanent interests of that class. The State formed by the Soviets has become the State of the entire Russian people. And it has done this through the tenacious perseverance of the Communist Party, the eager faith and loyalty of the workers, and the assiduous and never-ending work of propaganda, elucidation and education carried out by the exceptional men of the Russian Communist movement, directed by the lucid and unstoppable will of the master of them, Nikolai Lenin. The Soviet has demonstrated its immortality. It is the only form of organized society which responds precisely to all the many, varied needs of the great mass of the Russian people; their permanent and vital needs, economic and political. It is the only form of society which can realize and satisfy the aspirations and hopes of all the oppressed peoples of the world.

The cruel and long drawn-out war had left a sad inheritance of poverty, of barbarity, of anarchy; the organization of social services had fallen apart; human community itself had been reduced to a nomad horde, lacking work, lacking discipline, lacking the power of decision: the dumb débris of an immense process of decomposition. The new State is salvaging the worn-out fragments of society from the rubble and is putting them together again, welding them together; it is recreating a faith, a discipline, a soul, a thrust towards work and progress. A task which could be the glory of an entire generation.

It is not enough. History is not content with this hard test. The new State is being implacably assailed by formidable opponents. False currency is being coined to corrupt the peasants, to tempt their famished stomachs. Russia's every outlet to the sea is being cut off, all its trade links, all solidarity. It is being robbed of the Ukraine, of the Donetz basin, of Siberia, of every market for raw materials and foodstuffs. All along a ten-thousand-mile front, bands of armed men are threatening invasion: uprisings are being funded, betrayals, acts of vandalism, terrorism and sabotage. Even the most clamorous victories are being transmuted, through treachery, into sudden defeats.

This does not matter. The power of the Soviets is holding up: out of the chaos of defeat it is creating a powerful army which is becoming the backbone of the proletarian State.

Pressed on all sides by massive, hostile forces, it is finding in itself the intellectual vigour and historical flexibility to adapt to the needs of changing circumstances, without changing character, and without compromising the happy process of development towards communism.

The Soviet State has thus shown itself to be a fatal and irrevocable moment in the fatal process of human civilization. It is the first nucleus of a new society.

The other States cannot live with a proletariat Russia, yet they are powerless to destroy it: all the massed means of which international capital disposes – the monopoly on information, the possibility of slander, corruption, the land and sea embargo, boycotting, sabotage, shameless treachery (Prinkipo), violations of international law (like starting wars without any declaration), military pressure, the exploitation of superior technical resources – all these various means prove powerless against the faith of a whole populace. So it is historically necessary that the other States should either disappear, or else *become* Russia, become one with it.

This schism in the human race cannot last for long. Humanity is naturally tending towards internal and external unity; towards an order of peace and tolerance which would permit the reconstruction of the world. Russia has survived for two years after a disastrous war, with the blockade on, with no help from outside, relying on its own forces. The capitalist States, on the other hand, despite having the whole world on their side, despite stepping up the exploitation of the colonies in order to save their own lives, are still continuing to go downhill, piling up one disaster after another, and one destruction after the next.

So Russia is where history is; Russia is where life is; only in the regime of the Councils can the life and death problems which are hanging over the world find an adequate solution. The Russian Revolution had paid its dues to History: a price made up of death, of poverty, of hunger, of sacrifice, of unbroken will. Today, the duel is drawing to its climax. The Russian people has risen to its feet, in all its immensity: a giant, terrible in its ascetic thinness, towering over the crowd of pygmies who are furiously attacking it.

The Russian people has armed itself to the teeth for its Valmy. It cannot be defeated; it has already paid its dues. It must be defended against the hordes of drunken mercenaries, of adventurers and bandits who want to sink their teeth into its raw, living heart. The natural allies of the Russian people, its comrades throughout the world, must raise a war-cry in its support, to make its impetus unstoppable, to open the way for it to return into the life of the world.

L'Ordine Nuovo, 7 June 1919

Workers' Democracy

An urgent problem is clamouring at the door of every socialist who feels a keen sense of the historical responsibility weighing on the working class and on the Party which represents the critical and active consciousness of this class's mission.

How can the immense social forces that the war has unleashed be harnessed? How can they be disciplined and given a political form that has the potential to develop smoothly into the skeleton of the socialist State in which the dictatorship of the proletariat will be embodied? How can the present and future be welded together, in such a way as to meet the urgent needs of the present and also to work usefully to create and 'anticipate' the future?

This article is intended as a stimulus to thought and action. It is an invitation to the best and most conscious workers to reflect on the problem and – each within his own sphere of competence and action – to start collaborating towards a solution, bringing the problem to the attention of their comrades and the associations to which they belong. The concrete task of building the future cannot be undertaken without a collective, collaborative effort of explanation, persuasion and mutual education.

The socialist State already exists, potentially, in the social institutions characteristic of the exploited working class. These institutions must be linked together, co-ordinated, and ranked in a hierarchy of competences and powers – highly centralized, but still respecting the autonomy and articulations of each individual institution. In this way, a genuine workers' democracy can be created right now, in active, effective opposition to the bourgeois State; ready, right now, to take over from the bourgeois State in all its essential functions, of administrating and controlling the nation's assets.

At the moment, the workers' movement is led by the Socialist Party and the Confederation of Labour but, where the great working masses are concerned, the social power of both institutions is exercised by indirect means, by prestige and enthusiasm, by authoritarian pressure – even by inertia. The Party's sphere of influence broadens every day; it reaches previously unexplored strata of the population, awakening conviction and the desire to work effectively for the advent of communism in groups and individuals who have previously been absent from the political struggle. These disorderly and chaotic energies must be given a permanent form and discipline. They must be absorbed, co-ordinated, prepared for action. The proletarian and semi-proletarian classes must be transformed into an ordered society, which can educate itself, acquire experience and develop a responsible awareness of the duties which weigh on any class that accedes to the power of the State.

For the Socialist Party and the trade unions to absorb the whole of the working class will be the work of years, even decades. These institutions will not be immediately identifiable with the proletarian State; in fact, in Communist Republics, they have continued to exist independently of the State, with the Party acting as a driving force and the unions as instruments for control and the achievement of limited reforms. The Party must continue in its role as the organ of communist education, the furnace of faith, the depository of doctrine, the supreme power harmonizing the organized and disciplined forces of the worker and peasant classes, and leading them towards their goal. It is precisely because it has to fulfil this role with all due rigour that the Party cannot throw its doors open to the invasion of new supporters, not yet accustomed to responsibility and discipline.

But the social life of the working class has a rich and varied supply of different institutions and activities. It is these institutions and activities which we should be developing and co-ordinating, linking them together in a vast and flexible system capable of absorbing and disciplining the entire working class.

The workshop, with its internal commissions, the socialist clubs, the peasant communities – these are the centres of proletarian life we should be working in directly.

The workshop commissions are organs of worker democracy which must be freed from the constraints imposed on them by the bosses, and infused with a new life and energy. At the moment, these commissions have the task of curbing the power the capitalist exerts within the factory, and they perform an arbitrational and disciplinary function. In the future, developed and improved, they should be the organs of proletarian power, replacing the capitalist in all his useful managerial and administrative functions.

Workers should proceed, right now, to elect vast assemblies of delegates, chosen among the best and most politically aware comrades, under the slogan, 'All the power in the workshop to the workshop committees', together with the other, complementary slogan, 'All State power to the workers' and peasants' councils'.

In this way, the communists organized in the Party and the local committees would be presented with a vast arena for concrete revolutionary propaganda. The clubs, acting in accord with the urban Party sections, should carry out a survey of the working-class forces in their area, and they should become the seat for the local councils of workshop delegates: the nerve-centre assembling and co-ordinating all the proletarian energies of the area. The electoral systems could vary according to the size of the workshop; but the aim should be to elect one delegate for every fifteen workers, divided into categories (as is done in English factories), ending up, through a series of elections, with a committee of workshop delegates including representatives of every aspect of the work (manual workers, clerical staff, technicians). The local commission should also aim to incorporate workers in other categories, living in the area: waiters, cab-drivers, tram-drivers, railway-workers, road-sweepers, private employees, shop-workers, etc.

The local committee should be an expression of *the whole of the working class* living in that area: a legitimate, authoritative expression, capable of enforcing a discipline based on the power spontaneously delegated to it and able to order the immediate and complete cessation of all work in the area.

The local committees would grow into urban commissariats, subject to the control and discipline of the Socialist Party and the trade federations.

A system of worker democracy of this kind (integrated with equivalent peasant organizations) would give a permanent structure and discipline to the masses. It would be a magnificent education in politics and administration, and it would involve the masses, down to the last man, schooling them in determination and perseverance, teaching them to see themselves as an army in the field, which must hold together if it is not to be destroyed or reduced to slavery.

Every factory would build up one or more regiments of this army, with its own NCOs, its own liaison services, its own officer corps and general staff, with all powers delegated through free election and not imposed in an authoritarian manner. Through workshop meetings and a ceaseless work of propaganda and persuasion on the part of the most politically aware elements, it would be possible to bring about a radical transformation in worker psychology. The masses would become better prepared and equipped for the exercise of power. An awareness would develop of the duties and rights of comrades and workers – an awareness which would be all the more concerted and effective because it would have been generated from living, historical experience.

As we have already said, these rapid jottings are only intended as a stimulus to thought and action. Each single aspect of the problem really deserves a large-scale, in-depth consideration, with detailed explanations, and due consideration of other, subsidiary and lateral issues. But the full, concrete solution to the problems of socialist life can be provided only by communist practice: a collective, friendly debate, which modifies people's consciousness, uniting them and filling them with an overwhelming enthusiasm for action. To tell the truth, to reach the truth together, is a revolutionary, communist act. The formula, 'the dictatorship of the proletariat' must stop being simply a formula, a chance to show off one's revolutionary phraseology. Whoever genuinely wills an end must also will the means. The dictatorship of the proletariat means the establishment of a new State, a typically proletarian State, which channels the institutional experience of the oppressed class and turns the social life of the working classes into an all-encompassing and highly organized system. This State cannot be improvised: the Russian Bolsheviks toiled for eight months to broadcast their slogan, 'All power to the Soviets', and to make that slogan come true – and Russian workers had been familiar with the Soviets since 1905. Italian communists should capitalize on this Russian experience to save themselves time and effort. The task of reconstruction will itself demand so much time and labour that every day and every action possible should be directed to that goal.

L'Ordine Nuovo, 21 June 1919 (with Palmiro Togliatti)

The State and Socialism[1]

We are publishing this article by 'For Ever', even though it is a jumble of arrant nonsense and meaningless jargon. In the opinion of 'For Ever', the Weimar State is a Marxist State; we at the *Ordine Nuovo* are State-worshippers who want the State to exist *ab aeterno* ('For Ever' evidently meant to say *in aeternum*); the socialist State is the same thing as State socialism; there was such a thing as a 'Christian State' and a 'plebeian State under Caius Gracchus'; Saratov's Soviet could survive without co-ordinating its production and its action of revolutionary defence with the general system of the Russian Soviets, etc. All these assertions, all this nonsensical rubbish – all presented as a defence of anarchy.

Still, we are publishing 'For Ever''s article. 'For Ever' is not merely an individual: he is a social type. Seen from this point of view, he must not be ignored: he must be identified, studied, discussed and put behind us. In a spirit of loyalty and friendship (friendship cannot be divorced from truth and from all the pain that truth brings with it). 'For Ever' is a pseudo-revolutionary: anyone whose action rests entirely on overblown rhetoric, frenzied rantings and romantic enthusiasms is only a demagogue, not a revolutionary. The revolution needs men of sober mind, men who will see to it that there is bread in the shops, that the trains run on time and raw materials get to the factor-

---

[1] Reply to an article by Massimo Fovel ['For Ever'], 'In Defence of Anarchy'.

ies; men who will arrange for the exchange of industrial and agricultural products; men who will guarantee people's safety and personal
freedom in the face of crime, who will ensure the efficient running
of the whole complex of social services, and prevent the populace
falling into a state of desperation and mad internecine strife. Even
when it is a case of solving just one of these problems, in a village
of a hundred inhabitants, rhetorical enthusiasms and unbridled rant-
ing can only make you laugh (or cry).

But 'For Ever', even though he is a type, does not represent all
libertarians. There is a communist libertarian, Carlo Petri, on the
editorial staff of the *Ordine Nuovo*. With Petri, the debate is on a
much higher plane: where communist libertarians like Petri are concerned, we have absolutely no choice but to work with them – they
are a force of the revolution. Reading over Petri's article in the last
issue and the article of 'For Ever' which we are publishing here (with
the aim of establishing the dialectical terms of the libertarian idea:
being and not-being) we have noted down the following observations.
Naturally, Comrade Empedocles and Comrade Caesar, who are
referred to directly by Petri, are free to respond for themselves.

I

Communism is embodied in the proletarian International. Communism exists only when it is international, only insofar as it is international. In this sense, the socialist, proletarian movement is against the
State, because it is against the national capitalist States and against
the national economies, which stem from the national State and are
conditioned by it.

But if the national States will be eliminated in the Communist
International, that is not to say that the State itself will be eliminated –
the State understood as the concrete 'form' of human society.
Society, as such, is a pure abstraction. Within history, in the living,
flesh-and-blood reality of human civilization as it develops, society is
always a system of States, a balance between States: it is a system,
a balance of concrete institutions, within which society develops a
consciousness of its existence and its development and without which
society could not exist or develop at all.

The conquests of human civilization become permanent – become
real history, and not just a superficial, passing episode – only when

they are embodied in an institution and find a form in the State. The socialist idea remained a myth, an evanescent chimera, a mere whim of individual fantasy until it was embodied in the socialist proletarian movement, in the defensive and offensive institutions of the organized proletariat. It is within these institutions and by means of these institutions that the socialist idea has taken on a historical form and progressed. It is from these institutions that it has brought into being the national socialist State, which is set up and organized in such a way as to enable it to be integrated with the other socialist States. Or rather, it is set up in such a way that it is only able to survive and develop by working alongside the other socialist States to bring into being the Communist International, in which every individual State, every institution, every individual will achieve their full potential for life and freedom.

In this sense communism is not 'against the State'. On the contrary, it is implacably opposed to the enemies of the State – anarchists and trade-union anarchists. It condemns their propaganda as utopian and dangerous to the proletarian revolution.

A pre-established schema has been constructed, in which socialism is a 'gang-plank' to anarchy. This is a stupid prejudice, an arbitrary mortgage on the future. In the dialectic of ideas, anarchy is a continuation of liberalism, rather than socialism; in the dialectic of history, anarchy will be expelled from the sphere of social reality along with liberalism. As the production of material goods becomes increasingly industrialized and the concentration of capital is matched by a corresponding concentration of the working masses, the libertarian idea has fewer and fewer adherents. The libertarian movement is still widespread in those areas still dominated by a craft economy and a feudal system of land ownership. In the industrial cities and in rural areas where agriculture has become mechanized, the anarchists have tended to disappear as a political movement, even if they survive as an ideological ferment. In this sense, the libertarian idea will have its role to play for some time yet. It will continue the liberal tradition, insofar as the liberal tradition has achieved and realized conquests for humanity which are not destined to die with capitalism.

At the present moment, in the social turmoil brought about by the war, it seems that the number of adherents to the libertarian idea has multiplied. In our view, this is through no merit of the idea itself. The phenomenon is a regressive one: new elements have migrated into the cities, devoid of any political culture, out of step with the class struggle in the complex form that the class struggle has assumed with the development of industry. The virulent word-mongering of the anarchist agitators can get an easy grip on these instinctual, primitive consciousnesses; but nothing profound or permanent can be created by pseudo-revolutionary jargon. And those who are leading the way, who are imprinting the rhythm of progress on history, who are determining the sure and unswerving advance of communist civilization are not the 'boys on the street', or the *Lumpenproletariat*, or the bohemians, or dilettantes, or long-haired, frenetic romantics. They are the massed ranks of the working classes, the iron-clad battalions of the politically conscious, disciplined proletariat.

II

The entire liberal tradition is anti-State.

The literature of liberalism is one long polemic against the State. The political history of capitalism is characterized by a furious and unending struggle between the citizen and the State. Parliament is the organ of this struggle; and, precisely because of this, Parliament tends to absorb all the functions of the State – in other words, to do away with the State, by depriving it of any effective power, since the aim of popular legislation is to free local institutions and individuals from any subjection to or control by central power.

This liberal action is part of the general activity of capitalism, whose aim is to ensure that the conditions for competition are as solid and dependable as possible. Competition is the fiercest enemy of the State. The idea of the International itself is liberal in origin; Marx took it over from the Cobden school and the propaganda for free trade, though he did so in a critical way. The liberals are incapable of bringing about peace and the International, because private and national property generates splits, borders, wars, national States in permanent conflict with each other.

The national State is an organ of competition. It will disappear when competition has been eliminated and a new economic practice established through the concrete experiences of socialist States.

The dictatorship of the proletariat is still a national State and a class State. The parameters of competition and the class struggle have been changed, but competition and the classes continue to exist. The dictatorship of the proletariat has to resolve the same problems as the bourgeois State, of external and internal defence. These are the concrete, objective conditions that we have to take into account: to talk and act as though the Communist International already existed, as though the period of struggle between socialist and bourgeois States, of pitiless competition between communist and capitalist national economies, was already behind us, would be a disastrous error for the proletarian revolution.

Human society is undergoing an extremely rapid process of decomposition, corresponding to the process of dissolution of the bourgeois State. The concrete, objective conditions in which the dictatorship of the proletariat will have to act will be conditions of tremendous disorder and terrifying lack of discipline. It becomes necessary to form a rock-solid socialist State, capable of arresting this dissolution and disorder as soon as possible, reshaping the social body into a coherent form and defending the revolution against external attacks and internal rebellions.

The dictatorship of the proletariat, if it is to survive and develop, must take on a markedly military character. This is why the problem of a socialist army becomes one of the most crucial; and it becomes urgently necessary, in this pre-revolutionary period, to try and get rid of the sediment of prejudice left by past socialist propaganda against all forms of bourgeois domination.

We must re-educate the proletariat, get it used to the idea that in order to eliminate the State within the International we need a kind of State which is designed to achieve this end, and that to eliminate militarism we may need a new kind of army. That means training the proletariat in the practice of dictatorship, in self-government. The difficulties to overcome will be very many and it is impossible to predict with confidence that these difficulties will remain alive and dangerous only for a brief period. But even if the proletarian State only needs to exist for a day, we should still be working now to ensure that the conditions in which it will be operating will be such as to facilitate the performance of its task – the elimination of private property and the classes.

The proletariat is unschooled in the art of governing and ruling and the bourgeoisie will put up a formidable opposition to the socialist

State, whether open or underground, violent or passive. Only a politically educated proletariat, which does not let the setbacks it will inevitably encounter reduce it to despair and demoralization, which remains faithful and loyal to its State in spite of the errors that may be committed by single individuals and the backwards steps that the concrete conditions of production may make necessary – only this kind of proletariat will be capable of putting the dictatorship into practice, liquidating the malign heritage of capitalism and the War and bringing the Communist International into being. And, by its very nature, the socialist State demands a loyalty and a discipline different from, even opposite to those required by the bourgeois State. Unlike the bourgeois State, which is the more strong, at home and abroad, the less its citizens can control and follow the exercise of its powers, the socialist State requires an active and permanent participation by all comrades in the life of its institutions. It must also be remembered that the socialist State is a means to bring about very radical changes; and it is not possible to change a State with the ease with which one changes a government. A return to the institutions of the past will mean mass death, the unleashing of a white terror that will cause unlimited bloodshed: in the conditions created by the war, it would be in the interests of the bourgeois class to wipe out three-quarters of the working populace, in order to restore flexibility in the foodstuffs market and to put itself back in a strong position in the struggle for the easy life to which it has become accustomed. There can be no waverings of any kind, for any reason.

Right from this moment, we must awaken in ourselves and others this sense of responsibility, as keen and implacable as the executioner's sword. The Revolution is a great and fearsome thing, not a game for dilettantes or a romantic escapade.

When it has been defeated in the class struggle, capitalism will leave an unhealthy residue of anti-state ferments – or feelings which will go by that name, because some individuals and groups will want to exempt themselves from the work and discipline necessary to the success of the Revolution.

Dear comrade Petri, let us work to avoid any bloody clashes between subversive factions, to protect the socialist State from the cruel necessity of imposing discipline and loyalty with armed force, of eliminating one part in order to save the social body from decay and corruption. Let us work together, in our cultural task, to demonstrate that the existence of the socialist State is a necessary link in the chain of tasks the proletariat must perform in the name of its emancipation, its freedom.

L'Ordine Nuovo, 28 June–5 July 1919

The Conquest of the State

The tendency towards a concentration of capital, determined by the mode of production, produces a corresponding concentration of the human working masses. This fact lies at the root of all the revolutionary theses of Marxism; which lies at the root of the conditions of the new proletariat way of life, of the new order of communism, destined to replace the bourgeois way of life, the disorder of capitalism, generated by free competition and the class struggle.

Within the sphere of general capitalist activity, the worker, too, operates on the plane of free competition, as a citizen-individual. But the starting conditions in the struggle are not the same for everyone, at any given time: the existence of private property puts a social minority in a position of privilege, so that the struggle is uneven. The worker is continuously exposed to the most deadly risks: his very survival, his culture, the life and the future of his family are exposed to the sudden consequences of fluctuations in the labour market. So the worker attempts to escape from the sphere of competition and individualism. The principles of association and solidarity become crucial to the working class, and change the psychology and the way of life of workers and peasants. Institutions and organs arise which embody these principles, and these form the basis for the process of historical development that will lead to communism in the means of production and exchange.

The principle of association can and must be adopted as the crucial factor in the proletariat revolution. It is this historical tendency that determined the emergence and first development of the Socialist parties and the trade unions, in the period immediately preceding the present one (which we might call the period of the First and Second Internationals, or the period of recruitment).

The development of these proletarian institutions, and of the proletarian movement as a whole, was not, however, autonomous: it did not obey laws which were inherent in the life and the historical experience of the exploited working class. The laws of history were dictated by the propertied class, organized as the State. The State has always been the protagonist of history, because the power of the propertied class is concentrated in its organs. It is in the State that the propertied class disciplines itself, and forms itself into a unity that can stand above the clash of competition, in order to protect its privileged position in the supreme phase of competition: the struggle between the classes for power and pre-eminence in the leadership and ordering of society.

In the period in question, the proletarian movement was no more than a function of capitalist free competition. The proletarian institutions had to assume the form they did not because of any inner necessity, but because of external constraints, because of the formidable pressure of events and constraints arising from capitalist competition. It is because of this that we have seen the internal conflicts, the deviations, the fluctuations, the compromises that have marked the existence of the proletariat movement during the whole period prior to the present one: the period that culminated in the collapse of the Second International.

Certain currents within the socialist and proletarian movement had emphasized, as a crucial factor in the revolution, the need to organize workers according to the kind of work they did. The Syndicalist movement appeared, for a moment, to possess the true interpretation of Marxism, the true interpretation of the truth.

The error of the Syndicalist movement is this: it assumes that the trade unions will continue to exist in their current form and with their current functions, as though they constituted a perennial form of association while, in fact, their form and functions have been determined by external, rather than internal factors and, for this reason, they cannot have a constant and predictable line of development. Syndicalism, which presented itself as the beginning of a 'spontaneous', libertarian tradition, has in fact been no more than one of the disguises of the abstract spirit of Jacobinism.

This is the root of the errors in the Syndicalist current, which showed itself to be incapable of taking over the Socialist Party's task of educating the working class for the revolution. The workers and the peasants felt that, as long as the propertied class and the democratic-parliamentary State are dictating the laws of history, any attempt to escape from the sphere of influence of those laws is foolish and ridiculous. It must be accepted that, within the general configuration that society has assumed as a result of industrial production, the only way in which we can participate actively in life and act to modify our environment is in our capacity as citizen-individuals, members of the democratic-parliamentary State. The experience of liberalism is not a useless one, and it is possible to progress beyond this experience only if we first experience it. The apoliticism of the apoliticals was simply a degeneration of politics: it is as much a political act to reject the State and set oneself against it as it is to participate in the general historical activity that is brought together in Parliament and the municipal councils, the popular institutions of the State. What changes is the *quality* of the political act concerned. The Syndicalists were working outside reality, and thus their politics were fundamentally mistaken. The Parliamentary Socialists were working at the heart of things: they could make mistakes (indeed, they did make many very serious mistakes), but the general direction that their activity took was not in error. For this reason, it was they who won the 'contest'. The great masses, whose intervention can objectively modify social relations – the great masses chose to organize themselves around the Socialist Party. In the final analysis, notwithstanding all its mistakes and all its defects, the Party succeeded in its mission. It made something of the proletariat, which had previously been nothing; it gave it an awareness; and it gave a direction to the liberation movement, a real, a purposeful direction, which corresponded in general lines to the process of historical development of human society.

The gravest mistake of the socialist movement was similar to that of the Syndicalists. As they participated in the general activity of human society, within the State, the Socialists forgot that their position ought to be essentially one of criticism, of antithesis. They allowed themselves to be absorbed by reality, rather than dominating it.

Marxist Communists should be characterized by what we might call a 'maieutic' mentality. It is not their role to abandon themselves to the flow of events determined by the laws of bourgeois competition: rather, they should maintain a critical distance. History is a continual process of becoming, and so it is essentially unforeseeable. But that does not mean that 'everything' is unpredictable in the process of historical becoming; that is, that history is the domain of chance and irresponsible whim. History is, at one and the same time, freedom and necessity. Institutions, in whose development and activity we can see history embodied, emerge and remain in existence because they have a task and a mission to accomplish. Certain objective conditions for the production of material goods and for men's spiritual consciousness have arisen and developed. If these conditions – which because of their mechanical nature are almost mathematically calculable – change, then the whole complex of relationships that regulate and inform human society changes with them, as does the level of human consciousness. The whole configuration of society is transformed, and traditional institutions go into decline: they are inadequate to their task and become obstructive and dangerous.

If human intelligence were incapable of grasping some rhythm, establishing some pattern in the process of historical becoming, civilization would be impossible. Political genius may be recognized precisely in this capacity to master the greatest possible number of concrete terms, necessary and sufficient to pin down a process of development. It is the capacity, in other words, to anticipate the immediate and the more distant future, and to act on this intuition to prescribe the activity of a State, hazarding the future of a whole people. In this sense, Karl Marx has proved by far the greatest political genius of our age.

The socialists have accepted, often supinely, the historical reality that is a product of the capitalist initiative. They have fallen into the mistaken way of thinking that also affects liberal economists: a belief in the perpetuity of the institutions of the democratic State, in their fundamental perfection. In their view, the form of democratic institutions can be corrected, touched up here and there, but, fundamentally, it must be respected. An example of this kind of smug and narrow thinking is Filippo Turati's Minos-like[1] pronouncement that Parliament stands to the Soviet as a city does to the barbarian horde.

The current catchphrase, 'the conquest of the State', arises out of this misunderstanding of the nature of the historical process, along with the entrenched habit of compromise and the 'cretinous' tactics of parliamentarism.

We, on the other hand, are convinced, in the light of the revolutionary experiences of Russia, Hungary and Germany, that a socialist State cannot be incarnated in the institutions of a capitalist State. Where those institutions are concerned, the socialist State represents a radically new departure, even if it makes perfect sense within the history of the proletariat. The institutions of the capitalist State are organized with the purpose of facilitating free competition: simply to change the people in charge will do nothing to direct the activity of these institutions towards a different end. The socialist State does not signify communism, not yet; it does not signify the establishment of a communal economic practice and way of life. It is a transitional State, whose task is to suppress competition by suppressing private property, the classes and the national economies. This task cannot be performed by a parliamentary democracy. The formula 'the conquest of the State' should be understood in this sense: the creation of a new type of State, born out of the associative experience of the proletarian class, to replace the democratic–parliamentary State.

And that brings us back to where we started from. As we have said, the institutions of the socialist and proletarian movement, in the period preceding the present one, did not develop autonomously, but as the result of the general configuration of a human society ruled by the sovereign laws of capitalism. The war has turned the strategic situation of the class struggle on its head. The capitalists have lost their pre-eminence; their liberty is limited; their power has been cut down to nothing. The capitalist tendency to concentration of resources has reached its furthest limit possible, with the achievement of a world monopoly on production and commerce. The corresponding concentration of the working masses has given an unprecedented power to the revolutionary proletarian class.

The traditional institutions of the movement have become incap-

---

[1] [Translator's note] The adjective *minossico* (obviously ironic here) implies a stern and unrelenting judgement. Minos, mythical king of ancient Crete, was assigned the task of judging the dead in Virgil's *Aeneid* and Dante's *Inferno*.

able of containing this great blossoming of revolutionary life. Their very structure is unsuited to the task of disciplining forces that have become a part of the conscious historical process. These institutions are not dead. Created in response to free competition, they must continue in existence until every last remnant of competition has been suppressed, until the classes themselves and the parties have been suppressed and the national dictatorships of the proletariat have fused into the Communist International. But alongside these institutions, a new type of institution must begin to be created and developed: State-like institutions devised, precisely, to *replace* the private and public institutions of the democratic-parliamentary State. Institutions devised to take over the role of the capitalist, in administrating and running industry; and to guarantee the autonomy of the producer in the factory, on the shop-floor. Institutions capable of taking over the management of all the different functions inherent in the complex system of production and exchange: those functions that link the various divisions of a factory together, to form the basic economic unit; those functions that link together the various activities of the agricultural industry, as well, and that must be co-ordinated, through horizontal and vertical planning, in the harmonious edifice of the national and international economy, freed from the suffocating and parasitical tyranny of private ownership.

Never has the revolutionary drive of the proletariat of Eastern Europe been stronger, or its enthusiasm more fervent. But it seems to us that a lucid and precise awareness of the end is not being matched by an equally lucid and precise awareness of the means required, as things stand at the moment, to achieve that end. The conviction has by now become rooted in the masses that the proletarian State is embodied in a system of workers', peasants' and soldiers' Councils. But no very clear idea has yet developed of the tactics necessary to ensure the actual creation of this State. It is necessary, therefore, to set up a network of proletarian institutions, without delay: institutions rooted in the consciousness of the great masses, and which will be able to rely on the permanent discipline and loyalty of those masses; institutions would provide a framework, rich with dynamism and potential, within which the class of workers and peasants, in its totality, could develop. It is certain that if a mass movement of a revolutionary character were to emerge today, in the present conditions of proletarian organization, the results would boil down to no more than a purely formal correction of the democratic State: all that would happen is that the powers of the Chamber of Deputies would be enhanced (via a constituent assembly) and a bunch of bungling, anticommunist socialists would take charge. The experiences of Germany and Austria must have something to tell us. The forces of the democratic State and the capitalist class are still immense. We should not attempt to hide from ourselves the fact that capitalism keeps going especially through the work of its lackeys and sycophants; and that disreputable breed is still very far from extinct.

To sum up, the creation of the proletarian State is not a thaumaturgical act. It too is a process of becoming, a process of development. It presupposes a preparatory work of organization and propaganda. Greater support and greater powers must be given to those proletarian institutions that already exist within the factories, and similar ones must be created in the villages as well. And it must be ensured that the men who are active in them are communists, aware of the revolutionary mission that their institution must fulfil. Otherwise all our enthusiasm, and all the faith of the working classes will not be enough to prevent the revolution from degenerating wretchedly into a new Parliament of tricksters, fools and incompetents, so that new and more terrifying sacrifices will be necessitated in future, to bring about a genuine proletarian State.

L'Ordine Nuovo, 12 July 1919

Unions and Councils

The proletarian organization whose function is to express the aspirations of the worker and peasant masses, from its headquarters in the Confederation of Labour, is undergoing a constitutional crisis similar in character to the crisis in which the democratic-parliamentary State is vainly floundering. The crisis, in both cases, is one of power and sovereignty. The solution to one crisis will prove to be the solution to the other, because, once they have resolved the problem of the will to power within the sphere of their own class organization, the working masses will be in a position to create the organic framework of their own State, and to successfully challenge and overturn the parliamentary State.

The workers feel that 'their' organization has become such an enormous apparatus that it has finished up by obeying laws of its own: laws dictated by its structure and complicated working mechanisms, which are quite alien from the masses that have acquired consciousness of their historic mission as a revolutionary class. They feel that their will to power is not being expressed, in any very clear and precise way, by the existing institutional hierarchies. They feel that, even on their own territory, in the home they have built for themselves with such tenacity, with such patient efforts, cementing it with their blood and tears – even here, the human is being crushed by technology, bureaucracy is drying up the creative spirit, and a glib and banal dilettanteism is trying in vain to cover up a complete absence of any precise views about the needs of industrial production, and a complete lack of understanding of the mentality of the proletarian masses. The workers are angered by what is happening but, as individuals, they are powerless to change anything. The words and the wills of individual men are too puny a thing compared with the iron laws inherent in the bureaucratic structure of the trade-union apparatus.

The leaders[1] of the organization are not aware of this profound and widely felt crisis. The more obvious it becomes that the working class is not organized into forms that are consistent with its true, underlying historical structure, that it is not integrated in a configuration that is modified continually in accordance with the internal laws that govern that class's real process of historical development, the more pig-headedly the leaders persist in their blindness, and the more set they become on resolving dissent and conflict in a purely 'legalistic' way. Incorrigible bureaucrats that they are, they believe that an actual, objective condition, rooted in a psychology that develops out of the real experience of the shop floor, can be changed simply by rousing speeches, and slogans voted unanimously in meetings drowned out by brutish uproar and empty rhetorical outpourings. Now they are attempting to 'rise to the challenge of the times' and, just to show that they are even capable of 'tough thinking', they are dusting off all those old and worn-out syndicalist ideological clichés, harping on about how the Soviet is the equivalent of the trade union, and how the existing system of trade-union organization already constitutes the framework of a communist society, the system of forces within which the dictatorship of the proletariat must take on a concrete form.

Trade unions, in the form in which they currently exist in the countries of Western Europe, are not only a very different kind of organization from the Soviet; they are also remarkably different from the kind of trade union that is developing with ever greater momentum within the Communist Republic of Russia.

The craft unions, the Camere del Lavoro, the industrial federations and the Confederazione Generale del Lavoro all represent a type of proletarian organization specific to the period of history dominated by capital. In a certain sense, it may be claimed that this kind of institution is an integral part of capitalist society and performs a

---

[1] [Translator's note] Gramsci uses the English term 'leader' here.

function that only makes sense within a regime of private property. During this period of capitalism, in which individuals are valued only inasmuch as they own goods and trade their property, workers too have been compelled to obey the iron laws of general necessity, and they have become traders in the only commodity they possess: their work-power and their professional skills. As they have become more exposed to the risks of competition, the workers have brought this commodity of theirs together in ever larger and more comprehensive 'firms', and they have created this enormous cattle-market, this apparatus for concentrating labour. They have imposed wages and working hours, and disciplined the market. They have hired from outside, or created from within, a loyal administrative staff, trained in this kind of speculation, capable of mastering market conditions, drawing up contracts, assessing commercial risks and initiating economically advantageous projects. The essential nature of the trade union is competitive, not communist. It cannot be the instrument for a radical renewing of society. All it can do is supply the proletarian movement with skilled bureaucrats and technical experts on general industrial matters: it cannot form the foundation of proletarian power. It does not offer any scope for selecting those individuals of the proletariat who will be capable and worthy of leading society. The cadres who will embody the *élan vital*, the rhythms of progress of a communist society, will not emerge out of the trade union movement.

The dictatorship of the proletariat can be realized only in a type of organization that is geared to the activity of the producer, rather than to that of the salaried worker, the slave of capital. The Factory Council is the nucleus of this kind of organization. All branches of labour are given a representation in the Council, proportionate to the contribution that each individual trade and each branch of labour makes to the manufacture of the object that the factory is producing for the collectivity. This means that the Council is a class institution, a social institution. Its *raison d'être* lies in labour, in industrial production – in something permanent, that is, rather than in something like salaries and class-divisions: something transitory, something that we are, in fact, striving to overturn.

Because of this, these Councils can bring about the unification of the working class. They can give the masses a cohesion and a shape that mirrors the cohesion and shape that the masses assume within the general organization of society.

The Factory Council is the model for the proletarian State. All the problems that are inherent in the organization of the proletarian State are also inherent in the organization of the Council. In both Council and State, the concept of a citizen gives way to the concept of a comrade. The experience of collaborating to produce efficiently and usefully develops solidarity among the workers and reinforces the existing links of affection and comradeship. Everyone is indispensable, everyone is in his proper place, and everyone *has* a place and a function. Even the most ignorant and primitive of workers, even the vainest and most 'civil' of engineers will finally come to an awareness of this truth, through the experiences of factory organization. Everyone will finish up by acquiring a communist consciousness, which will enable him to understand what a great step forward the communist economy represents with respect to the capitalist economy. The Council is the most appropriate organ for mutual education and for fostering the new social spirit that the proletariat has managed to distil out of its fruitful, living experience in the community of labour. In the trade union, a spirit of workers' solidarity developed out of the struggle against capitalism, out of suffering and sacrifice. In the Council, that solidarity becomes something positive, something permanent. It is manifest even in the most insignificant moments of industrial production. It is expressed in the joyous awareness of forming an organic whole: a homogeneous, compact system which, through useful work and the disinterested production of social wealth, asserts its sovereignty and realizes its power and its freedom to mould history.

The existence of such an organization – an organization in which the working class is structured as a unified, productive class, an organization in which worthy cadres and individuals will spring up naturally, of their own accord – will have important and fundamental consequences for the constitution of the trade unions and for the spirit which animates their activity.

Like the trade union, the Factory Council is organized according to the separate trades that workers are engaged in. In each section of the workplace, the workers are divided into crews, and each crew constitutes a work unit (divided according to trade). The Council is made up of representatives elected by the workers for each separate trade, each crew, in the workplace. But the trade union is based on the individual, whereas the Council is based on the organic and concrete unit of a whole trade, as it is realized in the discipline of the industrial process. The work-crew (the individual trade) feels itself to be a distinct entity within the homogeneous body of the working class. At the same time, though, it feels itself to be integrated within the system of discipline and order whose exact and precise functioning enables production to develop. Where its economic and political interests are concerned, the single trade is an integral part of the class, one with it. Where it is distinct from the rest of the class is in matters of its technical interest, the development of the particular instruments that trade uses in its work. In the same way, all the various industries are homogeneous and united, in their general end, of perfecting production, distribution and the social acquisition of wealth; but each industry has its own, particular interests where the technical organization of its own, specific activity is concerned.

The existence of Councils gives workers direct responsibility for production; it encourages them to improve their way of working; it introduces a conscious and voluntary discipline and it creates the mentality of the producer, the maker of history. Workers then carry this new consciousness into the trade union and the trade union is then able to go beyond the simple activity of class struggle, and to devote itself to the fundamental task of re-shaping economic life and the technical realities of work, of creating the forms of economic life and working practice appropriate to a communist society. In this sense, the trade unions, which are made up of the best workers, and the workers who have achieved the highest degree of consciousness, can enact the supreme moment of the class struggle and the dictatorship of the proletariat: they can create the objective conditions in which the classes will no longer be able to exist, and will never again be reborn.

This is what the industrial trade unions are doing at the moment in Russia. They have become the organs within which all the individual enterprises in a given industry come together, are connected up and articulated, forming a great industrial entity. Wasteful competition is being eliminated, and the main services of administration, supply, distribution and storage are being unified in vast centres. Work systems, manufacturing secrets and new applications immediately become the common property of everyone in the industry. The multiplicity of bureaucratic and disciplinary functions inherent in the system of private property relations and the individual firm is reduced to what is required by strictly industrial needs. The applications of these union principles to the textile industry in Russia has enabled the bureaucratic staff to be cut from 100,000 to 3,500.

An organization that takes the factory as its basic unit will unify the class (the *whole* class) into a coherent and homogeneous entity, precisely fitted for the industrial process, capable of dominating that process and mastering it once and for all. It is within this kind of factory organization that the dictatorship of the proletariat can be realized: the Communist State, which will destroy class domination in the political superstructures and throughout the entire social fabric.

The trade unions and the industrial unions are the backbone of the great body of the proletariat. They shape individual and local experiences and bring them together in a larger whole, realizing the ideal of a national levelling of the conditions of work and production, which is the basis on which communist equality must be built.

But, for it to be possible for the trade unions to start moving in this *positive* class and communist direction, it is necessary that the workers should channel all their energy and commitment into consolidating and extending the system of Councils, and bringing the working class together into an organic unity. It is on this homogeneous and united foundation that all the superstructures of the communist dictatorship and the communist economy will spring up and develop.

L'Ordine Nuovo, 11 October 1919

The Trade Unions and the Dictatorship of the Proletariat

The international class struggle has reached its highest point so far in the victory of the workers and peasants of two national proletariats. In Russia and Hungary, the workers and peasants have established a dictatorship of the proletariat. And, in both Russia and Hungary, this dictatorship had to wage a bitter struggle not only against the bourgeoisie, but also against the trade unions. Indeed, the conflict between the dictatorship and the unions was one of the causes of the collapse of the Hungarian Soviet, because the unions, even if they never openly attempted to overthrow the dictatorship, consistently played the part of the 'defeatists' of the revolution and never ceased to sow the seeds of demoralization and cowardice among red soldiers and workers. An examination, however brief, of the reasons for this conflict and the conditions in which it took place cannot fail to be useful for the revolutionary education of the masses. For, even if the masses must be persuaded that the trade union is perhaps the most important proletarian organ of the communist revolution – because the socialization of industry depends on the unions, and the unions are responsible for creating the conditions in which private enterprise must disappear, never to re-emerge – they must also be convinced of the need, before the revolution, to create the psychological and material conditions in which any conflict, any power dualism between the various organs that embody the class struggle against communism would be impossible.

The class struggle has assumed a distinctly revolutionary character throughout Europe and the rest of the world. The idea championed by the Third International, that the class struggle must be directed towards the establishment of a dictatorship of the proletariat, has won out over democratic ideology and is spreading irresistibly among the masses. The Socialist Parties are joining the Third International, or at least, are acting in accordance with the basic principles agreed at the Moscow Congress. The trade unions, on the other hand, have remained faithful to 'true democracy', and never miss an opportunity to induce or force workers to declare their opposition to the dictatorship and to reject any show of solidarity with Soviet Russia. This attitude on the part of the unions was rapidly overcome in Russia, because the development of the trade and industrial unions was accompanied by a parallel, but more accelerated development of workshop Councils. In Hungary, on the other hand, it has eroded the foundations of proletarian power; in Germany, it has led to the mass slaughter of communist workers, and the emergence of the Noske phenomenon; in France, it has led to the failure of the general strike of 20–21 July, and the consolidation of the Clemenceau regime; it has so far prevented any direct intervention in the political struggle on the part of English workers and everywhere it is threatening to create a profound and dangerous division in the forces of the proletariat.

The Socialist Parties are becoming ever more markedly revolutionary and internationalist in character. The trade unions, on the other hand, are tending to embody the theory (!) and tactics of reformist opportunism, and becoming purely national organisms. This is creating a quite intolerable state of affairs, a state of permanent confusion and chronic weakness for the working class – and this, in turn, is compounding the general instability of society and fermenting moral disintegration and a descent into barbarism.

The trade unions have organized workers according to the principles of the class struggle, and they were themselves the first organic forms created by this struggle. The organizers of the trade union movement have always said that only the class struggle can lead the proletariat to freedom, and that the aim of the trade union organization is precisely that of suppressing individual profit and the exploitation of one man by another, since what it aims at is to eliminate the capitalist (the private owner) from the industrial process of production and, in this way, to eliminate the classes. But the trade unions could not accomplish this end at once, and so they directed all their energy towards the immediate end of improving the material conditions of the proletariat, demanding higher salaries, shorter working hours and a body of social legislation. Movement followed movement, strike followed strike, and the conditions of workers' lives objectively improved. But all the results of union action, all its victories, are still based on the old foundations. The principle of private ownership remains intact and powerful; the capitalist order of production and the exploitation of man by man remain intact – indeed, they are expanding in new directions. The eight-hour day, the increase in wages, the benefits of social legislation do not affect profit. Any upset that union action may cause to the profit rate on an immediate level is corrected and finds a new level within the play of free competition in those nations with a global economy, like England and Germany, while those with a more limited economy, like France and Italy, have recourse to protectionism. In other words, capitalism just makes up any increase in the general costs of industrial production at the expense of the amorphous national or colonial masses.

Trade unions have thus shown themselves to be incapable of overthrowing capitalist society, acting within their own sphere and with their own methods. Union action is incapable of bringing about the emancipation of the proletariat, of leading the proletariat towards that exalted and universal end that it had originally proposed.

According to syndicalist doctrine, what the trade unions should have been doing was educating workers to take charge of production. Because the industrial unions are a complete reflection of a given industry, it was argued, these unions will become the worker cadres equipped to run that particular industry. Trade-union appointments will serve as a means of selecting the best workers – the most motivated, the most intelligent, those best equipped to master the complex mechanism of production and exchange. The worker-leaders of the leather industry will be those most capable of running that industry, and so on for the metal industry, the publishing industry, etc.

What a terrible illusion! Trade-union leaders were never selected for their industrial competence, but rather for their legal, bureaucratic or public-speaking skills. And the more these organizations expanded, the more frequent their interventions in the class struggle and the more wide-reaching and profound their action, the more necessary it became to reduce the office of leadership to a purely administrative and financial one. Technical, industrial skills became more and more irrelevant, and bureaucratic and commercial skills were all that mattered. In this way, a veritable caste of union bureaucrats and journalists grew up, with a group mentality of their own, in absolute contrast with the mentality of the workers. And this caste has finished up by taking on the same position with respect to the working masses as the civil service has *vis-à-vis* the State. In both cases, it is the bureaucracy that really rules and governs.

The dictatorship of the proletariat aims to eliminate the capitalist regime of production and private ownership, because only in this way can man's exploitation of man be eliminated. The dictatorship of the proletariat aims to eliminate class differences and the class struggle, because only in this way can the social emancipation of the working class be realized. To achieve this end, the Communist Party is teaching the proletariat how to marshal its power as a class and how to use this armed power to overcome the bourgeoisie and to bring about the conditions in which the exploiting class can be suppressed, never to be reborn. The task of the Communist Party within the dictatorship is, then, as follows: to organize the class of workers and peasants powerfully and definitively into a ruling class, to keep a check on whether all the organs of the new State are really working to further the revolution, and to break down the old rights and relationships inherent to the principle of private property. But this work of destruction and surveillance must be accompanied by a positive work of creation and production. If this positive work does not bear fruit, then political power is useless and the dictatorship cannot work. No society can survive without producing – still less the dictatorship, which in fact needs a particularly intense rhythm of production, since it is coming into being in the conditions of economic chaos brought about by five years of full-scale war and months and months of armed terrorism on the part of the bourgeoisie.

And this is the vast and glorious task that the trade unions should be confronting. It is they who should be putting into practice a programme of socialization, and starting up a new order of production, in which enterprises are not grounded on their owners' desire for lucre, but on the collective interests of the social community – interests which, in the case of each branch of industry, lose their indistinct, generic character and take on a concrete form in the appropriate trade union.

In the Hungarian Soviet, the trade unions did not attempt any kind of creative action. Where politics is concerned, the trade-union officials raised continual problems for the dictatorship, setting themselves up as a State within the State. Where economics is concerned, they remained inert. More than once, factories had to be socialized against the wishes of the trade union, even though socialization was their duty *par excellence*. But the leaders of the Hungarian organizations were mediocrities; their mentality was a bureaucratic–reformist one and they lived in constant fear of losing the power they had had over the workers up to that point. Simply because the function for which the unions had developed prior to the dictatorship was one that presupposed the predominance of the bourgeois class, simply because their officials did not have any technical and industrial skills, the unions claimed that the proletariat was too immature to take over direct responsibility for production and championed the idea of 'true' democracy – in other words, keeping the bourgeoisie on in its principal positions as a ruling class. They wanted to prolong and promote the age of agreements, labour contracts, social legislation, simply in order to ensure a market for their own skills. They advocated waiting for the international revolution, unable to grasp the fact that in Hungary the international revolution was taking the form of the Hungarian revolution, in Russia, of the Russian revolution, and, throughout Europe, of general strikes, military revolts and working-class living conditions made impossible by the aftermath of the war.

In the final session of the Budapest Soviet, one of the most influential leaders of the Hungarian trade unions put the position of the defeatists of the revolution in the following way: 'When the Hungarian proletariat assumed power and proclaimed the Soviet Republic, its hopes rested on three events: (1) the imminent outbreak of a world revolution; (2) the help of the Red Army of Russia; and (3) the Hungarian proletariat's spirit of sacrifice. But the world revolution was slow in breaking out, the Red troops failed to reach Hungary and the Hungarian proletariat's spirit of sacrifice turned out to be no greater than the spirit of sacrifice of the proletariat of Western Europe. At the present historical juncture, the Soviet government is withdrawing to allow the nation a chance to enter into negotiations with the Entente. It is withdrawing to avoid drawing the Hungarian proletariat into bloodshed, to save and preserve the Hungarian people in the interests of the world revolution, because *some day, whatever happens now,* the great hour of the world Socialist revolution must still arrive.'

In the last issue of the communist paper *Vörös Ujsàg* (2 August), the situation created for the Hungarian proletariat by its traditional organs was described as follows:

'Does the Hungarian proletariat know what is in store for it if it does not immediately eliminate the assassins it is harbouring? Does the Budapest proletariat know what destiny awaits it, if it cannot find the strength to throw off this band of plunderers which has found its way into the proletarian State? The White terror and the Romanian terror will join forces to rule over the Hungarian proletariat; the agonies of hunger will be appeased only by the whip, and our industrial production will be encouraged by pillaging our machines and destroying our factories.

The "aristocracy" of the working class, *all those* who, in the course of the proletarian dictatorship, addressed the proletariat *even once,* will have to answer for their actions to Romanian bayonets and machine-guns. "True" democracy will be established in Hungary, because all those with something to say will be equally at rest in the tomb and the others will all enjoy the same rights to the lash of the Boyars' whip. The disputes between Party and unions will cease, because for a long time to come there will be neither a Communist Party nor trade unions in Hungary. The debate over whether the dictatorship should use force or persuasion will cease, because the bourgeoisie and the Boyars will already have made their minds up about the methods *their* dictatorship will adopt: hundreds of gallows will announce the fact that the dispute has been decided in favour of the bourgeoisie, through the weakness of the proletariat.'

L'Ordine Nuovo, 25 October 1919

Syndicalism and the Councils

Are we syndicalists? Is the movement of workshop delegates that has started up in Turin nothing more than the latest in the endless series of local variants on the syndicalist theory? Is it fair to see it as a minor turbulence heralding the coming devastations of the cyclone that is our very own, Italian brand of syndicalism – that blend of demagogy, blatant pseudo-revolutionary word-mongering, irresponsible indiscipline and maniacal agitation on the part of a few individuals of limited intelligence (small brains, big mouths), who have, in the past, sometimes managed to get their greedy hands on the will of the masses, that will take its place in the annals of the Italian workers' movement, with the label 'Italian Syndicalism'?

Where the concrete experience of proletarian revolution is concerned, syndicalist theory has failed completely. The trade unions have shown themselves inherently incapable of bringing about the dictatorship of the proletariat. The normal pattern of development of a trade union is marked by a constant decline in the revolutionary spirit of the masses. As the union enhances their material strength, so their appetite for conquest diminishes or disappears, their vital energies are sapped and heroic intransigence gives way to the practice of opportunism, of 'bread-and-butter' demands. The quantitative advance brings about a qualitative impoverishment, and an easy compromise with the social forms determined by capitalism. It introduces a new mentality among the workers: the stingy, narrow mentality of the lower and middle ranks of the bourgeoisie. And yet the most basic task of the union is to recruit the working masses 'in their entirety', to absorb all industrial and agricultural workers into its ranks. So the means are not appropriate to the end; and, since the means are, in any case, nothing other than one moment of the end that is in the making, it must be concluded that trade unionism is not a means to the revolution, is not a moment of the proletarian revolution, is not the revolution in the making. Trade unionism is only revolutionary insofar as the grammatical possibility exists of yoking the two words together.

Trade unionism has revealed itself as nothing but a form of capitalist society, not a potential successor to capitalist society. Trade unionism organizes workers not as producers, but as wage-earners: that is, as creatures of the capitalist regime of private ownership, as vendors of the commodity that is labour. Trade unionism divides up workers according to the tools they use in their work or the materials they work with – in other words, according to the form that capitalism, the regime of economic individualism, stamps on them. Using one tool rather than another, working on one kind of material rather than another, generates different capacities and different attitudes to work and earnings. The worker then becomes fixed in this particular capacity and attitude, and sees his work not as a moment in the process of production, but simply as a means to earn his living.

By bracketing this worker together with those of his companions within the trade or industry who use the same tools or work with the same materials, the trade union or industrial union reinforces this mentality, making it all the more difficult for the worker to conceive of himself as a producer, and leading him, instead, to see himself as a 'commodity' within a national and international market, which sets a price, a value, on him, through the play of competitive forces.

The worker can come to conceive of himself as a producer only if he conceives of himself as an inseparable part of the whole system of labour that finds its final expression in the finished product, only if he *lives* the unity of the industrial process: a process involving collaboration between manual workers, skilled workers, administrators, engineers, technical managers. For a worker to conceive of himself as a producer, he must first become aware of his place within the production process of a particular factory (for example, in Turin, a car plant) and think of himself as a necessary and essential moment in this process. But then he must go on from this phase, and look at the whole activity of the motor industry in Turin, and to start conceiving of Turin as a production unit characterized by the car. He must become aware that a great part of the general working activity of Turin exists and has developed solely because the motor industry exists and has developed there. He must start regarding the workers in these various industrial activities as part of the motor industry as well, in that they create the necessary and sufficient conditions for the existence of this industry. Starting out from the nucleus of the factory, seen as a unity, an act that creates a given product, the worker can move on to understand ever greater units, up to an entire nation, which, taken as a whole, is a gigantic apparatus of production, characterized by its exports, by the amount of wealth that it exchanges with an equivalent amount of wealth coming in from everywhere in the world, from all the other giant production apparatuses into which the world is divided. It is at this point that the worker becomes a producer, because he has acquired a consciousness of his function within the process of production, in all its various stages, from the single factory to the nation and the world. It is at this point that he begins to feel what it is to be a member of a class. He becomes a communist, because private ownership is not a function of productivity; he becomes a revolutionary because he sees capitalists, private owners of companies, as a dead weight, an obstacle that should be eliminated. It is at this point that he develops a conception of the 'State' – of a complex organization of society, a concrete form of society – because this complex form is nothing other than the form of the gigantic mechanism of production which – for all its various connections and inter-relations and the new and higher functions that are necessitated by its huge size – is still a reflection of the life of the individual workshop. The State represents, ordered into harmonious hierarchy, the complex of all those conditions necessary for the survival and development of the worker's own industry, his factory, his own identity as a producer.

The Italian practice of pseudo-revolutionary trade unionism is rejected by the Turinese movement of workshop delegates, along with the practice of reformist trade unionism. The former is, in fact, rejected twice over, because reformist trade unionism in itself represents a rejection of pseudo-revolutionary trade unionism. Indeed, if the most the trade union can do is to satisfy the workers' 'bread and butter' demands; if the most it can do, under a bourgeois regime, is to guarantee a stable market for wages, and to eliminate some of the uncertainties that were most dangerous to the physical and moral well-being of the worker, then it is evident that reformist trade union practice has gone further towards achieving these results than pseudo-revolutionary practice. Anyone who demands more from an instrument than it is able to do, or who tries to make out that an instrument is capable of more than its nature allows, is just being ridiculous, and cannot achieve anything but demagoguery. Italian pseudo-revolutionary trade unionists are often led to discuss whether it would be a good idea to restrict membership of trade unions (like the railway-workers' union) to 'revolutionaries' – the daring minority that drags the cold, indifferent masses behind it. In proposing this, they are rejecting the most basic principle of trade unionism, the organization of the masses in their entirety. Because deep down, subconsciously, they can intuit the inanity of what is supposed to be 'their own' propaganda, and the incapacity of trade unions to give a genuinely revolutionary form to the consciousness of the worker. Because they have never put the problem of the proletarian revolution to themselves with clarity and precision. They uphold the 'producers' theory, but they have never really developed the mentality of producers. They are demagogues, not revolutionaries; they are agitators, stirring the blood ... already roused by the fireworks of speeches, rather than educators, formers of workers' consciousness.

Is it true that the delegates' movement has grown up simply with the end of replacing Buozzi or D'Aragona with Borghi? The delegates' movement is the negation of all forms of individualism and the cult of personality. It is the start of a great historical process, in the course of which the working masses will acquire an awareness of their indissoluble unity – a unity based on production, on the concrete act of work. This awareness of theirs will take on an organic form, as a leadership emerges: a leadership thrown up from the very heart of the masses, which can therefore act as a conscious expression of the precise end to be reached, of a great historical process which – despite the errors that individuals may commit, despite the crises that may be brought about by national and international circumstances – will nevertheless lead, in an irresistible progress, to the dictatorship of the proletariat, the Communist International.

Syndicalist theory has never expressed this kind of conception of the producer and of the process of historical development of the society made up of producers. It has never given any indication that the organization of the workers should be structured with this kind of direction and meaning in mind. It has theorized one particular form of organization – the trade union or the industrial union. It has built on a reality, certainly, but it was a reality which bore the stamp of the capitalist regime of free competition and private ownership of the workforce. What it has finished up building, then, is nothing but a utopia, a great castle in the air.

The notion of the system of Workers' Councils, based on the power of the working masses, organized by workplace, by unit of production, takes its origins from the concrete historical experiences of the Russian proletariat. It is the result of the theoretical work of our Russian communist comrades – not syndicalists, but revolutionary socialists.

L'Ordine Nuovo, 8 November 1919

Out of the Dilemma

The only thing that the dilemma *La Stampa* is posing to Italian revolutionaries can tell us is quite how little the *Stampa* journalist understands about Italian reality – or how little he pretends to understand. The reality of Italy today consists of a movement of subterranean, uncontrollable forces, which have not yet begun to figure – and, at this point, never will – within the traditional political parties' picture of the situation. To reduce the problem of Italian life to the powerplay of party politics, to believe, or pretend to believe, that the Italian people can escape from the terrible vice-like grip of history with some act of parliamentary politics, is already, at the present moment, mere charlatanism and tomorrow it could become a tragic farce – the Italian people's last, definitive collapse into economic catastrophe, with a foreign heel grinding into the neck of Italian workers and peasants, who will be dropping dead at the machine or the furrow, after 12–14 hours of hard labour, all for a crust of bread thrown at them by a Senegalese or Papuan master.

The Italian State no longer functions as a political entity, because the apparatus of industrial and agricultural prodution which is the substance of the political State no longer functions. Forced to unite with economic apparatuses in a different league from it during the war, because of the necessities of war, the Italian economic apparatus has been shattered – it has lost its centre of gravity, its driving force.

The Italian economic apparatus has become a purely fiscal phenomenon, which is to say that it has reached that phase of decomposition
and collapse which could have been predicted as the dialectical phase
that was to follow – logically and chronologically – the phase of
maximum industrial development. The pedantic Marxist kicks out
against this fearsome reality; it strikes him as . . . anti-historical; he
feels that before reaching the proletarian revolution it is necessary
for the course of historical development to solder the earlier links in
the chain of progress. This was the intellectual position of the Russian Mensheviks, Zeretelli, Dan, Ciedidze, and this is the position of
the *Stampa* journalist. But real history has no use for intellectual
schemes or hypotheses about how events are going to unfold, other
than as hypotheses, indications which may serve to steer our practical
action in what may prove the right direction. And revolutionaries
adhere to real history, not the play of party politics: to the dialectic
of real economic forces, not the pious hopes and trepidations of
self-important asses.[1]

No government power based on Parliament will be able to force
the capitalists (entrepreneurs, bankers, speculators, the great landowners, the great bureaucrats) to give up the cut they take on production – even if the government has the collaboration of the Socialists.
No government power based on Parliament will be able to prevent
individual capitalists from joining together in industrial leagues or
concentrating for their credit on the major banks; nor will it be able
to stop these real forces, which have the instrument of production in
their hands, from halting production to get the worker and peasant
classes by the throat with the bony hand of hunger. No Parliamentary
government power can prevent the moneybags from corrupting the
functionaries of the civil service, the military and the Church, from
corrupting journalists and 'creating' just that public opinion which
suits them, from stirring up movements against the 'reformist' State,
the State that 'does not want to go against the grain of history'. No
Parliamentary government can have the strength to get a system of
production working normally when it has become corrupt and
decayed. We can rule out persuasion and Franciscan preaching: the
only way to achieve this end would be a regime of terror, or a vast

[1] See n. 1, p. 61.

bureaucratic apparatus of control (so-called nationalization), which would hit workers and peasants particularly hard, because it would be necessary to exact still further 'cuts' on production and the order of production would fall further into decay. Class collaboration leads to decay, to permanent disorder: a horrendous, seething, inchoate mass of barbaric and savage passions. This is the condition that Russia was thrown into by the Mensheviks' and populists' policy of compromise with the capitalists. This policy could not stop the capitalists from closing factories and starving workers. It could not stop the great landowners from hiring mercenaries to expel impoverished peasants from their lands. It could not stop the Kornilovist generals from attempting *coups de main* to impose uniformed dictatorships.

For Italian society to be saved from the abyss into which it is being forced by the hammer-blows from abroad and from reactionaries at home, we need a government that bases its power on the direct control of the industrial apparatus – a control exercised by those with the keenest interest in industrial and agricultural recovery: the workers and peasants themselves. We need a government, then, that represents the workers and peasants, that represents their vital interests and their interests alone. And this government must be a functional state machinery made up of the workers and peasants – the two most numerous orders of the working class, with the collaboration of those other less numerous but no less indispensable orders: the skilled workers of industry and administration and intellectual workers. This machinery of state is in the course of construction and historical necessity will accelerate its development. A population of forty million inhabitants does not die like an individual who has been poisoned. The task of the revolutionaries is to propel the most conscious workers and peasants along the road to historical realization and to tell the truth implacably. Are peasants and workers better than capitalists? Do they have the magic secret of order, productivity, saving? No, no: what they have is the strength of numbers and a real interest in order, productivity and efficiency – a real *existential* interest, not simply an interest in profit margins, because, if production stops, what that means for the workers is dying in their hundreds in the marketplace, while for capitalists it simply means . . . a trip to the South Seas. Since the Italian people has been led into this life-or-death dilemma, any other dilemma is mere charlatanism – a shifty word-game, the captious mouthings of factionists greedy for power for its own sake, eager to get back into government to practise their shady self-interested politics, their shady and ghoulish politics of personal feuding.

Avanti!, 29 November 1919

The Historical Role of the Cities

The communist revolution will be carried out by the working class, understood in the Marxist sense of the term, as a social stratum made up of urban workers who have been unified and moulded by the factory and the capitalist industrial system. Just as the city, this organ of industry and civic life, was the instrument of capitalist economic power and the bourgeois dictatorship, so will it also be the instrument of communist economic power and the dictatorship of the proletariat. The proletarian dictatorship will preserve this magnificent apparatus of industrial and intellectual production, this driving force of civil life, from the ruin which is looming so threateningly over it. Bourgeois power, corrupted and devastated by the imperialist war and the economic consequences of that war, is now revealing the progress of its decay in the cities, which are steadily declining in comparison with the countryside. People are hungry, and, in the face of this elemental desire, which can only be satisfied by the country, all the great historical and spiritual conquests represented by the city become worthless and fall apart at the seams. The proletarian dictatorship will save the cities from ruin. It will provoke civil war in the countryside and will bind vast strata of impoverished peasants to the cities. In this way, it will prevent those miraculous engines of life and civil progress which are the cities of today from being destroyed piecemeal by the landholders and usurers of the countryside who, in their uncouth way, hate and despise modern industrial civilization.

The same situation that we saw in Italy in the national Risorgimento is now being reproduced in the development of the communist revolution. The effective historical forces, then as now, are, in particular, the cities of Turin and Milan, and a similar relationship pertains between these two cities. The national Risorgimento had its fulcrum in Milan. Milan and Lombardy were teeming with bourgeois forces eager for expansion: it was an existential necessity for their class to see Italy organized into a unified system, with a unified system of tariffs, weights and measures, currency, transport, maritime outlets, taxes and laws. But the Milanese bourgeoisie would never have been capable of creating a bourgeois state; it would never have been capable of freeing itself from the Austrian yoke. Barricades alone were not enough to achieve this, nor personal heroism, nor the Five Days; Milan alone was not enough – a liberal city, squeezed on all sides by the Austrian-sympathizing countryside. The decisive historical force, the historical force capable of creating an Italian State and firmly unifying the bourgeois class of all Italy, was Turin.

The bourgeois population of Piedmont was not as rich or as daring as its Lombardy counterpart, but it was disciplined, it was solidly unified in a State, it had a stern military and administrative tradition and it had managed, through the intelligence of its politicians, to become part of the European balance of power. The Piedmontese State was a reliable apparatus of conquest, capable of carving out an Italian neo-formation; and it was able to provide the new State with a powerful military and administrative nucleus, and to give an organic form – its own – to the Italian people. Turin was the nerve-centre of this powerful Piedmontese system. Turin was the force that unified the population of Piedmont and it was the crucible of the Italian capitalist revolution.

Today Turin is not the capitalist city *par excellence*, but it is the industrial city, the proletarian city *par excellence*. The working class of Turin is compact, well-disciplined and *distinct* as in few other cities in the world. Turin is like one great factory: its working population conforms to a single pattern and is powerfully unified by industrial production.

The Turin proletariat has been able to advance so far along the path of Soviet-style mass organization precisely because of this powerfully unified character of the city's industry; precisely because, through its experiences in the class struggle, it had already acquired a keen awareness of its homogeneity and unity. And the same awareness could rapidly be acquired by the entire working population of Piedmont, because Piedmont as well, with its tradition of patient, steady, industrious labour and its heritage of material and cultural wealth, built up over many centuries of political independence and self-government, continues to represent a highly individual and distinctive economic unit – an economic unit of an autonomous kind, which produces almost all the goods it consumes and exports enough to be indispensable not only to Italy, but to Europe itself.

The only possible source for the model of State organization that will encompass the entire nation and embody the dictatorship of the proletariat is this compact, disciplined Piedmontese system of industrial and agricultural production, which has been magnificently equipped by capitalism to exercise political dominance over the whole nation (the Giolitti phenomenon is at root nothing other than a consequence of the blind faith Italian capitalism has in the Piedmontese bourgeoisie's traditions of government and leadership). The state of economic ruin that Italy finds itself in and the poverty of its natural resources will mean that an immense productive effort will be required from the proletariat once it comes to power. For this reason, for it to be conceivable that a workers' dictatorship in Italy can govern and develop until the establishment of communism, the class of workers and peasants must set up a strong network of workers' and peasants' Councils to take over the national apparatus of production and exchange, to acquire a keen sense of their economic responsibility and to give the workers a powerful and alert self-consciousness as producers.

The regional economic system of Piedmont – a great producer of foodstuffs (grain, rice, chestnuts, wine), rich in natural electric power and a multiplicity of industries (food, textiles and clothing, engineering, building, timber, rubber, leather, chemical industries, etc.) – this regional system which produces more than it consumes and which is centralized in the great industrial apparatus of Turin can supply the working class with a model for its national proletarian economic State.

Because of their peculiar structure and the well-defined and coherent character of the proletariat produced by the capitalist means of production, Turin and Milan are being called to play the same role in the communist revolution and the creation of the workers' State as they played in the capitalist revolution and the creation of the bourgeois State.

But, in the communist revolution, as well, the fulcrum of the movement will be Milan. The bourgeoisie's most important and powerful financial forces are located in Milan and it is there that the proletariat will have to fight its most difficult battles. The nerve-centre of the immense capitalist profit factory which is the bourgeois State is located in Milan. From Milan, thousands and thousands of threads branch out throughout the entire national territory, subjugating the workers' and peasants' labour to the capitalists' safes. The only way for the proletariat to destroy the capitalist dictatorship is for it to take over the powerful financial and commercial concerns that have their headquarters in Milan and turn them into instruments of the economic and political power of the proletariat. Communist revolution in Milan means communist revolution in Italy, because Milan is, effectively, the capital of the bourgeois dictatorship.

In the service of counter-revolution, the Reggio Emilia weekly, *La Giustizia*, has reproduced and commented on a passage from J. Wanin's article published in the *Ordine Nuovo* of 6–13 December – the passage where it says, 'with rare exceptions (interesting exceptions, from this point of view), the capitalist countries today possess a State apparatus which is so concentrated that a political revolution can only be conceived of as a decapitation of this apparatus. The revolution must take place in the capital cities if it is to have a chance of success.' *La Giustizia* raises the question of Rome as an exception, not in order to point the workers towards a solution of the problem, but in order to discourage them, to try and convince them that revolution is impossible in Italy because the capital 'is not an industrial city and is not surrounded by proletarian communities'. But the truth is that the Italian State must be decapitated in Milan, rather than Rome, because the real capitalist governing apparatus is situated not in Rome but in Milan. Rome is the bureaucratic capital; in Rome, the proletarian dictatorship will have to struggle not against the economic power of the bourgeoisie, but simply against the sabotage of bureaucrats. [A rationing of foodstuffs and the presence of a solid corps of armed workers in Rome will guarantee the Italian Soviet government normal administration and the security which is indispensable to carry out the essential task of transferring the bureaucratic capital to the economic capital.][1] Rome as a city has no role whatsoever in Italian social intercourse. It stands for nothing and it will be subjected to the strict laws against parasites which the workers' State will enact.

L'Ordine Nuovo, 17 January 1920

[1] [Translator's note] The passage in square brackets was censored in some copies of *L'Ordine Nuovo*.

The Italian State

In an article published recently in the *Resto del Carlino*, Enrico Ferri, who is Professor of criminal law at the University and has been a Member of Parliament for several terms, 'opines that *it is incomprehensible why* the Ministry of the Interior should be in charge of the overall management of the prison system, rather than the Ministry of Justice'. From what it seems, Professor Enrico Ferri 'opines' that this is simply a matter of chance, an anomaly, and he therefore believes that the decision could be revoked by ministerial decree. In light of the fact that Professor Enrico Ferri was for years the leader of the workers' movement in Italy, it is not surprising that the Italian workers and peasants should be finding it so difficult to attain to a conception of the State as a historical development, as the ultimate organization of the propertied class, as an instrument in the hands of the working class: an instrument for suppressing the bourgeoisie, both politically and economically, in order to prepare the ground for the advent of communism and to ensure an uncontested freedom of development for communist society. If one thinks, as well, that the Honourable Filippo Turati, another leader (opposed to Ferri, because of doctrinal differences and differences in their understanding of Marx!), after five years of war and the massacre of fifteen million men, can achieve a great parliamentary success by regaling the assembly of representatives of the Italian people with an elegant speech on prostitutes' right to vote (the Honourable Filippo Turati's

profound Marxist spirit found expression, nonetheless, in his identification and definition of the social category of 'female employees in
the love industry'), any sense of surprise disappears completely and
the anarchic tendencies of the Italian proletariat become entirely
understandable. It becomes entirely comprehensible that, for the Italian working class, Karl Marx has been just a 'saint to hang over the
pillow': a name which means nothing except a medal, a postcard, a
liqueur.

What is the Italian State? And why is it what it is? What economic
forces and what political forces are at its base? Has it undergone a
process of development? Has the system of forces that brought it into
being remained the same ever since? What are the ferments within
the State which have determined its process of development? What
precise position does Italy occupy in the capitalist world and how
have pressures from outside influenced the internal process of development? What new forces has the imperialist war revealed and stimulated? What probable direction will the present lines of force in Italian
society develop in?

The opportunistic, reformist nihilism that has dominated the
Italian Socialist Party for decades, and that now looks on mockingly,
with the scoffing scepticism of senility, at the efforts of the new
generation and the tumult of passions aroused by the Bolshevik
revolution, ought to conduct a little examination of its conscience
regarding its responsibilities and its incapacity to learn, to understand
and to perform its educational function. We of the younger generation should reject these has-beens, despise them. What connection
is there between us? What have they created? What have they given
us to pass on to our successors? What memories have they left us of
love and gratitude for having opened up and illuminated the path of
exploration and learning, for having enabled us to progress, to take
a leap forward? We have had to do everything for ourselves, drawing
on our own strength, our own patience. The current generation of
Italian socialists has no-one to thank but itself. No-one who has not
worked or produced anything has any right to mock its errors and its
efforts – no-one whose only inheritance to our generation is a mediocre collection of mediocre little newspaper articles.

The Italian State which, being parliamentary, supposedly stands
in the same relation to the Soviet Republic as civilization does to the
barbarian hordes,[1] has never even made an attempt to disguise the

---

[1] The reference is to Turati: see p. 112.

ruthless dictatorship of the propertied class. It could be said that the Albertine Statute served only one precise end: to tie the fortunes of the Crown very closely to the fortunes of private property. The only checks, indeed, that exist in the machinery of State to curb the will of the government of ministers of the king are those concerned with the private property of capital. The Constitution has not created any institution to protect, at least formally, the great freedoms of the citizen body: individual liberty, freedom of speech and freedom of the press, freedom of association and assembly. In capitalist States which call themselves liberal democracies, the ultimate institution protecting the liberties of the people is the judicial power. In the Italian State, the judiciary is not a power, it is an order – an instrument of the executive power, an instrument of the Crown and of the propertied class. It is entirely understandable, then, that the overall management of the prison system, as well as the management of individual prisons, and the police force and all the repressive apparatus of the State should reside with the Ministry of the Interior. It is entirely understandable, as well, why, in Italy, the President of the Council of Ministers should always keep the Interior Ministry to himself – that is, why he should want to keep the whole national apparatus of armed force entirely in his hands. The President of the Council of Ministers is the right-hand man of the propertied class: the great banks, the great industrialists, the great landowners, the General Staff of the armed forces all have a hand in choosing him, and he engineers himself the parliamentary majority by fraudulent and corrupt means. His power is unlimited, not only in practice – as is undoubtedly the case in all capitalist countries – but also in the law. The President of the Council of Ministers is the only real power in the Italian State.

The Italian ruling class has not even had the hypocrisy to disguise its dictatorship. It has regarded the working people as though they were an inferior race, to be governed without too much standing on ceremony, like an African colony. The country is ruled as though there were a permanent state of siege. At any moment of the day or night, an order from the Minister of the Interior to the prefects is enough to set the police administration in motion. The police are unleashed into private homes and meeting-places. *Without any mandate from the courts*, which are passive, in the normal course of administrative routine, individual freedom is violated, home life violated and citizens are handcuffed and thrown together with common criminals in filthy, sickening prisons; they are defenceless against physical brutality and their contacts and private affairs are disrupted or destroyed. Through a simple order from a police commissioner, a meeting-place can be invaded and searched and a meeting can be dissolved. Through a simple order from a prefect, a censor can strike out a piece of writing whose content is completely outside the prohibitions envisaged by general decrees. Through a simple order from a prefect, the leaders of a union may be arrested: that is, there is an attempt to break up an association.

Tsarist Russia used to be cited as an example of a despotic state, but, in effect, there was not the slightest difference between the Tsarist State and the Italian State, between the Duma and the Italian Parliament. There *was* a difference in political culture and human sensibility between the Russian people and the Italian people. The Russians, whether liberals or socialists, denounced abuses of power to the world. The Italians, less well-endowed with human sensibility, only complained about the most *monstrous* incidents; less politically educated, they did not manage to detect in the various individual episodes a continuity traceable to the constitution of the State. Since justice does not exist in Italy as an independent power, since the repressive apparatus in Italy is not in the hands of justice, *parliamentary power does not exist, and legislation is simply a fraud*. In reality and in law, there exists only one power in Italy – the executive power. The Crown exists and the propertied class, which wants to be defended at all costs.

The Tsarist State was a State of landowners. That explains the boorishness of the ministers of the Tsar: country people call a spade a spade and beat down their enemies with clubs. The revolution of March 1917 was an attempt to introduce a balance between industrialists and landowners into the State. The liberal State is born out of the balance between these two forces of private property. The division of powers – that is the emergence alongside Parliament of a judiciary power that guarantees the political equality of the bourgeois parties of government and prevents the individual parties in power from using the machinery of the State to perpetuate their hold on power – is the characteristic of the liberal State. The Russian working people, once it had been stirred into motion in March 1917, prevented the revolution from crystallizing in its bourgeois, liberal phase. The industrial workers continued the work begun by the masters of industry, eliminated all masters and emancipated the proletariat.

The driving force behind the foundation of the Italian unitary State came from the bourgeois industrial nuclei of Northern Italy. The State consolidated itself as industry developed, at the expense of agriculture, brutally subjugating agriculture to the interests of industry. The Italian State was not liberal, because it was not born out of a system of balance. But the ministers of the King of Italy, well-schooled in English liberal terminology, preferred the sandbag of the London *apache* to the club of the Russian peasant as a means of dealing with the enemies of industry.

Even before the war, the internal relations of the Italian propertied class had changed. Salandra, who declared war, was the first President of the Council of Ministers in the history of the Italian State to come from the South; Nitti was the second. The executive power is being prised away from the old system of capitalist forces: the economic substance of the Italian State has become fluid; it is beginning to shift. Rural Italy is taking over the State; it has a major party, the Partito Popolare. One would expect these shifting forces of capitalism to result in a liberal State, a bourgeois republic – were it not for the fact that there exists a revolutionary working class, which is also on the move, determined to carry through its historical mission, to eliminate the propertied class and set up a workers' democracy.

Faced with a choice between the Soviet Republic and the bourgeois republic, between workers' democracy and liberal democracy, reformists and opportunists choose the bourgeois republic and liberal democracy. The new generation of Italian socialist intellectuals, which has no links with these has-beens, these petit bourgeois intellectuals, which is free from prejudice and the pull of tradition, which acquired its maturity amid the passions of the war and its revolutionary character in the study of the Bolshevik revolution, is called upon to create that form of production that is specific to its historical action – ideas, myths, bold thinking and revolutionary action – for the foundation of the Italian Soviet Republic.

L'Ordine Nuovo, 7 February 1920

The Drunken Soldier

In the writers of *La Stampa* there relives the immortal figure of the *lanzo*, the mercenary soldier in sixteenth-century comedy: 'Us *lanzi* have got it made: we do just what we want, then say we was drunk when we done it!' We writers for *La Stampa* have got it made: we claimed that Libya was the promised land for the famished hordes of the Southern peasantry, we claimed that Giuseppe Bevione, candidate for Turin's fourth electoral district was going to be the founder of a new and regenerative political tradition; we claimed that President Wilson, that great athlete of humanity, was going to reorganize the world so justice reigned and put all the freemasonries, imperialisms and racketeerisms of the two continents in their place. We have made fools out of our gullible readers, but so what? No problem, we can't be held to anything: *La Stampa* is 'a political newspaper, so its lifeblood is current affairs'.

And what is 'politics and current affairs' for the 'drunken soldiers' of *La Stampa*? It is the superficial jostling for power of the parliamentary parties, the collusion of individual capitalists with individual members of the workers' movement, the resolution of such urgent and fundamental historical problems as: 'Is Salandra or Nitti in power, rather than that hammer of all evils, Cavaliere Giovanni Giolitti?' Should the government send Amendola and Borghese of the *Corriere* to London to do its officious diplomatic scheming, or should it send Marcello Prati, Benedetto Cirmeni and Cesare Sobrero? Should the combinations of the national and international bank-safes be entrusted to Silvio Crespi or to Commendatore Volpi? Should the prefects, subprefects, judges, magistrates, procurators and police superintendents be chosen from among Giolitti's clientage, from among the trusted henchmen of the Cavaliere or the trusted henchmen of Salandra or Nitti?

It is only natural that the 'drunken soldiers' of *La Stampa* should refuse to descend to the 'philosophical' battlefield of *Avanti!* For *Avanti!*, politics means the class struggle, the movements of the great masses of the working population, as they are determined by the process of development of the capitalistically organized national and international economic apparatus. 'Current affairs' means following (and promoting) the process of disintegration of society and the State as they had been shaped by fifty years of bourgeois rule. 'Current affairs' means observing and pointing out the way in which this process is bearing out the theses of Marxist doctrine, which informs the programme of action of the Socialist Party of which *Avanti!* is the organ. 'Current affairs' means observing, pointing out and explaining how, in Italy as elsewhere, the Bank has unified two industrial categories which had previously been in conflict (the steelworkers and the mechanics); how the State has promoted the cartel of the major banks and has fallen into the hands of this colossal capitalist coalition; how industrial and financial capitalism, despite its electoral bloc, is no longer capable of keeping a firm grasp on State power since rural Italy, with its ill-defined peasant class, has produced a great parliamentary party which is aiming to take control of the State and organize it along Christian-social, aristocratic, demagogic lines. For *Avanti!*, politics and current affairs mean pointing out (and drawing pedagogic conclusions from these experiences and stimuli to action) how the working class is becoming ever more aware of its historical mission, foretold by Marx; how the working class, through a continual inner activity which is creating new institutions, a new psychology, a new way of life, is organizing itself into a ruling class: a class capable of founding a new type of State, the Soviet republic, to put communism into practice – the normal development of a centralized 'planned' economy, which the bourgeois State has organized for the War and is maintaining in place . . . for a Pyrrhic victory.

Avanti! is the paper of the Socialist Party, of the party of the working class – a mighty social organism, which moves forward by putting into action a discipline established in its congresses; an organism which is bound by millions and millions of links to the Italian working population, as it is organized in its unions, co-operatives and factories; as it is organized, in its most active avant-garde element, in the Party clubs and the local sections. The writers of *Avanti!* are loyal and dedicated footsoldiers of the Party. They are organized, responsible, bound to a discipline which has been formed in the course of thousands and thousands of debates and thousands and thousands of experiences of the national and international working class, It is understandable that the 'drunken soldiers' of *La Stampa* – lackeys of the bourgeois State, ideological agents of capitalism, employees of a journalistic firm which works like any commercial firm, to squeeze out material profit and especially political profit for the black hand of the directors of the big newspapers – it is understandable that the 'drunken soldiers' of *La Stampa* refuse to come down on to the philosophical battleground of *Avanti!* No-one who is fighting with the poisoned weapons of the irresponsible paid mercenary, against the workers and for the big money, can come down on to the field where the exploited are struggling, on to the battlefield of working-class struggle. The 'drunken soldier' is completely alienated from the feelings, the ideas, the aspirations, the 'philosophy' of the working class.

The Socialist Party, the political organization of the conscious avant-garde of the proletariat has the historical task of organizing the class of impoverished workers and peasants into a ruling class. Since *Avanti!* is actively performing this task – within the limitations of its purely journalistic action – the militants who write for *Avanti!* do not disdain to come down to the level of *La Stampa* to unmask the tricks of the agents of the bourgeoisie. The *Stampa* campaigns are themselves an episode in the class struggle. We have characterized this episode in the following manner: the Italian bourgeois State was formed under the impetus of capitalistic nuclei in Northern Italy which wanted to unite the system of relations of production and exchange of the national market, which was divided into a multiplicity of tiny regional and provincial states. Until the Left came to power, the Italian State extended suffrage only to the propertied class. It was a ferocious dictatorship which put Southern Italy and the islands to the sword and the fire – crucifying, quartering, burying alive the impoverished peasants whom salaried writers attempted to defame by branding them 'brigands'. The development of industry strengthened the unified State: the Left came to power, extended suffrage and introduced a pinch of 'democracy'. The industrial dictatorship was, however, no less ferocious than the dictatorship of the bourgeoisie and the landowners sated with ecclesiastical possessions. The State put itself at the service of industry and in '98 it suppressed the movements in which, for the first time, the working class rose up, simultaneously with the impoverished peasants of Sicily and Sardinia. Industrial 'democracy' revealed its true nature: in the special laws against the working class and in the power given to officials to suspend constitutional guarantees in Sicily and Sardinia (Giulio Bechi's book, *Caccia grosse* [*Big-game Hunting*], is the 'ingenuous' narration of a minor state official in Sardinia who declares the state of emergency and takes as hostages old people, women, babes in arms – and who is punished by the military authorities because he has offended the sensibilities of Sardinian intellectuals by writing perverse things about the colour of the sky, the landscape and the chastity of the women). The ultimate achievement of industrial development is Giolittism, which for *La Stampa* is the absolute high point of 'true' democracy. The democratic nature of the Italian State may be judged in the light of the following historical observation: liberal regimes are characterized by a balance between two great political parties, one conservative (representing landowners) and one democratic (representing industrial capital). The balance is guaranteed by the judiciary, which is independent of Parliament and the government and which has the task of opposing any undermining of bourgeois categories and which therefore historically embodies the democracy of the propertied class, which stands above the individual classes and categories of property itself. In Italy, since the Left came to power, such a balance has never existed and the judiciary, constitutionally, does not exist. The Italian State has never been democratic: it is despotic, a police State (there is only one power: the government, with one consultative body: Parliament). It has always been a dictatorship exercised by industrialists against both the industrial working class and the peasant classes. The war has politically weakened industrial capital: it has strengthened the working class in its historical role of revolutionary opposition to capital and it has created the conditions necessary for the birth of a great party of the peasant classes, the Partito Popolare – a party constitutionally opposed to the industrialists. In this way, the bourgeois State has entered a formidable political crisis which could tear it apart. In the normal course of events, it should become a liberal State, with a balance between industrialists and landowners; but for that to happen the control of the armed forces would have to pass from the hands of the government (the executive power) into the hands of a power independent of the government and the Parliament, into the hands of a judiciary order which had become a real power, by means of a constitutive assembly. The capitalist class wants to avoid this crisis; it wants to prevent 'its' government losing control of the armed forces even for a moment: the working class would rise up violently to widen the breach in the defences and seize State power by revolutionary means. And, at this point, up pops the living 'democracy' again – Cavaliere Giolitti, with his pack of petit bourgeois bloodhounds, the 'drunken soldiers' of *La Stampa* saying that the working class, if it had its head screwed on and did not allow itself to be taken in by hare-brained 'philosophers', should collaborate with the 'true' democracy to consolidate the bourgeois State, that is to consolidate the position of capital. It should set up an 'industrial' coalition on the English model, in opposition to the coalition of the peasant classes forged by the Partito Popolare. The Socialist Party should slip back from a revolutionary position to the position of the Labour Party before the War.

The working class has learned to be suspicious of its petit bourgeois 'friends', the intellectual agents of capital. Even if the Italian State were not a police state, even if it were a liberal democratic republic, the working class would have and has only one duty towards it: to overthrow it.

Avanti!, 18 February 1920

The Factory Worker

For a society to live and develop, it must adhere to some historically determined form of production. Where there is no production, no form of organized work (even at a very basic level), there can be no society and no historical life. Modern society has lived and developed to its current point because it adhered to a system of production: the system of production historically determined by the existence of two classes – the capitalist class, which owns the means of production, and the working class, which serves the other class and is yoked to it by the shackles of the pay-packet and the looming threat of starvation.

At the present stage of development, the capitalist class is represented by a class . . . in the forefront of progress, the plutocracy. The historical trajectory the capitalist class has followed is a process of corruption and deterioration. The capitalist class's traditional role in production has passed into the hands of an irresponsible middle class, without any kind of financial or emotional investment in production. They are bureaucrats of the 'State functionary' type: venal, grasping and corrupt – stockbrokers, small-time politicians down on their luck, human scum who live for the day, sating their basest desires and setting themselves ideals well suited to their swinish mentality: getting as many women as possible, having a lot of money to blow on high-class prostitutes, *bals tabarin* and gross, showy luxury; having their little slice of power, so they can torture those beneath them and make them suffer.

The working class, on the other hand, has been developing towards a completely new and unprecedented model of humanity: the factory worker, the proletarian who has shed all psychological traces of his agricultural or craft origins, the proletarian who lives the life of the factory, the life of production – an intense, methodical life. His life may be disorderly and chaotic where his social relations outside the factory are concerned, and his political relations within the system of the distribution of wealth. But, within the factory, it is ordered, precise and disciplined.

The capital-owning class has become divorced from labour and production. It has fallen apart, lost any sense of its original unity, which was a dialectical unity – unity in the individualistic struggle to compete for profit. The unity of the capitalist class has come to be identified with a State institution, the government. The individual has entrusted his role of struggle and competition into the hands of a band of adventurers and mercenary small-time politicians and has fallen back into a state of primitive, barbaric bestiality – a breeding-ground for base, greedy instincts.

The working class has come to be identified with the factory, with production: the proletarian cannot live without working and without working in an orderly, methodical way. The division of labour has unified the proletarian class psychologically: it has fostered within the proletarian world that body of feelings, instincts, thoughts, customs, habits and attachments that can be summed up in the phrase 'class solidarity'. Within the factory, every proletarian is led to conceive of himself as inseparable from his work-mates; how could the raw material piled up in the warehouses come to circulate in the world as an object of use to man in society, if a single link were missing from the system of labour in industrial production? The more the proletarian specializes in a particular professional task, the more conscious he becomes of how indispensable his companions are; the more he feels himself as one cell within a coherent body, possessed of an inner unity and cohesion; the more he feels the needs for order, method, precision; the more he feels the need for the whole world to become like a vast factory, organized with the same precision and method and order which he recognizes as vital in the factory where he works; the more he feels the need for the order, precision and method which are the life-blood of the factory to be projected out into the system of relations that links one factory to another, one city to another, one nation to another.

With this new mentality of his and this unique outlook on the world, the factory worker, the urban industrial proletarian, is the prototype of communism. He is the revolutionary force that embodies the mission of renewing human society. He is a founder of new States. It is in this sense (despite the cretinous misrepresentations of the journalists of *La Stampa*) that we asserted that Turin was the crucible of the communist revolution: because the working class of Turin is made up in the majority of proletarians, factory workers, revolutionaries of the type envisaged by Karl Marx – not petit bourgeois revolutionaries, throwbacks to the Risorgimento, revolutionaries of the type so dear to the hearts of democrats and anarchist muddlers. It is in this sense, as well, that we maintained that the working masses that go to make up the General Confederation of Labour are more 'revolutionary' than those organized by the Italian Syndicalist Union (USI), because the Confederation takes in the workers from the most specialized and best organized industries, the most 'revolutionary', avant-garde industries, while the USI is an organism that seems incapable of getting beyond an indistinct, gelatinous stage – the stage defined by a conception of the world that is characteristic of members of the petit bourgeois class who have never made it to become capitalists and of craftsmen and peasants who have not yet become proletarians.

For a society to live and develop, it must produce, and produce more than it consumes, whether or not it then goes on to organize the distribution of its products for consumption and accumulation in an iniquitous way. Society can live and thrive in the midst of iniquity, but it dies if it does not produce – even if justice reigns. Bourgeois society is dying because it is not producing; because, what with the new relations of distribution created by the war and the resulting plutocratic phase of capitalism, the labour of the producers is not enough to keep up with consumer demand, far from allowing any accumulation. Material wealth is being gradually annihilated, while, at the same time, the accumulation of share certificates for the appropriation of material wealth – paper money – is increasing. The capitalist system of distribution has become a kind of armed looting, which is being carried out by those in government. Capitalism has become divorced from the sphere of production and the management of industry has fallen into inept and irresponsible hands; it is only the working class now which retains a real love for labour and the machine. The working class now dominates production. It is the master of society, because, just by standing back and folding its arms, it is capable of severing the last nerves that still keep society twitching; also because only a truly heroic productivity drive would be capable of infusing society with new vigour and new development potential. The comfortably waged apostles, the outriders of capitalism, the greedy beggars at the door of the bourgeois soup-kitchen believe that their overblown patriotic or humanitarian outpourings – fit only for the pages of a cheap novel – will be enough to incite this productive heroism on the part of the proletariat, just as they managed to incite the proletariat to heroism in the war. But tricks like that only work once: and, in this case, they cannot call on the police to give them a hand! They will have to get used to the fact – either willingly, or with a little help from the red guards – that the proletariat will only increase production for the sake of communism, to translate their conception of the world into practice and turn their 'philosophy' into history, not to provide more leisure or luxury for the owners of paper money. The proletariat will increase production when it saws off all the many dead branches from the tree of life with the weapons of its State power. This pruning will, in itself, determine an increase in production – a better distribution, that is, and the possibility of accumulation.

L'Ordine Nuovo, 21 February 1920

Towards a Renewal of the Socialist Party[1]

1 What defines the character of the class struggle in Italy at the present moment is the fact that industrial and agricultural workers throughout Italy are irrepressibly set on forcing the question of the ownership of the means of production on to the agenda in an explicit and violent manner. The national and international crises which keep raging and which are steadily destroying the value of currency are a clear sign that capitalism is on its last legs. The existing order of production and distribution can no longer satisfy even the most elementary human needs and survives only because it is ferociously defended by the armed might of the bourgeois State. With its every move, the working population of Italy is surging towards a great economic revolution, which will introduce new modes of production and a new order in the productive and distributive process, giving the power of initiative in production to the class of industrial and agricultural workers and tearing it away from the hands of the capitalists and landowners.

---

[1] This memorandum was written by Gramsci for the Turin socialist group against the background of the preparations for the metal-workers' strike of April 1920. It was published in *L'Ordine Nuovo* after being presented to the national executive in Milan in May. It subsequently gained the approval of Lenin at the Congress of the Third International later that summer, thereby boosting the prestige of the *Ordine Nuovo* group within the PSI. Although clearly informed by Gramsci's ideas, one should bear in mind that as a Party document it had to take other views into account.

2   The industrialists and landowners have achieved a maximum
concentration of class discipline and power: any new directive
launched by the General Confederation of Industry is immediately
carried into effect in every factory in the land. The bourgeois State
has created a corps of armed mercenaries, ready to act as an executive
instrument of the will of this new and powerful organization of the
propertied classes, which aims to restore capitalist power over the
means of production through the widespread use of lock-outs and
terrorism, forcing the workers and peasants to submit to the expropriation of an increased quantity of unpaid labour. The recent lock-out
in the Turin engineering plants was one example of this determination on the part of the industrialists to hold a pistol to the head of the
workers. The industrialists took advantage of the lack of revolutionary
co-ordination and concentration in the Italian working-class forces
to attempt to break apart the whole structure of the Turin proletariat
and destroy the prestige and authority the factory institutions that
had begun the struggle for workers' control (Councils and shop-floor
delegates) enjoyed among the workers. The long drawn out agricultural strikes in the Novara and Lomellina regions show how the
landowners are prepared to bring production to a standstill in order
to reduce the agricultural proletariat to despair and starvation and
force it to submit to the harshest and most humiliating of working
and living conditions.

3   The present phase in the class struggle in Italy is the phase
that precedes *either* the conquest of political power on the part of the
revolutionary proletariat and the transition to new modes of production that will allow a recovery in productivity; *or* a tremendous reaction on the part of the propertied class and the governing caste. No
violence will be spared in subjecting the industrial and agricultural
proletariat to servile work. There will be a bid to smash the working
class's organs of political struggle (the Socialist Party) once and for
all and to incorporate its organs of economic resistance (trade unions
and co-operatives) into the machinery of the bourgeois State.

4   The reason why the worker and peasant forces lack revolutionary co-ordination and concentration is that the leading organs of the
Socialist Party have shown themselves to be utterly lacking in any
understanding of the phase of development that we are currently
passing through in national and international history, or of the mission incumbent on the revolutionary proletariat's organs of struggle.

The Socialist Party is watching the course of events like a spectator. It never has an opinion of its own to express that has any relation to the revolutionary theses of Marxism and the Communist International. It never launches slogans that can be adopted by the masses; that can give a clear lead; that can unify and co-ordinate revolutionary action. As the political organization of the vanguard section of the working class, the Socialist Party should develop a concerted line of action designed to enable the working class to win the Revolution and win it once and for all. Made up, as it is, of that part of the proletarian class that has not allowed itself to be demoralized and prostrated by the physical and spiritual oppression of the capitalist system, but has succeeded in preserving its autonomy and a conscious and disciplined spirit of initiative, the Socialist Party ought to embody the vigilant revolutionary consciousness of the entire exploited class. Its task is to draw the attention of all the masses to itself, to ensure that its directives become their directives and to win their permanent trust, so that it may become their guide and intellect. It is essential, then, that the Party should immerse itself in the reality of the class struggle, as it is waged by the industrial and agricultural proletariat. It needs to be in a position to understand all the various phases and episodes in this struggle and all the multifarious forms it takes, in order to resolve this diversity into unity, to give a real lead to all the various movements and to instil the conviction in the masses that there is an immanent order within the terrible chaos of the present: an order that, as it establishes itself, will regenerate human society and adapt the instruments of labour and make them capable of satisfying the basic needs of life and social progress. But even after the Congress of Bologna, the Socialist Party has remained a purely parliamentary party, stuck within the narrow confines of parliamentary democracy and only concerned with the superficial political declarations of the governing caste. It has not established an autonomous character for itself as a Party typical of the revolutionary proletariat and the revolutionary proletariat alone.

5   After the Congress of Bologna,[2] the central organs of the Party should immediately have mounted and carried through an energetic

---

[2] 5–8 October 1918. The Congress culminated in the defeat of the reformists and the adoption of Serrati's motion calling for adherence to the Third International. A small minority supported Bordiga's abstentionist position.

campaign to give homogeneity and cohesion to the Party membership: to give it the specific and distinctive physiognomy of a Communist Party belonging to the Third International. But no polemic against the reformists and opportunists was ever even started; neither the Party leadership nor [the Party newspaper] *Avanti!* advanced a genuinely revolutionary conception of their own to counterbalance the incessant propaganda the reformists and opportunists were disseminating in Parliament and the trade-union bodies. Nothing was done by the central organs of the Party to give the masses a Communist political education or induce them to oust the reformists and opportunists from the leadership of trade-union and co-operative institutions; nor was anything done to give the individual sections and the most active groups of comrades a unified direction and a unified strategy. And so we have got a situation where the revolutionary majority in the Party lack a mouthpiece for its thought or an executor for its actions in the Party leadership and newspaper, while the opportunist elements, in contrast, have organized themselves powerfully and exploited the prestige and authority of the Party to consolidate their positions in Parliament and the trade unions. The Party leadership has allowed them to marshal their forces and to vote in resolutions that go against the principles and tactics of the Third International and are hostile to the Party line. The leadership has given a completely free hand to lower-level bodies to pursue lines of action and propagate ideas contrary to the principles and tactics of the Third International. The Party leadership has systematically distanced itself from the life and activity of the Party sections and organizations and the individual comrades. The confusion that existed in the Party prior to the Congress of Bologna and which might have been explained as a result of wartime conditions, has not disappeared; on the contrary, it has increased to an alarming extent. It is only natural in such conditions that the masses should have lost their faith in the Party and that, in many places, anarchic tendencies should have tried to get the upper hand. The political Party of the working class justifies its existence only to the extent that, by powerfully centralizing and co-ordinating proletarian action, it counterposes a *de facto* revolutionary power to the legal power of the bourgeois State and so limits its freedom of initiative and manoeuvre. If the Party fails to unify and co-ordinate its efforts; if it reveals itself to be simply a bureaucratic institution, with no soul and no will, then the working class will

instinctively move to form another party for itself and will start shifting its allegiances towards the anarchist tendencies, precisely because
they conduct a constant and fierce attack on the centralization and
bureaucracy of the political parties.

6   The Party has played no part in the international movement.
The class struggle is assuming ever vaster forms all over the world.
Everywhere, workers are being driven to renew their methods of
struggle and frequently, as in Germany after the militarist coup, to
rise up in arms. The Party has not troubled itself to explain these
events to the Italian working people or to justify them in the light of
the ideas of the Communist International. It has not troubled itself
to mount a comprehensive educational programme designed to make
the Italian working people aware of the truth that the proletarian
revolution is a world phenomenon and that each individual event
must be considered and judged within a world context. The Third
International has already met twice in Western Europe, in December
1919 in a city in Germany and in February 1920 in Amsterdam. The
Italian Party was not represented at either of these two meetings and
the central organs of the Party did not so much as inform Party
activists about what was discussed and decided at the two confer-
ences. Polemics are raging within the Third International over the
doctrine and tactics of the Communist International. They have even
led (as in Germany) to internal splits in the Party. The Italian Party
has been completely cut off from this vigorous dialogue of ideas,
which is tempering revolutionary consciousnesses and forging a unity,
in spirit and action, among the proletariats of all nations. The central
organ of the Party has no correspondent of its own in France, or
England, or Germany or even in Switzerland – a strange state of
affairs for the paper of the Socialist Party which represents the interests of the international proletariat in Italy; and a strange state of
affairs, too, for the Italian working class, which has to get its information from the defective and tendentious reporting of the bourgeois
papers and news agencies. As the Party organ, *Avanti!* should be the
organ of the Third International. *Avanti!* should publish all the
reports, debates and analyses of proletarian problems that concern
the Third International. *Avanti!* should wage an incessant polemic,
conducted in a spirit of unity, against all opportunistic deviations and
compromises. But instead, *Avanti!* is a showcase for opportunistic
thinking, like the recent speech in parliament by the Honourable

Claudio Treves, which was woven around a petit-bourgeois notion of international relations and developed a theory that was counter-revolutionary and defeatist of proletariat energies. This lack of any concern on the part of the central organs to keep the proletariat informed of the events and the theoretical discussions taking place within the Third International can also be observed in the activity of the Party's publishing house. This carries on publishing trivial pamphlets or writings that propagate the ideas and opinions of the Second International, ignoring the publications of the Third International. Writings by Russian comrades which are crucial to an understanding of the Bolshevik revolution have been translated in Switzerland, England and Germany, but are unknown in Italy (to cite just one example, Lenin's *State and Revolution*). What is more, those pamphlets that *are* translated are translated extremely badly – they are often incomprehensible, because of their grammatical distortions and distortions in meaning.

7   From the above analysis, it should already be clear what kind of effort at renewal and organization we believe must be carried out as a matter of necessity within the Party structure. The Party must take on a precise and distinct character of its own. It must turn itself from a petit-bourgeois parliamentary party into the Party of the revolutionary proletariat as it struggles to achieve a Communist society by means of the workers' State. It must become a homogeneous, cohesive Party, with a doctrine of its own, a strategy of its own and a rigid, implacable discipline. Those who are not revolutionary Communists must be eliminated from the Party; and the leadership, freed from its concern with preserving unity and balance between the various tendencies and the various leaders,[3] must put all its energies into getting the workers' forces on to a war footing. All happenings in national and international proletarian life must be immediately analysed in manifestos and circulars from the leadership and lessons drawn from them for the purposes of Communist propaganda and the development of revolutionary consciousness. The leadership must keep in close contact with the sections and become the motor centre of proletarian action in all its manifestations. The sections must promote the formation of Communist groups in all factories, unions, co-operatives and barracks and these will ceaselessly propagate the

---

[3] [Translator's note] The English word 'leaders' is used here in the original.

Party's ideas and tactics, organize the setting up of Factory Councils to oversee industrial and agricultural production and develop the propaganda needed to win over the unions, the Camere del Lavoro and the General Confederation of Labour, in an organic fashion. In this way, these Communist groups will become the trusted elements whom the masses will delegate to form political Soviets and exercise the proletarian dictatorship. The fundamental and indispensable condition for attempting any experiment with Soviets is the existence of a cohesive and highly disciplined Communist Party that can coordinate and centralize the whole of the proletariat's revolutionary action in its central executive committee, by means of its nuclei within the factories, unions and co-operatives. In the absence of this condition, any proposal of such an experiment should be rejected as absurd and of interest only to those who are seeking to give the idea of Soviets a bad name. In the same way, we should reject the proposal for a Socialist mini-parliament, as this would rapidly become a vehicle for the reformist and opportunistic majority in the parliamentary group to promote their democratic utopias and counter-revolutionary schemes.

8   The leadership should immediately think out, draw up and distribute a programme for revolutionary government by the Socialist Party, laying out the concrete solutions that the proletariat, once it becomes the dominant class, will provide for all the essential problems – economic, political, religious, educational, etc. – that are currently besieging the various sections of the Italian working population. Rooting itself in the idea that the Party's strength and activity is founded solely on the class of industrial and agricultural workers who possess no private property and that it regards the other strata of the working population as auxiliary to the proletarian class, in the strict sense, the Party must launch a manifesto in which the revolutionary conquest of power is presented in explicit terms; in which the industrial and agricultural proletariat is invited to prepare and arm itself and in which the Communist solutions to current problems are laid out in their main lines: proletarian control over production and distribution, the disarming of mercenary armed bodies, control of local government by working-class organizations.

9   On the basis of these considerations, the Turin Socialist Section has decided to seek an understanding with all those groups of comrades from other sections who are interested in meeting together

to discuss these proposals and approve them. We envisage an organized accord that will pave the way, in the near future, to a congress devoted to problems of proletarian strategy and organization and that, in the meantime, will monitor the activities of the Party's executive organs.

L'Ordine Nuovo, 8 May 1920

The Factory Council

The proletarian revolution is not the arbitrary act of an organization that declares itself to be revolutionary, or of a system of organizations that declare themselves to be revolutionary. The proletarian revolution is an extremely long-term historical process that manifests itself in the emergence and development of certain productive forces (which we may sum up by the term 'proletariat') within a certain historical context (which we may sum up by the terms 'regime of private property, capitalist mode of production, factory system, organization of society in a democratic-parliamentary State'). At a certain point in this process, the new productive forces are no longer able to develop or organize themselves in an autonomous fashion within the official framework of the human community of the time. It is in this phase that the revolutionary act occurs. This consists in a violent effort to smash apart this existing framework and to destroy the entire apparatus of economic and political power within which the revolutionary productive forces had been trapped. It consists in a violent effort to shatter the machinery of the bourgeois State and to construct a new kind of State within whose framework the newly liberated productive forces can develop and expand; whose organization provides them with strong defences and the necessary and sufficient arms to eliminate their enemies.

The actual process of the proletarian revolution cannot be identified with the development and activity of revolutionary organizations of a voluntary and contractual nature, such as political parties and trade unions – organizations which have grown up on the terrain of bourgeois democracy and political liberty, as affirmations and developments of this political liberty. Insofar as they embody a doctrine that interprets the revolutionary process and predicts its development (within certain limits of historical probability), insofar as they are recognized by the great masses as their expression and their embryonic apparatus of government, these organizations are at present and will increasingly be the direct and responsible agents of the successive acts of liberation that the entire working class will attempt in the course of the revolutionary process. But, all the same, they do not embody this process; they do not supersede the bourgeois State; they do not embrace – *cannot* embrace – the whole seething spectrum of revolutionary forces which capitalism has unleashed in the course of its implacable development as a machine of exploitation and oppression.

During the period in which the bourgeois class is economically and politically predominant, the real developments in the revolutionary process take place subterraneously, in the darkness of the factory and in the darkness of the minds of the countless multitudes that capitalism subjects to its laws. The process is not something that can be controlled or documented at this stage: it will be so in the future, when the elements that go to make it up (feelings, desires, habits, the stirrings of initiative and a new way of life) will have developed and become purified as a result of developments in society and in the position the working class occupies within the sphere of production. Revolutionary organizations (the political party and the trade union) grow up on the terrain of political liberty and bourgeois democracy, as affirmations and developments of liberty and democracy in general, in a sphere in which there is such a thing as a relation of citizen to citizen. The revolutionary process takes place on the terrain of production, in the factory, where the relations are those between the oppressor and the oppressed, the exploiter and the exploited, where there is no such thing as liberty for the worker and no such thing as democracy. The revolutionary process takes place where the worker is nothing and wants to become everything, where the power of the proprietor is boundless, where the proprietor has power of life and death over the worker and over his wife and children.

When can we say that the historical process of the workers' revolution, which is immanent in the capitalist social system, which has its own inherent laws and necessarily unfolds through the confluence of a multiplicity of actions, all of which are uncontrollable, since they arise from a situation that is not of the worker's choosing and whose consequences he cannot predict – when can we say that this historical process of the workers' revolution has blossomed out into the light of day, and become something that can be controlled and documented?

We can say this when the whole of the working class has become revolutionary – no longer in the sense that it refuses in a general way to collaborate with the governing institutions of the bourgeois class and to function as an opposition within the framework of democracy, but in the sense that the whole of the working class, as it is to be found in a factory, launches a movement which must necessarily result in the foundation of a workers' State and the reorganization of human society into an absolutely original form, a universal form, which embraces the whole workers' International and hence the whole of humanity. And we say that the present period is revolutionary, because we can see that the working class, all over the world, is beginning to create, beginning with all its energies (despite the errors, hesitations and setbacks only natural in an oppressed class, with no historical experience behind it, which has to do everything for itself, from scratch) to generate working-class institutions of a new type, representative in character and constructed on an industrial basis. We say that the present period is revolutionary because the working class is beginning to exert all its strength and will to found its own State. That is why we say that the birth of the Factory Councils is a major historical event – the beginning of a new era in the history of the human race. For now the revolutionary process has burst forth into the light of day and entered into the phase where it can be documented and controlled.

In the liberal phase of the historical evolution of the bourgeois class and the society dominated by the bourgeoisie, the basic unit of the State was the proprietor, subjugating the working class to his profit in the factory. In the liberal phase, the proprietor was also an entrepreneur and an industrialist. Industrial power, the source of industrial power, lay in the factory and the worker could not succeed in freeing himself from the conviction that the proprietor was necessary, since the person of the proprietor was indivisible from that of the industrialist and that of the manager responsible for production and hence also for the worker's salary, his bread, his clothing, the roof over his head.

In the imperialist phase of the historical process of the bourgeois class, industrial power is divorced from the factory and concentrated in a *trust*, a monopoly, a bank, the bureaucracy of the State. Industrial power does not have to answer for what it does and so it becomes more autocratic, ruthless and arbitrary. But the worker – freed from his subjection to the 'boss', freed from his servile, hierarchical mentality, and driven also by the new conditions in society as a whole resulting from the new historical phase – the worker makes priceless advances in terms of autonomy and initiative.

In the factory, the working class becomes a given 'instrument of production' within a given organic system. Each individual worker comes to play a part in this system 'by accident' – by accident, that is, as far as his own will is concerned, but not where his destined work is concerned, because each worker represents a given necessity within the process of labour and production. This is the only reason why he is taken on and the only way in which he can earn himself a living: he is a cog in the division-of-labour machine, in the working class as it is organized as an 'instrument of production'. If the worker attains a clear consciousness of this 'given necessity' that he represents, and uses it as the basis for a representative apparatus which has all the hallmarks of a State (i.e. an apparatus which is not voluntary or contractual, for card-holders only, but absolute, organic and honed to a reality which has to be acknowledged if food, clothing, housing and industrial production are to be guaranteed) – if the worker, the working class can do this, it is achieving something of the deepest significance. It is starting history afresh, opening up the era of workers' States that must coalesce to form a Communist society: a society organized on the model of a large engineering works, in which every people, every part of humanity acquires an identity by virtue of carrying out a particular form of production and no longer by virtue of being organized as a State with given borders.

By constructing this representative apparatus, the working class is in effect expropriating the primary machinery, the most important instrument of production – the working class itself, which rediscovers itself, develops an awareness of its organic unity and pits itself, as a unified entity, against capitalism. The working class affirms in this way that industrial power, the source of industrial power, must return to the factory. It proposes the factory once more, this time from the workers' point of view, as the framework within which the working class constitutes itself as a specific organic body, as the nucleus of a new State – the workers' State – and as the base of a new representative system – the system of Councils. The workers' State, arising as it does in accordance with a given pattern of production, has within it the seeds of its own development, of its own dissolution as a State and its own organic incorporation into a global system – the Communist International.

Just as today, in the Council of a large engineering plant, every work crew (defined by the job it does) is amalgamated, from a proletarian point of view, with the other crews in the same shop; just as every stage of the industrial process is merged, from the proletarian point of view, with the other stages, throwing into relief the whole productive process – so, on a world scale, English *coal* will merge with Russian *oil*, Siberian *grain* with Sicilian *sulphur*, *rice* from Vercelli with *wood* from Styria . . . in a single organism, governed by an international administration that supervises the wealth of the whole world in the name of the whole of humanity. In this sense, the Factory Council is the first step in a historical process that will culminate in the Communist International, no longer as a political organization of the revolutionary proletariat but as a reorganization of the world economy and the whole human community, on both a national and a world level. The value and the historical reality of every revolutionary action that takes place now depends on whether it is conceived of as part of this process and whether it helps free this process from the bourgeois superstructures that restrict it and obstruct it.

The relations that should exist between the political party and the Factory Council, between the union and the Factory Council, are implicitly contained in the argument unfolded above. The Party and the unions should not project themselves as tutors or as ready-made superstructures for this new institution, in which the historical process of the revolution is taking on a controllable historical form. They should project themselves as the conscious agents of its liberation from the constraining forces concentrated in the bourgeois State. They should set themselves the task of organizing the general (political) external conditions in which the process of the revolution can move forward at the maximum possible rate and the liberated productive forces extend themselves to the full.

L'Ordine Nuovo, 5 June 1920

Two Revolutions

Any form of political power can only be historically conceived and justified as the juridical apparatus of a real economic power: as the defensive organization and the condition for development of a given order in the relations of production and distribution of wealth. This fundamental (and elementary) canon of historical materialism sums up the whole complex of theses we have sought to develop in an organic fashion on the problem of Factory Councils. It sums up the reasons why, in our discussion of the real problems of the proletariat class, we have given pride of place to the positive experiences generated by the working masses' wide-scale movement to set up, develop and co-ordinate the Councils. We have therefore asserted: (1) that the revolution is not necessarily proletarian simply because it sets out to overthrow and succeeds in overthrowing the bourgeois State; (2) nor is it proletarian and communist simply because it sets out to eliminate and does eliminate the representative institutions and the administrative machinery through which the central government exerts the political power of the bourgeoisie; (3) it is not proletarian and communist even if the wave of popular insurrection places power in the hands of men who call themselves communists (and are communists in all sincerity). The revolution is proletarian and communist only in the degree to which it is a liberation of the proletarian and communist productive forces that had been developing in the very heart of the society dominated by the capitalist class. It is proletarian and communist only in the degree to which it fosters and promotes

168

the expansion and organization of proletarian and communist forces capable of putting a start to the patient and methodical work needed to build a new order in the relations of production and distribution: a new order in which a class-divided society will become an impossibility and whose systematic development will therefore coincide with a gradual drying-up of State power and a systematic dissolution of the political organization that defends the proletarian class, as the proletariat dissolves as a class and becomes humanity itself.

The revolution that takes the form of a destruction of the bourgeois State apparatus and the construction of a new State apparatus concerns and involves all the classes oppressed by capitalism. Its immediate cause is the harsh fact that, in the conditions of famine left behind by the imperialist war, the great majority of the population (made up of artisans, small-holders and petit bourgeois intellectuals, of the wretchedly poor peasant masses and also of backward proletarian masses) has been left with no guarantee of the availability of the basic requirements of everyday life. This revolution tends to be prevalently anarchic and destructive in character: to take the form of a blind explosion of rage, a tremendous outpouring of furious undirected passions, which settle down into a new State power only when weariness, disillusionment and hunger finally force an acknowledgement of the need for a constituted order and a power that can make that order respected.

This revolution may result purely and simply in a constituent assembly, which seeks to patch up the wounds inflicted on the bourgeois State apparatus by the people's anger. It may go so far as to create soviets, the autonomous political organization of the proletariat and the other oppressed classes; but then these classes may not dare to go beyond this organization and start tampering with economic relations and they will therefore be swept back by the reaction of the propertied classes. The revolution may go so far as to destroy the entire bourgeois State machinery and to establish a state of permanent disorder, in which the existing wealth of the nation and its population start melting away and disappearing, crushed by the impossibility of any kind of autonomous organization. Or it may get so far as setting up a proletarian and communist power, which then wears itself out in repeated, desperate attempts to create by decree the economic conditions it needs to survive and grow stronger and which is finally swept away by the capitalist reaction.

We have seen these historical developments in Germany, Austria,

Bavaria, the Ukraine and Hungary. The revolution as a destructive act has not been followed by the revolution as a process of reconstruction along communist lines. The presence of the right external conditions – the Communist Party, the destruction of the bourgeois State, strong union organizations, the arming of the proletariat – has not been enough to make up for the absence of this other condition: the existence of productive forces of a sort to favour development and growth, a conscious movement of the proletarian masses to back their political power with economic power, a determination on the part of the proletarian masses to introduce proletarian order into the factory, to make the factory the basic unit of the new State and to build the new State in a way that reflects the industrial relations of the factory system.

This is why we have always maintained that the duty of the communist nuclei within the Party is not to let themselves become obsessed with particular issues (like the problem of electional abstentionism or what form a 'real' communist party should take) but to work instead to create the overall conditions within which all particular problems can be resolved as problems within the organic development of the communist revolution. Is it possible, in fact, for a communist party to exist at all (as a party of action, not an academic party of pure doctrinarians and politicos who think 'rightly' and express themselves 'rightly' where communism is concerned), if there does not exist among the masses that spirit of historical initiative and that aspiration to economic autonomy which the Communist Party should reflect and synthesize? And since the formation of the parties and the emergence of the real historical forces of which the parties are the expression are not things that happen at a stroke, out of nothing, but come about as the result of a dialectical process, is not the main task of the communist forces precisely that of giving consciousness and shape to those productive forces – communist in essence – which will have to develop and, through their growth, create the secure and lasting economic base for the proletariat's hold on political power?

Similarly, can the Party abstain from participating in the electoral struggles for the representative institutions of bourgeois democracy, if its task is that of politically organizing all the oppressed classes around the communist proletariat? To achieve this, it must become the 'governing' party representing these classes, in a democratic sense, given that only for the communist proletariat can it be a party in the revolutionary sense.

By becoming the trusted 'democratic' party of all the oppressed classes, by keeping in contact with all sections of the working people, the Communist Party can lead all sections of the populace to acknowledge the communist proletariat as the ruling class which must take over State power from the capitalist class. It can create the conditions in which the revolution as destruction of the bourgeois State can be identified with the proletarian revolution, the revolution that is to expropriate the expropriators and initiate the development of a new order in the relations of production and distribution.

So, by projecting itself as the party of the industrial proletariat, by working to equip the productive forces that capitalism has thrown up in the course of its development with consciousness and a precise direction, the Communist Party can create the economic conditions for the communist proletariat's hold on State power. It can create the conditions in which the proletarian revolution may be identified with the popular revolt against the bourgeois State, in which this revolt may become an act of liberation of the real productive forces that have built up in the heart of capitalist society.

These different series of historical events are not separate and independent; they are different moments in the same dialectical process of development, in the course of which the relations of cause and effect weave together, get reversed and get tangled. Our experience of revolutions has shown, however, how, since Russia, all other two-stage revolutions have failed and the failure of the second revolution has plunged the working classes into a state of prostration and demoralization that has allowed the bourgeois class to remarshal its strength and to begin a systematic extermination of the communist vanguards as they try to regroup.

For those communists who are not content to keep on chewing over the first basics of communism and historical materialism, but who live in the reality of the struggle and understand reality as it is, from the viewpoint of historical materialism and communism, the revolution as conquest of social power on the part of the proletariat can only be conceived as a dialectical process in which political power engenders industrial power and industrial power engenders political power. The Soviet is the instrument of revolutionary struggle that allows the autonomous development of a communist economic organization, reaching from the Factory Council to the Central Economic Council, which settles the plans for production and distribution and in this way succeeds in making capitalist competition redundant. The Factory Council, as an expression of the autonomy of the producer in the industrial sphere and as the basis of communist economic organization is the instrument for the final struggle to the death with the capitalist order, in that it creates the conditions in which the class divisions in society are eliminated and any new class divisions are rendered 'physically' impossible.

But for communists who are living at the heart of the struggle, this conception will not remain an abstract thought: it becomes a reason for struggle, a spur to a greater effort of organization and propaganda.

Industrial development has produced a certain degree of intellectual autonomy in the masses and a certain spirit of positive historical initiative. We must organize and shape these elements of the proletarian revolution, to create the psychological conditions for them to develop and spread throughout the working masses through the struggle for control of production.

We must strive to promote the organic creation of a communist party that will not be a collection of dogmatists or would-be Machiavellis, but a party of revolutionary communist action, a party with a precise awareness of the historical mission of the proletariat and capable of guiding the proletariat towards the accomplishment of this mission. A party, then, that will represent the masses who want to free themselves autonomously, by their own efforts, from political and industrial servitude, through the organization of the social economy – not a party that makes use of the masses for its heroic imitations of the French Jacobins. We must shape things in such a way – as far as it is possible to do this through party action – that there will not be two revolutions, but the popular revolt against the bourgeois State will find at the ready organized forces capable of beginning the process of transforming the national productive apparatus from an instrument of plutocratic oppression into an instrument of communist liberation.

L'Ordine Nuovo, 3 July 1920

The Communist Groups

We have often insisted on this general thesis: in the historical period
dominated by the bourgeois class, all forms of association (including
those devised by the working class to further its struggles), insofar
as they have emerged and developed on the terrain of liberal democracy, must of necessity form part of the bourgeois system and the
capitalist structure of society. For this reason, just as these associations emerged and developed with the emergence and development
of capitalism, so they are declining and falling into decay with the
decline and decay of the system of which they form a part. Many
developments in working-class life at the present historical moment
(the masses' rejection of organizational discipline, certain factories'
declarations in favour of anarchic and syndicalist theories, episodes
of disheartenment and acute demoralization, the ephemeral triumphs
of the various Masaniellis thronging the streets and *piazze*) would be
incomprehensible outside the general picture of the decomposition
of the traditional institutions of government. They *can* be explained
and justified, though, as part of the agonizing labour-pains that characterize any historical period in which an oppressed class is
attempting to free itself from the conditions of its servitude and striving to lay the foundations for the new order within which it can
realize its historical autonomy. It is this general thesis that we took
as the starting-point for our criticism of the trade-union organization,
which had always been conceived as the original form of the working

173

class and the autonomous framework within which the communist revolution would develop. We backed instead the 'originality' of the Factory Council, the only proletarian institution which, springing up, as it does, in a sphere *outside* the political relations of one citizen to another, a sphere in which freedom and democracy for the working class do not exist, where all that does exist, in all its harshness and cruelty, is the economic relation between the exploiter and the exploited, the oppressor and the oppressed, represents the endless striving for freedom that the working class is engaged in under its own steam, using its own methods and systems, for ends which cannot be other than specific to it, without intermediaries, without delegating power to functionaries and career politicians. The Socialist Party itself has not escaped this general process of dissolution and collapse of the traditional institutions of government of the class-divided society, but the Party, because of its greater flexibility (because it is not weighed down by the sedimentation of constituted interests), has been able to react rapidly, especially where the revolutionary tension is at its highest pitch (as in Turin). The Party is undergoing a crisis of organic transformation and the basic elements of its new structure are the communist groups within the factories.

The traditional structure of the Socialist Party is no different from that of any other party which has grown up on the terrain of liberal democracy. It consists of a general assembly of members, which appoints an executive committee enjoying the trust of the rank and file and an arbitration committee made up of Party elders. All the working principles that characterize democratic political association are found in the Party's structure: the division of powers in deliberative, executive and judiciary and the internal competition of the ... 'parties' (the revolutionary and reformist tendencies in the Party, which attempt to alternate in power by adjusting the 'scales' of opportunism). The Party also possesses the essential characteristics found in any assembly in which the sovereign will of democracy is expressed: irresponsibility, incompetence, fickleness and disorderliness – essential characteristics which have to be 'corrected', naturally, by officialdom and the bureaucratic will of the executive committees. This structure, characteristic of all associations that have grown out of bourgeois political democracy, is an expression of the historical substance which is the lifeblood of such associations: the desire to win a majority in the popular assemblies (local and provincial councils and the Chamber of Deputies) and to win this majority by the method that is proper to democracy – by reeling off generic and muddled policies to the electorate (and swearing to put them into practice at all costs).

The assembly is the form of political association that corresponds to the State based on territorial boundaries. It is a continuation of the arrangements of the barbaric peoples who expressed their sovereignty by beating their pikes on the ground and howling. The psychology of the political assemblies that express sovereignty in democratic regimes is 'crowd psychology', which means brute instincts and the irresponsibility of anonymity prevailing over reason and intellect. It can lead to lynchings if the less noble instincts get the upper hand; while in moments of lyrical exaltation it leads to people fighting to replace the horses pulling the fashionable ballerina of the moment along in triumph. This must be why the Italian national assembly's most intelligent and hard-working deputy has pronounced that Parliament stands in the same relation to the soviets as civilization to the barbarian hordes.[1]

Since the workers' State represents a moment in the development of human society in which the relations of political life tend to become identified with the technical relations of industrial production, the workers' State is not based on territorial boundaries, but on the organic structures of production: factories, workshops, shipyards, mines, farms. When it organizes itself within the workplace, the Socialist Party projects itself as the party of government of the working class within the new institutions that the working class is creating to realize its historical autonomy and become a ruling class. The historical substance underlying proletarian political association is no longer simply a determination to win a majority in the popular assemblies of the bourgeois State; it is also a determination to give concrete assistance to the working class in its wearisome labours of development. It becomes possible to foresee a radical transformation in the way the Party is organized. The assembly of members – individual atoms, whose responsibility is only to their consciences, which are troubled and clouded by thunderings and demagogic improvisations and the fear of being found lacking by the assizes of the proletariat – will be replaced by assemblies of delegates with an imperative

[1] The reference is to Turati: see p. 112.

mandate, who will replace generic and muddled debates by debates
on the concrete problems that concern the workers in the factories,
and, responding to the pressing need to keep up the propaganda and
the struggle in the factories, will turn the party assemblies, at last,
into a real preparation for the conquest of economic and political
power by the proletarian masses. It becomes possible to foresee the
transformation of the Socialist Party from an association born and
bred on the terrain of liberal democracy into a new type of organization specific to proletarian civilization.

It was enough just to say the word of command for communist
groups to be set up in Turin, for them to organize themselves immediately and begin to function in a real and vital fashion. During the
local metal-workers' strike that preceded last April's vast movement,
in some factories a communist group that had only just been set up
was forced to take control of the workers, because of the ineptitude
of the Council of Workshop Commissars, to prevent any disintegration of revolutionary discipline and stop dead any drift into disorder.[2]
The experience that has been gained so far in the principal workshops
already constitutes a precious heritage, which must be assessed in
the near future in a meeting of delegates from the various groups
and made available to all the comrades in the section. Only from
such a meeting can the unified programme of work that has now
become necessary emerge, at least in outline. The meeting will consist of the organic ordering of the elements of concrete experience
that each group will give as its particular contribution. It is already
possible, even now, to establish that the historical configuration of
the Socialist Party is being transformed by the formation of communist groups, and it becomes possible to understand the historical configuration of the Russian Communist Party. The Party, insofar as it
is made up of revolutionary workers, engages in the struggle alongside
the masses and is completely immersed in the burning reality of the
revolutionary struggle; but since the Party embodies Marxist doctrine,
for those workers who are in the Party, the struggle is a conscious
struggle for a precise, determinate end: it is a lucid act of the will, a
discipline already forged within the mind and the will. The workers
in the Party thus become an industrial vanguard within the workers'

---

[2] On 28 March, Turin metal industry employers declared a lock-out against the factory
councils because of a conflict over legal time and the actions of commissars.

State, just as they are a revolutionary vanguard in the period of struggle for the introduction of proletarian power. Revolutionary enthusiasm is carried over into the field of production.

Communism as a system of new social relations can only come into being when the material conditions are in place that permit it to come into being. This system of relations cannot be introduced by legislative or administrative means. The office of the Communist Party within the workers' State is that of acting on the great masses as a psychological catalyst, to lead them into realizing in reality – consciously, through an act of will – the new relations that the new conditions have made possible. The introduction of 'Communist Saturdays' as a new 'custom' for the Russian proletariat masses is due to the discipline of the workers of the Communist Party, who, through the factory groups, have become the first to put into effect the new mode of labour and production which alone can eliminate capitalism once and for all and which therefore represents the culmination of the revolutionary class struggle that began with the seizing of political power and with control over labour and production.

L'Ordine Nuovo, 17 July 1920

The Programme of *L'Ordine Nuovo*

I

When, in the month of April, 1919, we got together – three, four, five of us – and decided to start publishing this review, *L'Ordine Nuovo* (and those discussions and decisions of ours must still be around somewhere, because the proceedings were written up – that's right, the proceedings, no less – and a fair copy was made ... for posterity!), none of us (or perhaps just one!) was thinking in terms of changing the world, reforming the hearts and minds of the human multitudes, opening a new phase in history. None of us cherished rose-tinted illusions about how successful the project was going to be (or perhaps one of us may have fantasized about 6,000 subscribers in one month).

Who were we? What did we represent? What did we have to say that was new? Alas! The only sentiment that united us, in those meetings, was that aroused by a vague passion for a vague proletarian culture. We wanted to *do* something. We felt desperate, disorientated, swept up in the fervour of those months that followed the armistice, when it seemed as though Italian society was heading for an imminent cataclysm. Alas! The only really original thing that was said during those meetings was stifled. Someone who was a technician said: 'We need to study the way in which the factory is organized as an instrument of production. We must devote all our attention to capitalist

178

systems of production and organization and we must work to focus the attention of the working class and the Party on this topic.' Some-one else, who was interested in human organization, in human history and working-class psychology, said: 'We need to study what is going on among the working masses. Is there anything in Italy, any working-class institution, that can be compared with the Soviet, that shares some of its characteristics? Something which would allow us to claim that the Soviet is a universal form, not a purely Russian institution – that wherever there are proletarians struggling to win industrial auto-nomy for themselves, the Soviet is the form the working class adopts as the expression of this urge for freedom. The Soviet is the form of self-government of the working masses – is there so much as a germ, a vague hope, a timid step towards this form of Soviet-style self-government in Italy, in Turin?' This man, who had once been struck by a question put to him point-blank by a Polish comrade – 'Why has there never been a congress of the internal commissions in Italy?' – answered his own questions at those meetings of ours in the following way: 'Yes, there *is* the germ of a workers' government, the germ of a Soviet, in Italy, in Turin – the internal commission. Let us study this working-class institution, conduct some research into it. Let us study the capitalist factory as well, but not as a structure for material production, because that would need a specialized know-ledge we do not have. Let us study the capitalist factory as the neces-sary form of the working class, as a political organism and the "national territory" of workers' self-government.' This struck a new note – and it was rejected by none other than Comrade Tasca.

What was it that Comrade Tasca wanted? He was opposed to our launching any propaganda directly among the working masses. He wanted an agreement with the general secretaries of the federations and trade unions. He wanted there to be a meeting with these general secretaries to draw up a plan for official action. The *Ordine Nuovo* group would have been reduced in this way to the level of an irre-sponsible clique of arrogant upstarts and 'coachman-flies'.[1] So what was the programme of the first issues of *L'Ordine Nuovo*? The pro-gramme was the absence of any concrete programme, just a vague and hopeless aspiration to deal with concrete issues. What was the *idea* [behind] the first issues of *L'Ordine Nuovo*? No central *idea*, no

---

[1] See n. 1, p. 61.

hidden rationale behind the literary material that was published. What did Comrade Tasca mean by 'culture' – what did he mean in real terms, I am saying, not in any abstract sense? This is what Comrade Tasca meant by 'culture': he meant 'reminding', rather than 'thinking' – and reminding us of the tiredest, most threadbare debris of working-class thought. He meant letting the Italian working class know, 'reminding' the worthy working class of Italy – so backward, so rough and uneducated – that Louis Blanc had some thoughts about how work should be organized and that these thoughts have led to experiments in practice; 'reminding' them that Eugenio Fournière has compiled a careful academic composition, dishing up piping hot (or piping cold) a model for the Socialist State; 'reminding' them about the Paris Commune, in the spirit of Michelet (or of the worthy Louis Molinari) – without so much as hinting that the Russian communists, following in the footsteps of Marx, are currently tracing the Soviet, the system of Soviets, back to the Paris Commune; without so much as hinting that Marx's observations on the 'industrial' character of the Paris Commune had been used by Russian communists to understand the nature of the Soviet, to elaborate the *idea* of the Soviet and to map out their party's line of action, once it had become the party of government.

What was *L'Ordine Nuovo* in its first issues? It was an anthology, a simple anthology: a review that could just as well have come out of Naples, Caltanisetta, Brindisi – a review of abstract culture and abstract information, with a strong leaning towards horror stories and well-intentioned woodcuts. That was *L'Ordine Nuovo* in its first few issues for you – an incoherent mess, the product of a mediocre intellectualism, fumbling around looking for an end to aim at and a direction for its action to take. That was *L'Ordine Nuovo* for you as it was launched following the meetings we held in April 1919 – those carefully minuted meetings, those meetings in which Comrade Tasca rejected (because it did not conform to the sound traditions of the respectable and peace-loving happy family of Italian socialism), the proposal to devote our energies to 'unearthing' a Soviet tradition within the Italian working class, to uncovering the hidden seam of the real revolutionary spirit in Italy – real in the sense that it is at one with the universal spirit of the workers' International, that it is the product of a real historical situation, that it is the result of the creative efforts of the working class itself.

Togliatti and I staged an editorial *coup d'état*. The problem of the internal commissions was raised explicitly in issue no. 7 of the review. A few evenings before writing the article, I had outlined the argument to Comrade Terracini and Terracini had expressed his full agreement with it both in theory and practice. The article, written in collaboration with Togliatti and cleared by Terracini, was published and there followed just what we had predicted: Togliatti, Terracini and I were invited to give talks to study groups and factory assemblies; we were invited to discussions with the officers and dues collectors of the internal commissions. We went ahead; and the problem of the internal commissions became the central problem, the *idea* of *L'Ordine Nuovo*. It came to be seen as the fundamental problem of the workers' revolution; it was the problem of proletarian 'freedom'. For ourselves and our followers, *L'Ordine Nuovo* became the 'journal of the Factory Councils'.

The workers loved *L'Ordine Nuovo* (and we can assert this with heart-felt satisfaction). And why did the workers love *L'Ordine Nuovo*? Because in the articles of this paper they found something of themselves, the best part of themselves. Because they felt the articles of *L'Ordine Nuovo* to be filled with the same spirit of inner searching that they themselves were filled with: 'How can we become free?' 'How can we become ourselves?' Because the articles of *L'Ordine Nuovo* were not cold, intellectual artefacts, but something that sprang from our discussions with the best of the workers; they built on the actual feelings, desires and passions of the Turin working class – emotions that we had identified and sometimes sparked ourselves. Because the articles of *L'Ordine Nuovo* were almost like a 'recording' of real events, seen as moments in a process of inner liberation and self-expression on the part of the working class. That is why the workers loved *L'Ordine Nuovo* and that is how the *idea* of *L'Ordine Nuovo* emerged. Comrade Tasca did not contribute in the least to this process of creation and development: *L'Ordine Nuovo* developed its own *idea* independently of his intentions and his 'contribution' to the revolution. This to me explains his attitude today and the 'tone' of his polemic. He has not put any real work into arriving at 'his conception' and it does not surprise me that it proved an abortion, since it was unloved. Nor does it surprise me that he should have treated the subject with such clumsiness and barged in with such boorishness and lack of self-discipline, in his attempt to restore to our activity that 'official' character that he had supported and minuted so carefully a year before.

II

In the previous instalment, my aim was to trace the origin of Comrade Tasca's attitude to the programme of *L'Ordine Nuovo* – a programme which, as a result of our hands-on experience of the spiritual and practical needs of the working class, had come to be organized around the central problem of the Factory Councils. Since Comrade Tasca wanted no part of this experience – since, in fact, he was actually hostile to the idea – he failed to grasp the problem of the Factory Councils in its real historical terms and to understand the organic interpretation of the problem that, despite the odd hesitation and the odd understandable mistake, had been gradually taking shape in the work being done on it by myself and Togliatti and the other comrades who wanted to help us with it. For Tasca, the problem of the Factory Councils was simply a problem in the mathematical sense – the problem of how to organize at once the *whole* of the class of Italian workers and peasants. In one of his polemical pieces, Tasca writes that he considers the Communist Party, the trade union and the Factory Council as being on the same plane. Elsewhere he shows that he has failed to understand the meaning of the adjective 'voluntary' which *L'Ordine Nuovo* attaches to the party and trade-union organizations to differentiate them from the Factory Council, which is identified as a 'historical' form of association, of a kind whose only point of comparison, in the present day, is the bourgeois State. According to the conception developed by *L'Ordine Nuovo* – a conception which, as a conception, was necessarily organized around an idea, the idea of freedom (and concretely, on the plane of actual historical creation, around the hypothesis of the working class carrying out an autonomous revolutionary action) – the Factory Council is an institution that is 'public' in character, while the Party and the trade union are institutions that are 'private' in character.

In the Factory Council, the worker participates as a producer – that is, as a consequence of a universal characteristic of his, in consequence of his position and role in society, in the same way in which the citizen participates in the parliamentary democratic State. In the Party and the trade union the worker participates 'voluntarily', by signing a written undertaking, a 'contract' that he can tear up at any moment. The Party and the trade union, because of this 'voluntary', 'contractual' nature, can in no way be confused with the Council, which is a representative institution, which develops not arithmetically but morphologically, and, in its higher forms, aims to give a specifically proletarian profile to the apparatus of production and exchange that was developed by capitalism for the purpose of making profits.

It was because of this that *L'Ordine Nuovo* did not employ the political terminology of a class-divided society to refer to the development of the higher forms of the organization of the Councils, but instead relied on references to industrial organization. According to the conception developed by *L'Ordine Nuovo*, the system of Councils cannot be expressed by the word 'federation', or something similar. It can only be represented by translating on to the scale of an entire industrial zone the complex of relations in industry that link one job crew to another or one section to another in a factory. For us, Turin was an example ready to hand, and so in one article Turin was taken as the historical forge of the Italian communist revolution.

In a factory, the workers are producers in the sense that they collaborate in the preparation of the object being manufactured and are deployed in a way that is determined precisely by the industrial techniques being used, which are independent (in a certain sense) of the mode of appropriation of the values that are being produced. The workers in a car factory, whether they are metal-workers, vehicle-builders, electricians, joiners, etc., all take on the function of producers in that they are all equally necessary and indispensable in the construction of the car, in that, industrially organized as they are, they form a historically necessary and absolutely indivisible entity.

Turin developed as a city in the following way. The transfer of the capital to Florence and then Rome and the fact that the Italian State initially took the form of an extension of the Piedmontese State, meant that Turin was deprived of a petit bourgeois class, whose members went to provide the personnel for the new Italian State apparatus. But this transfer of the capital and this sudden disappearance of a characteristic element of modern cities did not bring about a decline in the city. On the contrary, Turin began to develop again and this new development occurred organically, in line with the growth of the mechanical engineering industry and the system of Fiat factories. Turin had given up its class of petit bourgeois intellectuals to the State; and as the capitalist economy developed, ruining Italy's small-scale industry and craft economy, a thronging proletarian mass converged on Turin, giving the city its present character, perhaps one of the most unusual in the whole of Europe. The city was and still is structured naturally around a single industry that 'controls' all the city's movements and regulates its outlets. Turin is the city of the *motor car*, in the same way that the Vercelli area is characterized economically by *rice*, the Caucasus by *oil*, South Wales by *coal*, etc. Just as in a *factory*, the workers form a pattern, governed by the production of a particular object, which unites and co-ordinates metal- and wood-workers, builders, electricians, etc., so in the city the proletarian class adopts a pattern determined by the prevailing industry, which by its existence orders and governs the entire urban complex. So, too, on a national scale, a people adopts the pattern determined by its exports and the real contribution the nation makes to the economic life of the world.

Comrade Tasca, slapdash reader of *L'Ordine Nuovo* that he is, has failed to grasp this theoretical argument, which, in any case, was nothing more than a translation for Italian historical conditions of the ideas developed by Comrade Lenin in several texts which have been published by *L'Ordine Nuovo* itself, together with the ideas of the American theorist of the revolutionary syndicalist organization, the IWW,[2] the Marxist Daniel De Leon. Indeed, in one passage, Comrade Tasca interprets in a purely 'commercial' and fiscal sense the representation of the economic production complexes designated with the terms 'rice', 'wood', 'sulphur', etc. In another passage, he asks himself how on earth the Councils are supposed to relate to one another. In a third, he identifies as the source of the idea developed in *L'Ordine Nuovo* Proudhon's idea of the factory destroying the government – even though the same issue of 5 June that included the article, 'The Factory Council' and the comment on the Congress of the Chamber of Labour, also featured an extract from Marx's text on the Paris Commune, in which Marx refers explicitly to the *industrial* character of the communist society of producers. It was in this work of Marx's that De Leon and Lenin found the fundamental source of inspiration for their ideas. It was on the basis of these elements that

---

[2] Industrial Workers of the World, a leftist organization founded in 1905 by a disaffected splinter group from the American Federation of Labor, with the aim of organizing unskilled workers.

the *Ordine Nuovo* articles were drafted and elaborated. Once again –
and here we are talking, precisely, about the issue of the paper that
gave rise to this polemic – Comrade Tasca showed that he had read
the articles in question extremely superficially and without any understanding of their historical and intellectual substance.

I do not wish to repeat, for the benefit of the readers of this
polemic, all the arguments that have already been advanced to
develop the idea of workers' freedom which is being realized initially
in the Factory Council. All I wanted to do here was simply to point
to certain fundamental themes, in order to prove how Comrade Tasca
has failed to grasp the inner logic of *L'Ordine Nuovo*'s development.
In an appendix which will follow these two short articles, I shall
analyse some of the points made by Tasca in his exposition, insofar
as it seems appropriate to clarify them and demonstrate their inconsistency. One point, though, must be cleared up immediately – where
Tasca, talking about finance capital, writes that capital 'takes off',
detaches itself from production and floats above it ... All this
mumbo-jumbo about banknotes 'taking off' and 'floating' (!) has
nothing whatsoever to do with the elaboration of the theory on Factory Councils. We stressed that the *person* of the capitalist had become
detached from production – not capital itself, whether financial or
otherwise. We stressed that the factory is no longer run by the owner
in person but by the bank, by way of an industrial bureaucracy which
tends to have no interest in production, just as the civil servant has
no interest in public administration. This served as a starting-point
for a historical analysis of the new hierarchical relations which have
gradually become established in the factory; also to pinpoint the
emergence of one of the most important historical conditions for the
industrial autonomy of the working class, whose organization in the
factory tends to embody the capacity to direct production. The business about 'flight' and 'floating' is a rather unfortunate fantasy on the
part of Comrade Tasca – who, incidentally, even though he refers to
a recent review he did for the *Corriere* of Arturo Labriola's book on
Capitalism to prove that he has 'worked on' the question of financial
capital (and it should be noted that Labriola supports precisely the
opposite theory to that of Hilferding, which was later adopted by the
Bolsheviks), when it comes down to it, shows himself up as having
understood absolutely nothing about it and having built his little castle
in the air out of vague reminiscences and empty words.

The polemic has been useful in showing that the points I raised about the Tasca report were entirely justified. Tasca had only the merest smattering of knowledge about the problem of the Councils, backed by an inconquerable craving to come up with some theory of his own, to initiate his own personal action, to open up a new era in the trade-union movement.

Our comments on the Trades Union Congress and on Comrade Tasca's intervention, designed to sway the vote on an executive motion, were dictated by our determination to preserve the integrity of our review's programme. The Factory Councils have their own laws: they cannot and must not accept the legislation of the very trade-union organs that it is their immediate aim to reform at a fundamental level. Similarly, the Factory Councils movement holds that the workers' representatives should come directly from the masses and be bound to them by an imperative mandate. The intervention of Comrade Tasca at a workers' congress, in his role as rapporteur, without a mandate from anyone, on a matter that concerns the working masses in their entirety and whose imperative resolution would have been binding for them, was so markedly in contrast with the whole spirit of *L'Ordine Nuovo* that the comment, harshly worded as it was, was entirely justified and absolutely necessary.

L'Ordine Nuovo, 14 and 28 August 1920

The Communist Party

I

Since Sorel, it has become a cliché to refer to the primitive Christian communities in assessing the modern proletarian movement. It must be said at once that Sorel is in no way responsible for the small-mindedness and intellectual crudity of his Italian admirers, just as Karl Marx is not responsible for the ridiculous ideological pretensions of 'Marxists'. Within the field of historical research, Sorel is an 'inventor': he cannot be imitated; he does not supply his aspiring disciples with a method that can be applied mechanically, by anyone, on any occasion, and produce intelligent findings as a result. For Sorel, as for Marxist doctrine, Christianity represents a revolution at the height of its development – a revolution, that is, that has gone as far as it can, as far as creating a new and original system of moral, legal, philosophical and artistic relations. To assume these developments as an ideological blueprint for *every* revolution is a crude and unintelligent travesty of Sorel's historical intuitions. All it can give rise to is a series of historical researches on the 'germs' of proletarian culture that we *must* be able to detect, if it is true (as it is for Sorel) that the proletarian revolution is immanent in modern industrial society and if it is true that from this revolution, as well, there will result a new set of rules for living and a wholly new system of relations, characteristic of the revolutionary class. What significance can be attached, then, to the assertion that, in contrast with the early Christians, the workers are not chaste, or sober, or very original in their lifestyle? Leaving to one side the kind of amateurish generalization that turns all 'Turinese metal-workers' into a mob of brutes, who eat their roast chicken every day and get drunk in brothels at night, who neglect their families and look to the cinemas and an aping of bourgeois manners to satisfy their ideals of beauty and morality – leaving to one side this kind of amateurish and puerile generalization, the statement can still in no way become the premise for a historical judgement. It is equivalent, in historical terms, to saying that, since modern Christians eat well, use prostitutes, get drunk, give false testimony, commit adultery, etc., etc., it must be a myth that ascetics, saints and martyrs ever existed. Every historical phenomenon, in other words, must be studied for its own peculiar characteristics, in the context of contemporary realities, as a development of the freedom that manifests itself in ends, institutions and forms that absolutely cannot be confused or compared (except metaphorically) with the ends, institutions and forms of historical phenomena in the past.

Every revolution that, like the Christian and the communist, comes about and can only come about through a stirring of the vast popular masses at their deepest level, cannot do other than break down and destroy the entire existing system of social organization. Who can imagine and foresee what the immediate consequences will be when the endless hordes who are currently deprived of will or power finally make their entry into the arena of historical creation and destruction? Because they have never before experienced this 'will' and this 'power', they will expect to see their newly gained will and power manifested in every public and private act. They will find the whole existing world mysteriously alien and will want to destroy it from the roots. But precisely because of the sheer immensity of the revolution, its character of unpredictability and boundless freedom, who would dare to hazard so much as a single definitive hypothesis on what sentiments, what passions, what initiatives, what virtues will be forged in this glowing furnace? Everything that exists at present, everything we see around us today that lies outside the scope of our own will and force of character – what changes will it all undergo? Will not every single day lived at this level of intensity be a revolution in itself? Will not every change that takes place in individual consciousness –

occurring, as it will, simultaneously across the whole mass of the people – have creative repercussions which are quite unimaginable?

Nothing can be predicted, in the realm of morality and sentiment, starting from what can be observed at present. Only one sentiment – which has now become a constant, a distinguishing feature of the working class – can be registered already: the sentiment of solidarity. But the intensity and strength of this sentiment can be counted on to sustain the will of resistance and self-sacrifice only for that period of time that even the people's meagre capacity for historical prediction can estimate, more or less accurately. They cannot be counted on, and thus relied on to sustain the historical will during the period of revolutionary creation and building of the new society, when it will be impossible to set a limit on how long resistance and sacrifice will be called for. Because, by then, the enemy to be fought and defeated will no longer be outside the proletariat – a defined and manageable external physical presence. It will be within the proletariat itself: in its ignorance, its sluggishness, its ponderous slowness in grasping new insights. The dialectic of the class struggle will have become internalized and in every conscience the newly created man will have to be on his guard every moment against the bourgeois lying in ambush. Because of this the workers' trade union, the body that realizes proletarian solidarity in practice and disciplines it, cannot serve as the model and the basis for predictions concerning the future of civilization. The trade union is lacking in elements necessary to encourage the development of freedom. It is destined to undergo radical changes as a consequence of general developments. It is determined, not determining.

The proletarian movement, in its present phase, is striving to bring about a revolution in the way in which material things and physical forces are organized. Its distinguishing features cannot be the sentiments and passions that are distributed throughout the masses, that sustain the will of the masses. The distinguishing features of the proletarian revolution can only be looked for in the party of the working class, the Communist Party, which owes its existence and development to its disciplined organization of the will to form a State, the will to give a new, proletarian order to the existing arrangement of physical forces and to lay the foundations of popular liberty.

At the present moment, the Communist Party is the only institution that may be seriously compared with the religious communities of primitive Christianity. To the extent that the Party already exists on an international scale, one can hazard a comparison and establish a scale of criteria for judging between the militants for the City of God and the militants for the City of Man. The communist is certainly not inferior to the Christian in the days of the catacombs. On the contrary! The ineffable end which Christianity promised to its champions is, in its evocative mysteriousness, ample justification for heroism, saintliness, a thirst for martyrdom. There is no need for the great human resources of character and will to come into play in order to awaken a spirit of sacrifice in someone who believes in a heavenly reward and eternal bliss. The communist worker who, week after week, month after month, year after year, without asking for anything in return, follows up his eight hours work at the factory with eight hours work for the Party or the union or the co-operative – from the point of view of human history, this communist worker is greater than the slave or artisan who risked everything to make it to his secret prayer meeting. Similarly, Rosa Luxemburg and Karl Leibknecht are greater than the greatest of Christian saints. Precisely because what they are fighting for is something concrete, human, defined, the warriors of the working class are greater than the warriors of God. The moral forces that sustain their will are the more infinite the more finite the end their will is directed towards.

How vast an expansion will come about in the sentiments of the worker who spends eight hours a day bending over his machine, repeating the ritual gestures of his job, as monotonous as the clicking of a circle of rosary beads, when he becomes a 'master' and the measure of all social values? Is it not a miracle that the worker can still manage to think at all when he is reduced to working away without understanding the how and why of what he is doing? This miracle of the worker who, day after day, gains in spiritual autonomy and the freedom to create within the realm of ideas, struggling against his weariness and boredom, against the monotony of a job that tends to mechanize and hence to stifle his inner life – this miracle is being organized in the Communist Party, in the will to struggle and the revolutionary creativity that are expressed in the Communist Party.

The worker in the factory merely executes given tasks. He does not follow through the overall process of work and production. He is not a point that moves to create a line: he is a pin stuck in a particular place and the line is made up of the sequence of pins that have been set up by an alien will for its own ends. The worker tends to carry over this way of being into all areas of his life: he readily adapts, in everything, to being a simple material executor, a 'mass' guided by a will that is alien to his own. He is intellectually lazy, he cannot see and does not wish to see beyond his immediate horizon, and so he lacks any reliable criterion for choosing his leaders and he lets himself be easily swayed by promises. He wants to believe he can get what he wants without any great effort on his part and without having to think too much. The Communist Party is the instrument and the historical form of the process of inner liberation through which the worker is transformed from *executor* to *initiator*; from *mass* to *leader* and *guide*, from pure brawn to a brain and a will. The founding of the Communist Party gives a glimpse of that seed of liberty that will germinate and grow to its full extent when the workers' State has prepared the necessary ground. The slave or artisan of the classical world 'came to know himself' and realized his own liberation when he joined a Christian community, where he felt himself to be equal, a brother, because all were sons of the same father. It is just the same for the worker, when he joins the Communist Party, where he collaborates in 'discovering' and 'inventing' new ways of life, where he collaborates 'consciously' in the world's activity; where he thinks, looks ahead, has a responsibility; where he organizes, rather than simply being organized; where he feels himself to be part of a vanguard that runs ahead pulling the whole popular mass along with it.

Even in purely organizational terms, the Communist Party has shown itself to be the particular form of the proletarian revolution. No previous revolution involved political parties: they were born after the bourgeois revolution and they have entered their decline on the terrain of parliamentary democracy. Here, as elsewhere, there is confirmation of the Marxist idea that capitalism throws up forces that it then cannot succeed in keeping under control. The democratic parties served to show up able politicians and secure their success at the polls. Today the men in government are imposed by the banks, the great newspapers, the industrial confederations; the parties are crumbling into a multitude of personal cliques. The Communist Party, arising out of the ashes of the socialist parties, is repudiating its democratic and parliamentary roots and revealing its essential characteristics which are completely new within history. The Russian Revolution is a revolution brought about by men who were organized by the Communist Party – men who forged themselves a new personality within the Party, developed new sentiments and realized a moral life which is destined to become the universal consciousness and the ultimate end of all men.

II

Political parties are the reflection and the nomenclature of the social classes. They emerge, develop, decline and renew themselves as the various strata of the warring social classes undergo changes of genuine historical significance, as they acquire a new and clearer awareness of themselves and their own interests. What has become characteristic of the present historical period, as a consequence of the imperialist war, which profoundly altered the structure of the national and international apparatus of production and exchange, is the rapidity of the process by which the traditional parliamentary parties, which emerged on the terrain of liberal democracy, are now falling apart and new political organizations are rising up alongside them. This general process obeys an implacable inner logic of its own, which is shown up in the disintegration of the old classes and groupings and in the bewilderingly rapid shifts in the position of whole strata of the population throughout the entire territory of the State and often throughout the entire territory under capitalist domination.

Even those social classes which historically have been the slowest and most sluggish in differentiating themselves, like the peasant class, have not escaped the chemical action of the reagents dissolving the body of society. On the contrary, it seems as though the slower and more sluggish these classes have been in the past, the more eager they are now to race on to the ultimate consequences in the dialectic of the class struggle – civil war and the violation of economic relations. In Italy, we have seen a powerful party of the rural class, the Partito Popolare, emerging as if from nowhere, in the space of two years. When it was set up, this party claimed to represent the economic interests and political aspirations of all the different social strata of rural Italy, from the baron with his *latifondi*,[1] to the medium-

---

[1] [Translator's note] *Latifondi*: large, often under-cultivated landed estates, characteristic of southern Italy.

sized landowner, from the small landholder to the tenant farmer, from the sharecropper to the penniless peasant. We have seen the Partito Popolare win almost a hundred seats in parliament with bloc lists completely dominated by the representatives of the barons, the great forest owners and the owners of large and medium-sized estates – a tiny minority of the rural population. We have seen internal struggles between tendencies in the Partito Popolare breaking out almost immediately and quickly becoming endemic – a reflection of the process of differentiation that was taking place in the original electoral body. The great masses of small landowners and peasants were no longer content to be the passive infantry-mass enabling the medium-sized and larger landowners to secure their interests. Under their energetic pressure, the Partito Popolare split into a right, a left and a centre, and we have seen the extreme left of the *popolari*, under pressure from the poorest peasants, adapting a revolutionary stance and entering into competition with the socialist party, which has also become the representative of the vast peasant masses. We are already witnessing the break-up of the Partito Popolare, whose parliamentary wing and Central Committee no longer represent the interests and the newly acquired self-consciousness of their mass electorate or the forces organized in the white unions.[2] These are now represented by the extremists who, not wanting to lose control of them and unable to delude them with legal action in Parliament, are forced to resort to violent struggle and to invoking new political institutions of government.

The same process of rapid organization and even more rapid dissolution has also been apparent in the other political current that claimed to represent the interests of the peasants: the war veterans' association. It is a reflection of the tremendous internal crisis that is racking the whole of rural Italy, and that reveals itself in the massive strikes in the centre and the north, in the take-over and distribution of the great *latifondi* of Apulia and in the appearance of hundreds and thousands of armed peasants in the towns of Sicily.

This profound stirring of the peasant classes is shaking the framework of the democratic parliamentary state to its very foundations. Capitalism, as a political force, is being reduced to corporate associations of factory owners. It no longer possesses a political party whose ideology also extends to the petit bourgeois strata in the cities and

---

[2] The Catholic trade unions, as opposed to the socialist ('red') unions.

the countryside and so ensures the survival of a broadly based legal state. In fact, capitalism has been reduced to relying for its political representation on the major newspapers (a print-run of 400,000, a thousand electors) and the Senate, which is immune, as an institution, from the actions and reactions of the great popular masses, but which also lacks authority and prestige in the country. Because of this, the political power of capitalism is tending to become even more closely allied with the upper ranks of the military – with the Royal Guard and the swarm of adventurers who have emerged since the Armistice, aspiring, every one of them, to become the Kornilov or the Bonaparte of Italy. The political power of capitalism can today only find expression in a military *coup d'état* and an attempt to impose a rigid national dictatorship to drive the brutalized Italian masses into reviving the economy by sacking neighbouring countries sword in hand.

With the bourgeoisie worn down and exhausted as a ruling class, with capitalism exhausted as a mode of production and exchange, with the peasant class failing to provide a unified political force capable of forging a State, the working class is being ineluctably summoned by history to take upon itself the responsibilities of a ruling class. Only the proletariat is capable of creating a strong state that can make itself respected, because the proletariat has, in communism, a programme of economic reconstruction that finds its necessary premises and conditions in the phase of development reached by capitalism in the 1914–18 Imperialist War. Only the proletariat, through its creation of a new organ of public authority, the system of Soviets, can give dynamic expression to the fluid and incandescent mass of workers and restore order amid the general upheaval of the productive forces. It is natural and historically justified that it should be precisely in a period such as this that the problem of forming a Communist Party should arise – a party representing a proletarian vanguard which has a precise consciousness of its historical mission, which will establish the new social order and be both initiator and protagonist of the new and unprecedented historical period.

Even the traditional political party of the Italian working class, the Socialist Party, has not escaped the process of decomposition of all forms of association, this process which is characteristic of the period we are living through. This has been the colossal historical error of the men who have been in charge of the controlling organs of our association from the outbreak of the World War to the present day –

believing that they could preserve the old structure of the party when it was crumbling from within. In fact, the Italian Socialist Party, if you look at its traditions, at the historical origins of the various currents it is made up from, at its pact, tacit or explicit, with the General Confederation of Labour (a pact which has the effect, in all its congresses, Councils and deliberative assemblies, of giving an unwarranted power and influence to trade-union bureaucrats), at the unlimited autonomy conceded to its parliamentary group (which gives deputies, too, a power and influence at congresses, Councils and high-ranking discussions which is similar to that of the union bureaucrats and equally unjustified) – if you look at all these things, the Italian Socialist Party is not different at all from the British Labour Party: it is revolutionary only where the general statements contained in its programme are concerned. It is a conglomeration of parties: when it moves, it cannot help but move sluggishly and slowly. It runs the permanent risk of becoming an easy prey for adventurers, careerists and ambitious men without integrity or political capability. With its heterogeneous character, with the endless snags in its machinery, worn and sabotaged as it is by *serve-padrone*,[3] it can never be in a position to take upon itself the burden of and responsibility for the revolutionary initiatives and actions demanded of it by the ceaseless pressure of events. Here we have the explanation for the historical paradox that, in Italy, it is the masses who propel and 'educate' the party of the working class and not the Party which guides and educates the masses.

The Socialist Party claims to be the champion of Marxist doctrines. One would therefore expect the Party to possess, in these doctrines, a compass to steer it through the confusion of events. One would expect it to have that capacity for historical foresight that characterizes the intelligent followers of Marxist dialect. One would expect it to possess a general plan of action, based on this historical foresight, and to be in a position to issue clear and precise orders to the working class, engaged in its struggle. But instead, the Socialist Party, the champion of Marxism in Italy – just like the Partito Popolare, the party which represents the most backward classes in the Italian population – is exposed to all the pressures of the masses and it shifts and

---

[3] [Translator's note] *Serva-padrona*: maid who is really the mistress of the house (character in Italian comic opera).

alters its position following the shifts and alterations of the masses. This Socialist Party, which proclaims itself to be the guide and edu- cator of the masses, is in fact nothing more than a wretched clerk, recording the way in which the masses are operating of their own accord. This poor Socialist Party, which proclaims itself to be at the head of the working class, is nothing more than the baggage-train of the proletarian army.

If this strange behaviour on the part of the Socialist Party, this bizarre state that the party of the working class finds itself in, has not yet led to a catastrophe, it is because there exist in the ranks of the working class – in the urban Party sections, in the unions, in the factories, in the villages – energetic groups of communists who are conscious of their historical role, energetic and shrewd in their actions, well equipped to guide and educate the proletarian masses around them. It is because there exists, at the heart of the Socialist Party, a potential Communist Party, which only needs an explicit organization – a centralization, a discipline of its own, in order to be able to develop rapidly, to take over and renew the membership of the party of the working class and to give a new direction to the Confederation of Labour and the co-operative movement.

The immediate problem in this period – after the metal-workers' struggle and before the congress in which the party is going to have to adopt a serious and precisely defined attitude to the Communist International – is precisely that of how to organize and centralize these communist forces which already exist and are in operation. The Socialist Party is crumbling at a rate of knots, falling further into decay by the moment. In a very short space of time, the tendencies in the Party have rearranged themselves completely. Faced with the responsibilities of historical action and the obligations the party accepted by joining the Communist International, individuals and groups within it have become confused and shifted their ground. Centrist and opportunist equivocation has captured a section of the Party's leadership, spreading confusion and doubt in the sections. Amid this general falling-off of conscience, will and faith, this tem- pest of baseness, cowardice and defeatism, the duty of communists is to form tight-knit groups, to rally and stand at the ready for the orders which will come. Acting on the basis of the theses approved by the Second Congress of the Third International, and on the basis of steadfast discipline to the supreme authority of the worldwide workers' movement, sincere and dedicated communists must carry out the preparatory work, which is needed to set up, at the earliest possible opportunity, the communist fraction of the Italian Socialist Party, which must then, at the Florence Congress, for the good name of the Italian proletariat, become, in name and in fact, the Communist Party of Italy, a section of the Third Communist International. The communist fraction must have an organic and powerfully centralized leadership apparatus. It must have its own disciplined branches wherever the proletariat works, assembles and struggles and a whole range of services and organs for supervision, activity and propaganda, which will enable it to function and develop right from the first as a real party.

After saving the working class from disaster in the metal-workers' strike through their energy and spirit of initiative, the communists must now follow through their attitudes and action to their logical conclusion. They must save (by reconstructing it) the primordial fabric of the party of the working class. They must give the Italian proletariat a Communist Party which is capable of organizing the workers' State and the conditions needed to bring about a communist society.

L'Ordine Nuovo, 4 September and 9 October 1920

Red Sunday[1]

The scribblers of the bourgeois class are writhing with fury at finding themselves constrained to record the activity of the working class in the occupied factories. Working-class activity, working-class initiatives in the fields of production, internal order, military defence! Social hierarchies have been smashed, historical values turned upside down. The 'implementing' classes, the 'instrumental' classes have become the 'managerial' classes: they have become their own bosses and found their representatives within their own ranks – men who can be invested with the power of government, men who can take on all the tasks involved in turning an elemental and mechanical aggregation into an organic whole, a living creature. All this has got the scribblers of the bourgeoisie writhing in fury, believing as they do that the bourgeois class has been divinely invested with the powers of decision and historical initiative!

What the workers have done has an immense historical importance, which must be grasped in all its aspects by the working class. This is a day the workers will devote to examining their consciences, to discussing and mulling over the events that have taken place. One day like this has to be worth ten years of normal activity for the workers: ten years of normal propaganda, of absorbing revolutionary notions and ideas at the normal rate.

[1] This article appeared on the first Sunday following the occupation of the factories in September 1920.

What has happened in these past few days? The metal-workers' federation has called on the workers to engage in a trade union struggle to win wage improvements. The industrialists refused to acknowledge that there was any real validity in the workers' demands. The leaders of the organization, even though they are not communists, even though they sign manifestos against Bolshevik methods of emancipating the proletariat, nevertheless, after examining the real situation, found that they had to shift the struggle on to a new domain – a domain where, even if violence was not necessary in the immediate term, it was necessary to start planning and organizing violence without delay. In the meantime, a new fact immediately emerged from this new method of struggle. While workers were struggling to improve their economic situation through strike action, their only real role in the struggle was that of trusting their distant leaders and developing virtues of solidarity and resistance which rested, precisely, on this generic trust. But when, in the course of the struggle, the workers occupy the factories with the aim of keeping production going, the moral position of the masses immediately takes on a new aspect and a new value. The trade-union leaders are no longer in charge: they disappear in the immensity of the larger picture and the mass has to solve the problems of the factory for itself, with its own resources and its own men.

The factory, under the capitalists, was a miniature State, ruled by a despot. The ruler enjoyed a singular suffrage – a single man with a single vote – and he exercised this privilege in choosing the manual workers, clerks, foremen as specialists and distributing them among the workshops, offices and labs. The factory was a despotically organized State, with all power resting in the hands of the proprietor or his representative. The multiplicity of States constituted by all the various capitalist factories came together in the bourgeois State, which secured the discipline and obedience of the non-property-owning population by giving it a semblance of power and sovereignty, by summoning it every five or seven years to nominate its deputies to Parliament and the municipal councils. Today, with the workers' occupation, this despotic power in the factories has been destroyed and the suffrage broadened, as the right to choose industrial executives has passed into the hands of the working class. Every factory has become an illegal state, a proletarian republic living from day to day, awaiting the outcome of events. But even if a great uncertainty still hangs over the future of these proletarian republics, given that the enemy forces have not yet revealed themselves or given any hint of their real intentions, the mere fact that these republics exist – are 'alive' – has an immeasurable importance and historical value. Life has a logic, an inner energy of its own which goes beyond the will and the whims of individuals. Now that these proletarian republics are alive, they are having to cope with all the problems that face any autonomous and independent power that exercises sovereignty over a delimited territory. The political capacity, the initiative, the revolutionary creativity of the working class are now being put to the test.

The first problem, the fundamental and unavoidable problem facing the citizens of the factory-State is that of military defence. It is facing them in an unprecedented way. The bourgeois State builds its army on three social strata: the bourgeoisie, the petite bourgeoisie and the working people. The people provides the military mass, the haute bourgeoisie and the aristocracy the upper ranks of the officer class, while the petite bourgeoisie fills the junior commands. The capitalist army is organized in the same way as the capitalist factory, where the class of proprietors (or those assimilated to them through financial interests) has despotic command, the proletariat is the passive infantry-mass and the petite bourgeoisie fills the subordinate command posts.

In the factory-republic, there exists only one class, the proletariat: the class that used to provide the passive infantry-mass for industry and the army. Now this class has to create its own army – an articulate, organized, disciplined army, capable of resisting the enemy forces and defeating them. The workers tend to see defence as an obligation that everyone shares in and this is certainly the right way to think about it. But then they are led to conclude that this duty should be carried out by everyone, indiscriminately; and this is a mistake. Military defence needs to be organized in a special corps, with its own commands and functions, though the concept of hierarchy can no longer have any application in these formations, since 'there exists one class only'. These formations should not be restricted in numbers, because defence can at any moment give way to attack and military initiative.

This problem of military defence is linked to another: will it not come about that the multiplicity of proletarian republics constituted by the factories occupied and controlled by the workers will be led inevitably, by the inner dialect of historical development, to join together, form themselves into a united confederation and counterpose a central power of their own to the central power of the bourgeois State? The working class is today confronting the concrete problem of setting up a city-wide Soviet. If such a Soviet is created, it will need to have an army force at its disposal, which can and must be provided by regularly constituted and commanded factory formations, which can be amalgamated, through a relay of commands, into a city militia. But, conversely, the creation of military nuclei in the factory raises the problem of the Soviet, since defence has no limits, and must proceed according to its own logic.

These problems should be discussed today by the workers in the factories, in the general assemblies, which are the organ of power and sovereignty of the proletarian factory-republics. The preparatory and propaganda work for the nomination of workers' deputies must be carried out now, so that, at a given moment, when the march of events has swept history along to a point where the new, the unprecedented can happen, the new organs of the proletariat in its struggle for emancipation will be ready to spring forth from every factory or group of factories. And the same considerations apply to this other revolutionary creation as to the armed force.

In the bourgeois state, the functions of supreme command (the government) are in the hands of the capitalists or the high-ranking social class which is linked to the proprietors through financial interests. The subordinate posts – the posts as national deputies – are in the hands of the petite bourgeoisie, which allows itself to be dominated economically and morally by the capitalists. The mass of working people is manipulated politically to satisfy the material interests of the proprietors and the idealogical ambitions of the petite bourgeoisie. To keep this class hierarchy intact, the Constitution maintains that it is illegal for deputies to be bound by imperative mandates. The bourgeoisie relies on the pressures of the political environment and the enticing possibilities for satisfying personal ambition to corrupt deputies – even worker deputies – as long as they are not bound by an imperative mandate.

In the constitution of the proletarian central power, all these conditions are changed. There exists one class only, which elects its deputies from among its own ranks, the electoral college being the factory and all mandates imperative and binding. This means that the old hierarchies are destroyed and that the workers' power is built up from a purely industrial and administrative base. The anarchists should be the first to welcome the organization of power, since their ideals are being given a concrete expression.

Today, on the metal-workers' Red Sunday, the workers must construct the first cell of the proletarian revolution which is arising out of the general state of affairs with all the irresistible force of a natural phenomenon.

L'Ordine Nuovo, 5 September 1920

Part Three
Socialism and
Fascism

Russia and the International

Soviet Russia has captured the sympathies of the working class the whole world over and is capturing them more every day. This is natural enough. The Russian proletarian revolution is dividing the world into two camps: on one side, those who are for it, who want to see it develop and triumph throughout the whole world; on the other, those who are against it, who want to see it choke to death on the blood of the revolutionary Russian proletariat; who see that as the way to crush the universal world revolution. On the one side there are the industrial working class and the semi-proletarian classes (that is, the rural poor) of all nations. On the other, there are the capitalists and bankers, the great landowners, the speculators of the whole world.

The sympathies Soviet Russia has won for itself among the international proletariat are so great that even the capitalist governments organizing the economic blockade against Russia no longer dare to struggle openly against its government and are constrained to recognize it and arrange commercial links with it.

Another particularly important fact, which needs to be underlined, is this: there is not a single workers' party or workers' organization – not even those that practise opportunism and reformism – that would now dare to declare itself openly opposed to Soviet Russia, even if, in practice, within their own national context, these parties are propping up the power of the bourgeoisie.

Why are reformist and opportunistic parties and organizations constrained in this way to hide their real, deep-rooted opposition to Soviet Russia under a hypocritical show of friendship? Because if they did not do so, they would very quickly lose the support of the working masses. It is a utilitarian motive, then, that is prompting them to declare themselves for Russia. The centrists and semi-reformists are behaving in just the same fashion: even though they claim to be against the Communist International, its principles, its tactics, its centralized organization, they still present themselves to the working class as defenders of the Russian proletarian revolution. If they did not do this they would be lost and the masses would desert them. They are pursuing a hypocritical policy of friendship and sympathy for Russia in order to be able to continue their work of spreading confusion, to delay the proletarian revolution.

This is true for every nation and especially for Italy. Let us leave the reformists to one side, because by now all conscious workers know what to think of their politicking – they know them to be enemies of the Russian proletarian revolution, even though they do not dare to speak out frankly against it.

Let us talk, instead, about the centrists and semi-reformists – those who disguise their treachery as a desire to hold the party together and who have given themselves the name of unitarian-communists. These are people who trumpet their ardent support for Soviet Russia and their firm adherence to the Communist International after declaring open war on both! Why are Comrade Serrati and his supporters making so much noise about their solidarity with Russia? Because Russia, its revolution, its principles and its methods of struggle enjoy a vast popularity among the Italian proletarian masses. Because the Italian proletariat's attitude to Soviet Russia is one of admiration and acclaim; because it feels utterly in solidarity with Soviet Russia, because it is determined to support Soviet Russia to the end, using all the means at its disposal. It is because of this that Comrade Serrati and the unitarian-communists are adapting to circumstance, in order not to lose their influence over the proletariat.

But they are making a show of friendship and solidarity not simply towards Russia and the Russian revolution, but also towards the Communist International. And in fact, in the consciousness of the Italian proletariat, the Russian revolution is bound together quite inseparably with the Communist International. Guided by its consciousness and its proletarian instinct, the Italian proletariat makes no distinction between the Russian revolution and the Communist International; rather, it sees them together, united, as they are in real life. So Comrade Serrati and his supporters are constrained, here as well, to trim their sails to the mood of the proletariat so as not to lose their ascendency. They do not have the courage to say frankly and openly that, since they are opposed to the 21 conditions the International has set, to its thinking on the colonial question and the question of nationalism, to its thinking on the agrarian question, even to the very principle of centralization which underlies the Communist International, this means that they are against the International itself.[1]

When it comes down to it, both the reformists and opportunists who have the courage to say so openly and the centrists and semi-centrists who do not dare to state their opposition to the Communist International openly, but who reject its most essential resolutions and work against it – both groups are, in practice, enemies of Soviet Russia and the Russian proletarian revolution, because to declare oneself opposed to the international communist workers' organization, whether covertly or openly, is to be an enemy of Russia and the Russian revolution.

What is the Communist International, in fact? It is the embodiment, in the international arena, of the principles and methods of the Russian revolution.

The Russian proletarian revolution is the first great proletarian revolution, which concluded triumphantly with the seizure of power by the proletariat in the largest capitalist nation on earth and with the establishment – unprecedented in history – of a dictatorship of the proletariat. This historical experience of the Russian revolutionary class has an immense importance for the entire international proletariat and its struggle for emancipation. Furthermore, the Russian revolution is not simply the product of particular conditions specific to that country; rather, it is a product of the Imperialist World War. Today, in all the capitalist countries, the economic crisis,

---

[1] The Second Congress of the Third International (19 July – 7 August 1920) set down a number of conditions (known as the 21 points) for the admission of socialist parties to the Comintern. Serrati and his 'maximalist' group found them acceptable, as did the communists gathered around Bordiga and Gramsci, but were opposed to expelling those, such as Togliatti's reformist faction, who disagreed with them. Hence Gramsci's irritation.

unemployment, inflation and monetary devaluation are common phenomena that bring conditions everywhere close to those of Russia before 1917. However, not only the outbreak, but also the subsequent development of the Russian revolution is linked to and depends on the economic crisis the world is going through – a crisis which is becoming broader and deeper by the day. The conditions for the world revolution are maturing rapidly and only the victory of the universal revolution can guarantee the definitive victory of the Russian revolution.

Now, what the Communist International is doing is nothing other than organizing the international proletariat, drawing on the priceless and overwhelming experience of the Russian revolution to prepare for the universal revolution.

Crushing the Russian revolution, then, means crushing the world revolution. This is something the capitalist governments know only too well and it is because of this that they are fighting Soviet Russia to the end. But it is something that the international proletariat is also coming to understand, increasingly, and the proletariat is shedding its last doubts that support for the Russian revolution is indivisible from adherence to the Communist International.

Those who are struggling against the Communist International, whether openly or surreptitiously, are in effect struggling against Soviet Russia: they are enemies of Russia and enemies who are all the more dangerous because they are fighting within the very ranks of the working class. It is they who are to blame if the bourgeoisie is still managing to keep a portion of the workers under its influence.

The supreme duty of the Italian communists is that of unmasking and combating this dangerous policy of the centrists. 'Off with your masks!' we must cry in the faces of the false friends of Russia and the International, 'you are working against the International, you are pitting yourselves against it and that means that you are enemies of the first great proletarian revolution. The Italian proletariat, when it understands this truth, cannot do other than condemn what you are doing.'

L'Ordine Nuovo, 9 January 1921

The Livorno Congress[1]

The Livorno Conference is destined to become one of the most important historical events in contemporary Italian life. At Livorno, the question of whether the Italian working class has the capacity to form an autonomous class party from its own ranks will finally be decided. It will finally emerge, as well, whether the experiences of four years of imperialist war and two of extreme hardship for product- ive forces all over the world have succeeded in giving the Italian working class an awareness of its historical mission.

The working class is both a national and an international class. It must place itself at the head of the working people struggling to free themselves from the yoke of industrial and financial capitalism on both a national and an international scale. The national task of the working class is determined by the process of development of Italian capitalism and Italian capitalism's official expression, the bourgeois State. Italian capitalism came to power by pursuing the following line of development: it subjugated the countryside to the industrial cities and it subjugated central and southern Italy to the North. In the Italian bourgeois State, the question of the relations between the cities and the countryside is not simply a question of the relations

[1] This article appeared on the eve of the Seventeenth Congress of the Italian Socialist Party, held at Livorno, on 15–21 January 1921. It was at this conference that the communist faction broke away from the maximalist and reformist groups to form the PCd'I.

between the great industrial cities and the country immediately surrounding them in the same region: it is a question of the relations between one part of the national territory and another, which is quite distinct from it and characterized by certain instantly recognizable features. Capitalism exercises its predominance and its exploitative practices in the following two ways: directly, in the factory, over the workers; but also indirectly, in the State, over broader swathes of the Italian working people, made up of impoverished peasants and semi-proletarians. What is indisputable is that only the industrial working class can resolve the central problem of Italian national life, the Southern question, by seizing political and economic power from the hands of the capitalists and the bankers. Only the industrial working class can bring to a conclusion the long and laborious task of unification that started with the Risorgimento. The bourgeoisie has unified the Italian people where territorial considerations are concerned. The working class has the task of finishing the bourgeoisie's work off and unifying the Italian people economically and spiritually. This can only be brought about by smashing the existing machinery of the bourgeois State, which rests on a hierarchical predominance of industrial and financial capitalism over the nation's other productive forces. This overturning of the State can only come about through the revolutionary struggle of the industrial working class which is directly subjugated to capitalism. It can only happen in Milan, Turin, Bologna – in the great cities from which all those millions of threads go out which make up the network of domination that industrial and financial capitalism has cast over all the productive forces of the country. In Italy, as a result of the particular configuration of the country's economic and political structure, not only is it the case that the industrial working class, by emancipating itself, will emancipate all the other oppressed and exploited classes. It is also true that these other classes will never be able to achieve emancipation unless they ally themselves closely with the industrial working class and maintain this alliance even through the harshest sufferings and the cruellest trials.

The special significance of the break between communists and reformists that will take place at Livorno is this: that the revolutionary industrial working class will break with those degenerate socialist currents that have decayed into State parasitism. It will break from those currents that sought to exploit the North's dominance over the

South to create proletarian aristocracies; those currents that have erected a further, co-operative system of protectionism alongside the bourgeois protectionist system of tariffs (which is the legal expression of the predominance of industrial and financial capitalism over the other productive forces of the nation), thinking that they could emancipate the working class at the expense of the majority of the working people of Italy.

The reformists point to the 'exemplary' socialism of Reggio Emilia: they would have us believe that the whole of Italy and the world can become one great Reggio Emilia. The revolutionary working class repudiates any such spurious form of socialism: the emancipation of the proletariat cannot come about through privileges won for a proletarian aristocracy by parliamentary compromise and ministerial blackmail. The emancipation of the workers can only come about through an alliance between the industrial workers of the North and the impoverished peasants of the South, with the aim of overthrowing the bourgeois State to found a workers' and peasants' State and to build a new apparatus of industrial production which will serve the needs of agriculture, which will industrialize Italy's backward agriculture and thus raise the national standard of living to the benefit of the working masses.

The Italian workers' revolution and the participation of the Italian working population in world affairs can only come about in the context of a world revolution. The seeds of a global workers' government already exist, in the Executive Committee of the Communist International, which emerged at the Second Congress. At Livorno, the vanguard of the Italian working class, the communist fraction of the Socialist Party, will underline the fact that disciplined loyalty to the first world government of the working class is necessary and indispensable: indeed, it will ensure that this question has first place on the agenda at the congress. The Italian working class accepts a maximum of discipline, because it wants to see the working class of all other nations accept and observe the maximum of discipline.

The Italian working class knows that it can emancipate neither itself nor the other classes that are being oppressed and exploited by capitalism, unless there exists a system of revolutionary forces throughout the world, collaborating to the same end. The Italian working class is prepared to help the other national working classes in their efforts towards liberation, but it would also like some guarantee that these other classes will help it in return. This guarantee can only come through the existence of a powerfully centralized international power, that enjoys the full and sincere confidence of all its members and is in a position to mobilize its forces with the same speed and precision with which the world power of capitalism can mobilize its forces, on its own account and in the interests of the bourgeoisie.

It should be obvious, then, that the issues that are currently tormenting the Socialist Party and that will be decided at the Congress of Livorno are not simply internal party questions or conflicts between individuals. What is going to be discussed at Livorno is the destiny of the working people of Italy. A new era in the history of the Italian people will be opening there.

L'Ordine Nuovo, 13 January 1921

Socialists and Fascists

The political position of Fascism is determined by the following basic circumstances:

(1) In the six months of their militant activity, the Fascists have amassed an extremely heavy baggage of criminal acts, which will only remain unpunished as long as the Fascist organization is strong and feared.

(2) The Fascists have only been able to carry on their activities because tens of thousands of functionaries of the State, especially in the public security forces (police, royal guards, carabinieri) and in the magistrature, have become their moral and material accomplices. These functionaries know that their impunity and their careers are closely bound up with the fortunes of the Fascist organization and so they have every interest in supporting Fascism in its every attempt to consolidate its political position.

(3) The Fascists possess sufficient stocks of arms and ammunition, spread over the whole national territory, to create an army of at least half a million men.

(4) The Fascists have organized a hierarchical system on a military model, which finds its natural, organic apex in the general staff.

It is quite natural and only to be expected that the Fascists do not want to go to prison and that instead they will use all their might, all the might at their disposal, to escape punishment and to achieve the ultimate end of every political movement: to hold political power.

What do the socialists and the leaders of the Confederation intend to do to prevent the Italian people from being subjected to the tyranny of the general staff, the great landowners and the bankers? Have they decided on a plan? Do they have a programme? It does not look like it. Could it be that the socialists and the leaders of the Confederation have decided on some 'clandestine' plan? But this would be ineffective, because only an insurrection of the great masses can defeat a reactionary *coup de force*, and mass insurrections, while they do need clandestine preparation, also need legal, open propaganda, to provide a lead, to point people in the right direction and prepare them mentally.

The socialists have never seriously faced up to the possibility of a *coup d'état*, or asked themselves what provisions they should make for defending themselves and going over to the offensive. Following their usual habit of mindlessly chewing over their collection of little pseudo-Marxist formulae, the socialists reject the idea of a 'voluntarist' revolution, 'believing in miracles', etc. But if the proletarian uprising were to be *forced* on the masses by the will of the reactionaries, who have no such 'Marxist' scruples, how should the Socialist Party behave then? Would it concede victory to the forces of reaction, without putting up any resistance? And if resistance was successful, if the armed proletariat in revolt succeeded in defeating the reactionary forces, what message would the Party give it then: to hand over its arms or to press on with its struggle to the end?

We believe that these questions, at the present moment, are anything but academic and abstract. It may be, of course, that the Fascists – who are Italians after all and have all the indecisiveness and weakness of character of the Italian petite bourgeoisie – will imitate the tactic adopted by the socialists in the occupation of the factories; that they will draw back and abandon those of their followers who have committed or abetted crimes to the punitive justice of a government committed to restoring legality. This may be what will happen: but it is bad tactics to put one's faith in the errors of one's enemies and to imagine those enemies as being incapable and inept. Anyone who has strength uses it. Anyone who risks being sent to prison will go through hell and high water to cling on to his freedom. A Fascist *coup d'état*, which is to say a *coup d'état* by the Fascist general staff, the great landowners and the bankers, is the menacing spectre that has loomed over this legislature from the start. The Communist Party has its line: to launch the slogan of insurrection and lead the armed populace to freedom – a freedom guaranteed by the workers' State. What is the slogan of the Socialist Party? How can the masses retain any trust in this party, whose only political activity has been reduced to a low moan and which is only really interested in the 'magnificent' speeches its deputies make in Parliament?

L'Ordine Nuovo, 11 June 1921

Why the Bourgeoisie Can No Longer Govern the Country

The more the task of running the productive forces slips out of the control of the capitalist leaders, the more the hopes of the bourgeois classes slide off into the domain of pure faith, of the indefinable and the supernatural.

Now that it has been given to understand that the revolution has become impossible, public opinion is awaiting some kind of divine revelation. It is waiting for the 'Unknown Leader' to come along and solve the riddle and kill the sphinx. But what can this 'Unknown Leader' do? What real forces can he base his government on – forces with a real importance in the economic life of production? The 'Unknown Leader' might succeed in winning over a majority in parliament and gaining parliamentary support for his government initiatives. But, outside the Chamber, who is going to put the concrete projects arising from these initiatives into *practice*? What class will take on itself to modify the miserable reality this country has plummeted into?

This is the insoluble problem that is facing all capitalist countries. This is the *raison d'être* of the crisis in government and authority that is slowly snaking through the whole of Central and Western Europe and ruining the whole world.

The parliamentary political parties are rooted essentially in the various stratifications of the lower and middle bourgeoisie – a class which, even though it still has a numerical importance and a demo-cratic importance, no longer has an essential role in production.

Turati's orders may reach the heads of the agrarian workers' leagues, the administrative counsellors of co-operative institutions, the foremen in the workshops. But they do not reach down to the working masses: they do not result in a single additional hoeful of earth being tilled in the field, or accelerate the rhythm of production, or set industrial workforces thrilling with the pleasure of creation.

Mussolini's orders can induce a band of Fascists to jump into a lorry and go and blow up a Camera del Lavoro headquarters, or to go to a fruit and vegetable market and impose price cuts. But they will not convince the peasants in a league that has gone over to Fascism to improve a field, or drain a marsh; they will not persuade a single market-gardener to graft a new plant and they will not prevent small landowners from feeding their fruit to their animals rather than taking it into the cities and exposing themselves to Fascist bullying.

Tovini's orders can induce parish priests across Italy to repeat from thousands and thousands of pulpits the words of the 'Unknown Leader' heading the government about peace, labour, harmony, pro-duction. But the crowds coming out of the churches will go back to their everyday lives – just as grasping as before, just as selfish, just as eager to get rich at the expense of their fellow-men.

Certainly heads of agrarian workers' leagues, co-operative counsel-lors, foremen, priests and Fascist leaders, all of whom do have a certain measure of popular influence, can succeed, during the elec-tion period, in ensuring victory at the polls for the friends of Turati, Mussolini and Tovini. They can convince or constrain vast masses of workers, peasants and white-collar workers to give their vote to these friends of Turati, Mussolini and Tovini. But in the sphere of production, in the activity that gets trains and ships and waggons moving, that gets industrial products made, all these people are worthless – they have no power to rule and no powers of persuasion.

These people, who are currently in command politically, are not and never will be in charge economically. They cannot bring unity: they are condemned to tear each other apart, plot against one another, mistrust one another. They speak but do not put their words into practice; they command and no-one obeys them; they impose their commands and finish up destroying to avenge themselves on a reality that refuses to obey them. This is the crisis in government and authority that is wrecking the whole capitalist world. The age of the Caesars is coming to an end in the domain of production: the masses are no longer content to work away passively, they are tired of treading the roads of the earth for a fistful of salt in defence of the Holy Roman Empire of capitalism. They want to have a home of their own, a family of their own: they want to build a heredity that will guarantee life and liberty for their children. The capitalist Holy Roman Empire is falling apart: the centurions are clamouring to take the place of Caesar. We are still waiting for the new forces to emerge which will establish a new order and give the masses the power to govern themselves, which will infuse society with a new faith in labour and a new joy in the creation of wealth. The irony of the centurions posing as Emperors is chastened by this implacable reality: the impossibility of governing, the uselessness of any kind of striving for change within the present social set-up, the decay of the political capacities of a class that has been forced to take refuge within the realm of the unknowable and the supernatural, to place all its hopes of salvation in the advent of a thaumaturgical 'Unknown Leader'.

L'Ordine Nuovo, 2 July 1921

La Stampa and the Fascists

La Stampa chose to speak out yesterday 'to open the eyes of those whose senseless facilitation of the violence of others has earned them the primary responsibility for the creation of an atmosphere that favours events like those we deplore today'. The question to put to *La Stampa* is: 'Who was at the head of the Italian State when Fascism was being organized on a grand scale and we were seeing the first punitive expeditions and the first shameless flaunting of guns, bombs and knives? Who was at the head of the Italian State when the Fascists began their violent seizure of the socialist municipal administrations? Who was at the head of the Italian State when the Fascist newspapers were publishing – openly and with impunity – their first death-sentences, and the first announcements of their planned arson and lootings and persecutions?' At the head of the Italian State at that time was Giovanni Giolitti, the statesman the *Stampa* was championing, the man who was supposed to be restoring Italy, politically, economically and morally. Giovanni Giolitti allowed the series of punitive expeditions to multiply, he allowed the Fascists to build up deposits of arms and munitions (just think that, in Turin itself, one Sunday, in a street near the Porta Nuova station, passers-by could see Fascists calmly and peaceably unloading guns and hand-grenades from a lorry). He allowed arson, he allowed looting, he allowed kidnappings, he allowed beatings, he allowed threats; he allowed the Fascists to do precisely what suited them best; he allowed them to start thinking they could get away with anything; he allowed things to get to a point where it seemed quite natural and spontaneous for the Fascists to take it on themselves to invade Sarzana,[1] ignoring the injunctions of the public forces of order. It is Giovanni Giolitti who bears the main responsibility for the crimes committed by Fascism; in fact, he is guilty of high treason for having allowed the laws of the State to be trodden underfoot with complete impunity, whole populations to be terrorized, massacred and tortured by armed gangs and private property to be destroyed by sacking and arson. And *La Stampa* needn't try coming out with stories about Bolshevik acts of violence and other rabble-rousing nonsense of the kind: in 1920, 2,500 'Bolsheviks' were killed in the streets and the *piazze* by the public forces of order entrusted with combating their 'acts of violence' and gunning them down for their 'acts of violence'. There has never been any impunity or tolerance for Bolshevik violence: crowds have been mown down in vast numbers; revolutionaries implacably arrested and condemned. And *La Stampa* needn't try bringing up the occupation of the factories, either: the factory occupations were a spontaneous mass movement and as such constrained the government to relative neutrality. Fascism developed gradually, gathering speed as it became more and more confident of enjoying juridical impunity and journalistic acclaim. Fascism is the spiritual offspring of Giovanni Giolitti: it is the purest and most sincere form of Giolittism.

And *La Stampa* – when did *La Stampa* ever speak out against the spread of Fascism? All you have to do is remember the epic-cum-lyric description *La Stampa* gave of the great Fascist exploit of the attack on the Camera del Lavoro. *La Stampa* published an interview with one of the heroes of the day, puffing up the heroism of Maramotti in language worthy of a cheap novel – Maramotti, who died after breaking into a private house, setting fire to it and attempting to kill the legitimate inhabitants.[2] And we can all remember the other cheap novel *La Stampa* dreamt up over the killing of the Fascist Campiglio, just as we can all remember the grim story with which it regaled the public after the killing of Sonzini and Scimula. How many workers

---

[1] At Sarzana an armed force of 600 Fascists sought to free ten of their companions jailed for violent crimes. For the first time they were opposed by the authorities; a force of eleven carabinieri fired on them, killing three of their number and successfully dispersing the crowd.
[2] Maramotti was a Fascist who died while burning down the Turin Camera del Lavoro.

have been murdered as a result of the morbid excitement stirred up by these fictions, which the *Stampa* writers have concocted with such cool, Jesuitical calculation?

And *La Stampa* has not changed. It still supports the Fascists, even now. Just read *La Stampa*'s report of Mussolini's threatening speech in Parliament. *La Stefani* has printed some of this speech:

> [Mussolini] observes that the deplorable system of verbal contumelies must be avoided at all costs and, above all, that it should no longer be thought that the changing attitudes of the government were capable of bowing the *political and military forces of Fascism.*

No-one could miss and no-one did miss the importance and the gravity of Mussolini's threat. The *Momento*, the paper of the Partito Popolare, which has a whole string of ministers and under-secretaries in the Bonomi cabinet; the *Momento*, which is at least a semi-official paper and certainly not one to throw words around lightly at a moment of such upheaval, when passions are running so high – the *Momento* thought it necessary to make this kind of explicit comment on Mussolini's very clear threat:

> The Honourable Mussolini expressed his regret that the Honourable Turati should have stated at a certain point in his interesting speech that the Fascists are speaking a different language from the other parts of the House. But, in all truth, when someone starts talking with such breathtaking audacity about there being 'political and military forces' at some faction's disposal, then it is clear that that faction is making itself out to be a State within the State – or rather, outside the State. So how, then, can there be any possibility of an understanding? But the Honourable Mussolini's declaration raises a question which must be of concern to the government in general and the minister of war in particular. *Where are these 'forces' the leader of the Fascists is referring to being recruited? Are they being recruited from the ranks of the regular armed forces? One only has to put the problem in these terms to realize its immense import and the need to resolve it without delay.* The army belongs to the nation and cannot be the instrument of a political party. *If there are men in uniform who do not feel inclined to serve the Fatherland and its legitimate government, then they should be instantly expelled from the army.*

Now then, *La Stampa* completely suppressed the Honourable

Mussolini's threatening expression. In *La Stampa*, 'the political and military forces of Fascism' become simply 'the forces of Fascism'.

The Honourable Mussolini's speech has been expurgated. *La Stampa*'s readers must be kept in ignorance of the explicit threat made by the official head of the Fascist movement in the State government. They must not be allowed to form an idea of the gravity of the situation in Italy as it has been created by the Honourable Giolitti, the restorer of political order, economic order, moral order. This tactic of *La Stampa*'s is a confirmation of the Honourable Giolitti's connivance with Fascism. Thousands and thousands of proletarian lives have been cut short on the orders of these political and journalistic brigands. Because when a government permits a crime to take place, it becomes the instigator of that crime and when a paper like *La Stampa* writes in the way it has been writing, it becomes a genuine threat to public safety, an incitement to atrocities and crimes.

L'Ordine Nuovo, 24 July 1921

Moral Problems and the Class Struggle

The peace treaty between Fascists and Socialists has been signed by the General Confederation of Labour as well.[1] This action on the part of the supreme organ of the trade-union movement is perfectly in keeping with the strategy the Italian labour leaders[2] have been following for years, in pursuit of their political ideal of a 'democratic' State based on the principles of parliamentary representation by class and function and the concentration of all economic activities in the State–union bureaucracy. The milestones along the way have been their participation in the industrial mobilization during the war, their adhesion to the Grand Commission,[3] their proposals for a constituent assembly in the immediate post-war period, their plans for a Labour Parliament and the transformation of the Senate by professional representation, their downgrading of the Camere del Lavoro and the labourite centralism in the secretariat of the Confederation, the transformation of the trade unions on the model of the *gilde*, State–union control of industry, the decision to remain in the Amsterdam International and the consequent collaboration with the International Labour

---

[1] On 3 August 1921, the PSI parliamentary group signed a '*patto di pacificazione*' (Pacification Pact) with Fascist deputies to end all violence between their respective followers. The pact proved abortive as Fascist raids continued unabated.

[2] [Translator's note] The term 'labour leaders' is in English in the original.

[3] The *Commissionissima*, as it was known, was convened in August 1918 to study the immediate needs of the Party following the War.

Office of the League of Nations, etc., etc. The peace accord entered into with the official intervention of the State, though it is a sacrifice – maybe even a painful one – for the few maximalists in the Socialist Party, is a victory for the labourites who lead the Confederation and pull all the strings in this Barnum's side-show.

The Italian Socialist Party, which has never been able to purge itself of its original sin – its democratic, parliamentary, petit bourgeois character – has never presented much of a real threat to our ruling classes. With the war and the Russian Revolution, the class struggle everywhere in Europe has taken on the ferocious character of an all-out effort to overthrow bourgeois power and establish a proletarian dictatorship. This drastic situation had exactly the effect that the men of good-will would have wanted to avoid. Well-meaning muddling became ever more impotent in the face of historical destiny.

The result has been a schism in world socialism. In Italy, since that time, we have seen existing differences of opinion growing ever more bitter, resulting in some extremely heated debates on the relations between the labourite-dominated unions and the Socialist Party, and resulting as well in the communists leaving the Socialist Party. The schism marked the political demise of 'maximalism' and resulted in the PSI coming under the thumb of the men of the Confederation. The mask of revolution was kept up for purposes of pure demagoguery.

These events are predictable within the development of the class struggle, which tends to result in a polarization between collaborationist labourism and the revolutionary, class party, the communist party.

The difference of opinion between revolutionaries and reformists over the role of the unions was at root a disagreement between the trade-union bureaucracy – which arrogated to itself all the political functions of worker organization – and the organized masses. This explains why Fascism should have developed along essentially anti-union lines – even while its parliamentary leaders were proclaiming their respect for the workers' organizations, to please the parliamentary leaders of socialism (with whom they have now made their peace, as though they had never been at odds with them). The bastions of reformist syndicalism have fallen one after the other at the first breath of a white reaction. Camere del Lavoro have been burnt down by the score, organizations dissolved or prevented from functioning, leaders arrested or exiled – sometimes even killed – and major achievements trampled underfoot; but the tactics of the reformists have not changed. They have continued to regard the State as the only means of restoring normality to union action by force of law; to regard it, what is more, as the only social reality. And so it is, today, that the reformist leaders of the General Confederation of Labour have not felt the need to make even the most summary examination of their conscience before underwriting the peace treaty with the Fascists.

On the contrary, the presence of representatives of the State was actually requested by them and, as always, docilely accepted by the maximalists. The labourites of the General Confederation of Labour have signed the peace treaty in the knowledge that, by doing so, they are performing an act of collaboration, an anti-class, counter-revolutionary act – contributing to the restoration of the authority of the law and the State and bringing the day closer when they can get their hands on 'power', by liquidating the last remains of the intransigent maximalism that is still blocking their way.

Avanti!, commenting on the 'pact' of Rome has described it as a straightforward 'truce', adopted for tactical reasons and to be regarded in the same light as an act of war; because 'there can be no cessation of the class struggle', but simply changes in the form of the struggle, dictated by circumstances. But *Avanti!* is the organ of maximalism – that is, the stage of the Barnum's side-show – whereas for a more accurate view of events, it is much more useful to understand the thinking of those pulling the strings.

Commenting on the treaty in *Battaglie sindacali*, the organ of the General Confederation of Labour, Gino Baldesi says exactly the opposite of what *Avanti!* said:

> It is not like the peace negotiated between two warring armies. The 'pact' of Rome is a 'moral' pact, which aims to sweep the life of society clean of all those corrupting elements which had infiltrated it and were threatening our very existence.

The union leaders are not even worried, as *Avanti!* is, about whether the treaty will be put into effect or not:

> Whether the followers, associates, and supporters of the signatories obey them or not is of secondary importance. Indeed, if we had to judge by the agendas approved by the Fascists in the regions worst affected, we would be saddened by how timid the

leaders are about opposing their good will to the very determined contrary will of their followers.

The labourites always have their answer: the State. If the treaty is not put into practice, they will make sure that it is, by going directly to the government if necessary. '*The laws exist and they must apply to everyone. Anyone who does not respect the treaty will have to answer to the law.*'

So, while *Avanti!* considers the treaty as a class act, Stenterello,[4] who knows the score, sees it as having no practical value other than as a condemnation of violence and a valorization of the law, of the State, of the 'healthy' principle of collaboration.

Baldesi is thinking about 'moral problems'. For Stenterello, Fascism is a moral problem. G. M. Serrati should send him some of his twopenny pamphlets of propaganda for beginners, to teach him that in the class struggle the only 'moral' problem is the victory of the proletariat.

L'Ordine Nuovo, 7 August 1921

---

[4] Stenterello is a traditional mask-character in Italian comic theatre: tall and thin, at once clumsy and fatuous. In an earlier article in *Avanti!* (10 March 1917), Gramsci argued that 'Stenterello is the prototype of the Italian bourgeoisie: gossipy, vain, empty . . .'

The Two Fascisms

The crisis of Fascism, on whose origins and causes so much is being written at the moment, can be easily explained if we look seriously at the actual development of the Fascist movement.

The *Fasci di combattimento* came into existence in the immediate post-war period and had the same petit bourgeois character as the various war-veterans' associations that emerged in that period. Because of their determined opposition to the socialist movement – partly an inheritance of the conflicts between the Socialist Party and the interventionist associations during the War – the *Fasci* won the support of the capitalists and the authorities. The fact that their emergence coincided with a need on the part of the landowners to form a white guard to combat the growing power of the workers' organizations meant that the system of armed bands created and armed by the big landowners could adopt this same name of *Fasci*. And, as these bands developed, the name became associated with *their* identity as a white guard of capitalism pitted against the class organs of the proletariat.

Fascism has never shaken off this original flaw in its make-up. Until now, the fervour of the armed offensive prevented any exacerbation of the rift between the urban, petit bourgeois nuclei, which are predominantly parliamentary and collaborationist, and the rural ones, formed by large and medium-sized landowners and the farmers themselves, which are principally concerned with the struggle against the peasants and peasants' organizations, resolutely anti-trade union and reactionary in character, and more willing to put their trust in direct armed action than the authority of the State and the efficacy of parliamentarism.

Fascism had its greatest development in the agricultural regions (Emilia, Tuscany, the Veneto, Umbria), achieving unconditional power in these regions through the financial support of the capitalists and the protection of the civil and military authorities of the State. But if, on the one hand, its ruthless offensive against the class organs of the proletariat has been of benefit to the capitalists – who, in the course of one year, saw the whole apparatus of struggle of the socialist trade unions fall apart and become redundant – it is nevertheless undeniable that the worsening violence has ended up by creating a widespread hostility to Fascism among the middle and popular strata of society. The Sarzana, Treviso, Viterbo and Roccastrada episodes, deeply shook the urban Fascist nuclei personified by Mussolini and they began to see a danger in the exclusively negative tactics pursued by the *Fasci* in rural areas.[1] On the other hand, however, these tactics had already started bearing some excellent fruit, since they had dragged the Socialist Party into a position of flexibility and willingness to collaborate in the country and in Parliament.

From this moment, the latent rift begins to reveal itself in all its true seriousness. The urban, collaborationist nuclei see themselves as having achieved the objective they had set themselves, of shifting the Socialist Party from its position of class intransigence, and they are eager to get their victory down in writing in the pacification pact. The agrarian capitalists, in contrast, cannot renounce the only tactic which ensures them a free hand in exploiting the peasant classes, without any trouble from strikes and organizations. The whole polemic that is stirring up the Fascist camp, between supporters and opponents of pacification, comes down to this basic disagreement, whose origins must be sought in the very origins of the Fascist movement.

The claims of the Italian socialists – that it was they who provoked the split in the Fascist movement with their skilful policy of com-

---

[1] The reference here is to a series of Fascist outrages in working-class areas against socialist and communist organizations during July 1921, which had the effect of losing them some public support.

promise – are nothing other than a further proof of their demagogy. In reality, the Fascist crisis is nothing new, it has always existed. Once the contingent factors which were holding the anti-proletarian ranks together ceased to operate, it was inevitable that the rifts in the party would emerge more clearly. The crisis, then, has done nothing more than clarify a pre-existing *de facto* situation.

Fascism will get out of the situation by splitting in two. The parliamentary section of the party, headed by Mussolini, which draws on the support of the middle classes (white-collar workers, small shopkeepers and small businessmen), will attempt to organize its supporters politically, leaning necessarily in the direction of collaboration with the socialists and *popolari*. The intransigent section of the party, which represents the need for the direct, armed defence of capitalist agrarian interests, will continue with its characteristic anti-proletarian activity. For this latter section – the most important where the working class is concerned – the 'truce agreement' which the socialists are priding themselves on as a victory will be utterly without value. The only real result of the 'crisis' will be the departure from the *Fasci* of a faction of petit bourgeois supporters who have vainly attempted to justify Fascism with a general political 'party' programme.

But Fascism, true Fascism, as the peasants and workers of Emilia, Tuscany, the Veneto, know it through the painful experience of the past two years of white terror – Fascism will continue, though it may have to change its name.

The task of the revolutionary workers and peasants is to take advantage of the period of relative calm brought about by the internal disputes among Fascist bands to infuse the oppressed and defenceless masses with a clear consciousness of the real situation in the class struggle and the means that are needed to defeat the arrogant reactionary movement of capitalism.

L'Ordine Nuovo, 25 August 1921

Legality

How far do the boundaries of legality extend? When can we say that these boundaries are no longer being respected? Certainly, it is not easy to fix any kind of boundaries, given the extremely elastic character of the concept of legality. For any government, everything that occurs in the domain of anti-government activity transgresses the boundaries of legality. And yet it can be argued that legality is determined by the interests of the class which holds power in any society. In capitalist society, legality is represented by the interests of the bourgeois class. When an action in any way affects private property and the profits that derive from it, then that action immediately comes to be considered illegal. This is what happens in substance. Where matters of form are concerned, legality presents itself in a rather different light. Since the bourgeoisie, on achieving power, conceded an equal right to vote to both bosses and employees, legality has, to all appearances, come to seem like a collection of norms freely recognized by all sections of the community. Now, some people have confused the substance of legality with the form and this has given rise to the liberal-democratic ideology. The bourgeois State is the liberal State par excellence. In it, everyone can express his opinion freely by means of his vote. That is what formal legality in the bourgeois State really comes down to: the exercise of the right to vote. Obtaining the vote for the popular masses appeared in the eyes of the ingenuous ideologues of liberal democracy as the decisive conquest in the social progress of humanity. It was never recognized that there were two sides to legality: an inner, substantive one and an outward, purely formal one.

By confusing these two faces of legality, the ideologues of liberal democracy have managed to pull the wool over the eyes of the popular masses for a certain period of time, convincing them that the right to vote would eventually result in their liberation from all the chains that bound them. Unfortunately, the short-sighted champions of liberal democracy were not the only ones to fall for this illusion. Many people who considered themselves and still consider themselves Marxists have believed that the emancipation of the proletarian class would come about through the sovereign exercise of that great conquest, universal suffrage. Some rash souls even used the name of Engels to justify this belief of theirs. But reality has destroyed all these illusions. Reality has shown quite incontrovertibly that there is only one true face to legality and that legality exists only within the boundaries set by the interests of the ruling class – which means, in capitalist society, the interests of the owning class. In fact, the experiences we have had of this, in recent times in particular, contain many important lessons.

The working class, by exercising its right to vote, had won control over a great number of communes and provinces. The organizations that represented it had achieved an impressive growth in membership and had succeeded in forcing through agreements that were advantageous for the workers. But as soon as the vote and the right to organize became means of attack against the bosses, this latter dropped any pretence at formal legality and started obeying nothing but its true law – the law of its own interest, the law of its conservation. The communes were violently stripped away from the working class; working-class organizations were dissolved by the use of armed force; the industrial working class and the peasantry were ousted from their positions, having become too much of a threat to the existence of private property. And thus we saw the birth of Fascism, which grew and established itself as a movement by making illegality into the only thing that was legal. No organizations, except the Fascist organization; no right to vote, except the right to vote for the agrarian and industrial representatives of Fascism. This is the kind of legality that the bourgeoisie is prepared to recognize when it is constrained to renounce the other, formal kind. The experience of these recent times, then, is not without lessons for those who used to believe quite genuinely in the efficacy of the legal guarantees offered by the bourgeois liberal State.

There comes a point in history when the bourgeoisie is constrained to repudiate what it has itself created. This point has arrived in Italy. To refuse to learn the lessons of this experience is either the ultimate in ingenuousness, something which deserves the severest sanctions; or else bad faith, something which should be punished without mercy. In fact, this seems to be the case with those socialist organizers who are now expressing their amazement that, for example, the Right Honourable Beneduce is not succeeding in ensuring that labour contracts are respected. For people who still like to think of themselves as players on the field of class struggle, this is incredible. Is it right that an organizer who claims not to have renounced the principles of class struggle, should be asking a minister what resources he has at his disposal to prevent the bosses from reneging on labour agreements? This kind of request can only engender doubts and uncertainties in the working class. It is only natural that the minister of employment should have no resources beyond being an instrument in the hands of agrarians and industrialists. While socialist organizers cannot come up with anything better than asking the employment minister to make the bosses respect agreements, the working class will have to continue to put up with every kind of infringement of its rights, without even being able to organize a defence for itself.

The industrialists are resigning from the arbitration committees. This too is a logical consequence of the situation. The industrialists now want to claw back their power in its entirety. They no longer want to accept this kind of limitation on their free will. They accepted the arbitration committees just as long as the revolutionary impetus of the masses was threatening their existence. But now that the situation seems favourable for any kind of reactionary tactic, the bosses cannot even be bothered to maintain the occasional scruple. They have openly set themselves on the path to the complete and despotic recovery of their power over the working masses. And what do the socialist organizers come up with, when confronted with these tendencies on the part of the ruling class? All the organizers are capable of doing is publicly denouncing the bosses' failure to respect agreements and the impotence of the employment minister. But in the meantime the working class is suffering all the ill effects of both the attitude of the bosses and the wavering of its own leadership. While the organizers are putting their questions to the minister of employment, more and more people are going hungry, hardship is increasing, and the forces of reaction are gaining strength. Those socialist organizers who during the war used to go and shake the bloody hands of generals in the mobilization committees are the same people who are demanding the help and intervention of employment ministers. Then, they became accomplices of the murderers who had caused the war, reining in the revolutionary impetus of the masses with the decisions of the arbitration committees. Now, they are leaving the working class defenceless, while the bosses are everywhere ignoring agreements and transgressing them at will.

Only the proposal of the Communist Union Committee offers a way of organizing a workers' defence against the capitalist assault. Only by uniting all the forces of the working class into a tightly organized army can we put up any serious opposition to the capitalists, who, acting on their orders, are aiming to reduce the whole of the working class to servitude. But where our respected socialist organizers are concerned, even just to demand respect for the agreements is now considered too revolutionary.

L'Ordine Nuovo, 28 August 1921

April and September 1920

With the anniversary of the occupation of the factories, a stale old piece of gossip has come back into circulation concerning the Turin communists who, according to some, are those chiefly responsible for the fact that the movement did not extend any further. The Honourable Buozzi alluded to this responsibility in his recent speech to the internal commissions of the Milanese metal-workers; another allusion is contained in a report from Turin in the Anarchist paper *Umanità nova*. The 'rumour' even found its way across the borders and Jacques Mesnil picked it up in an article on the Italian socialist movement published in Charles Rappaport's *Revue communiste*.

Let us put things straight once and for all. When, in September 1920, the functionaries of the Confederation found themselves faced with the mighty revolutionary uprising provoked by the initiative of the Central Committee of Fiom, they plunged desperately into the task of patching things up and looking for someone to saddle with the responsibility for their own blindness and lack of foresight, their own unreadiness, their own ineptitude. They had launched hundreds of thousands of workers on to the battlefield of illegality and armed insurrection, while forgetting one very simple thing: the need to procure weapons for the workers and to prepare the working class to withstand a bloody struggle. In Milan, where the headquarters of the movement were, they had not even bothered to make an inventory and a proper collection of the weapons and ammunition available in the factories. In Lecco, seven days after the occupation, the police were still able to confiscate 60,000 small bombs which had been left in the warehouses of some factory – 60,000 bombs which would have provided quite a respectable weaponry for the Milanese workers.

All of a sudden, the union functionaries came out in favour of the workers' offensive: indeed, they would have liked the offensive to start in Turin and for Turin to head the insurrection movement. But September 1920 was too close to April 1920. In April 1920, the Turinese proletariat, which had been dragged into a desperate struggle by the industrialists, as a result of a particular commitment they had taken on at the conference of the Confederation of Italian Industry held in Milan on the preceding 7 March, had been completely left in the lurch by the General Confederation of Labour. The Turinese, that April, had been isolated from the rest of Italy – stigmatized to the rest of Italy as a band of anarchists, hot-heads, undisciplined maniacs. The point had even been reached, that April, where there were allegations being made about the source of the 'funds' the Turinese had available for hiring a car. How would it have been possible not to mistrust the motives of those who, in September, were asking the Turinese to give the insurrection movement a kick-start, if these were the same people who, the previous April, had used all the means and all the dirty tricks at their disposal to blacken their name? How was it possible for the Turinese not to regard this offer as a cunning trap to ensure that the Turinese revolutionary movement would be definitively crushed by the police who had concentrated an imposing apparatus of troops in Turin?

This was the real situation. The Turin communists supported the need for an extension of the movement and voted for the agenda proposed by Schiavello and Burro. But they refused – entirely justifiably – to take responsibility for the initiative themselves. It would have been possible, in Turin, within the context of a national struggle, to withstand the impetus of the government forces with a good chance of victory. But it would not have been possible to take on the responsibility for an armed struggle with no assurance that the rest of Italy would have joined in and with no assurance that the Confederation would not have played its usual trick and allowed all the military forces of State power to converge on Turin, as it had in April. On this occasion as on others, the Turin communists acted wisely and showed themselves to be capable of cool reasoning and quite immune from that rash spirit of adventure they were accused of by the grand old men of opportunism and reformism. They had done their duty, they had planned things, as far as was possible, given their limited powers and the limited local resources available to them. But they refused to let themselves be trapped by the exponents of confederal mandarinism, who had launched the working masses on to the battle-field of armed struggle and forgotten to provide them with arms – the same people who had stupidly allowed 60,000 bombs to be con-fiscated in Lecco and who were then asking, in their confusion and hysteria and mad terror, for 'a few machine-guns with which to arm Milan'.

L'Ordine Nuovo, 7 September 1921

The Mainstay of the State

In the good old days, when people still remembered the Risorgimento and the great achievement of the Constitution still meant something to the great mass of the Italian population, an interesting polemic took place between the liberals and the republicans on the nature and significance of the oath of allegiance to the king that all deputies have to take in Parliament. This was what the liberals said: if deputies refuse to take this oath, if they succeed in getting it abolished, then the State itself will lose the main support it rests on. The Constitution is a reciprocal pact of allegiance between the people and the sovereign. If the people, through their representatives, withdraw from their obligation of allegiance; if the people, by abolishing the oath, demand the freedom to act against the Constitution, then the sovereign, too, is legally absolved of his obligations and becomes free to organize on his own behalf and orchestrate a *coup d'état* to overthrow the Constitution.

The government represents the sovereign within the national Parliament; indeed, the government is responsible for the sovereign before the national Parliament and before the people. If the government allows the Constitution to be violated with impunity; if the government allows the formation of armed bands in the country; if the government allows private associations to build up deposits of weapons and arms; if the government allows tens of thousands of private citizens, armed and in military formation, wearing helmets and carrying guns, to march undisturbed through the whole country, invade the capital and openly flaunt their 'power', what can this mean except that the government, which is responsible for the sovereign, has broken its oath of allegiance to the Constitution? What can it mean except that a *coup d'état* is being planned by those State organs grouped round the executive power? What can it mean except that in Italy we are already living in the kind of atmosphere that will automatically produce a *coup d'état*?

The pact between the people and the sovereign has thus already been denounced by the State power which represents the latter. So, automatically, all oaths of allegiance are denounced. What links are now binding State employees to the government? What links are now binding army officers to the supreme command? The logic of events is leading the populace to divide into two camps: those in favour of and those against a reactionary *coup d'état* – or rather those in favour of a reactionary *coup d'état* and those in favour of a popular insurrection capable of putting down the reactionary *coup d'état*. The eventuality is envisaged in the Constitution itself: it recognizes the people's right to armed insurrection when the State powers are infringing the Constitution itself. And, indeed, why ever should a pact, which must necessarily be a two-sided thing, remain in force for one party if the other has infringed its terms? Why should a State employee or an officer remain faithful to a law that no longer exists? Why should he preserve State secrets and not communicate them to the revolutionary parties, if keeping these secrets means favouring the *coup d'état* – which means the abolition of the statutory laws and freedoms, even at a formal level – while giving these secrets away to the revolutionary parties means contributing to the salvation of popular liberty and keeping faith with the spirit of the oath he took?

The bourgeois State depends for its survival in great part on the work and the sacrifices of thousands of civil servants and soldiers who perform their duty, often with real passion, who have a keen sense of honour and who have taken seriously the oath they had to swear on taking up office. If this crucial nucleus of sincere and loyally devoted people did not exist, the bourgeois State would collapse in an instant, like a house of cards. It is they who are the real, the only mainstay of the State – certainly not the others, the State extortionists, prevaricators, fools and parasites. Now: who is going to profit from the *coup d'état*? The only people who will profit will be these others, the extortionists, prevaricators, fools and parasites: *coups d'état* have very often – indeed, almost always – been nothing other than the means by which the dregs of the State apparatus try to cling on to the positions they have won for themselves, to the great detriment of society. These people are quite without scruples: they care absolutely nothing for oaths or for honour; they hate workers in general and especially those who work in the same office as them and are a living reproach to their own dishonesty and parasitism.

Today, the historical situation is this: only one great social class is in a position to offer a real opposition to the attempts by the unleashed forces of reaction to smother liberty – the class of workers, the proletariat. The role of this class now is that of the liberals in the Risorgimento. This class has a party of its own: the Communist Party, which is owed the collaboration of all sincere and disinterested elements within the Italian State who want to keep faith with their role as custodians of popular liberties against all the aggressions of the dark forces of the past which will not lie down and die.

L'Ordine Nuovo, 13 November 1921

The Essence of the Crisis

The fall of Bonomi, it is said, was caused by some dark manoeuvring in the corridors of power (the only thing in the whole business that is not shrouded in darkness is the ambition of a group of political operators). There is nothing wrong with that. Where the nation is concerned, Parliament in its entirety is a dark corridor, with no way out, where even the most profound and far-reaching events and conflicts have to be dealt with in this kind of shady manner, because the people there are incapable of conceiving of an alternative way of doing things. But it is not always true that beneath this form there is no substance worthy of a more serious consideration. Is this so in the present case?

It is something we have already stressed on a number of occasions that the political events of the past few months signal a series of very substantial transformations taking place in Italy. At the root of this transformation has been an attempt to ensure the adherence to the Italian State of profound strata of the working masses of the cities and the countryside and, by doing so, to rescue the State from the crisis that is racking it. The instruments of this action have been the two characteristically 'social-democratic' parties: the Popular Party and the Socialist Party. There has, however, been a curious division of labour between the two parties. In some places and on some issues, they have been fighting one another; in others, collaborating; in still others, dividing their roles and zones of influence as appropriate.

But, overall, the *popolari* and Socialists have been and are carrying out a common task: that of preparing the ground for the future Italian social-democratic State. The means that both groups have been employing to reach their end are demagoguery and lying, hypocritical opportunism. This has been happening to such an extent that in some areas, especially in rural areas and in the smaller regions, there are whole strata at the lower end of the working population which no longer make a distinction between the two parties. Collaboration is already taking place and the fact that it is happening from below first, rather than its coming from above, from the ruling organs, is an index of the way in which this collaboration corresponds with a new situation which is coming about and which must be taken into consideration.

But if this is one reality, the other reality that must be reckoned with is the traditional structure of the Italian State, resulting from the dominance of a ruling class whose interests are directly opposed to those of the masses and which is prepared to use violence and deception to maintain its domination over them. The *popolari* have been faced for quite a while now with the problem of how to reach an arrangement with this ruling class; they have even succeeded in solving this problem without losing their character as a party allied with and representative of vast organized masses. Through their actions so far, both in Parliament and in the country, the *popolari* have already demonstrated what social democracy will be like: the way in which the new regime will combine all the shadiest features of our traditional corrupt political cliques with the new characteristics of the social-democratic State – unprincipled, unscrupulously populist, hypocritical, corrupt and corrupting. Bonomi, from this point of view, may be seen as a true precursor.

Before reaching this end, though, it is necessary to pass through various settling-in periods. One of these was represented by the crisis of Fascist violence. Today, even in the Fascist Party, there are obvious symptoms of the social-democratic malady. The attitude the Fascists took to the banking question will do as an example. Besides, organized violence outside the legal framework of the State is a characteristic of all the apparently 'democratic' regimes that have taken shape in the post-war period.

Another phase in this settling-in period is represented by the crises in Parliament. The leading elements in the old and new ruling clique are having to be welded together. So some men are having to be eliminated and others promoted; certain rights that have been won are having to be recognized; and the eagerness of the newcomers reined back. It is a laborious process, from which, eventually, the new caste of rulers must emerge.

Obviously, this way of considering the question leads one to deny any value to the official parliamentary distinctions, which talk about a government of the right or a government of the left or an intermediate government of 'transition'. And if this is all empty jargon, party manifestos are not of any great importance either – nor, even, are the politicians themselves. The basic tenets that everyone, more or less, agreed on are not difficult to detect. What matters most is not what these tenets were, but rather the general process by which the Italian State, without changing its essential nature, is shifting its ground in the hope of strengthening itself and enjoying a new period of calm.

One novel element in all this, people say, is the attitude of the socialists. But this is not true. The socialists slot neatly into this general process, and after what we have said above about the analogy between the action of the *popolari* and that of the socialists it should not be necessary to explain this further for the moment. The only difference lies in the fact that the socialists do not have a place in the government – something which condemns them to be even more hypocritical and dishonest than the others; to have not just two, but three or four different masks with which to disguise their real face. The socialists now ask nothing more than to be able to do their bit in the common task of rebuilding and reinforcing the State. However they talk – whether they speak out shamelessly like Stenterello or reheat some old rubbish of Turati's, whether they hoist the pennon of intransigence or squawk like the parrot of *Avanti!* – every single one of their words and attitudes serves the bourgeoisie and the State, because it helps prevent the masses from getting a clear view in the deluge of events going on around them and from noticing the chains that the new preachers of liberty, reform and positive advances are preparing to clinch round their wrists.

For us, then, this is the crucial point about the present situation. It must be made clear to the masses of workers and peasants in Italy that any support they give to the demagogues of the social-democratic parties – the Socialist Party and the *Partito Popolare* – is a contribution to the reconstruction of the organism that for decades has been depriving them of freedom and well-being and condemning them to servitude, suffering and death. The struggle against social democracy, the struggle against the treacherous Socialist Party, is all part of the struggle to liberate the Italian proletariat from servitude of any form.

L'Ordine Nuovo, 5 February 1922

Letter to Trotsky on Italian Futurism

Here are the answers to the questions you put to me about the Italian Futurist movement.

Since the War, the Futurist movement in Italy has lost its distinctive features entirely. Marinetti is hardly doing anything for the movement. He has got married and he prefers to dedicate all his energies to his wife. The participants in the movement at the present moment include monarchists, communists, republicans and Fascists. A political weekly called *Il Principe* was set up recently in Milan, to put the case for, or try and put the case for, the same solution that Machiavelli advocated for sixteenth-century Italy – that is, that the struggle between the local parties which are leading the nation into chaos should be swept aside by an absolute monarch, a new Cesare Borgia, who would place himself at the head of all the warring parties. The editors are two Futurists, Bruno Corra and Enrico Settimelli. And Marinetti, who was arrested in 1920 for making a forceful speech against the king during a patriotic demonstration, is now contributing to this weekly.

The most important exponents of Futurism before the War have now become Fascists, with the exception of Giuseppe Papini, who has become a Catholic and written a *Story of Christ*. During the War, the Futurists were the most resolute supporters of 'war to the bitter end' and imperialism. Only one Futurist, Aldo Palazzeschi, was against the war. He broke with the movement and, even though he was one of the most interesting writers around, he eventually gave up writing altogether. Marinetti, who had always sung the praises of war, published a manifesto in which he showed that war was the only way the world could clean out its system. He took part in the War as captain of an armoured car battalion and his latest book, *L'alcova di acciaio* [*The Steel Bedchamber*] is an enthusiastic hymn to armoured cars in war. Marinetti has written a pamphlet, *In disparte dal comunismo* [Outside Communism], in which he develops his political doctrines – if the fantasies of this sometimes witty and always remarkable man can be termed doctrines. Before I left Italy the Turin section of the *Proletkult* had asked Marinetti to the opening of an exhibition of paintings by workers who are members of the organization, to speak on the significance of this art. Marinetti was very happy to accept the invitation; he visited the exhibition alongside the workers and then expressed his satisfaction at having realized that the workers had a far greater sensibility than the bourgeoisie to the problems of Futurism. Before the War, the Futurists were very popular among the workers. The review *Lacerba*, which had a print-run of twenty thousand copies, had a circulation which was four-fifths made up of workers. In the many Futurist art shows in the theatres of the great Italian cities, it often turned out that the workers would be defending the Futurists against upper-class or bourgeois youths, who were fighting against them.

Marinetti's Futurist group no longer exists. Marinetti's old review, *Poesia*, is now edited by a certain Mario Dessi, a man entirely lacking in any intellectual and organizational ability. In the South, especially in Sicily, there are many Futurist newsletters, which Marinetti writes for; but these little newsletters are published by students who confuse Futurism with an ignorance of Italian grammar. The strongest group among the Futurists are the painters. In Rome, there is a permanent exhibition of Futurist painting, which has been organized by a failed photographer, a certain Antonio Giulio Bragaglia, an agent for the cinema and for artists. Of the Futurist painters, the best-known is Giacomo Balla.

D'Annunzio has never officially taken up a stance on Futurism. It should be mentioned that, when it first emerged, Futurism adopted an explicitly anti-D'Annunzian character. One of Marinetti's first books was called *Les dieux s'en vont, D'Annunzio reste*. And even though, during the War, the political programmes of Marinetti and

D'Annunzio coincided on many points, the Futurists still remain anti-D'Annunzian. They scarcely took any notice of the *movimento fiumano*,[1] though later on they took part in the demonstrations.

It can be said that since the peace the Futurist movement has lost its character entirely and dissolved into various currents, which arose as a result of the War. The young intellectuals were on the whole extremely reactionary. The workers, who saw in Futurism the elements of a struggle against the old Italian culture – academic, dried-up, alien from the people – are now in the midst of an armed struggle for freedom and have little interest in the old debates. In the major industrial cities, the *Proletkult* programme, which aims to awaken workers' literary and artistic creativity, absorbs the energy of those who still have the time and the inclination to worry about this sort of thing.

Moscow, 8 September 1922

[1] In September 1919, D'Annunzio led a military expedition of some 2,000 'legionaries', made up of nationalists, anarcho-syndicalists, ex-servicemen and assorted adventurers, and occupied Fiume (Rijeka), a former Hungarian port on the Croatian coast to which the Italian government had unsuccessfully laid claim at the Versailles Peace Conference earlier in the year. There he presided over a comic-opera regime, which in many respects provided the prototype for some of the more baroque features of the Italian Fascist regime, until expelled by the Italian navy on Christmas Day, 1920.

Part Four
The Construction
of the Italian
Communist Party

Our Union Policy

In the 15 September issue of *Sindacato rosso*,[1] comrade Nicola Vecchi[2] recycles an old [*vecchia*] thesis of his: 'We must create a national class trade-union organism, which will be autonomous and independent from all the parties and temporarily independent from all the Internationals.'

What should our attitude be to such a proposal? How can we communists best direct our propaganda in order to stem any possible currents of opinion among the masses aligned with comrade Vecchi's thesis? What is our union policy in concrete terms, in the present situation: how, in other words, are we proposing to keep in contact with the great proletarian masses; to interpret their needs; to learn their desires and help them focus those desires; to assist the proletariat in its progress towards emancipation – a progress which is continuing despite all the repressions and violence of the hateful Fascist tyranny?

We are, in principle, against the creation of new unions. In all capitalist countries the trade-union movement has developed in a particular way, giving rise to the birth and development of a particular kind of large organization, which has grown out of the history, traditions, habits and ways of thought of the great majority of the prolet-

---

[1] Journal of the communist elements within the General Confederation of Labour.
[2] Exponent of the anarcho-syndicalist faction within the *Unione Sindacale*, who favoured closer links with the communists and Comintern.

arian masses. Every attempt that has been made to organize revolutionary syndicalist elements separately has failed in itself and has only
served to reinforce the hegemonic positions of the reformists within
the great trade-union organization. What benefit have the syndicalists
got from their creation of the *Unione Sindacale* in Italy? They have
only managed to exercise a very patchy and sporadic influence over
the mass of industrial workers – that is, over the most revolutionary
class of the working population. In the whole period from the assassination of Umberto I to the Libyan War, they have only won control
of the great agrarian masses of the Po Valley and Puglia; and the sole
result of this has been that these masses, which had at that time only
just entered the arena of the class struggle (that period, in fact, saw
a transformation of agrarian culture which increased the number of
farm-labourers by about fifty per cent) – these masses became distanced in their ideology from the industrial proletariat and, where
they had been anarcho-syndicalist up to the Libyan War (that is, in
the period in which the proletariat was becoming more radical), they
became reformists afterwards. In fact, from the armistice up to the
occupation of the factories, they constituted the passive infantry-mass
that the reformist leaders used to put a spoke in the wheels of the
revolutionary vanguard on every decisive occasion.

The example of America is even more typical and more telling
than that of Italy. No other organization has ever stooped to the level
of abjection and counter-revolutionary servility reached by Gompers'
organization.[3] Did this mean that American workers were abject servants of the bourgeoisie? By no means. And yet they remained
attached to the traditional organization. The IWW (revolutionary
syndicalists),[4] failed in their attempt to win over the masses controlled
by Gompers from the outside; they cut themselves off from these
masses and let themselves be massacred by the white guards. On the
other hand, the movement led by Comrade Foster, from within the
American Federation of Labor, using slogans reflecting the real, current situation and the deepest feelings of American workers, is winning over one union after another and showing up very clearly how
weak and shaky the power of Gompers' bureaucracy really is.

[3] The reformist American Federation of Labor headed by Samuel Gompers.
[4] See n. 2, p. 184.

We are, then, in principle, against the creation of new trade unions. The revolutionary elements can represent the working class as a whole, as the most highly developed point of that class's consciousness, only for as long as they remain part of the masses, sharing their mistakes, their illusions and disillusionments. If some ruling of the reformist dictators were to compel the revolutionaries to leave the General Confederation of Labour and organize themselves separately (an eventuality which obviously cannot be ruled out), then a new organization should declare itself committed to and be truly directed towards the sole goal of achieving reintegration with the movement, to restore the old unity between the class as a whole and its most conscious avant-garde.

The General Confederation of Labour, as a whole, still represents the Italian working class. But what is the current system of relations between the working class and the Confederation? To give an accurate reply to this question means, I think, looking for the real base our union activity rests on and then establishing what our role is and what our relations with the great masses are.

The General Confederation of Labour, as a union organization, has been cut down to its lowest level – a tenth, perhaps, of its numerical strength in 1920. But the reformist faction that controls the Confederation has kept its organizational cadres almost intact and has kept all its most active militants in place – intelligent, capable people who, let us admit it frankly, show themselves capable of working better, with more tenacity and perseverance than our own comrades.

The great majority – indeed, almost all – of the revolutionary elements who, over the past years, had acquired organizational and leadership capabilities and become accustomed to systematic work, have been massacred, or have emigrated or been dispersed.

The working class is like a great army suddenly deprived of all its junior officers: such an army would find it impossible to maintain discipline, structure, the spirit of struggle and a unified direction simply through the existence of a general staff. Any organization is an articulated whole, which can function properly only if there is an appropriate numerical relationship between the mass and the leaders. We do not have the cadres, the links, the services necessary to extend our influence across the great mass, to strengthen it and turn it back into an efficient instrument of revolutionary struggle. The reformists are in an incomparably better position than we are in this respect and they are exploiting the situation ably.

The factory continues to exist and it organizes its workers as a matter of course, assembling them and bringing them into contact with each other. The production process has kept up its 1919–20 level, characterized by an ever more massive role for capitalism, which results in turn in a more decisive importance for the worker. The increase in retail prices brought about by the need to keep 500,000 Fascist bullies permanently mobilized, is certainly not a very striking proof that capitalism has recovered its cutting edge in industry. The worker is, then, naturally strong within the factory, concentrated and organized within the factory. Outside the factory, in contrast, he is isolated, weak and out on a limb.

In the period before the imperialist war, the opposite situation obtained. The worker was isolated within the factory and allied with others outside it: he was pressing from the outside to win better factory legislation, to get working hours reduced and to achieve industrial freedom.

Today the proletarian factory is represented by the internal commission. The question immediately arises: why do the capitalists and Fascists, who destroyed the unions, not destroy the internal commissions as well? Why, when the unions have been losing ground, from an organizational point of view, under the pressures of the reactionary movement, has the internal commission, on the contrary, actually broadened its sphere of influence? It is a fact that in almost every Italian factory, it has come about that there is a single internal commission and that all workers – not simply the organized workers – vote in the elections for the internal commissions. The whole of the working class, then, is now organized in the internal commissions, which have definitively shaken off their strictly corporatist character.

This is, objectively, a great conquest, with extremely far-reaching implications. It serves to indicate that despite everything, despite all its pain, even while it is being ground down by the iron heel of the Fascist mercenaries, the working class – even if only at the lowest, microscopic level – is developing towards unity, towards a greater organizational homogeneity.

Why have the capitalists and the Fascists allowed this situation to come about? Why are they allowing it to continue? For capitalism and Fascism, it is necessary that the working class should be deprived of its historical function as the leader of the other oppressed classes of the population (the peasants, especially in the South and the islands, the urban and rural petite bourgeoisie). It is necessary, in other words, to destroy that system of working-class organization outside the factory that is organized on a national scale (unions and political parties), that exerts a revolutionary influence on the oppressed and deprives the government of its democratic power-base. But the capitalists, for industrial reasons, cannot wish to see every form of organization destroyed: within the factory, it is impossible to maintain discipline and keep production running smoothly without at least a minimum of constitutionality, a minimum of consensus on the part of the workers.

The most intelligent Fascists, like Mussolini, are the first to recognize that their ideology, standing as it does 'above class divisions', cannot extend beyond the sphere of that stratum of the petite bourgeoisie that has nothing to do with production and so no consciousness of social tensions. Mussolini is convinced that the working class will never lose its revolutionary consciousness and he considers it necessary to allow a minimum of organization. To keep trade-union organizations within strict limits, by the exercise of terror, is a way of ensuring that the reformists get control of the Confederation. It suits the Fascists that the Confederation should exist in an embryonic form, together with a scattered system of internal commissions, so that the reformists come to control and represent the whole of the working class.

This is the situation in Italy. This is the system of relations that exists today in Italy between the proletarian class and the organizations. The tactical implications for us are clear:

(1) We should work in the factory to create revolutionary groups which can gain control of the internal commissions and press them into extending their sphere of action ever further.

(2) We should work to forge links between the factories and to get things moving in a new direction, corresponding to the natural line of development of the factory organizations, from the internal commission to the Factory Council.

It is only in this way that we can keep our feet on the ground and keep in close contact with the great masses. It is only in this way, by keeping in the real world of hard work, in the white-hot crucible of working-class life, that we can succeed in rebuilding our organizational cadres and see new, able and conscious elements begin to emerge from the great masses, full of revolutionary ardour because conscious of their own value and their incontrovertible importance within the world of production.

Lo Stato operaio, 18 October 1923

Against Pessimism

There can be no better way of commemorating the fifth anniversary of the Communist International, the great world association of which we Italian revolutionaries feel ourselves more than ever to be an active and integral part, than by examining our consciousness – examining the very little we have done already and the immense task that lies ahead of us. This will be a way of clarifying our situation and, especially, of dispersing the dark, heavy clouds of pessimism which now loom over even the most able and responsible militants and which represent a great danger – perhaps the most serious danger we are facing at the moment – because of the political passivity, intellectual torpor and scepticism about the future such pessimism induces.

This pessimism is closely linked to the general situation in our country; the situation explains it, but does not justify it, of course. What difference would there be between us and the Socialist Party, between our will and that party's tradition, if we too were only capable of working and being actively optimistic in periods when everything is coming up roses, when the situation is favourable, when the working masses are moving forward spontaneously, through an irresistible impulse, and the proletarian parties can settle back into the brilliant position of La Fontaine's fly which thinks it is pushing the coach?[1] What difference would there be between us and the Socialist

---

[1] See n. 1, p. 61.

Party if we too abandoned ourselves to fatalism – even if for different reasons and with a different perspective on things; even though we have a greater sense of responsibility and have showed that this is the case by our active concern to prepare adequate organizational and material forces to meet any eventuality? What difference would there be between them and us if we too were to lull ourselves with the comfortable illusion that events cannot fail to unfold according to a fixed line of development – the line that we have predicted for them – inescapably running into the system of dykes and canals we have mapped out for them, and flowing down all the right channels, picking up form and historical power as they go? This is the central knot of the problem, which seems so inextricably tangled, because passivity can look from the outside like brisk activity and because there does appear to be a line of development, a seam that workers are worthily sweating in and toiling away to excavate.

The Communist International was founded on 5 March 1919, but its ideological and organic formation took place only at the Second Congress, in July–August 1920, when the Statutes and the 21 Conditions were approved. It was after the Second Congress that the campaign began in Italy for the reorganization of the Socialist Party – began on a national scale, that is, since it had already been initiated in the previous March by the Turin section, with the resolution drawn up for the Party's imminent National Conference, which was scheduled to be held, precisely, in Turin. Until the Second Congress, however, the campaign did not have any very significant repercussions (the Florence Conference of the abstentionist faction, held in July before the Second World Congress, rejected the proposal made by a representative of *L'Ordine Nuovo* that the faction should be given a broader base by turning it into a communist faction, without the abstentionist precondition which in practice had lost much of its *raison d'être*).

The Livorno Congress and the split that occurred there were presented as being linked to the Second Congress and its 21 Conditions, as being the inevitable outcome of the 'formal' proceedings of the Second Congress. This was an error and today we are in a position to measure its full extent by the consequences it has had. In reality, the proceedings of the Second World Congress were a living response to the situation in Italy and throughout the world. But we, for a whole series of reasons, did not determine our actions by what was happening in Italy; by the events in Italy which proved the Second Congress correct; which were a part and indeed one of the most important parts of the political reality that lay behind the rulings and the organizational measures decided on at the Second Congress. Instead, we just kept strictly to formal questions, questions of pure logic, pure consistency; and we were defeated, because the majority of the politically organized proletariat disagreed with us and refused to go along with us, even though we had the great authority and prestige of the International on our side and were relying on this factor. We had not been capable of conducting a systematic campaign, of a kind that could have reached down to all the constituent elements in the Socialist Party and forced them to reflect. We had not been capable of translating every Italian event of the years 1919 and 1920 into a language which could be understood by every Italian worker and peasant. We were not capable, after Livorno, of confronting the question of why the congress had had the outcome it did. We were not capable of confronting the question in practice, in such a way as to find a solution; in such a way as to continue our specific mission, which was to win over the majority of the Italian people. We were – it must be said – swept along by events. We were, without wanting to be, an aspect of the general dissolution of Italian society, which had become a kind of glowing crucible in which all traditions, all historical structures, all prevailing ideas were being melted down, sometimes to nothing. We had one consolation, which we clung to tenaciously – that fact that we were all in this together, but that we could claim to have predicted the cataclysm with mathematical precision, while everyone else was wallowing in the most blissful and idiotic of illusions.

After the Livorno split, we entered a situation where we were acting out of necessity. This is the only justification for our attitudes and activity after the Livorno split: we were being confronted by necessity in its crudest and most extreme form – the choice between life and death. We had to organize ourselves as a party among the flames of civil war, cementing our sections together with the blood of the most dedicated militants. We had to transform our groups, even as we were forming and recruiting them, into guerrilla detachments – detachments for the cruellest and most difficult guerrilla war that a working class has ever had to fight. Yet we succeeded: the Party was built and built to last. It is a phalanx of steel, too small, certainly, to enter into a struggle against the enemy forces, but large enough to become the framework for a broader formation, for an army which – to use the language of Italian history – can follow up the rout of Caporetto with the battle on the Piave.

This is the problem that faces us today, inexorably: how to build a great army for the forthcoming battles, building on the base of those forces which, since Livorno, have shown themselves to be capable of resisting the attack so violently launched by Fascism, without hesitations or backward steps. The development of the Communist International since the Second Congress has paved the way for this; once more, in the proceedings of the Third and Fourth Congresses, supplemented by those of the Enlarged Plenums of February and June 1922 and of June 1923, the International has responded to the Italian situation and the needs that arise from it. The truth is that we, as a Party, have already made a few steps forward in this direction: all that remains to us to do now is to register these steps and press boldly on.

What is the significance of the events that have taken place in the heart of the Socialist Party, first with the split from the reformists, secondly with the expulsion of the editorial group of *Pagine rosse*[2] and thirdly and finally with the attempt to expel the entire Third-Internationalist faction? Their precise significance is this: that while, as the Italian section, our Party was forced to limit its activity to the physical struggle of the defence against Fascism and to the preservation of its original structure, as an international Party it was working – continuing to work – to open up new paths towards the future, to broaden its sphere of political influence and to shift that part of the masses that had been standing by, looking on with indifference or hesitation, out of its position of neutrality. The activity of the International was for a time the only activity that allowed our Party to have an effective contact with the broad masses and that kept up a ferment of debate and the first stirrings of movement in significant strata of the working class – something it was impossible for us to achieve in any other way in the circumstances. It was undoubtedly a great success that we managed to tear some blocs away from the Socialist Party's gang, and that, when the situation seemed at its worst, we managed to create out of the amorphous socialist jelly some nuclei

---

[2] A journal founded on 29 June 1923 and edited by Serrati. It was suppressed in August 1924 when the group merged with the Communists.

of comrades who were prepared to declare that in spite of everything they had faith in the world revolution, and to acknowledge – in their actions, if not in their words (which, it appears, can be more painful than actions) – that they had been mistaken in the years 1920–21–22. This was a defeat for Fascism and the forces of reaction. It was, if we want to be honest about it, the only physical and ideological defeat Fascism and reaction have suffered in these three years of Italian history.

It is necessary to react forcefully against the pessimism of certain groups within our Party – groups which include some of our most responsible and able comrades. Pessimism represents our most serious danger at the present moment, in the new situation that is emerging in our country and that is due to be sanctioned and clarified in the first Fascist legislature. There are massive struggles on the horizon, perhaps more bloody and arduous than those of the past few years. The maximum possible energy is needed from our leaders, the greatest possible degree of organization of the mass of Party members, a great spirit of initiative and a very great swiftness of decision. Pessimism for the most part adopts the following refrain: we are returning to a pre-Livorno situation and we shall have to do all the same work again that we did before Livorno and that we thought was over and done with. We must convince every comrade of how mistaken this position is, in both political and theoretical terms. Certainly, it will be necessary to keep struggling hard. Certainly, the task of the basic nucleus of our Party formed at Livorno is not yet finished and will not be finished for a good while yet (it will still be a vital and ongoing task even after the victory of the revolution). But we shall not find ourselves back in a pre-Livorno situation, because the Italian and world situation in 1924 is not what it was in 1920 and we ourselves are not the same as we were in 1920 and would never want to go back to that state. Because the Italian working class has changed a great deal and it will no longer be the easiest thing in the world to make it reoccupy the factories using stove-pipes for cannons, after deafening its ears and stirring its blood with the vile demagogy of the maximalist fair-grounds. Because now our Party exists – which is something, after all, as it has proved – and we have boundless faith in it, as the best, soundest and most honourable part of the Italian proletariat.

L'Ordine Nuovo, 15 March 1924

The Mezzogiorno and Fascism

An important event in the current Italian political struggle has been the National Fascist Party's attempt to resolve the problem of the relations between the State/government and the South of Italy.

The Mezzogiorno[1] has become a reservation for the constitutional opposition. The Mezzogiorno has once again signalled its 'territorial' difference from the rest of the State, its determination not to allow itself to be absorbed unresistingly into an exaggeratedly unitary system, which would only mean an intensification of the old oppressions and exploitations. It has entrenched itself in a series of constitutional, parliamentarist, formalistically democratic positions, which must nevertheless have a certain value and significance if the National Party has felt the need to make the concessions it has made, simply in order to deprive the movement of its heads, its gurus, Orlando and De Nicola. Mussolini, when it comes down to it, has done nothing more than apply Giolitti-style tactics in a new situation that is infinitely more difficult and complex than any previous situation, with a population that has at least partially revived and started participating in public life and in a period in which, with the decrease in emigration, class problems are taking on an ever more violent character and becoming 'territorial' problems, because capitalism keeps its distance from the region, as does the government which administrates the interests of capitalism.

[1] The Italian South.

Many comrades often ask themselves in amazement the reason why the two great newspapers of the North of Italy, *Il Corriere della Sera* and *La Stampa*, should be opposed to Fascism. Is it not the case that Fascism has created the very situation these two papers wanted to see? Did these two papers not themselves contribute heavily to the successes of Fascism in the years 1920–1? Why are they now working in the opposite direction, working to deprive Fascism of its popular base, to dig the ground away from under its feet, by spreading confusion and pointing the petit bourgeois masses towards 'ideals of freedom'?

Obviously, the *Corriere* and the *Stampa* are not two 'pure' newspapers, simply trying to keep and enlarge their circle of subscribers and readers by insisting on the themes dear to the mentality of the masses; if this were the case, these two papers would already have made their acquaintance with the steel and petrol of the Fascist squads and 'occupation' by editors loyal to the new masters. The *Corriere* and the *Stampa* have not been occupied, have not allowed themselves to be occupied, because there are three categories of national 'institutions' that have not been occupied or allowed themselves to be occupied: the general staff of the army, the banks (or rather, the Bank – the Banca Commerciale, which exercises an uncontested monopoly) and the General Confederation of Industry.

The *Stampa* and the *Corriere* are traditionally the representatives of these 'institutions', the two parties of these national institutions. The *Stampa*, more 'left-wing', is now openly canvassing the possibility of a Radical–Socialist government as a possible successor to Fascism and it would not even be averse to a MacDonald-style experiment in Italy. *La Stampa* recognizes the problem of the South and sees the solution as being to draw the cream of the workers into the Piedmontese and Northern governing hegemony. What this means is effectively decapitating the revolutionary forces of the South at a national level, and preventing any possibility of an alliance between the peasant masses of the South, who will never be capable of overturning capitalism alone, and the industrial working class of the North, who would be locked in a compromising and dishonourable alliance with the exploiters.

The *Corriere* has a more 'unitary' conception of the situation, more 'Italian', so to speak – that is, more commercial and less industrial. The *Corriere* supported Salandra and Nitti, the two first Southern presidents (the Sicilian presidents represented Sicily, rather than the Mezzogiorno, because the Sicilian question is notoriously distinct from the question of the Mezzogiorno). The *Corriere* favoured the Allies, rather than Germany, like *La Stampa*; it has been a consistent supporter of free trade, rather than supporting it only during the electoral periods of the Giolitti government, like *La Stampa*; and it was not afraid during the War, as *La Stampa* was, that the State apparatus was going to pass from the hands of Giolitti's masonic bureaucracy into the hands of Salandra's 'Puglian compatriots'. The *Corriere* is more attached to conservatism. It might just support an alliance with the reformists, but only if the latter were prepared to jump through a lot of hoops. The *Corriere* wants an 'Amendola' government – that is, it wants the petite bourgeoisie of the South and not the cream of the Northern factory workers to be incorporated officially into the real power system. It wants to see a rural democracy in Italy, with Cadorna as its military leader, rather than Badoglio, as *La Stampa* would prefer, and with a kind of Italian Poincaré as its political leader, rather than a kind of Italian Briand. *Il Corriere*, unlike *La Stampa*, is not afraid that we are going to have another period like the 1890s – a period in which the insurrections of the Southern peasants are automatically linked to workers' insurrections in the industrial cities; when the Fasci Siciliani find their echo in the '98 revolt in Milan. The *Corriere* has faith in 'natural forces' and the cannons of Bava-Beccaris. The *Stampa* believes that Turati–D'Aragona–Modigliani are much more reliable arms than the cannons for taming the revolts of the peasants and clearing occupied factories.

Fascism's only response to *Il Corriere* and *La Stampa*'s precise and organic points have been purely mechanical and ridiculously choreographic words and actions.

Fascism is responsible for the destruction of the system of workers' protectionism known as 'Reggio co-operativism', 'Prampolian evangelism', etc., etc. Fascism has deprived the 'democrats' of their strongest weapon in the fight to turn the hatred of the peasant masses against the industrial forces, and it will now turn against the capitalists. 'Red parasitism' no longer exists, but this has not brought about any improvement in conditions in the Mezzogiorno. 'Red parasitism' has been replaced by a 'nationalist parasitism': how is it possible to prevent the Southern peasant from seeing in Fascism the concentrated syntheses of all those who have oppressed and exploited him?

With the collapse of the Emilia-Romagnan reformists' house of cards, the Royal Guards had to be dissolved, since they could not continue to be fed on the heady brew of anti-worker feeling.

The industrialists did do something to help Mussolini: the General Confederation of Industry, in its June 1923 conference, spoke in these terms, through the mouthpiece of its president, the Honourable Benni: 'So it appears that another long and complex initiative which we have started up on behalf of the Mezzogiorno will be carried through to a successful conclusion. We want to make our contribution, by some practical action, towards the resurgence of Southern Italy and the islands, where the first promising signs of a salutary economic revival are already beginning to appear. It is not a simple task, but it is one to which industrialists, as a class, must dedicate themselves, because it is in the interests of everyone that the structure of the nation should become even more unified, on the foundations of economic interests.' The industrialists helped Mussolini with their fine words, but these fine words were soon afterwards followed by rather more expressive deeds: the take-over of the cotton manufacturers of the Salerno region and the transport of all the machines, disguised as scrap iron, to the Lombard textile zone.

The Southern question cannot be resolved by the bourgeoisie, except in a temporary, makeshift manner, using corruption and fire and the sword. Fascism has exacerbated the situation and also clarified it to a great extent. The fact that this problem has not been addressed clearly, in all its implications and with all its possible political consequences, has obstructed the activity of the working class and it contributed a great deal to the failure of the revolution of the years 1919–20.

Today, the problem is even more complex and difficult than it was in those years, but it remains the central problem facing any revolution in this country – any revolution that wants to survive – so it must be tackled with courage and resolve. In the present situation, with the depression we are seeing at the moment in the proletarian forces, the Southern peasant masses have assumed an enormous importance in the revolutionary arena. Either the proletariat, through its political party, will succeed in creating a network of allies in the Mezzogiorno, or else the peasant masses will look for political leaders in their own region – in other words, they will put themselves entirely in the hands of the Amendolian petite bourgeoisie and become a storehouse of counter-revolutions, prepared to resort to separatism and appeals to foreign armies in the case of a purely industrial revolution in the North. The guiding idea of the workers' and peasants' government must then take special account of the Mezzogiorno. The problem of the Southern peasants must not be confused with the more general question of the relations between the cities and the rural areas within an economic whole which is organically subjected to the capitalist regime. The Southern question is also a territorial question and it is from this perspective that it must be considered if a programme of worker and peasant government is to be established that will win large-scale support from the masses.

L'Ordine Nuovo, 15 March 1924

The Party School

At the moment when the first courses are beginning at a Party school, we cannot help thinking back over the numerous educational initiatives we have already seen within the Italian workers' movement and the rather peculiar fate they have met with. Let us leave on one side the initiatives that have taken a different direction from ours – the direction of proletarian 'universities' without party colours. These have been, at best, rhetorical academies lacking in any inner principle of cohesion and unity; very often, they have been a vehicle for anti-proletarian forces and ideologies seeking to influence the working class. They have met the fate they deserved: they have followed one after another, sometimes intersecting, but without leaving any real mark.

But not a great deal more can be said, either, for those attempts that have been made on our own terrain and on our own orders. For one thing, they were always piecemeal in character; for another, they never led to satisfactory results. Let us remember for example what was done on the initiative of *L'Ordine Nuovo* in 1919–20. The school that was set up then in Turin amid a great wave of enthusiasm and in extremely favourable conditions, did not even survive for long enough to complete the programme that had been planned at the outset. In spite of this, it did have a very positive influence on our movement; but certainly not what the promoters of the school and the students had been hoping for. Out of the other initiatives, none, as far as we are aware, achieved the same kind of success and influence. It never proved possible to get beyond the limited group, the closed circle, the efforts of a few isolated individuals. It never proved possible to fight off the aridity and sterility which characterize small-scale bourgeois 'cultural' movements.

The fundamental reason for these failures is the absence of any link between the 'schools' that are planned or started up and an actual, objective movement. The only case in which this link existed is that of the *Ordine Nuovo* school mentioned above. In this case, however, the objective movement in question – the Turinese factory and Party movement – was such a massive one that it overpowered and almost annihilated in its path the attempt to set up a school to refine the theoretical capacities of the militants. A school large enough to reflect the importance of that movement would have demanded not just the activity of a few individuals, but a systematic, ordered effort by an entire Party.

Considered in this light (considered, that is, in relation to its fundamental cause), the ill fate that has met every attempt so far to create schools for the militants of the proletariat is revealed as being not so much an evil as a sign of the impregnability of the workers' movement – its impregnability in the face of what would be the real evil for it. It would be a bad thing indeed if the workers' movement were to become a hunting-reserve or a practice-ground for arrogant and maladroit pedagogues and exchange its character of impassioned militancy for one of objective study and disinterested 'culture'. Neither 'objective study' nor 'disinterested culture' can have any place in our ranks – which is to say nothing resembling what, in the humanistic, bourgeois conception of education, is considered the normal aim of teaching.

We are a militant organization and, in our ranks, the aim of studying is to enhance and refine the capacities for struggle of both individuals and the organization as a whole; to understand more fully our enemies' positions and our own, so that we can ensure that our day-to-day action is in accordance with these positions. Education and culture are, for us, no more than a theoretical consciousness of our immediate and long-term ends and the manner in which we can best succeed in translating them into practice.

To what extent does this kind of consciousness already exist within our Party today? To what extent has it spread through the Party ranks and infused both comrades in leadership roles and the ordinary militants whose task is to bring the words of the Party to the masses on a day-to-day level and to ensure that the Party's orders become effective and that its directives are carried out in practice? This has not yet happened to a sufficient extent, in our view, to enable us to carry out in full our work as guide to the proletariat. It has not yet happened to a sufficient extent to keep pace with the increase in our membership, our organizational resources and the political possibilities that the current situation offers us. The Party school must set itself the task of filling the gulf between what there should be and what there is not. This school is therefore closely linked with a movement of forces which we have a right to consider as representing the best that the Italian working class has been able to produce. It is the proletarian vanguard, which is forming and educating its cadres, adding a further weapon – of theoretical consciousness and revolutionary doctrine – to the battery it is assembling to confront its enemies and the battles that await it. Without this weapon, the Party does not exist. And without the Party, there is no possibility of victory.

L'Ordine Nuovo, 1 April 1925

The Party Grows in Strength by Combating Anti-Leninist Deviations[1]

Let us examine, coolly and calmly, these 'points from the left' which are claiming to offer our Party and the International new and 'original', Italian solutions to problems of strategy and organization, worthy of being adopted in place of Leninism.

The Italian situation

There is no paragraph in the 'points' explicitly dedicated to the situation in Italy. It is possible, however, to infer an opinion on the Italian situation from the paragraph dedicated to the question of cells – and it cannot be denied that this opinion does have a certain originality. What it comes down to is this: the situation in Italy now is not that of Russia in the years from 1905 to 1917. In other words, there is not a revolutionary situation. In Russia, there was the Tsarist terror, while in Italy, of course, we are not experiencing terror of any kind. In Russia, there were no great organizations of the masses (unions,

---

[1] Reply to the 'Programme of the *Comitato d'intesa* [lit. 'Committee of Agreement']', published on the same page of *L'Unità*. This grouping was formed in 1925 and consisted of the left-wing Bordiga supporters, who opposed the Comintern policy (advocated by Gramsci) of anti-Fascist alliances. They were decisively defeated at the Lyons Congress of January 1926, where they only obtained 10 per cent of the vote. The name *Comitato d'intesa* appears to have been coined as an attempt to avoid identifying the grouping openly as a faction in a Party in which factions were outlawed.

etc.), while in Italy, of course, there is the highest degree of freedom of organization – the masses can come together, freely discuss the issues that concern them, plan demonstrations. In Russia, there was no possibility of making progress by peaceful means. In Italy, on the other hand, the masses are taking new strides forward by the day.

Comrade workers of Milan, of Turin, of Trieste, Bari, Bologna – does this not strike you as an 'original' view of the situation in Italy? So original that it had never occurred to you to think of things in this way; but now the veil has fallen from your eyes and you are in a position to judge fairly between the Central Committee of the Party and this 'Committee of Agreement' which claims that it is possible to make progress by peaceful means. For extremism to set itself up as a faction promoting peaceful progress – that's a real piece of originality for you!

The Party

According to Leninist doctrine, the Communist Party is the vanguard of the proletariat: in other words, the most advanced section of a particular class and only of that class. Naturally, other social elements may enter the Party as well (intellectuals and peasants), but that does not alter the fact that the Communist Party is an organic part of the proletariat.

According to the 'Committee of Agreement', the Party is not part of a class, but a 'synthesis' of proletariats, peasants, deserters from the bourgeois class and also 'others' (these points go in for an extremely mysterious use of 'etc.'). For the 'Committee of Agreement', the Party is, therefore, an inter-class organization, a synthesis of interests which in fact cannot be synthesized in any way. Naturally this highly 'original' hotchpotch of ideas is passed off as Marxism. According to Marxism, the proletarian movement, which is created objectively out of the development of capitalism, becomes revolutionary – that is, it starts considering the problem of how to win political power for itself – only when the working class has become conscious of being the only class capable of resolving the problems that capitalism has thrown up as it develops, but which capitalism has not succeeded in – and cannot succeed in – solving. How does the working class acquire this consciousness? Marxism affirms and demonstrates, in opposition to syndicalism, that this does not happen spontaneously, but only because the representatives of political science and industrial technology – who are in a position to do this because of the particular position their class occupies (intellectuals are a class that serves the bourgeoisie but is not part of the bourgeoisie) – construct a proletarian political science on the base of the existing bourgeois political science. From the study of technology as it has developed under a capitalist regime, they arrive at the conclusion that no further development is possible unless the proletariat takes power and turns itself into a ruling class, imprinting the whole of society with its specific class characteristics. Intellectuals are necessary, then, in the construction of socialism. They have served, as representatives of political science and technology, to give the proletariat a consciousness of its historic mission. But this has been an individual, not a class phenomenon – as a class, it is only the proletariat which becomes revolutionary and socialist before the conquest of power and which struggles against capitalism. Furthermore, once socialist theory has emerged and been developed scientifically, the workers too assimilate it and develop it further. The Communist Party is, precisely, that part of the proletariat that has assimilated socialist theory and is continuing to propagate it. The task that, at the beginning of the movement, was performed by individual intellectuals (like Marx and Engels), but also by workers possessed of scientific capacities (like the German worker Dietzgen), is today performed by the combined action of Communist Parties and the International.

According to the 'Committee of Agreement', we should conceive of the Party in just the same way as it might have been conceived of at the beginning of the movement: as a 'synthesis' of individual elements, rather than a mass movement. Why is this? In this conception there is a tinge of powerful pessimism about the capacities of workers. Only intellectuals can be 'true' Communist revolutionaries; only intellectuals can be 'politicians'. Workers are workers and are doomed to remain so for as long as they are oppressed by capitalism. Under capitalist oppression, the worker cannot develop fully; he cannot escape from the blinkered narrowness of his role. And what does that make the Party? The Party is simply a small group of leaders (in this case, the 'Committee of Agreement') who 'reflect' and 'synthesize' the interests and the generic aspirations of the masses – even the masses within the Party.

Leninist doctrine asserts and demonstrates that this conception of the Party is a false one and an extremely dangerous one. It has led, among other things, to the phenomenon of trade-union 'mandarinism' – in other words, to counter-revolution.

According to Leninist doctrine, even if it is true that the working class as a whole cannot become entirely communist until after the conquest of power, it is nevertheless true that a vanguard of the working class *can* achieve this state even before the revolution. Workers enter the Communist Party not only in their capacity as workers (metal-workers, carpenters, building workers, etc.). They enter it as *Communist* workers – as political activists, that is, as theorists of socialism, not simply as generic rebels. And, in the Party, through its discussions, through its readings and through the Party schools, they develop continually and become leaders. Only in the trade union does the worker enter simply in his capacity as worker, rather than as a political activist who adheres to a particular theory.

Just how important these questions are and just how grave the consequences could be if they were resolved in the wrong way (or, as the 'Committee of Agreement' would say, in an 'original' way) can be seen if we look at the question of cells, which the Party wants to adopt as its foundation, rather than the old sections and the old territorial assemblies. The 'Committee of Agreement' is against cells. Why? The reason is clear: workshop cells are constituted and must always tend to be constituted by workers alone. But the worker cannot be a revolutionary – although he *is* a revolutionary in the territorial assembly, evidently because in these assemblies there are also lawyers, teachers, etc.

The whole paragraph in the Committee's Programme on the Party's organizational systems is a mass of errors and nonsensical statements. When, for example, was the British Labour Party ever organized on a cell basis? When were trade unions ever organized in cells? And why are trade unions necessarily counter-revolutionary? The trade unions are not revolutionary in themselves, but nor are they counter-revolutionary: trade union leaders may be either revolutionary or counter-revolutionary. The Labour Party is not organized on a cell basis. It is a federation of trade unions and political parties.

If things were as the 'Committee of Agreement' claims they are, why then did the Russian Bolshevik Party maintain and extend its cell organization even after the fall of Tsarism? Why is it still organized in cells even today, when the working class is in power and the trade unions (which, in the 'Committee of Agreement''s book, are counter-revolutionary) have full freedom of organization and assembly? And why is it that the cell system should be described as federalist, while the system of territorial assemblies is not? We all know what federalism is: it means, for example, a parity of the powers of all the constitutive organizations, however many members each represents. In the French trade-union movement, votes are cast on a union basis, not on the basis of the membership numbers, so that a hairdressers' association in a small town counts for as much as the metal-workers' union of Saint-Etienne (this system used to be in force in the Italian *Unione Sindacale*). Federalism means that representatives go to the congresses with an imperative mandate. The Committee of the Opposition[2] is federalist, in that the little Sardinian Action Party has the same powers as the 'enormous' Maximalist Party.

This whole paragraph on cells is a heap of rubbish completely lacking in common sense and showing no kind of historical perspective. In fact, the 'Committee of Agreement''s conception of the Communist Party is a retrograde conception, belonging to the initial period of capitalism, while the Leninist conception, as reflected in the organizational system of cells, is the conception that belongs to the imperialist phase of capitalism – that is, the phase in which the revolution is organized. Up to the time of the Paris Commune, it could be said that 'the Party is the organ that synthesizes and unifies the impulses that the class struggle has excited in both individuals and groups'. It could be claimed, in other words, that the Party's task is simply to register the progress of the working class and conduct ideological propaganda. But we are not in 1848 now. There exists today a broad and far-reaching mass revolutionary movement, and the Party guides the mass and directs the class struggle and does not simply play the notary. Still, it is pretty 'original' that such an outdated, reactionary position should be passed off as leftism.

Charlatanism and demagogy

The paragraph given over to the past activity of our Party is simply a farrago of commonplaces, liberally seasoned with bad faith, charlat-

[2] Following the murder of Matteotti by Fascists on 10 June 1924, all sections of the opposition in Parliament withdrew (the so-called Aventine Succession) and met separately in another part of Rome. The PCd'I returned to Parliament on 12 November 1924, judging the Aventine group impotent.

anism and demagogy. It really does take some cheek to claim that the Central Committee of the Party was steered back on to the right path only by the resolute (!) pressure of the periphery and the left. Precisely the opposite is true. The periphery was resolutely opposed to our parliamentary group's decision to leave the Committee of the Opposition and even more resolutely opposed to our return to Parliament. Within the parliamentary group, the only comrades who energetically backed the proposal for a return to Parliament were Comrades Gramsci and Maffi. Of the extreme left, it was only Comrade Borin who declared himself in favour of this proposal. Comrade Fortichiari, if he was present, did not speak. Damen and Repossi declared themselves resolutely – nay, 'fiercely' – opposed to the proposal and they claimed to be representing the feelings and views of the periphery in the debate.

That the 'Committee of Agreement''s claim is untrue can be seen from this fact: the Central Committee showed no hesitation in this as in the other questions – to the extent that even in the federal congresses of Naples and Milan, the two centres where extremism does have some kind of following, it was announced right from September that the parliamentary group would return to Parliament if the Committee of the Opposition threw out our proposal for an anti-Parliament. In Naples, Comrade Bordiga declared himself in agreement with the Central Committee on the issue of the return to Parliament and opposed to the proposal for an anti-Parliament, but no-one else spoke on the matter except Comrade Fiore, an extremist, who declared himself opposed to the return – he, too, insisting that the periphery had not understood. In Milan, only one comrade spoke on the issue, an extremist, Bernardi, who declared himself opposed to the return. Is it not a sign of bad faith and charlatanism to come along today and say that the periphery and the 'left' put pressure on the Central Committee? The truth is that the extremists of today, who have never had policies of their own, at that time were allowing themselves to be led by the more backward masses; they were 'synthesizing and unifying' a tendency of the right, which favoured a common front between the opposition parties. It was the Central Committee of the Party which dared go against the current and react against the passivity of the mass; and, through its political action, it succeeded in securing the revolutionary proletariat's independence from the bourgeoisie and making the proletariat an autonomous and decisive factor in the situation.

But this is a question that deserves to be dealt with in a different context and in more depth. For the moment, we just want to make one comparison – between the tactics of the Central Committee in this period and those of the Executive that was in charge of the Party in the years 1921–2. (It is only the demagogy and bad faith of the 'Committee of Agreement' which constrains us to touch on this matter.) In this present period, the Party has developed and its influence has increased because the Central Committee, working from the concrete current situation, has shown itself capable of foreseeing how events would develop. In 1921–2 the Executive (putting to one side its work in organizing the Party) showed itself incapable of foreseeing developments. It ruled out *a priori* the possibility of a Fascist *coup d'état*; it had no idea of how to find its bearings in the complex of actions and reactions that the class struggle had brought about in Italy; it let itself be caught unawares by decisive events. We do not wish to indulge in demagogy ourselves, though it would be far easier for us in this field than it is for the 'Committee of Agreement' where last year's situation is concerned. Is it not the height of demagogy, for example, to assert that 'the language of the press ought to have been more appropriate to the situation'? For the 'Committee of Agreement', the sequestrations and official menaces count for nothing, or the suspension of *L'Unità* last December and January . . .

Against Leninism. Against the Communist International

We have here just given an outline of the exhaustive reply that should be made to this document, which is the fundamental 'charter' of the 'Committee of Agreement' and which, if the Committee had its way, would become the 'charter' of the Party and the International. There is nothing new or original in this document. It is an undigested mass of old errors and old deviations from Marxism, which can only seem like 'originality' to those who do not know the history of the workers' movement. What is striking about this document is not so much its political errors as the intellectual decadence of those who have compiled it. It should be examined and discussed simply in order to show up more vividly, in contrast, the energy and intellectual vigour and profound historical rightness of Leninist doctrine, which did not permit Kornilovian Fascism to attain power in Russia but instead managed to guide the proletariat to revolutionary victory.

It can be ruled out *a priori* that such a document 'synthesizes' a position of the 'left'. This document is much more likely to lead, on the contrary, to the most dangerous kinds of right-wing deviations: one only has to think of its genuinely reactionary conception of the proletariat and its political capacities. From this point of view, it could be said that the current dispute between the Central Committee and the extremists does have some class content.

The Central Committee represents the ideology of the revolutionary proletariat, which is conscious of having become a class worthy of exercising power. The 'Committee of Agreement' represents a last-ditch attempt on the part of dwindling groups of revolutionary intellectuals, still steeped in a petit bourgeois mistrust of the worker, whom they regard as an inferior being, incapable of emancipating himself by his own efforts, rather than as a protagonist in the great task of emancipating all those oppressed by capital. And so the struggle is already won 'historically' before it has even been fought.

L'Unità, 5 July 1925

Cell Organization and the World Congress

In his article on the nature of the Communist Party, Comrade Bordiga writes:

> At the Second Congress, at which Lenin established the basis of the International, even though the experience of cells in Russia was already there to be drawn on, not a single reference was made to this organizational criterion (today presented as basic and indispensable) in any of those classic documents: the Statutes of the International, the Twenty-One Conditions for Admission, the Theses on the Duty of the Party and the Theses on the Duties of the International. What we have here is a 'discovery' made much later, whose place within the development of the International will be examined in due course.

Comrade Bordiga's assertion is incorrect. In the *Theses on the Fundamental Tasks of the Second Congress of the Communist International* and, to be more precise, in the second chapter, 'What Immediate and Universal Preparation for the Dictatorship of the Proletariat Should Consist In', Lenin wrote:

> The dictatorship of the proletariat means that all workers and all the exploited – those who have been subjugated, downtrodden, oppressed, intimidated, scattered and betrayed by the capitalist class – come under the full leadership of the only class the history of capitalism has prepared for such leadership. We must therefore begin preparing the way for the dictatorship of the prolet-

ariat, everywhere and immediately, proceeding in the following manner. Groups or cells of Communists must be created in every organization, federation and association without exception, first and foremost in proletarian organizations, but also in the non-proletarian organizations of the working, exploited masses (political, union, military, co-operative, cultural, sporting, etc.). These cells will be formed openly, in the first place, but there will also be clandestine cells, which will be essential wherever there is reason to expect their suppression on the part of the bourgeoisie, or the arrest or exile of their members. These cells, which are to be closely linked to one another and to the Party centre, must pool their experience; carry out their work of agitation, propaganda and organization; and *adapt themselves completely* to all fields of public life and *to every variety and category of the working masses*. And, working on all these fronts, they must systematically educate themselves, the Party, the class and the masses.[1]

In the *Twenty-One Conditions for Admission to the International* (Paragraph 9), it says:

Any party that wishes to be part of the Communist International must conduct systematic and unflagging communist activity within the unions, the workers' councils, the factory councils, the co-operative societies and all other workers' organizations. Communist cells should be organized within these organizations, to win the unions, etc. to the communist cause through their sustained and unflagging work. It is the duty of these cells everywhere, in their day-to-day work, to unmask the treachery of the social-patriots and the vacillation of the centrists. The communist cells must be completely subordinate to the Party.[2]

In the *Theses on the Duties of the Communist Party in the Proletarian Revolution* (Paragraph 18), it says:

The basis of the Communist Party's whole organizational activity everywhere must be the creation of a communist cell. This is the case even where the number of proletarians and semi-proletarians is very small. In every Soviet, in every union, in every consumers' co-operative, in every firm, in every residents'

---

[1] For the text of the passage referred to, see Lenin, *Collected Works* (London: Lawrence and Wishart, 1966), Vol. 31, pp. 191–2.
[2] *Collected Works*, Vol. 31, p. 209.

association; wherever anyone is working on behalf of communism – even if it is only two or three people – a communist cell should be set up immediately. It is only this kind of communist solidarity which will permit the vanguard of the working class to pull the entire working class along behind it. All the cells of the Communist Party that work in extra-Party organizations are absolutely subordinate to the Party organization, whether the Party is at that time operating inside or outside the law. Communist cells of various types must be subordinated one to another in an extremely rigorous hierarchical ordering, following the most precise system possible.

The Second Congress raised the problem of the organization of the Communist Parties in cells. The European parties found the way in which the problem was presented unclear. There was a confusion between cell organization as the basis of the Party and the organization of Communist factions in unions, co-operatives, etc. And it is true that these two organizational forms are not clearly distinguished in the statements cited above, even though the distinction is clearly made in the final summary of the *Theses on the Duties of the Party*. Point IV of the summary says: 'Wherever there are even just a dozen proletarians or semi-proletarians, the Communist Party must have an organized cell.' Point V: 'In every extra-Party institution, there must be a cell of the Communist Party strictly subordinated to the Party.' It is clear that in these two points a distinction is being made between the *cell*, the organizational basis of the Party, and the *faction*, the Party's organism of work and struggle within the mass associations.

That this is the case is shown by the theses written by Lenin in 1915 for Zimmerwald's left wing – that is, for the revolutionary nucleus that was to form the Communist International in 1919. And it is shown by the speech Lenin gave at the Third Congress in the special sub-section dedicated to the organization and structure of the Communist Parties. Lenin asks himself the question, 'Why is only the Russian Communist Party organized by cells? Why have the directives of the Second Congress which indicated the cell system as the right system for the Communist Parties not been put into effect?' And Lenin affirms in reply to these questions that the responsibility for this lies with the Russian comrades and with himself, in that the theses of the Second Congress used a language that was too Russian and not sufficiently 'European'. In other words, Russian experiences were alluded to without any attempt to update or explain them, on the assumption that these experiences had been noted and understood. The theses of the Third Congress on the structure of the Communist Party, written either directly by Lenin or under his supervision, are not a 'discovery', then, as Comrade Bordiga claims, but a translation into a language which would be comprehensible to 'Europeans' of the rapid and allusive pronouncements contained in the theses of the Second Congress.

But why does Comrade Bordiga want to make this distinction within the history of the International between the Second Congress and the following three? In his article on the 'Trotsky Question', Comrade Bordiga maintains that the history of the International can be divided into two parts: up to Lenin's death and after Lenin's death. In his article on the nature of the Party, on the other hand, the second phase starts right from the Third Congress – that is, from a period in which Lenin was alive and at the peak of his intellectual and political powers. In the course of the discussion, the following point will have emerged clearly (and it is a fundamental one for the Party debate): that, for Comrade Bordiga, the Italian revolutionary ment is finding itself once more in a phase similar to the phase between the Second Congress and Livorno – in other words, in a phase in which factions must be organized because we may find ourselves (or rather we already are) faced by the problem of a split. How else can one explain the allusions Comrade Bordiga has been making to the *Ordine Nuovo* group, in the 'points from the left' and the article on the nature of the Party – malevolent, grudging, rancorous allusions, not intended to smooth over the differences but rather to exacerbate them and make them appear insurmountable? Apart from anything else, however, Comrade Bordiga has forgotten one 'minor point': that even if the Second Congress is taken as a touchstone for understanding the current situation of our party, it is certainly not the *Ordine Nuovo* group which can be diminished in the role it has always performed in the intellectual formation of the Italian Communist movement. At the Second Congress, Comrade Lenin declared that he was going to make his own the theses presented by the *Ordine Nuovo* group at the Socialist Party's national conference in April 1920 and he wanted the deliberations of the congress to show that: (1) the *Ordine Nuovo* theses corresponded to all the fundamental principles of the Third International; (2) the theses of the *Ordine Nuovo* group should be examined at the Socialist Party Congress. No 'extremist' will want to deny that between Comrade Lenin's judgement and Comrade Bordiga's, we regard Comrade Lenin's as more important and as dictated by a deeper and sounder Marxist spirit than that of Comrade Bordiga.

L'Unità, 28 July 1925

The Organizational Basis of the Party[1]

In my previous article on cells, to which Comrade Mangano is referring, I wanted not so much to show as simply to *remind* readers of
something very simple, which should always be borne in mind by any
comrade who wishes to participate seriously in the Congress debate –
that is, anyone who sincerely intends to contribute to the education
of the Party, rather than simply to confuse matters. I wanted to
remind readers that the model of organization by cells is very closely
linked to the doctrine of Leninism and that, in the international
sphere, Comrade Lenin pointed to this type of organization right
from 1915, right from the time of the Zimmerwaldian left.

One of the most striking characteristics of Leninism is its formidable coherence and consistency. Leninism is a unified system of
thought and practical action, in which everything hangs together and
everything confirms everything else, from the general conception of
the world right down to the most minute problems of organization.
The fundamental nucleus of Leninism, where practical action is concerned, is the dictatorship of the proletariat and all the tactical and
organizational problems of Leninism are linked to the question of

---

[1] This piece is a reply to a commentary by Romeo Mangano on Gramsci's article, 'Cell
Organization and the World Congress', which appeared immediately after Gramsci's,
with the title 'Contro le cellule' ['Against Cells']. Mangano regarded cells as undermining the authority of the Party and a return to the *Ordine Nuovo* model Gramsci had
advocated in 1919–20.

how best to prepare and organize for the proletarian dictatorship. If what Comrade Bordiga has claimed were true – i.e., that cell organization as the basis of the Party were a 'discovery' of the Third Congress – then an extremely serious inconsistency would have been revealed within Leninism and the International and it would genuinely become necessary to ask ourselves whether there had been a deviation towards the right and social-democracy at the Third Congress – a shift from the terrain of revolutionary action, that is, towards a terrain of simple organizational activity, which has nothing to do with paving the way for the proletarian dictatorship.

This, indeed, is the polemical proposition of the extremist comrades. They want to 'show' that the organization of the Party on a cell basis is not an essential part of Leninism, by claiming that cell organization is a 'discovery' which dates from after the Second Congress; they can then go on to show that the International changed course at the Third Congress, in that the Communist Parties, from the Third Congress onwards, have been allotted basic and essentially organizational tasks, rather than tasks of action. According to the extremists, this explains why, when a suitable opportunity for action has presented itself, various parties have failed in their historic mission (to bring about an armed uprising and the conquest of power). They were distracted by secondary tasks of internal organization or organization of the broad masses (the question of cells, the tactic of the united front and the workers' government, the struggle for proletarian unity, etc.).

In my previous article, to which Mangano is referring, I have 'shown' that one of the arguments on which the polemical proposition of the extremists is based is unfounded. It will not be difficult to show that the others are equally inconsistent.

The question of cells is certainly, at one level, a technical problem of the general organization of the Party, but it is first and foremost a *political question*. The question of cells is the question of how to lead the masses or, in other words, how to pave the way for the proletarian dictatorship. The cell model is the best technical organizational solution available to the fundamental problem of our age.

The arguments in favour of and against cells that have so far been put forward in the debate (whether it is safer to organize on a street or a factory basis; whether intellectuals *as a class* will find it easier to lure the proletariat off the path and contaminate its ideology under

a cell system or a system of regional assemblies) concern secondary
issues, points of detail, which have only a secondary influence on the
reception of an organizational structure based on cells rather than on
regional assemblies.

The fundamental question is that of how to lead the masses: a
question that I myself have expounded in the following way before
our Central Committee (cf. *L'Unità* of 3 July), without the extremists
so much as uttering a syllable in response:

> In some respects, the revolutionary parties of Western Europe
> find themselves only now in the conditions in which the Bolsh-
> eviks found themselves right from the initial formation of their
> Party. In Russia, before the War, the kind of great workers'
> organizations which have characterized the whole period of the
> Second International in Europe before the War did not exist. In
> Russia, it was not only a general theoretical desideratum but a
> practical imperative of organization and struggle that the Party
> should be the expression of all the vital interests of the working
> class. The factory and street cells led the masses both in the
> union struggle for better working conditions and in the political
> struggle for the overthrow of Tsarism.
>
> In Western Europe, on the other hand, there was an ever more
> apparent division of labour between the union organization of
> the working class and its political organization. In the union
> camp, the reformist and pacifist tendency was rapidly gaining in
> strength – or, in other words, the bourgeois influence on the
> proletariat was steadily increasing. For the same reason, the
> activity of the political parties was shifting ever more towards the
> parliamentary sphere – that is, towards forms that were indistin-
> guishable from those of bourgeois democracy. During the War
> and in the period after the War and immediately before the estab-
> lishment of the Communist International and the splits in the
> Socialist camp that led to the formation of our parties, the syndic-
> alist–reformist tendency was consolidating itself as the organiza-
> tion controlling the unions. All this resulted in the kind of situ-
> ation in which, as we were saying, the Communist Parties of
> Western Europe are in the same position as the Bolshevik Party
> in Russia before the War.
>
> Let us observe what is happening in Italy. As a result of the
> repressive action of Fascism, the trade unions in our country had
> declined into impotence, both in terms of numbers and the power
> to struggle. Taking advantage of this situation, the reformists

took complete charge of the unions' central apparatus and started devising all kinds of measures and provisions to prevent any minority from setting itself up, organizing itself, developing and becoming a majority capable of taking the leadership. But the great mass – quite properly – wants unity and this unitary sentiment is reflected in the traditional Italian trade-union organization: the General Confederation of Labour. The mass wants to struggle and organize itself, but it wants to struggle in the ranks of the General Confederation of Labour and organize itself within the General Confederation of Labour. The reformists are opposed to the organization of the masses. Just recall D'Aragona's speech at the recent congress of the Confederation in which he stated that the Confederation should be made up of no more than a million members. If one thinks that the Confederation itself claims to be the sole organ representing all Italian workers – that is, not only the industrial and agricultural workers, but also the peasants – and that there are at least 15 million workers to be organized in Italy, it becomes apparent that the Confederation's programme involves organizing one fifteenth, or 7.5 per cent, of Italian workers, whereas we would like to see 100 per cent of workers being organized within the trade unions and the peasants' organizations.

But if the Confederation, for reasons of internal politics – that is, to ensure that its leadership remains in the hands of the reformists – only wants 7.5 per cent of Italian workers to be organized, it also – this time for more general political reasons, so that the Reformist Party can collaborate efficiently with a bourgeois democratic government – wants the Confederation, as a whole, to have some influence over the unorganized mass of industrial workers and peasants and it wants to guarantee an enduring social base for the parties with which it intends to collaborate, by preventing any attempt to organize the peasants. So the Confederation is manoeuvring especially in the area of the internal commissions, which are elected by the whole mass of the workers, both organized and unorganized. It would like to see organized workers – at least those outside the reformist tendency – prevented from presenting lists of candidates for the internal commissions and it would like to see the communists voting for the lists of the reformist minority as a matter of discipline, even where the communists have a majority in the local union organization and among the organized workers within individual workshops. *If we were to accept this reformist organizational programme, it would result in our Party being effectively absorbed into the reformist party and our sole remaining activity would be our activity in Parliament.*

On the other hand, how can we struggle against the application and realization of such a programme, without bringing about a split, which is the last thing we want to do? The only way out is for us to organize cells and develop them in the same way as they did in Russia before the War. *The reformists, as a trade-union faction, are holding the pistol of discipline at our heads and preventing us from centralizing the revolutionary forces, both where the union struggle and the political struggle are concerned.*

It is clear, then, that our cells must work directly within the factories to centralize the masses around the Party, urging them to reinforce the internal commissions where they exist and to create agitation committees in the factories where internal commissions do not exist or where they are not doing their job; urging them, as well, to work for the centralization of the factory institutions, as mass organs not confined to trade-union activity, but forming part of the general struggle against capitalism and its political regime. Certainly, the situation we find ourselves in is far more difficult than that which confronted the Russian Bolsheviks, because we have to battle against not only the reactionary forces of the Fascist State, but also the reactionary forces of the reformists within the unions. And precisely because the situation is more difficult, our cells will have to be stronger, both in organizational and ideological terms. In any case, a process of 'Bolshevization', in the organizational sense, is an inescapable necessity. And let no-one say that the Leninist criteria for Party organization are peculiar to the Russian situation and that it is a purely mechanical approach to try to apply them to Western Europe. To oppose the organization of the Party in cells is simply to reveal oneself to be still attached to the old social-democratic thinking. It means, when it comes down to it, being on the right – that is, in a position where one does not wish to combat social democracy.

If the question is put like this, as it should be, the secondary arguments that can be brought against cell organization lose a great deal of their weight. No organizational form can be absolutely perfect. The crucial thing is to establish the type of organization that best corresponds to the circumstances and needs of the proletarian struggle, not to go off in search of the absolutely ideal form.

Comrade Mangano considers it something of a find of his when he recalls Comrade Lenin's speech at the Third Congress on the 'European' Communist parties' 'striking ignorance' about the structure of their own parties. The question is far more complex than Comrade Mangano suspects, or could possibly suspect, given his determination to maintain his own state of 'striking ignorance' and to dismiss contemptuously as 'centrist' or 'opportunist' any lessons that could be learnt from the experiences of the proletariat in other countries or in Italy itself.

I recall a 'minor' episode in 1920. In June 1920, there was a national conference of the FIOM in Genoa to decide on the plan of campaign for the metal-workers' agitation which would lead, in the following September, to the factory occupations. We, the wretched *Ordine Nuovo* crew, the 'centrists', 'opportunists', etc., etc., who have always had the contemptible habit of concerning ourselves with the real progress of working-class affairs, having been informed that the battle-plan for the occupation of the factories had been drawn up at the Genoa conference, got Comrade Terracini to raise with the leadership of the Socialist Party the issue of whether the Party should intervene in the agitation and we proposed creating cells as the organizational base of the Party itself within the factories. The proposal was rejected following a speech by the then extremist Baratono, who considered that the creation of cells would have meant breaching the pact of alliance [with the unions], in that the Party, by forming cells, would have been supplanting the unions (or, in other words, the reformists) in the leadership of the masses. When we had been defeated before the Party leadership, one of the *Ordine Nuovo* group – to be precise, the author of this article – went to the national conference of the abstentionist faction held in Florence in the July, as representative of the Turinese Socialist section, to propose setting up a communist faction based on the organizational and political principles of the Communist International (cells, factory councils). Here, as well, the proposal was rejected because it was felt that 'purely organizational forms' were useless for leading the masses (while statements of Parliamentary abstentionism, on the other hand, were quite sufficient). And in this way the working class came to occupy the factories without any kind of revolutionary political leadership and the way was clear for the reformists to lead the masses to give up the struggle.

This Italian episode, like the entire 'European' experience after the Second Congress, shows just how difficult it was for the old Socialist Parties to understand what the dictatorship of the proletariat meant in concrete terms. It also shows that just declaring oneself for the dictatorship and thinking that one is working for it does not mean that one is really for it and really working to bring it about.

According to Comrade Mangano, the fact that it has taken a long time for us to understand means not that we should hurry to make up for lost time, but that we should give up on any attempt to understand and to act.

L'Unità, 15 August 1925

A Study of the Italian Situation

I

There are three basic factors in the Italian political situation which need to be studied.

1. The positive, revolutionary factor, i.e. the progress achieved by the united front tactic. The current situation in the organization of Committees of Proletarian Unity and the tasks of the communist factions in these committees.[1]

2. The political factor represented by the disintegration of the Fascist bourgeois–agrarian bloc. Internal situation in the ruling party and significance of the crisis it is passing through.

3. The political factor represented by the tendency to construct a left democratic bloc that has its pivot in the Republican Party, in that a republican stance is supposed to provide the basis for this democratic coalition.

---

[1] In the autumn of 1924, the PCd'I launched the policy of Workers' and Peasants' Committees. These were linked to the Factory Councils of 1919–20 and were an attempt to organize the united front from below amongst the masses. Tasca and others close to the trade unions accused the scheme of '*Ordine Nuovism*' and wanted to concentrate on protecting the established labour organizations and working through them. Their view had gained support from the 'Trade Union Commission' at the Lyons Congress of March 1926, amongst others from Bordiga and the representative of the Comintern.

United Front Tactics

One reason why the first point needs to be studied is to check the correctness of the political line decided on at the Third Congress. The essential feature of the Third Congress of our Party was that it not only raised, in general terms, the problem of the need to establish the leading role of the Communist Party within the working class and of the working class within the working population of Italy, but it also sought to define, in practical terms, the political elements by means of which this leading role might be established. In other words, it sought to identify those parties and associations that acted as vehicles for bourgeois and petit bourgeois influence over the working classes and that had the potential for being radically redirected and their class values overturned. And so now we need to check, by results, whether the Party was correct in identifying the agitation committees as the organizational terrain most suited for the immediate regrouping of the forces set in action by the tactic of the united front.

On the positive side, we may say that our Party has succeeded in winning a clear position of political initiative among the working masses. In this last period, all the journalistic organs of the parties that control the Italian popular masses have been filled with polemics against the advances our Party has made. All these parties are on the defensive against our actions; in fact, they are indirectly being led by us, since a good 60 per cent of their activity is either devoted to resisting our offensives or else is devised to give the masses some kind of gratification that will lure them away from our sphere of influence.

It is clear that in the conditions of repression and control represented by Fascist politics, the results of our tactics cannot be measured statistically at the level of the great masses. Still, it is undeniable that when certain elements within the democratic and social-democratic parties shift, even minimally, towards the tactical terrain marked out by the communists, this shift cannot be put down to chance and dismissed as having a purely individual significance. In practical terms, the question can be framed like this: in all parties, especially in democratic and social-democratic parties in which the organizational structure is very loose, there are three layers. The numerically very restricted upper layer, that is usually made up of parliamentary deputies and intellectuals, often closely linked to the ruling class. The bottom layer, made up of workers and peasants and members of the urban petite bourgeoisie, which provides the mass of Party members or the mass of those influenced by the Party. And an intermediate layer, which in the present situation is even more important than it is in normal circumstances, in that it often represents the only active and politically 'live' layer of these parties. It is this intermediate layer that maintains the link between the leading group at the top and the mass of members and sympathizers. It is on the solidity of this middle layer that the Party leaders are counting for a future renewal of the various parties and a reconstruction of these parties on a broad basis.

Now, it is precisely on a significant section of these middle layers of the various popular parties that the influence of the movement in favour of a united front is making itself felt. It is within this middle layer that we are seeing this capillary phenomenon of the disintegration of the old ideologies and political programmes and the first stirrings of a new political formation on the terrain of the united front. Old reformist or maximalist workers who exercise a wide influence in certain factories or urban neighbourhoods. Peasant elements in the villages and small provincial towns who represent the most advanced figures of the rural world – the people to whom the peasants of the town or village turn for counsel and practical advice. Minor intellectuals in the cities who as representatives of the left Catholic movement radiate an influence in the surrounding areas which cannot and must not be measured by their modest stature, but rather by the fact that outside the city they appear as a tendency of that party which the peasants were accustomed to follow. These are the kind of elements over which our Party exercises an ever increasing influence and whose political spokesmen are a sure index of movements at a grass roots level that are often more radical than may appear from these individual shifts.

Particular attention must be paid to the part played by our youth organization in the activity for the united front. It is necessary to bear in mind, then, that a greater flexibility must be allowed in the actions of the youth organization than is allowed to the Party. It is obvious that the Party cannot go in for fusion with other political groups or for recruiting new members on the basis of the united front. The purpose of the united front is to foster unity of action on the part of the working class and the alliance between workers and peasants; it cannot be a basis for party formations. For the young communists, on the other hand, the question is rather different. By their very nature, the young communists represent the elementary stage in the formation of the party. To join the 'youth movement', it is not required that one is already a communist in the full sense of the word, but simply that one has a desire to struggle and to *become* a communist. This factor must serve as a general point of reference in order to define more clearly the tactics appropriate for the young communists.

One factor that deserves careful attention, because it has considerable historical significance, is the following. It is certainly significant that a maximalist, a reformist, a republican, a member of the *Partito Popolare*, a member of the Sardinian movement or a Southern democrat should support the programme of the proletarian united front and the alliance between workers and peasants. But it is far more significant that a member of Catholic Action should openly support such a programme. In fact, the opposition parties, albeit in an inadequate and ill-defined manner, tend to establish and maintain a distance between the popular masses and Fascism. Catholic Action, on the other hand, today represents an integral part of Fascism; it seeks to use religious ideology to win the support of broad popular masses for Fascism. Indeed, it is destined, in a certain sense, in the minds of a very strong tendency within the Fascist Party (Federzoni, Rocco, etc.), to take the place of the Fascist Party itself in its function as a mass party and an organism for political control over the populace. So every success on our part, however limited, in the field of Catholic Action means that we are managing to sabotage Fascist policy in a field that seemed entirely closed off to proletarian initiative.

To conclude on this point, we may assert that the political line of the Third Congress has been verified as correct and that the balance-sheet for our actions for the united front is extremely positive.

It is necessary to include a special point on trade-union activity, understood both in the sense of the position that we occupy today within the class unions and also in the sense of a real trade-union activity to be carried out; also in the sense of our position with respect to the corporations.

Where the second point is concerned, it is necessary to establish with precision the internal situation within the Fascist bourgeois–agrarian bloc and within the Fascist organization properly speaking.

The Two Tendencies within Fascism

On the one hand, the tendency of Federzoni, Rocco, Volpi, etc., which wants to draw the conclusions from this whole period since the march on Rome. It wants to liquidate the Fascist Party as a political organism and to incorporate into the State apparatus the bourgeois position of strength created by Fascism in its struggles against all the other parties. This tendency is working together with the Crown and the general staff. It wants to incorporate into the central forces of the State on the one hand Catholic Action (in other words, the Vatican), putting an end *de facto* and perhaps even formally to the rift between the House of Savoy and the Vatican; and on the other hand the more moderate elements of the former Aventine opposition. It is certain that, while Fascism in its nationalist wing, given the past and the traditions of the old Italian nationalism, is working towards Catholic Action, the House of Savoy, on the other hand, is once again trying to exploit its traditions in order to attract the members of the Di Cesarò and Amendola groups into government spheres.

The other tendency is officially represented by Farinacci. Object-ively, it represents two contradictions within Fascism: (1) The contra-diction between landowners and capitalists, whose interests clash, in particular, over tariffs. It is certain that today's Fascism typically represents the clear predominance of finance capital within the State: capital which seeks to subjugate all the productive forces of the coun-try. (2) The second contradiction, which is far more important, is that between the petite bourgeoisie and capitalism. The Fascist petite bourgeoisie sees the Party as its instrument of defence, its Parliament, its democracy. It seeks to put pressure on the government through the Party, to prevent itself from being crushed by capitalism.

One factor that must be kept in mind is the state of total enslave-ment to America in which Italy has been placed by the Fascist govern-ment. In the liquidation of its war debts to both America and Britain, the Fascist government did not take the trouble to obtain any guaran-tee of the negotiability of Italian obligations. The Italian stockmarket and exchequer are continually exposed to the political blackmail of the American and British governments, which can at any moment release vast quantities of Italian currency on to the market. The

Morgan debt, moreover, was incurred under even worse conditions.[2] Of the hundred million dollars of this loan, the government has only thirty-three million at its disposal. The other sixty-seven million the Italian government can only make use of with the generous personal consent of Morgan – which means that Morgan is the real head of the Italian government. These factors may have the effect of lending a nationalist intonation to the petite bourgeoisie's defence of its interests through the Fascist Party: a nationalist intonation opposed to the old nationalism and the present leadership of the party, which has sacrificed national sovereignty and the political independence of the country to the interests of a small group of plutocrats. In this connection, one thing our Party must do is to put a special emphasis on the slogan of the United Soviet States of Europe, as an instrument of political initiative among the Fascist rank and file.

In general, it can be said that the Farinacci tendency in the Fascist Party is lacking in unity, organization and general principles. It is more of a widespread state of mind than a tendency properly speaking and it will not be very difficult for the government to break up its constitutive nuclei. What is important from our point of view is that this crisis, insofar as it represents the detachment of the petite bourgeoisie from the bourgeois–agrarian alliance, cannot be other than a source of military weakness for Fascism.

The general economic crisis is the fundamental factor in the political crisis. It is necessary to study the elements that make up this crisis because certain of them are inherent in the general Italian situation and will have a negative effect in the period of proletarian dictatorship as well. These principal elements can be defined as follows: of the three elements that traditionally make up the assets in the Italian balance of trade, two – remittances from emigrants and the tourist industry – have collapsed. The third element, exports, is going through a crisis. If to these two negative factors (remittances from emigrants and the tourist industry) and the third, partially negative factor (exports) is added the need for heavy imports of grain owing to the failed harvest, it becomes clear that the prospects for the coming months are looking catastrophic.

It is necessary to bear these four elements in mind to understand the impotence of the government and the ruling class. Certainly, even

[2] J.P. Morgan lent over 100 million dollars to Italy in early 1926.

if the government can do nothing or next to nothing to increase remittances from emigrants (take account of the initiative proposed by Mr. Giuseppe Zuccoli, the expected successor to Volpi at the Ministry of Finance) and to boost the tourist industry, something *can* be done to increase exports. At all events, a major policy initiative is possible in this area, which, even if it did not heal the wound, would at least help to stop the flow of blood. Some people are thinking in terms of a labour policy based on inflationism. Naturally, this possibility cannot be absolutely ruled out, but (1) if it did come to pass, its results in the economic field would be relatively minimal; (2) in the political field, on the other hand, its results would be catastrophic.

In reality, it is necessary to bear the following factors in mind: (1) Exports represent only a part of the credit side of the Italian balance of trade, at most two-thirds; (2) To wipe out the deficit, it would be necessary not only to obtain the maximum yield from the existing productive base, but also to enlarge the productive base itself by buying new machinery abroad, which would increase the trade deficit even further; (3) Raw materials for Italian industry are imported from abroad and have to be paid for in hard currency. A large-scale increase in production would mean that an enormous mass of circulating capital would be needed for buying raw materials; (4) It must be kept in mind that Fascism as a general phenomenon has reduced the wages and salaries of the Italian working class to a minimum. Inflation makes some sense in a country with high wages, as an alternative to Fascism: it lowers the standard of living of the working classes and thus restores freedom of manoeuvre to the bourgeoisie. Inflation makes no sense at all in Italy, where the standard of living of the working class is already at subsistence level.

Among the elements of the economic crisis: the new organization of joint-stock companies with preferential voting, which is one of the sources of rupture between petite bourgeoisie and capitalism; also the imbalance which has appeared recently between the gross capital of the joint-stock companies, which is being concentrated in fewer and fewer hands and the gross national savings. This imbalance shows that the sources of savings are drying up, since current incomes are no longer sufficient for needs.

The Democratic Coalition

On the third political factor. It is clear that a certain regrouping is taking place in the democratic field, more radical than anything we have seen in the past. Republican ideology is becoming stronger, in the same way that we have already seen when we were looking at the united front: in other words, within the middle layers of the democratic parties (and in this case, to a considerable degree, among the upper layers as well).

Old former Aventine leaders have refused the invitation to resume contact with the monarchy. It is said that even Amendola himself went over to republicanism entirely in the last years of his life and carried out personal propaganda along these lines. The *popolari* have apparently developed republican leanings as well, etc. It is certain that great efforts are being made to bring about a neo-democratic regrouping on the terrain of republicanism: a regrouping designed to take power as soon as Fascism collapses and to set up a dictatorship opposed to both the reactionary right and the communist left. This republican democratic reawakening has been helped along by recent events in Europe, like the Pilsudski adventure in Poland and the death-throes of the French cartel. Our party must confront the general problem of the broad perspectives within national politics.

We can define the main factors here as the following. Even though it is true that, politically, the successor to Fascism may be a dictatorship of the proletariat (since no intermediate party or coalition is capable of giving even the most minimal satisfaction to the economic demands of the working classes, who will burst violently on to the political scene the moment the existing relations are destroyed), it is nevertheless not certain – in fact, it is not even probable – that the passage from Fascism to the dictatorship of the proletariat will be a direct one. It must be borne in mind that the existing armed forces, given their composition, cannot be won over immediately and that they will be the deciding factor in the situation.

It is possible to line up hypotheses in order of increasing probability. It is possible that we may pass from the present government to a coalition government, in which men like Giolitti, Orlando, Di Cesarò and De Gasperi will provide a greater immediate flexibility. Recent events in the French Parliament show quite what flexibility bourgeois policy is capable of, where what is at stake is postponing the revolutionary crisis and dislodging, wearing down and dividing enemies. A sudden, lightning economic crisis – something not improbable in a situation like that in Italy – could bring the democratic republican coalition to power, since it would present itself to the officers of the army, to a part of the Fascist militia itself and to State functionaries in general (a factor which must be given considerable weight in situations like that in Italy), as capable of checking the revolution.

These hypotheses only serve to provide us with a general perspective. They serve to establish the following points: (1) Right from today, we must reduce to a minimum the influence and organization of the parties that may make up the left coalition, in order to increase the probability of a revolutionary collapse of Fascism (in that the energetic and active elements in the population will be in our camp when the crisis strikes); (2) in any case, we must aim to ensure that the democratic interlude lasts as short a time as possible, by setting out from this very moment to make conditions as favourable as possible for us.

It is from these indications that we must derive the guidelines for our immediate practical activity. Intensification of the general activity of the united front and organization of ever increasing numbers of agitation committees, to be centralized at least on a regional and provincial level. Within the committees, our fractions must seek first of all to obtain the maximum representation of the various left political currents, systematically avoiding all party sectarianism. Issues must be presented in an objective manner by our fractions, as an expression of the interests of the working class and the peasants.

Tactics where Maximalist party is concerned. Need to raise the Southern problem more energetically. If our Party does not start working seriously in the South, the South will be the strongest base for the left coalition.

Tactics where Sardinian Action Party is concerned, in view of its forthcoming congress. For Southern Italy and the islands, creation of regional working parties in the rest of Italy.

II

Where the international situation is concerned, it seems to me that the dominant issue is that of the English general strike[3] and the

---

[3] Of 4–13 May 1926.

conclusions to be drawn from it. The English strike has posed two fundamental problems for our movement.

(1) The problem of general perspectives: that is, the problem of a precise assessment of the phase that the capitalist order is currently passing through. Is the so-called period of stabilization now over? What point are we at regarding the capacity for resistance of the bourgeois regime? Clearly, it is interesting and necessary, not only from a theoretical and scientific but also from a practical and immediate point of view, to establish precisely the point that the capitalist crisis has reached. But clearly, as well, any new political orientation based on a new assessment of the precise degree of the capitalist crisis would be pointless if this new assessment were not to be reflected immediately in genuinely new political and organizational directives.

The question we should be asking, it strikes me, is the following one. In the international field – and this, in practical terms, means two things: (1) in the field of that group of capitalist States which are the keystone of the bourgeois system; and (2) in the field of those States that represent, as it were, the periphery of the capitalist world – are we about to pass from the phase of political organization of the proletarian forces to the phase of technical organization of the revolution? Or, on the other hand, are we about to pass from the former of the phases mentioned to an intermediate phase, in which a given form of technical organization can accelerate the political organization of the masses and thus accelerate the passage to the concluding phase of the conquest of power? These problems, in my view, should be discussed. But it is obvious that it will not be possible to find a solution to them at a purely theoretical level. They can only be solved on the basis of concrete data regarding the real efficiency both of the revolutionary and the bourgeois forces.

This study must be based on certain observations and criteria. (1) The observation that in the advanced capitalist countries, the ruling class possesses political and organizational resources that it did not possess, for example, in Russia. This means that even the most serious economic crises do not have immediate repercussions in the political sphere. Politics is always one step behind – or many steps behind – economics. The State apparatus is far more resistant than it is often possible to believe; and, at moments of crisis, it is far more capable of organizing forces loyal to the regime than the depth of the crisis might lead one to suppose. This is especially true of the most important capitalist States.

In typical peripheral States, like Italy, Poland, Spain or Portugal, the State forces are less efficient. But in these countries one finds a phenomenon that merits the closest attention. This is what this phenomenon consists of, in my view: in countries like these, between the proletariat and capitalism there is a broad band of intermediate classes, which seek to promote (and, in a certain sense, succeed in promoting) policies of their own, with ideologies that often influence broad strata of the proletariat, but that have a particular hold over the peasant masses. Even France, though it occupies a leading place in the first group of capitalist States, has certain characteristics that bring it closer to the situation of the peripheral States.

What seems to me to be characteristic of the present phase of the capitalist crisis is the fact that, unlike in 1920–2, today the political and military formations of the middle classes are radical and left-wing in character, or at least present themselves to the masses as radical and on the left. Allowing for its particular characteristics, the development of the Italian situation can, I think, in a certain sense, provide a model for the various phases other countries have been going through. In 1919 and 1920, the military and political formations of the middle classes were represented in Italy by primitive Fascism and D'Annunzio. It is well known that in those years both the Fascist movement and D'Annunzio's movement were prepared to go as far as allying themselves with the revolutionary proletarian forces to overthrow the Nitti government, which appeared to be the go-between for American capitalism's bid to enslave Italy (Nitti was the precursor of Dawes in Europe).

The second phase of Fascism – 1921 and 1922 – was clearly reactionary. From 1923, a capillary process began, in the course of which the most active elements within the middle classes moved over from the reactionary Fascist camp to the camp of the Aventine opposition. This process crystallized in a manner that might have proved fatal for Fascism in the period of the Matteotti crisis. Because of the weakness of our movement – a weakness which was in itself significant – the phenomenon was curtailed by Fascism and the middle classes were swept back into a renewed state of political fragmentation. Today, the capillary phenomenon has started up again, on a far greater scale than in the post-1923 movement; and it is being accompanied by a regrouping of revolutionary forces around our party, which means that a new crisis like the Matteotti one would be unlikely to end with a new 3 January.

These phases, which Italy has been passing through in what I would call a classic and exemplary manner, can be found in all those countries we have called peripheral capitalist countries. The present phase in Italy – a regrouping of the middle classes on the left – can be found in Spain, Portugal, Poland and the Balkans. Only in two countries, Czechoslovakia and France, do we find a continuity in the presence of the left bloc – a fact that in my view merits particularly close study.

It seems to me that the conclusion to be drawn from these observations – which will naturally need be revised and set out in a systematic manner – might be the following. In reality, we are entering a new phase in the progression of the capitalist crisis. This phase is taking a different form in the countries of the capitalist periphery and in the advanced capitalist countries. Czechoslovakia and France provide the connecting links between these two series of States. In the peripheral countries, there is the problem of the phase I have referred to as intermediate, lying between the phases of political and technical preparation for the revolution. In the other countries, France and Czechoslovakia included, it seems to me that the problem is still one of political preparation. For all the capitalist countries, there is a fundamental problem: how to pass from the united front tactic, understood in a general sense, to a specific tactic, which deals with the concrete problems of national life and works on the basis of the popular forces as they are historically determined.

In technical terms, the problem concerns the appropriate slogans and forms of organization. If I were not afraid of being accused of *Ordine Nuovoism*, I would say that one of the most important problems today, particularly in the major capitalist countries, is that of the Factory Councils and workers' control, as the basis for a new regrouping of the proletarian class which would permit a more effective struggle against trade-union bureaucracy and allow the immense masses of non-unionized workers not only in France, but in Germany and England as well, to be incorporated into our movement.

Where England is concerned, in any case, it seems to me that the problem of the regrouping of the proletarian masses might even be tackled on the terrain of trade-unionism itself. Our English Party should have a programme for the reorganization of the trade unions along democratic lines. Only when the local trade-union branches in England start co-ordinating their activities in the manner of our Camere del Lavoro and give these Camere del Lavoro adequate powers, will it be possible: (1) to liberate English workers from the influence of union bureaucracy; (2) to reduce the influence exercised within the Labour Party by MacDonald's party (ILP), which at present functions precisely as a local centralizing force in a context of political fragmentation; (3) to create a terrain upon which it will be possible for the organized elements in our party to exercise a direct influence on the mass of English workers. I think that this kind of reorganization of the trade unions, with the impulse coming from our Party, would have the significance and importance of a genuine Soviet germination. Moreover, it would be in the line of the historical tradition of the English working class, from Chartism to the Action Committees of 1919.

The second fundamental problem posed by the English general strike is that of the Anglo-Russian Committee. I think that despite the indecision, weakness and, if you like, treachery of the English left during the general strike, the Anglo-Russian Committee should be maintained, because it is the best terrain on which to revolutionize not only the English trade-union world, but also the Amsterdam unions. There is only one eventuality in which there should be a break between the communists and the English left: if England was on the eve of the proletarian revolution and our Party was strong enough to lead the insurrection on its own.

NB These notes have been written solely in order to prepare the work of the Steering Committee. They are far from being definitive; they simply represent the draft for an initial discussion.[4]

---

[4] Gramsci gave this paper to the executive of the PCd'I at the meeting of 2–3 August 1926, having first made preliminary soundings amongst his colleagues.

The Soviet Union on the Path to Communism

Over the last week, the bourgeois newspapers have dedicated quite a number of articles to the situation in Russia. The Honourable Baldesi has summed up the general tendency of the coverage in *La Stampa*, *La Tribuna* and *Il Mondo*, in an article in *Il Mondo* itself, in which he claims that communism in Russia has now been proved to have failed and that the re-establishment of capitalism is now just round the corner. For a start, as a good social-democrat, the Honourable Baldesi is highly displeased that the Bolsheviks should have had a socialist revolution in October 1917 at all, because, according to him, after the overthrow of Tsarism, what was wanted was a democratic, bourgeois government – one of those regimes that so delight the proletarians of every nation. So great is his displeasure, in fact, that, despite the fact that he appears to be favourable to agrarian reform, it has slipped his mind that it was only the proletarian revolution which gave the land to the peasants. It has slipped his mind, in other words, that the various governments that succeeded one another in Russia between February and October 1917 were imperialist and bourgeois governments, which would never have enacted that agrarian reform democrats and reformists claim to be so enthusiastic about.

It was only the alliance of workers and peasants and the Bolshevik revolution which brought about that massive upheaval of the foundations of the Russian economy. No democratic regime, not even in the post-war period, has done anything of the kind; in Western Europe, it would have been unthinkable. The hesitant attempts in Romania and Poland are failing miserably. In his examination of the present economic conditions in Russia, the Honourable Baldesi, like all his friends, are failing, above all, to take account of conditions before the War. We have found statistics about the population, taxes and national income of the various countries in the pre-war period in a book of Harvey Fischer's, *I debiti interalleati* [*The Allied Debt*], published by the Bankers' Trust of New York. The national *per capita* income was $351 in the USA, $226 in Britain, $182 in France and only $43 in Russia. In terms of national income, Russia was even below Greece, Turkey, Bulgaria and Serbia. And then there was the War, followed by the revolution and the civil war.

It was not the revolution, which took place in a matter of days in Moscow and Leningrad and across the country, which devastated Russia and reduced it to a vast terrain strewn with burnt-out ruins. Rather, it was the intervention of the great powers in support of the white armies – those liberal, democratic regimes dear to the hearts of *Il Mondo* and the Honourable Baldesi. It was the fault of the white – bourgeois, liberal, democratic – armies of France and England, if the peasants stopped cultivating the earth and the railways were destroyed, the factories abandoned, the cities sacked. And if, in spite of everything, the Soviet regime has triumphed, that in itself indicates that this regime enjoyed the consensus of the vast majority of the Russian people. No other regime in any country in Europe could have met the challenge which the Soviet regime has faced.

So one only has to think about the situation in which the revolution was started to understand why, if the Russian workers have not exactly been in clover, it is ridiculous and senseless to put the blame on communism. On the contrary, the results which have been achieved so far must be considered little short of miraculous: the fact, that is, that industrial and agricultural production have been brought back up to their pre-war levels and that the conditions of workers have been improved. Because the crisis referred to above, the current crisis, is primarily caused by the fact that the peasants, no longer oppressed by the rents and taxes and masters, are now eating more grain than they were before the War and at the same time are able to acquire more industrial products for their own consumption. In the pre-war period, Russian landowners exported a vast amount of grain, while keeping the millions of peasants who produced it in a state of permanent hunger. Today these peasants have increased their standard of living, to such an extent that the national industries, which have got back to pre-war levels of production, are unable to satisfy their demand.

But the fundamental argument of our opponents is the New Economic Policy and its future effects. However, they are not taking into account the fact that if, in the Russian economic revival, private capital has been growing, collective capital has taken on an even greater importance. All the collectivized major industry, all the factories – steelworks, metallurgical works, textile mills, etc. – are the property of the State and are run by the State; and they employ ninety-five per cent of Russian workers. But that does not concern our opponents. They note that there are thousands of shops and workshops and blacksmiths' forges in Russian villages; that there are even small factories being started up (these are allowed no more than fifteen workers if they are mechanized and fifty if they are not); and they claim, finally, that capitalism is winning out in Russian industry. They pretend to be unaware of the fact that all the export trade is monopolized by the State through the banks, which are all collective organs. They try to feign ignorance of the fact that the State's whole efforts are directed towards developing the socialist elements in production and that those capitalist elements which have been acknowledged as useful and which clearly cannot be suppressed immediately, by some drastic action, are nevertheless rigorously controlled.

And then there is agriculture. We have already made the point that only the Bolshevik revolution could have had the strength to give the land to the peasants. In no bourgeois regime – not even one where the Honourable Baldesi was prime minister – will the rural masses ever have the chance to own the land. So, for the bourgeoisie, it is a historical inevitability (and the Honourable Baldesi, as a social-democrat is of the same opinion) that medium and large landed estates should be formed and that there should be a process of wealth concentration – a process whose end result will be, inevitably . . .'. yes, the *latifondo*. Then, after a couple of centuries, there will be another peasants' revolution; and so on.

We deny that this process is inevitable if the might of the State is pitted against it and the might of a collectivized industrial and finan-

cial economy. Another process is taking place in Russia: the development of small-holdings which collaborate with one another. It is
through co-operation – co-operation in production, in sales, in credit,
in purchasing, good production, etc. – that the Russian peasants will
avert the danger of agrarian capitalism becoming re-established and
will instead build up an economy in which collective structures will
be ever more important.

No communist has ever promised workers he could create the land
of milk and honey overnight. No communist has ever believed that
a communist regime could be brought about in six months. The
transitions from slave to feudal regimes and from feudal to capitalist
regimes have taken a mammoth toll of human effort over extremely
long periods. Even today, in the most flourishing capitalist regimes,
there are still traces of a feudal economy. There is no reason to think
that communism can be brought about with a touch of a magic wand.

The profound difference between Russia and the other countries
whose regimes are so dear to the hearts of the various Baldesis of
the democratic and reformist camps is this: that in Russia all the
might and all the will of the State is directed towards bringing about
communism, whereas in other countries all the force and will of the
State is dedicated to preserving capitalism and stopping communism.
That is the case even in countries where the reformists are in power:
in the famous Belgium, for example, where the Honourable Vander-
velde is a slave to bureaucracy and a . . . *servant* of democracy and is
shifting the burden of the economic crisis on to the petite bourgeoisie
and the workers, just like a Poincaré, or worse.

These are elementary truths, which we can understand must seem
unpalatable to the bourgeoisie. If, on the other hand, we could still
believe in the good faith of the social-democrats in Italy and elsewhere, it would be very difficult for us to understand the pleasure it
seems to be giving them to describe the alleged failure of communism
in Russia – the failure, that is, of the only revolution which has put
Marxist theory and the capacities of the proletariat to the test. Is
there a socialist bone still left in their bodies? They know full well
that if some new crisis brings about a new proletarian society, it is
not they who will have the honour and burden of realizing the
workers' ideal. Their only chance of scraping themselves a living now
is to reassure the various bourgeoisies of the contribution they could

make to defending their predominance, if the need for such a defence was ever felt.

It is perfectly natural, therefore, that, in *Il Mondo* (in the organ, that is, of those democrats who bear the responsibility for our defeat in the crisis which followed Matteotti's assassination; those democrats who chose defeat rather than a revolutionary proletarian revival), the failure of communism should be proclaimed by the Honourable Baldesi – that same Baldesi who, on the day of the march on Rome, fulfilled his duty as a socialist deputy and a leader of the General Confederation of Labour by going round telling all the ushers in the Parliament building that, if the Honourable Mussolini really insisted, he would be prepared to accept a ministerial portfolio at great personal sacrifice. A worthy representative, then, of the party which is doing everything it can to shake off the chains of Matteotti's martyrdom, with which it has been shackled by a cruel twist of fate.

L'Unità, 7 September 1926

Letter to the Central Committee of the Soviet Communist Party[1]

(Rome, 14 October 1926)

Dear comrades,

The Italian Communists and all the conscious workers of our country have always followed your debates with the greatest interest. On the eve of every congress and every conference of the Russian Communist Party, we were confident that, despite the fierceness of the polemics, the unity of the Russian Party was not in danger. On the contrary, we were confident that, having achieved a greater ideological and organizational homogeneity through such debates, the Party would be better prepared and equipped to overcome the many difficulties connected to the exercise of power in a workers' State. Today, on the eve of your Fifteenth Conference, we no longer have the same confidence we had in the past. We cannot free ourselves of a sense of anguish; it seems to us that the present attitude of the opposition bloc and the heat

---

[1] Gramsci's letter was a response to the struggle that took place within the Russian Communist Party in the second half of 1926, between the majority Stalin–Bukharin faction and the Trotsky–Zinoviev–Kamenev oppositional minority. Togliatti, writing from Moscow on 18 October 1926, judged the letter inopportune, believing Gramsci to have exaggerated the effect of the split on Communist Parties elsewhere and to have underestimated the importance of following the correct line as laid down by the majority faction. Gramsci, replying on 26 October 1926, reiterated his position, stressing the need for unity, and urged Togliatti to forward his letter.

of the polemics within the Communist Party of the USSR make it
incumbent on brother parties to intervene. It is precisely this conviction
which has prompted us to address this letter to you. It may be that the
isolation in which our Party is forced to live has led us to exaggerate the
dangers so far as the internal situation in the Communist Party of the
USSR is concerned. But, in any case, our assessment of the international repercussions of this situation is certainly not exaggerated and as
internationalists we wish to carry out our duty.

The internal situation in our brother party in the USSR strikes us
as different and far more serious than in previous debates because
today we are seeing an ever-widening split within the Leninist central
group which has always been the leading nucleus of the Party and
the International. Quite independent of the numerical outcome of
the vote in congress, this kind of split can have the gravest repercussions – not only if the opposition minority fails to accept with the
utmost loyalty the fundamental principle of revolutionary party discipline, but also if, in the course of its struggle, it transgresses certain
boundaries which lie above any formal democratic criteria.

One of Lenin's most precious lessons was that we should pay great
attention to the opinions of our class enemies. Well, dear comrades,
you can be quite sure that the most powerful press organs and statesmen of the international bourgeoisie are setting great store by the
radical character of the current conflict within the fundamental nucleus of the CPSU. They are counting on this split within our brother
Party, convinced that it must lead to the disintegration and slow
death-agony of the proletarian dictatorship; that it will bring about
the downfall of the revolution as the invasions and the revolts of the
white guards could not. The very coolness and circumspection with
which the bourgeois press is now seeking to analyse Russian events –
the fact that it is now seeking, as far as possible, to avoid the violent
demagogy which characterized it in the past – are symptoms that
should cause Russian comrades to reflect and make them more aware
of their responsibility.

There is another reason as well why the international bourgeoisie
is counting on a possible split or a worsening of the internal crisis in
the Communist Party of the USSR. The workers' state has not been
in existence in Russia for nine years. It is a certainty that only a small
minority, not only among the working classes but even among the
Communist Parties themselves in other countries, is capable of

reconstructing the development of the revolution in its entirety and tracing, even in the details of everyday life in the Soviet Union, the continuity of the red thread leading to the general prospect of the construction of socialism. And that is the case not only in countries where freedom of association no longer exists and the freedom of the press has been completely suppressed or subjected to unprecedented restrictions, as in Italy (where the courts have confiscated and outlawed the printing of the books of Trotsky, Lenin, Stalin, Zinoviev and most lately the *Communist Manifesto*), but even in those countries where our Parties are free to keep their members and the masses in general adequately informed. In these countries the great masses cannot understand the debates that take place in the Communist Party of the USSR, especially if they are as violent as the present one and concern not some question of detail but the political line of the Party in its entirety. Not just the working masses in general, but the masses within our Parties themselves regard the Republic of the Soviets and the Party in power there as a single combat unity working within the general perspective of socialism and they want to see it continuing in this role. It is only because the masses in Western Europe regard Russia and the Russian Party in this light that they accept it freely, as a historical necessity, that the CPSU should be the leading Party in the International. It is only because of this that the Republic of Soviets and the CPSU are a formidable element of revolutionary organization and a formidable driving force.

The bourgeois and social-democratic parties, for the same reason, are exploiting the internal disputes and conflicts that exist within the CPSU. They want to combat this influence of the Russian revolution; to combat the revolutionary unity that is being forged around the CPSU throughout the world. Dear comrades, it is extremely significant that in a country like Italy – where the Fascist State and party organization succeeds in stifling any significant sign of autonomous life on the part of the great mass of workers and peasants – it is significant that the Fascist papers, especially the local papers, are full of articles, technically well constructed for propaganda purposes and using a minimum of demagogy and striking a minimum of abusive attitudes, which set out to demonstrate, with an obvious attempt at objectivity, that, to go by what the best known leaders of the opposition in the CPSU themselves are saying, the State of the Soviets is now firmly back on the path to becoming a purely capitalist State, so that in the world duel between Fascism and Bolshevism, Fascism will come out on top. If, on the one hand, this campaign shows that the Republic of the Soviets still enjoys limitless sympathy among the great masses of the Italian people – who, in some regions have for six years now been receiving only a trickle of illegal Party literature – it also, on the other hand, shows that Fascism, which knows the real internal situation in Italy extremely well and has learnt how to deal with the masses, is attempting to use the political stance of the Joint Opposition to break down once and for all Italian workers' staunch aversion to Mussolini's government and to foster a state of mind in which Fascism will appear as, if nothing more, an ineluctable historical necessity, notwithstanding the brutalities and other evils it brings with it.

We believe that in the entire International our Party is the one which feels most keenly the repercussions of the grave situation that exists in the CPSU. And this is not only for the reasons outlined above, which are so to speak external, relating to the general conditions of revolutionary development in our society. You know that all the parties of the International have inherited both from the old social democracy and from the differing national traditions that exist in the various countries (anarchism, syndicalism, etc., etc.) a mass of prejudices and ideological impulses which represents the main breeding-ground for deviations, both on the right and the left. It took much painful experience and many painful, debilitating crises but, in these last years and especially after the Fifth World Congress, our parties were gradually beginning to settle down into a stable Leninist configuration; gradually turning into true Bolshevik parties. New proletarian cadres were created from below, from the shopfloor, while the intellectual elements were subjected to a rigorous selection process and a strict and uncompromising assessment on the basis of their practical work, on the terrain of action. This restructuring took place under the guidance of the CPSU as a united entity and of all the great leaders of the CPSU.

Now, the gravity of the present crisis and the threat of an open or latent split is halting this process of development and restructuring in our parties; crystallizing deviations on the right and left and yet again putting off the moment when the world party of workers will achieve organic unity. It is to this factor in particular that we believe it our duty as internationalists to call the attention of the most responsible comrades in the CPSU. Comrades, in these past nine years of world history, you have been the organizing and driving element behind the revolutionary forces in all nations. The role you have performed has no precedent for scope and profundity in the entire history of the human race. But today you are destroying your work. You are going backwards and running the risk of losing the leading role that the CPSU had won for itself through the contribution of Lenin. It appears to us that the violent passions aroused by Russian internal affairs are making you lose sight of the international implications of Russian affairs themselves. You are forgetting that your duties as Russian militants must be carried out – and *can* only be carried out – within the framework of the interests of the international proletariat.

The Political Bureau of the Italian Communist Party has examined all the problems now under discussion in the CPSU as thoroughly and carefully as it was possible for us to do. The questions you are facing today may be facing our Party tomorrow. In our country too, the rural masses make up the majority of the working population. Moreover, all the problems inherent in the hegemony of the proletariat will present themselves in an even more complex and acute form in Italy than in Russia itself, because the density of the rural population in Italy is vastly greater; because our peasants have an extremely rich tradition of organization and have always succeeded, as a mass, in making their specific weight felt in national political life; and because the organizational apparatus of the Church in Italy has two thousand years of tradition behind it and has specialized in propaganda and the organization of the peasants in a way which has no parallel in other countries. If it is true that industry is more developed in our country and that the proletariat has a considerable material basis, it is also true that this industry has to import its raw materials and is therefore more exposed to crises. The proletariat will only be able to carry out its leading function, then, if it is rich in the spirit of sacrifice and if it has freed itself completely from any remaining trace of reformist or syndicalist corporatism.

It is from this realistic and, we believe, Leninist point of view that the Political Bureau of the Italian Communist Party has examined your debates. Up till now, we have expressed a Party view only on the strictly disciplinary question of factions, since we wished to respect the request you made after your Fourteenth Congress not to carry the Russian debate over into the other sections of the International. We now state that we consider basically correct the political line of the majority of the Central Committee of the CPSU; and the majority of the Italian Party will certainly take the same position, if it becomes necessary to debate the whole question. We do not wish to agitate or direct propaganda at you or at the comrades of the Joint Opposition – it would be useless. We will not, then, make a list of all the specific questions with our opinion noted in the margin. We repeat that we are struck by the fact that the attitude of the opposition concerns the entire political line of the Central Committee and goes to the very heart of Leninist doctrine and the political action of our Soviet Party. It is the principle and the practice of the hegemony of the proletariat which are being brought into question; the fundamental relations of alliance between the workers and peasants which are being disturbed and threatened – that is, the pillars of the workers' State and the revolution.

Comrades, it has never happened before in history that a dominant class, in its entirety, should be experiencing worse living conditions than those of certain elements and strata of the dominated and subjected class. History has reserved this unprecedented contradiction as the destiny of the proletariat. It is in this contradiction that the greatest dangers for the dictatorship of the proletariat lie, especially in countries where capitalism has not developed very far or succeeded in unifying the proletarian forces. It is from this contradiction, which, moreover, is already apparent in certain forms in those capitalist countries in which the proletariat has objectively achieved a prominent position in society, that reformism and syndicalism are born, and the corporate spirit and the stratifications of the labour aristocracy. However, the proletariat cannot become the dominant class if it does not overcome this contradiction by sacrificing its corporate interests. It cannot maintain its hegemony and its dictatorship if, even once it has become dominant, it does not sacrifice these immediate interests for the general and permanent interests of its class. Certainly, it is easy to be demagogic on the subject, stressing the negative sides of the contradiction: 'Is it you who is the ruler, o ill-clothed and ill-fed peasant? Or is it the Nepman in his furs, enjoying all the bounty of the earth?' And so the reformists, after a revolutionary strike which has increased the cohesion and discipline of the mass but which went on for long enough to impoverish the individual workers still further, are now saying: 'What good did it do you to struggle? You are ruined and impoverished!' It is easy to be demagogic on this subject; in fact, it is difficult not to be when the question has been posed in terms of the corporate spirit, rather than in Leninist terms, in terms of the doctrine of the hegemony of the proletariat, which historically finds itself in one particular given position rather than any other.

This, for us, is the essential element in your debate. This is the root of the errors of the Joint Opposition and the origin of the latent dangers contained in its activities. In the ideology and practice of the Joint Opposition we see the rebirth of that whole tradition of social democracy and syndicalism which, up till now, has prevented the Western proletariat from organizing itself as a ruling class.

Only a firm unity and discipline in the Party that governs the workers' State can ensure proletarian hegemony under the regime of the New Economic Policy – that is, amid the full development of the contradiction to which we have referred. But unity and discipline in this case cannot be mechanical and enforced; they must be sincere and arise from conviction. They must not be the kind of unity and discipline one would expect from an enemy unit that has been imprisoned or besieged and whose only thought is of escape or an unexpected sortie.

This, dearest comrades, is what we wanted to say to you, in the spirit of brothers and friends, even if younger brothers. Comrades Zinoviev, Trotsky and Kamenev have played a very important part in educating us for the revolution; they have on occasion corrected us with great energy and rigour; they have been our masters. It is to them that we are addressing ourselves in particular, as those principally responsible for the present situation, because we like to feel certain that the majority in the Central Committee of the CPSU is not set on winning a crushing victory in the struggle and that it is disposed to avoid excessive measures. The unity of our brother party in Russia is necessary for the development and triumph of the world revolutionary forces. All communists and internationalists must be prepared to make the greatest sacrifices in the face of this necessity. The damage caused by an error of a united Party can be easily mended. The damage caused by a split or a prolonged period where a split is imminent may be irreparable and fatal.

With communist greetings,
The Political Bureau of the PCdI

Some Aspects of the Southern Question[1]

What gave rise to these notes was an article on the Southern question published in the 18 December issue of *Il quarto stato*, under the name of 'Ulenspiegel',[2] and prefaced by a rather absurd introduction by the editors of the journal. In his article, 'Ulenspiegel' mentions Guido Dorso's recent book (*La rivoluzione meridionale*, pub. Piero Gobetti (Turin, 1925)) and refers to Dorso's comments on our Party's stance with regard to the Southern question. In their presentation, the editors of *Il quarto stato* – who proclaim themselves to be 'young people *perfectly acquainted* with the Southern problem *in its broad outlines* [sic]' – register their collective protest against the fact that some 'merit' is being allowed to the Communist Party. Nothing wrong with that so far: young people of the *Quarto stato* stamp have been forcing even worse opinions and objections on to long-suffering pieces of paper since time began. But then these 'young people' go on to say (and I quote), 'We have not forgotten the magic formula of the Turin communists, which was: divide up the great landed estates among the rural proletariat. This formula is worlds removed from any sane, realistic vision of the Southern problem.' And at this point, we really

[1] This text is based on a manuscript Gramsci was working on at the time of his arrest and, as a result, it remains unfinished. The Southern Question was to form the focus of a series of articles that he was preparing for publication, all of which appear to have gone missing.
[2] Pseudonym of Tommaso Fiore, a writer for Piero Gobetti's *La Rivoluzione liberale*.

have to get things straight, because the only 'magical' thing here is the effrontery and superficial dilettanteism of the 'young people' who write for *Il quarto stato*.

The 'magic formula' is a pure fabrication. And the 'young people' of *Il quarto stato* cannot have much respect for their enormously intellectual readers if they feel they can risk turning the truth upside down with such glib presumptuousness. Here, in fact, is an extract from *L'Ordine Nuovo* (No. 3, January 1920), in which the viewpoint of the Turin communists is summarized:

> The Northern bourgeoisie has subjugated the South of Italy and the Islands and reduced them to the status of colonies to be exploited. The Northern proletariat, in emancipating itself from capitalist slavery, will emancipate the Southern peasant masses, who are enslaved to the banks and the parasitic industrialism of the North. The economic and political regeneration of the peasants must not be sought in the division of uncultivated or poorly cultivated lands, but in solidarity with the industrial proletariat, which, in turn, relies on the solidarity of the peasants and has an 'interest' in ensuring that capitalism is not reborn economically from landed property and that Southern Italy and the Islands do not become a military base for capitalist counter-revolution. By introducing workers' control over industry, the proletariat will orient industry towards the production of agricultural machinery for the peasants, clothing and footwear for the peasants and electrical energy for the peasants; it will prevent industry and the banks from carrying out any further exploitation of the peasants and chaining them as slaves to their strongboxes. By smashing the factory autocracy and the oppressive apparatus of the capitalist State, by setting up a workers' State that will subject the capitalists to the law of useful labour, the workers will smash all the chains that shackle the worker to his poverty and despair. By establishing a workers' dictatorship and taking over industry and the banks, the proletariat will swing the enormous weight of the State bureaucracy behind the peasants in their struggle against the landowners, against the elements and against poverty. It will provide the peasants with credit, set up co-operatives and guarantee security of person and property against looters. It will carry out public works of reclamation and irrigation. It will do all this because it is in its interests to encourage an increase in agricultural production and to win and keep the solidarity of the peasant masses. It is in its interests to orient industrial production towards

the useful end of peace and brotherhood between town and country, between North and South.

That was written in January 1920. Seven years have gone by and we are seven years older politically as well. There are certain concepts that might be expressed better today: a clearer distinction could and should be made between the period immediately following the conquest of State power, which is characterized by simple workers' control over industry, and subsequent periods. But the important thing to note here is that the basic concept of the Turin communists was not the 'magic formula' of dividing up the great estates, but rather a political alliance between Northern workers and Southern peasants, to oust the bourgeoisie from State power. What is more, it was precisely the Turin communists (even though they *did* support a division of the land, as an adjunct to the solidary action of the two classes), who warned against the illusion of seeing a mechanical division of the great estates as a 'miracle solution'. In the same article of 3 January, we find:

> What good does it do an impoverished peasant to occupy an uncultivated or poorly cultivated piece of land? Without machinery, without accommodation on the site, without credit to tide him over until harvest-time, without co-operative institutions to buy the harvest from him (if he makes it through to the harvest without hanging himself first from the stoutest bush or the least sickly wild fig-tree on his untilled land!) and preserve him from the clutches of the usurers – without all these things, what can a peasant achieve by occupying the land?

Yet, despite this, we were still in favour of the highly realistic and by no means 'magical' formula of giving the land to the peasants. But we wanted this distribution to take place within the context of a general revolutionary action on the part of the two allied classes, under the leadership of the industrial proletariat. The *Quarto stato* contributors invented out of thin air the 'magic formula' they attribute to the Turin communists. By doing so, they showed up their journalistic lack of seriousness and a lack of scruples worthy of a bar-room philosopher. And these, too, are political factors that carry some weight and have some influence.

In the proletarian camp, the Turin communists have had one undeniable 'merit': that of bringing the Southern question to the

attention of the vanguard of the working class and identifying it as
one of the essential problems of national policy for the revolutionary
proletariat. In this sense, they have been instrumental in shifting the
Southern question out of its indistinct, intellectualistic phase – the
phase of so-called 'concretism' – and into a new phase. The revolutionary worker from Turin or Milan has become the protagonist of
the Southern question, in place of people like Giustino Fortunato,
Gaetano Salvemini, Eugenio Azimonti and Arturo Labriola (to stick
to the names of the gurus of the 'young people' of *Quarto stato*).

The Turin communists had raised, in concrete terms, the question
of the 'hegemony of the proletariat': in other words, the question of
the social basis of the proletarian dictatorship and the workers' State.
For the proletariat to become the ruling, the dominant class, it must
succeed in creating a system of class alliances which allow it to mobilize the majority of the working population against capitalism and the
bourgeois State. In Italy, within the real class relations that exist here,
this means succeeding in obtaining the consent of the broad peasant
masses. But the peasant question in Italy is historically determined;
it is not a question of 'the peasant and agrarian question in general'.
In Italy, as a result of the particular character of Italian tradition and
the particular turn Italian history has taken, the peasant question has
taken on two characteristic and peculiar forms: the Southern question
and the question of the Vatican. For the Italian proletariat, then,
winning over the majority of the peasant masses means taking on
board these two questions, from a social point of view; understanding
the class needs they represent; incorporating these needs into its
revolutionary transitional programme; and incorporating them among
the objectives for which it is struggling.

The first problem the Turin communists needed to resolve was
that of how to modify the political stance and the general ideology
of the proletariat itself, as a national element that exists within the
overall structure of State life and is unconsciously subjected to the
influence of bourgeois education, the bourgeois press and bourgeois
tradition. It is well known what kind of ideology has been disseminated on a vast scale by bourgeois propagandists among the masses in
the North: that the South is the ball and chain that is holding back the
social development of Italy; that Southerners are biologically inferior
beings, semi-barbarians or complete barbarians by natural destiny;
that if the South is backward, the fault does not lie with the capitalist

system or any other historical cause, but with Nature, which made Southerners lazy, inept, criminal and barbaric – only tempering this cruel fate with the purely individual explosion of a few great geniuses, who stand like solitary palm-trees in an arid, barren desert. The Socialist Party was to a great extent the vehicle for this bourgeois ideology within the Northern proletariat. The Socialist Party gave its blessing to all the 'Southernist' literature of the clique of writers who made up the so-called positivist school: men like Ferri, Sergi, Niceforo, Orano and their lesser followers, who, in articles, sketches, short stories, novels, impressions and memoirs repeated the same refrain in different forms. Yet again, 'science' was used to crush the abject and the exploited, but this time it was a science dressed up in Socialist colours and claiming to be the science of the proletariat.

The Turin communists reacted energetically against this ideology; and precisely in Turin, where war veterans' accounts and descriptions of 'brigandage' in the South and the Islands had had the greatest influence on the popular tradition and the popular mind. They reacted energetically, taking practical action, and they succeeded in obtaining results of great historical significance. They succeeded in creating, precisely in Turin, the embryo of what will prove to be the solution to the Southern problem.

In fact, even before the war, an episode had taken place in Turin which contained in potential all the action and propaganda developed by the communists in the post-war period. When in 1914, through the death of Pilade Gay, the fourth constituency of the city was left vacant and the question arose of who should be the new candidate, a group from the Socialist section, including the future editors of *Ordine Nuovo*, aired the possibility of nominating Gaetano Salvemini as candidate. Salvemini was at that time the most radical spokesman for the peasant masses of the South. He was outside the Socialist Party; indeed, he was conducting an extremely energetic campaign against the Socialist Party – an extremely risky one, as well, because his claims and his accusations were provoking hatred among the Southern working masses not only for figures like Turati, Treves and D'Aragona, but for the industrial proletariat in its entirety. (Many of the bullets that the royal guards fired against the workers in 1919, '20, '21, '22 were cast from the same lead that served to print Salvemini's articles.) Nevertheless, this Turinese group wanted to use Salvemini's name to take a stand, as was made clear to Salvemini himself by

Comrade Ottavio Pastore, who had gone to Florence to obtain his consent to the candidature. 'The workers of Turin want to elect a deputy for the peasants of Apulia. The Turin workers know that in the 1913 general elections, the overwhelming majority of the peasants of Molfetta and Botonto supported Salvemini, but the administrative pressures of the Giolitti government and the violence of the hired thugs and the police prevented the Apulian peasants from expressing themselves. The workers of Turin are not demanding any kind of commitments from Salvemini: neither to the Party, nor to a pro-gramme, nor to the discipline of the Socialist parliamentary group. Once he was elected, Salvemini would be answerable to the peasants of Apulia, not the workers of Turin, who would conduct their elect-oral propaganda according to their own principles and would not be held in any way to Salvemini's political activity.'

Salvemini decided against accepting the candidature, though he was shaken by the proposal, even moved by it (at that time there was still no talk about communist 'perfidy' and we all behaved in a decent and amicable manner). He proposed Mussolini as a candidate and undertook to come to Turin to support the Socialist Party in its electoral struggle. And indeed, he held two large-scale rallies in the Camera del Lavoro and Piazza Statuto, amid the masses who saw and applauded in him the representative of the Southern workers, oppressed and exploited in an even more hateful and bestial manner than the Northern proletariat.

The approach that can be seen in potential in this episode and that did not have any further consequences at the time purely because of Salvemini's decision, was taken up again and put into effect by the communists in the post-war period. Let us recall the most salient and symptomatic events.

1919 saw the foundation of the 'Young Sardinia' association, the first prelude to what would later become the Sardinian Action Party. 'Young Sardinia' set itself to unite all Sardinians, both on the island itself and the mainland, into a regional bloc capable of keeping up an effective pressure on the government to ensure that the promises made to soldiers during the War were honoured. 'Young Sardinia''s organizer on the continent was a certain Professor Pietro Nurra, a *Socialist*, who is today very probably part of the group of 'young people' who find some new horizon to explore every week in the pages of *Quarto stato*. Lawyers, teachers, civil servants flocked to the movement with the enthusiasm that greets every new opportunity for fishing for crosses, titles and medals. The constituent assembly, held at Turin for Sardinians living in Piedmont, was impressive for the sheer number of people who took part. The majority was made up of humble folk: men of the people with no obvious qualifications; unskilled factory workers; hard-up pensioners; former carabinieri, prison guards and revenue officers, now involved in all kinds of small-scale business enterprises. All were fired with enthusiasm at the idea of finding themselves back among their fellow countrymen and hearing speeches about their native land, to which they were still bound by countless ties of family and friendship, of memories, suffering and hope – the hope of returning to their country, but to a more prosperous, richer country, where it was possible to make a living, albeit a modest one.

The Sardinian communists, who numbered precisely eight, went to this meeting and presented the chairman with a motion of their own and asked to deliver an answering speech. After the rousing, rhetorical speech of the official speaker, larded with all the frills and flourishes of provincial oratory; after those present had all wept at the recollection of their past sorrows and the blood shed in battle by the Sardinian regiments and all worked themselves up into a frenzy of enthusiasm at the thought of a united bloc made up of all the generous sons of Sardinia, it was very difficult to 'pitch' the opposition motion right. The most optimistic predictions were, if not actual lynching, at the very least a little trip to the police station, after being saved from the consequences of the 'noble wrath of the crowd'. But the reply, even though it provoked overwhelming astonishment, was nevertheless listened to attentively; and once the spell was broken, rapidly but methodically, the revolutionary conclusion was reached. The dilemma – 'do you poor wretches really want to form a bloc with the Sardinian gentry, who have ruined you and who are the local overseers of capitalist exploitation? Or do you want to form a bloc with the revolutionary workers of the mainland, who want to overthrow all forms of exploitation and emancipate all the oppressed?' – this dilemma was somehow forced into the minds of those present. The vote, by division of the assembly, was a tremendous success. On one side, the little group of flashily dressed *signori*, top-hatted civil servants, professional people, livid with rage and fear, with three dozen policemen as a garnish to consensus; on the other the whole mass of poor wretches, with their neat little wives in their Sunday best crowding round the tiny communist cell. An hour later, at the Camera del Lavoro, the Sardinian Socialist Education Club was set up with 256 members. The formation of 'Young Sardinia' was put off *sine die* and never took place.

This was the political basis for the action conducted among the soldiers of the Sassari Brigade, a brigade made up almost entirely of Sardinians. The Sassari brigade had taken part in the suppression of the insurrectionary movement in Turin in August 1917 and it was confidently believed that it would never fraternize with the workers, because of the legacy of hatred any repressive action leaves in the crowd – even for those who were merely the material instruments of the repression – and in the regiments, because of the memory of the soldiers who fell beneath the blows of the insurgents. The Brigade was welcomed by a crowd of ladies and gentlemen, offering the soldiers flowers, cigars and fruit. The soldiers' state of mind is captured in the following anecdote, told by a leather-worker from Sassari, who was involved in the first propaganda soundings: 'I approached a bivouac in Piazza X (in those first days the Sardinian soldiers were camping in the squares as though in a conquered city) and I spoke with a young peasant who had greeted me warmly because I was from Sassari like him.

"What have you come to do in Turin?"

"We have come to fire against the gentlemen who are on strike."

"But it's not the gentlemen who are on strike; it's workers – poor people."

"They're all gentlemen here: they wear collars and ties and earn thirty lire a day. Don't tell me who the poor are – I know them and I know how they dress. There are poor people in Sassari, all right. All of us 'diggers' are poor and we earn one and a half lire a day."

"But I'm a worker and I'm poor."

"You're just poor because you're Sardinian."

"But if I go on strike with the others, are you going to fire against me?"

The soldier thought for a minute, then putting his hand on my shoulder said: "Listen, when you go on strike with the others, just you stay at home!"'

This was the attitude of the vast majority in the Brigade, which contained only a small number of workers – miners from the Iglesias field. Yet, after a few months, on the eve of the general strike of 20–

21 July, the Brigade was sent away from Turin, the older soldiers were dismissed and the unit divided in three: one third was sent to Aosta, one third to Trieste and one third to Rome. The Brigade was moved away at night, without warning. There was no elegant crowd applauding them at the station and the songs they were singing, even if they were still war-songs, were saying something rather different from those they were singing when they arrived.

Have these events had no consequences? On the contrary, they have had results that can still be felt today and that continue to work away in the hearts and minds of the popular masses. They illumin- ated, for an instant, brains that had never thought in that way and that remained marked by the experience and radically changed. Our archives have been scattered and we have ourselves destroyed many papers to avoid provoking arrests and persecutions. But we can remember dozens – hundreds – of letters which arrived at the editor- ial offices of *Avanti!*, sent from Sardinia: letters which were often collective, signed by all the Sassari Brigade veterans from a particular town in Sardinia. The political stance we supported propagated itself along unrecorded – and unrecordable – paths. The formation of the Sardinian Action Party was heavily influenced by it at the rank and file level and it would be possible to cite episodes rich with content and significance in this connection.

The last recorded repercussion of this activity took place in 1922, when 300 carabinieri of the Cagliari legion were sent to Turin for the same purposes as the Sassari Brigade had been. At the editorial offices of *L'Ordine Nuovo*, we received a statement of principle signed by a very large number of these carabinieri. This letter echoed in every way our own position on the Southern question. It was the decisive proof of the correctness of our approach.

For this approach to be politically effective, the proletariat had to make it its own: that goes without saying. No mass action is possible unless the mass itself is convinced of the ends it wishes to achieve and the methods to apply. The proletariat, if it is to govern as a class, must throw off all traces of corporatism and all syndicalist prejudices and incrustations. What does this mean? That not only must the distinctions that exist between one trade and another be overcome, but it is also necessary, in order to win the trust and support of the peasants and of some categories of urban semi-proletarian, to over- come certain prejudices and conquer certain forms of egotism which may and do persist within the working class even when trade particularism has been banished. The metal-worker, the joiner, the builder, etc., must not only start thinking as proletarians and not as metal-workers, joiners, builders, etc.; they must also take a further step forward. They must think as workers who are members of a class that aims to lead the peasants and the intellectuals: a class that can only win and only build socialism if it is aided and followed by the great majority of these other social strata. If this is not achieved, the proletariat does not become the leading class and these strata (which in Italy represent the majority of the population) remain under bourgeois control, making it possible for the State to resist the impetus of the proletarian attack and to wear it down.

Now, what has happened in the field of the Southern question shows that the proletariat has understood its duties in this respect. Two events should be cited, one which took place in Turin, the other in Reggio Emilia – in other words, in the citadel of reformism, of class corporatism, of the kind of working-class protectionism that is always being cited by 'Southernists' in their propaganda among the peasants of the South.

After the factory occupation, the management of Fiat proposed to the workers that they should take over the running of the company as a co-operative. Naturally enough, the reformists favoured the proposal. An industrial crisis was looming and the spectre of unemployment was haunting working-class families. If Fiat became a co-operative, there would be a certain degree of job security for the skilled workers and particularly for the most politically active workers, who were convinced they were marked out for dismissal. The Socialist Party section, led by the Communists, intervened energetically in the debate. They said to the workers:

'A large-scale concern like Fiat can only be taken on as a co-operative by the workers if the workers are determined to enter into the system of bourgeois political forces which governs Italy today. The Fiat management's proposal is all part of the Giolittian political plan. What is this plan? The bourgeoisie, even before the War, could no longer govern peacefully. The uprising of the Sicilian peasants in 1894 and the Milan insurrection of 1894 were the *experimentum crucis* of the Italian bourgeoisie. After the bloody decade of 1890–1900, the bourgeoisie had to renounce a dictatorship which was too exclusive, violent and direct: the Southern peasants and the Northern workers were rising against it *simultaneously*, if not in a co-ordinated fashion.

'With the new century, the ruling class introduced a new policy of class alliances, of class political blocs – in other words, of bourgeois democracy. It had to choose. Either it could have a rural democracy, which would mean an alliance with the Southern peasants, a policy of free trade, universal suffrage, administrative decentralization and low prices for industrial products; or else a capitalist–worker industrial bloc, which would mean no universal suffrage, tariff barriers, the maintenance of a highly centralized State (an expression of bourgeois domination over the peasants, especially in the South and the Islands), and a reformist policy on industrial wages and trade-union liberties. It chose – and not by chance – this latter solution. Giolitti personified bourgeois rule and the Socialist Party became the instrument of Giolitti's politics.

'If you look closely, it was in the decade from 1900 to 1910 that the most radical crises occurred in the Socialist and workers' movement, as the masses reacted spontaneously against the policies of their reformist leaders. Syndicalism was born: the instinctive, elemental expression – primitive, but healthy – of the workers' reaction against the bloc with the bourgeoisie and in favour of a bloc with the peasants and, *first and foremost, with the peasants of the South.* That is just what it is: indeed, in a certain sense, syndicalism is a weak attempt on the part of the Southern peasants, represented by their most advanced intellectuals, to lead the proletariat. Who is it that forms the leading nucleus of Italian syndicalism? And what is its ideological essence? The leading nucleus of syndicalism is made up almost entirely of Southerners: Labriola, Leone, Longobardi, Orano. The ideological essence of syndicalism is a new kind of liberalism, more energetic, more aggressive, more pugnacious than the traditional variety. If you look closely, there are two basic questions underlying all the successive crises of syndicalism and the gradual passing-over of the syndicalist leaders into the bourgeois camp: emigration and free trade, both of which are closely bound up with Southernism. The phenomenon of emigration gave rise to Enrico Corradini's idea of the 'proletarian nation'; the Libyan War appeared to a whole swathe of intellectuals as the beginning of the 'great proletariat''s offensive against the capitalist, plutocratic world. A whole group of syndicalists passed over to nationalism – indeed, the Nationalist Party was originally set up by ex-syndicalist intellectuals (Monicelli, Forges-Davanzati, Maraviglia). Labriola's book, *History of a Decade* (the ten years from

1900 to 1910) is the most typical and characteristic expression of this anti-Giolittian and Southernist neo-liberalism.

'In the ten years in question, capitalism was strengthened and developed and it directed a part of its activity towards agriculture in the Po Valley. The most characteristic feature of these ten years was the mass strikes of the agricultural workers of the Po Valley. A profound upheaval took place among the Northern peasants; a far-reaching process of class differentiation (the number of *braccianti* [day labourers] increased by fifty per cent, according to the 1911 census figures) and a corresponding realignment of political currents and mental attitudes. Christian democracy and Mussolinism were the two most outstanding products of the period. Romagna was the regional crucible of these two new activities; the *bracciante* seemed to have become the social protagonist of the political struggle. The left-wing organs of social democracy (*L'Azione* of Cesena) and Mussolinism too soon fell into the hands of 'Southernists'. The Cesena *Azione* was a regional edition of Gaetano Salvemini's *L'Unità*. *Avanti!*, under Mussolini's editorship, slowly but surely transformed itself into a platform for syndicalist and Southernist writers. People like Fancello, Lanzillo, Panunzio and Ciccotti became assiduous contributors. Salvemini himself did not hide his sympathies for Mussolini, who even became the darling of Prezzolini's *Voce*. Everyone remembers, in fact, how when Mussolini left *Avanti!* and the Socialist Party, he was surrounded by this cohort of syndicalists and Southernists.

'The most notable repercussion of this period in the revolutionary field was the Red Week of June 1914; Romagna and the Marches were the epicentre of Red Week. In the field of bourgeois political activity, the most notable repercussion was the Gentiloni pact. Since the Socialist Party, as a result of the agrarian movements in the Po Valley, had returned after 1910 to a strategy of intransigence, the industrial bloc, backed and represented by Giolitti, lost its effectiveness. So Giolitti shifted his rifle to the other shoulder. He replaced the alliance between the bourgeoisie and the workers by an alliance between the bourgeoisie and the Catholics, who represented the peasant masses of Northern and Central Italy. As a result of this alliance, Sonnino's Conservative Party was completely destroyed, leaving only a tiny cell in Southern Italy, around Antonio Salandra.

'The War and the post-war period saw a series of extremely important capillary processes taking place within the bourgeois class.

Salandra and Nitti were the first two Southern heads of government (not including Sicilians, of course, such as Crispi, who was the most energetic representative of the bourgeois dictatorship in the whole nineteenth century). They attempted to put into effect the industrial bourgeois–Southern landowner plan, Salandra on a conservative basis and Nitti on a democratic one (both these heads of government were substantially helped by the *Corriere della Sera* or, in other words, by the Lombard textile industry). Salandra was already attempting during the War to shift the technical forces of the State organization towards the South – in other words, to replace Giolitti's State personnel with a new personnel that would embody the new political course of the bourgeoisie. You remember the campaign conducted by *La Stampa*, especially in 1917–18, for a close collaboration between Giolittians and Socialists to prevent the "Apulianization" of the State; that campaign was led in *La Stampa* by Francesco Ciccotti – in other words, it was *de facto* an expression of the accord between Giolitti and the reformists. The question was not a trivial one and the Giolittians, in their fierce defensive obstinacy, went beyond the bounds of what is permitted to a party of the haute bourgeoisie: they stooped to those displays of antipatriotism and defeatism that none of us has forgotten.

'Today, Giolitti is in power once more and once again the haute bourgeoisie is putting itself in his hands, panicked by the impetuous movement of the popular masses. Giolitti wants to tame the Turin workers. He has beaten them twice: in last April's strike and in the occupation of the factories, with the aid of the General Confederation of Labour – that is, of corporative reformism. He now believes he can bring the workers into the framework of the bourgeois State system. What will happen, in fact, if the skilled workforce of Fiat accepts the management's proposals? The present industrial shares will become debentures: in other words, the co-operatives will have to pay a fixed dividend to debenture-holders, whatever the state of the business. The Fiat company will be bled completely dry by the institutions of credit, which remain in the hands of the bourgeoisie, in whose interest it is to get the workers at its mercy. The workforce will necessarily have to bind itself to the State, which will "come to the aid of the workers" through the activity of working-class deputies – through the subordination of the working-class political party to government policies. That is Giolitti's plan carried through to its natural conclusion. The Turin proletariat will no longer exist as an independent class, but simply as an appendage of the bourgeois State. Class corporatism will have triumphed, but the proletariat will have lost its position and role as leader and guide. The mass of poorer workers will see it as privileged, while the mass of peasants will see it as an exploiter on the same level as the bourgeoisie, because the bourgeoisie – as it has always done – will represent the privileged nuclei of the working class to the peasant masses as the sole cause of their sufferings and their abject poverty.'

The skilled workforce of Fiat accepted our point of view almost unanimously and the management's proposals were rejected. But this experience was not enough in itself. In a whole series of actions, the Turin proletariat had shown itself to have reached an extremely high level of maturity and political capacity. The technical and supervisory grades and white-collar workers in the factories were able to improve their conditions in 1919 only because they were supported by the workers. To break the militancy of the higher grades, the employers proposed to the workers that they should themselves nominate new squad and shop foremen, through an election. The workers rejected the proposal, even though they had ample cause for conflict with the supervisory grades, who had always acted for the bosses as instruments of repression and persecution. Then the newspapers mounted a furious campaign to isolate these grades, pointing to their very high salaries, which sometimes went up to 7,000 lire a month. The skilled workers also gave their support to the agitation of the manual workers, who would not have won their demands without them. Within the factories, all privileges and all forms of exploitation of the less skilled by the more skilled categories were swept away. By means of these actions, the proletarian vanguard won its social position as a vanguard. This was the basis for the development of the Communist Party in Turin. But outside Turin? Well, we wanted expressly to take the issue beyond Turin and, more precisely, to Reggio Emilia, where the greatest concentration of reformism and class corporatism was to be found.

Reggio Emilia had always been the target of the 'Southernists'. A phrase of Camillo Prampolini: 'Italy is divided into Northerners and filthy Southerners' [*L'Italia si divide in nordici e sudici*] could be taken as the most characteristic expression of the violent hatred disseminated among Southerners against the workers of the North. In Reggio

Emilia, a problem arose similar to the one at Fiat: a large company was to pass into the hands of the workers as a co-operative enterprise. The Reggio reformists were full of enthusiasm for the project and trumpeted its praises in their papers and at their meetings. A Turinese communist went to Reggio, took the floor at a factory meeting and outlined the problem of North–South relations in its entirety. The miracle was achieved: the workers, by an overwhelming majority, rejected the reformist, corporative position. It was revealed that the reformists did not represent the true spirit of workers of Reggio; they only represented their passivity and other negative sides. They had succeeded in establishing a political monopoly, thanks to the high concentration in their ranks of organizers and propagandists with a certain professional aptitude; and, in this way, they had prevented a revolutionary current from developing and becoming organized. But the presence of one skilled revolutionary was enough to rout them and to reveal that the workers of Reggio are valiant fighters and not a herd of pigs raised on government fodder.

In April 1921, 5,000 revolutionary workers were laid off from Fiat, the Factory Councils were abolished and wages in real terms cut. Something similar probably happened in Reggio Emilia. In other words, the workers were defeated. But did this mean that their sacrifice was in vain? We do not believe so: on the contrary, we are convinced that it was not in vain – though, certainly, it would be difficult to cite a whole series of great mass events which would prove the immediate, lightning effectiveness of these actions. Apart from anything, in the case of the peasants, such evidence is always difficult, if not impossible, to come by; still more so where the peasant mass of the South is concerned.

The South can be defined as an area of extreme social disintegration. The peasants, who make up the great majority of the population, have no cohesion among themselves (of course, some exceptions must be made: Apulia, Sardinia, Sicily – areas which have distinctive features within the broad picture of the structure of the South). Southern society is a great agrarian bloc made up of three social strata: the great amorphous, scattered mass of the peasantry; the intellectuals of the lower and middle strata of the rural bourgeoisie; and the great landowners and major intellectuals. The Southern peasants are in perpetual ferment, but as a mass they are incapable of giving a unified expression to their aspirations and needs. The middle layer of intellectuals receives the impulses for its political and ideological activity from the peasant base. The big landowners in the political field and the major intellectuals in the ideological field hold together and dominate, in the last analysis, this whole complex of phenomena. Naturally, it is in the ideological field that this centralization is at its most precise and efficacious. Thus Giustino Fortunato and Benedetto Croce represent the two keystones of the whole Southern system and, in a certain sense, they are the two central figures of Italian reaction.

The Southern intellectuals are one of the most interesting and important social strata in Italian national life. One only has to think that more than three-fifths of the State bureaucracy is made up of Southerners to realize how true this is. Now, to understand the particular mentality of the Southern intellectuals, certain facts must be borne in mind:

1. In every country, the stratum of intellectuals has been radically modified by the development of capitalism. The old model of intellectual was the organizing element in a society with a prevalently peasant and artisanal basis. In order to organize the State and to organize commerce, the ruling class produced a particular type of intellectual. Industry has introduced a new model of intellectual: the technical organizer, the specialist in applied science. In societies in which the economic forces have developed in a capitalist direction, up to the point where they have absorbed the greater part of national activity, it is this second model of intellectual which has prevailed, with all its characteristics of order and intellectual discipline. By contrast, in those countries in which agriculture continues to play a major or even a leading role, the old model remains predominant. It provides the bulk of the State personnel and locally, too, in the villages and little country towns, it plays the part of intermediary between the peasant and the administration in general. In Southern Italy, this model predominates, with all its characteristic features: democratic in the face it turns towards the peasantry; reactionary in that turned towards the great landowners and the government; much given to political intrigue, corrupt and untrustworthy. One could not understand the traditional cast of the Southern political parties if one did not take the characteristics of this social stratum into account.

2. The Southern intellectual comes in the main from a class which is still very strong in the South: the rural bourgeoisie. This means

the small or medium landowner who is not a peasant, who does not work the land, who would find it shameful to farm his own land but who wants to extract from the little land he has – leased out either for rent or on a share-cropping basis – enough to live respectably, to send his sons to university or the seminary and to give a dowry to his daughters, who must marry an officer or a civil functionary of the State. From this class background, the intellectuals derive a fierce antipathy to the working peasant, considered as a work machine that can be bled dry and then replaced, given the excess working population. They also derive from their class an atavistic, instinctual feeling of blind fear of the peasants and their destructive violence; and from this in turn they derive the habit of refined hypocrisy and an extremely refined art of deceiving and subduing the peasant masses.

3. Since the clergy belongs to the social group of intellectuals, it is necessary to note the features that distinguish the Southern clergy as a whole from the Northern clergy. The Northern priest is generally the son of an artisan or a peasant; he has democratic sympathies and is more tied to the peasant masses. Morally he is more upright than the Southern priest, who often cohabits more or less openly with a woman; and he therefore exercises a spiritual office that is socially more far-reaching, guiding a family's whole activity. In the North, the separation of Church and State and the expropriation of ecclesiastical goods were more radical than in the South, where the parishes and convents have retained or rebuilt considerable assets, both fixed and moveable. In the South, the peasant thinks of the priest (1) as a bailiff, with whom the peasant comes into conflict on the question of rents; (2) as a usurer who demands extremely high rates of interest and brings the religious element into play in order to make sure he collects his rent or interest; (3) as a man subject to all the usual passions (women and money) and who, therefore, from a spiritual point of view, does not inspire confidence in his discretion and impartiality. Confession, then, has only a minimal guiding role and the peasant, even though he is often superstitious in a pagan way, has little time for the clergy. All this explains why the *Partito Popolare* has never had a leading role in the South (except in a few areas of Sicily) and does not possess a network of institutions and mass organizations. The peasant's attitude to the clergy can be summed up by the popular saying, 'The priest is a priest when he's at the altar; anywhere else, he's a man like all the rest.'

The Southern peasant is linked to the great landowner through the mediation of the intellectual. The peasant movements, in that they do not take the form of mass organizations that are autonomous and independent, at least in a formal sense (i.e. organizations capable of selecting peasant cadres of peasant origin and of reflecting the differentiations and advances taking place in the movement) always end up by finding themselves a place within the normal articulations of the State apparatus – the communal and provincial councils and the Chamber of Deputies. This process takes place through the composition and decomposition of local parties, whose personnel is made up of intellectuals, but which are controlled by the major landowners and their agents – men like Salandra, Orlando, Di Cesarò.

The War appeared to introduce a new element into this type of organization with the war-veterans' movement, in which the peasant–soldiers and the officer–intellectuals made up a more united bloc and one which was to a certain extent opposed to the great landowners. It did not last long; the last trace of it is the National Union conceived by Amendola, which still retains some glimmer of existence thanks to its anti-Fascism. However, given the complete absence of any tradition of *explicit* organization on the part of *democratic* intellectuals in the South, even something like this grouping must be given due attention and taken into account, since, with a change in the overall political conditions, it could develop from a tiny trickle of water into a swollen and muddy torrent.

The only region in which the war-veterans' movement had a clearer profile and succeeded in creating a more solid social structure for itself is Sardinia. And this is understandable: the reason is, precisely, that in Sardinia the class of great landowners is extremely small, has no function and does not possess the extremely ancient cultural and governmental traditions of the mainland South. The pressure exerted from below by the masses of peasants and shepherds is not counterbalanced by the crushing weight of the higher social stratum of the big landowner, so the ruling intellectuals feel that pressure in all its strength and make greater strides forward than the National Union.

The situation in Sicily has features that differentiate it very clearly from the situation of both Sardinia and the mainland. The big landowners are much more cohesive and resolute than in the mainland South. Moreover, there is a certain amount of industry in Sicily and a highly developed commerce (Sicily is the richest region of the South of Italy and one of the richest in Italy). The upper classes are keenly aware of their importance in national life and they make their weight felt. Sicily and Piedmont are the two regions which have provided the Italian State with the greatest number of political leaders; they are the two regions which have had a dominant role from 1870 onwards. The Sicilian popular masses are more advanced than those of the rest of the South, but their progress has taken a typically Sicilian form. A Sicilian mass socialism exists, with a tradition and a development all its own. In the 1922 Chamber it had about twenty deputies out of the fifty-two elected on the island.

We have said that the Southern peasant is linked to the great landowner through the mediation of the intellectual. This model of organization is the most widespread throughout the whole of the mainland South and in Sicily. It results in a monstrous agrarian bloc which, as a whole, functions as an intermediary and overseer for Northern capitalism and the great banks. Its sole aim is to preserve the *status quo*. There is no glimmer of intellectual light within this bloc, no programme, no urge towards betterment and progress. If any idea or programme has been put forward, it is always one that originated outside the South, in the conservative agrarian political groups (especially the Tuscan ones) which were allied in Parliament with the conservatives of the Southern agrarian bloc. Sonnino and Franchetti were among the few intelligent bourgeois thinkers who saw the Southern problem as a national problem and outlined a government plan to solve it.[3]

What was Sonnino and Franchetti's point of view? That it was necessary to create an economically independent middle stratum in the Italian South, that would fulfil the role of 'public opinion' (as they then put it), limiting the cruel and arbitrary actions of the landowners, on one side, and moderating the rebelliousness of the impoverished peasants, on the other. Sonnino and Franchetti had

[3] Sidney Sonnino and Leopoldo Franchetti were prominent conservative politicians from Tuscany. In 1876, they carried out a private investigation of the socio-economic, political and administrative problems of the South, which first brought them to public attention. They published their findings in 1877, in a two-volume study entitled *Inchiesta in Sicilia*; Sonnino's volume was subtitled *I contadini* [*The Peasants*] and Franchetti's *Le condizioni politiche e amminstrative della Sicilia* [*Political and Administrative Conditions in Sicily*].

been terrified by the popularity that the Bakuninist ideas of the First International had achieved in the South of Italy. Their fear led them to make blunders that were often grotesque. In one of their publications, for example, they cite the fact that an inn or cheap *trattoria* in a Calabrian town (we are quoting from memory) was named after 'The Strikers' [*scioperanti*], as evidence of how widespread and deep-rooted Internationalist ideas were. This fact, if it is true (and it must be, given the intellectual probity of the authors) can be explained more simply if one recalls how many Albanian colonies there are in the South and how the word *skipetari* ['Albanians'] has undergone the strangest and most curious deformations in the various dialects (so that in certain documents of the Venetian Republic we read about military formations made up of *S'ciopetà*). Now then, it is not so much that Bakunin's theories were widely known in the South as that the situation itself was such that it could have suggested Bakunin's theories to him. Certainly, the impoverished peasants of the South were thinking about 'smashing everything up' long before Bakunin's brain dreamed up the theory of 'pandestruction'.

The government plan of Sonnino and Franchetti never even came anywhere near being put into practice. Nor could it: the nexus of relations between North and South in the organization of the national economy and the State is such that the birth of a broad middle class, in the economic sense (or, in other words the birth of a broad capitalist bourgeoisie) would be almost impossible. Any accumulation of capital on the spot, any accumulation of savings, is made impossible by the fiscal and customs system and by the fact that the capitalists who own firms do not transform their profits into new capital locally, because they are not local people. When emigration reached the gigantic proportions it did in the twentieth century and the first remittances began flooding in from America, liberal economists triumphantly shouted 'Sonnino's dream is coming true. A silent revolution is taking place in the South which, slowly but surely, will change the whole social and economic structure of the country.' But the State intervened and the silent revolution was smothered at birth. The government offered treasury bonds at fixed interest and the emigrants and their families turned from being agents of the silent revolution into agents for financing the State's subsidies to the parasitical industries of the North. Francesco Nitti, as a democrat, standing formally outside the Southern agrarian bloc, might have seemed just the man to put Sonnino's programme into effect. On the contrary, he was the most effective agent of Northern capitalism, raking in the last resources of the savings of the South. The thousands of millions swallowed up by the *Banca di sconto* almost all came from the South. The great majority of the 400,000 creditors of the *Banca italiana di sconto* were Southern savers.

Over and above the agrarian bloc, there is also an intellectual bloc at work in the South, which in practice has served up till now to prevent the cracks in the agrarian bloc from becoming too dangerous and causing a landslide. Giustino Fortunato and Benedetto Croce are the exponents of this intellectual bloc and they can therefore be considered as the most active reactionaries of the entire peninsula.

We have said that Southern Italy is an area of extreme social disintegration. This formula can be applied not only to the peasants but also to the intellectuals. It is a striking fact that, in the South, alongside the vast landed estates, there have always existed and still exist great accumulations of culture and intelligence in single individuals or small groups of great intellectuals, while there is no organization of culture at a lower level. The South has the Laterza publishing house and the review *La Critica*. It has academics and cultural bodies of the greatest erudition. But it does not have small or medium-sized reviews and it does not have publishing houses around which middle-ranking groups of Southern intellectuals might form. Those Southerners who have tried to escape from the agrarian bloc and approach the Southern question in a radical way have found a welcome in reviews published outside the South and have grouped themselves around these reviews. One might even say that all the cultural initiatives by middle-ranking intellectuals that have taken place this century in Central and Northern Italy have been characterized by Southernism, because they have been strongly influenced by intellectuals from the South: all the reviews of the group of Florentine intellectuals (*La Voce; L'Unità*); the reviews of the Christian democrats (*L'Azione*, of Cesena); the reviews of the young Emilian and Milanese liberals published by G. Bonarelli (*La Patria* in Bologna or *L'Azione* in Milan) and, finally, Gobetti's *Rivoluzione liberale*.

Well, the supreme political and intellectual moderators of all these initiatives have been Giustino Fortunato and Benedetto Croce. In far wider circles than the stifling sphere of the agrarian bloc, they have managed to ensure that the way in which the Southern question was approached did not go beyond certain limits, did not become revolutionary. As men of the highest culture and intelligence, raised on the traditional terrain of the South but linked to European and hence world culture, they had all the gifts necessary to satisfy the intellectual needs of the most sincere representatives of the educated youth of the South, to calm down any passing itch they might feel to rebel against existing conditions and to steer them along a middle way of classical serenity of thought and action. The so-called neo-Protestants or Calvinists have not understood that in Italy, since a mass religious reformation would be impossible given the conditions of modern civilization, the only historically possible reformation has already taken place, with the philosophy of Benedetto Croce. The direction and method of thought have been changed and a new conception of the world has been constructed, transcending Catholicism and every other form of religion based on myth. In this sense, Benedetto Croce has fulfilled an extremely important 'national' function. He has detached the radical intellectuals of the South from the peasant masses and made them participate in national and European culture. Through this culture, he has ensured the absorption of these intellectuals by the national bourgeoisie and hence by the agrarian bloc.

L'Ordine Nuovo and the Turin communists, even if, in a certain sense, they can be related to the intellectual formations already mentioned – even if they too have felt the influence of Giustino Fortunato and Benedetto Croce – nevertheless represent at the same time a complete break with that tradition and the beginning of a new development, which has already borne fruit and will continue to do so. As has already been pointed out, the Turin communists have identified the urban proletariat as the modern protagonist of Italian history and hence also of the Southern question. Having served as intermediaries between the proletariat and certain strata of left-wing intellectuals, they have succeeded in modifying the latter's mental outlook – if not completely, then certainly to a considerable degree.

This is the principal feature of the figure of Pietro Gobetti, if one thinks carefully about it. Gobetti was not a communist and would probably never have become one. But he had understood the social and historical position of the proletariat and his thought could no longer develop in isolation from this element. In our work together on the paper, we placed Gobetti in contact with a living world that he had previously only known through the formulae of books. And since his most striking characteristics were intellectual honesty and a complete lack of any petty vanity and mean-mindedness, he could not but convince himself that a whole series of traditional ways of regarding and thinking about the proletariat were false and unjust.

What was the effect on Gobetti of these contacts with the proletarian world? They were the source and stimulus for a new conception that we do not wish to go into here: a conception that in great part goes back to syndicalism and the way of thinking of the intellectual syndicalists. In this view of the world, the principles of liberalism are projected from the order of individual phenomena to that of mass phenomena. The qualities of excellence and prestige in the life of individuals are carried over into the classes, which are regarded almost as collective individualities. This outlook generally leads, in the intellectuals who share it, to a position of pure contemplation and registration of merits and demerits; to an odious and stupid position as referees of contests and allocators of prizes and punishments. In practice, Gobetti escaped this destiny. He showed himself to be an extraordinarily talented cultural organizer and he performed a role in these recent times that should not be ignored or undervalued by the workers. He dug out a trench beyond which those groups of honest and sincere intellectuals, who in 1919–21 had felt that the proletariat would have made a better ruling class than the bourgeoisie, could not retreat. Some people in good faith and all honesty, others in extremely bad faith and dishonestly, went round repeating that Gobetti was nothing but a communist in disguise: an agent if not for the Communist Party, at least for the communist group of *L'Ordine Nuovo*. There is no need to deny such fatuous rumours. The figure of Gobetti and the movement he represented were spontaneous products of the new historical climate in Italy. That is their significance and importance. We have sometimes been reproached by comrades in the Party for not having fought against the *Rivoluzione liberale* current of ideas. Indeed, this lack of conflict was taken as evidence of the organic link, of a Machiavellian nature (as people say) between us and Gobetti. We could not fight against Gobetti because he was developing and representing a movement that should not be fought against, at least where its main principles were concerned.

Failing to understand that means failing to understand the question of intellectuals and the function they perform in the class struggle.

335

Gobetti, in practice, served us as a link: (1) with those intellectuals raised on the terrain of capitalist technique who had adopted a left position, favourable to the dictatorship of the proletariat, in 1919–20; (2) with a series of Southern intellectuals who, through more complex relationships, approached the Southern question in a different way from the traditional one, introducing the Northern proletariat into the equation (out of these intellectuals, Guido Dorso is the most substantial and interesting figure). Why should we have fought against the *Rivoluzione liberale* movement? Perhaps because it was not made up of pure communists who had accepted our programme and doctrine down to the last full stop? It could not have been asked of them to do this because it would have been a paradox, politically and historically.

Intellectuals develop slowly, far more slowly than any other social group, because of their very nature and historical function. They represent the entire cultural tradition of a people; they seek to express and synthesize the whole of its history. That is true in particular of the old type of intellectual, born on peasant soil. It is absurd to think that such intellectuals, *en masse*, can possibly break completely with the past and transplant themselves entirely on to the terrain of a new ideology. It is absurd where intellectuals *en masse* are concerned and perhaps absurd as well for very many intellectuals taken individually, however many sincere efforts they may make and wish to make.

Now, we are interested in the mass of intellectuals and not only the individuals. Certainly, it is important and useful for the proletariat that one or more intellectuals, as individuals, should adhere to its programme and its doctrine; should merge with the proletariat, becoming one with it and feeling themselves to be an integral part of it. The proletariat, as a class, is short of organizing elements; it does not have its own layer of intellectuals and it will only be able to form such a stratum, very slowly and laboriously, after the conquest of State power. But it is also important and useful that a break should take place within the mass of intellectuals: a break of an organic nature, historically characterized. It is important that there should be formed, as a mass formation, a left tendency in the modern sense – that is a tendency oriented towards the revolutionary proletariat.

This formation of intellectuals is needed if we are to see an alliance between the proletariat and the peasant masses: even more so, an alliance between the proletariat and the peasant masses of the South.

The proletariat's destruction of the Southern agrarian bloc depends on its succeeding in organizing increasingly significant masses of impoverished peasants into autonomous and independent formations, through the efforts of its Party. But the degree to which it will succeed in this indispensable task depends, as well, on its capacity to split apart the intellectual bloc that constitutes the flexible but extremely resistant armour of the agrarian bloc. The proletariat was helped towards the accomplishment of this task by Piero Gobetti and we think that the dead man's friends will continue with the work he undertook, even without his guidance. The task undertaken is enormous and difficult, but worthy of every sacrifice (even that of life, as in Gobetti's case) on the part of those intellectuals in both North and South (and there are many of them, more than is generally believed) who have understood that only two social forces are essentially national and bearers of the future: the proletariat and the peasants . . .

Drafted between September and November 1926

Index

Index

crowd psychology, 175
Cultural Association, proposals for, 35–8
culture, political and educative role of,
    xii, xv–xvii, xviii, xxvii, 8–12, 180; *see
    also* Cultural Assocation
Cuoco, Vincenzo, xxviii
customs policy, 29, 80, 82; *see also* tariffs
Czechoslovakia, 299

Damen, Comrade, 273
D'Annunzio, Gabriele, xlvi, 245–6, 298
D'Aragona, Ludovico, 130, 262, 284,
    317
Daudet, Léon, 75, 76, 79
Dawes, Charles Gates, 298
De Leon, Daniel, 184
De Nicola (of National Party), 260
De Sanctis, Francesco, xvii, 10
De Tullio, Commendatore, 81, 83
demagoguery, 130, 224, 241, 273, 274,
    311, 312
democracy, 60, 62, 63, 122, 125; rural,
    262, 323; workers', 96–100
democratic parties, 289–90; democratic
    coalition, 295–6
Dessi, Mario, 245
determinism, 43, 44, 46
Di Cesaró, G. A. C., 292, 295, 330
Di Gasperi, Alcide, 295
dialectical process, 66, 170, 171
dictatorship, 60–1, 63, 64, 68, 84, 88; *see
    also* dictatorship of the proletariat
dictatorship of the proletariat, 92, 96,
    104–6, 113, 130, 136, 311, 316,
    336; definition of, 99; establishment
    of, in Russia, 207; Lenin on, 276–7,
    281–2; realization of, in Factory
    Councils, 117, 119, 120; Socialist
    Parties' understanding of, 287; as
    successor to Fascism, 295; trade
    unions and, 121–6 *passim*; *see also*
    revolution, proletarian
Diderot, Denis, 10
Dietzgen (German worker), 270
Dimier, Louis, 79
discipline, required by proletariat, xvi, xx,
    26, 97, 119, 211, 312
division of labour, xxiii, 152, 166
Dorso, Guido, 313, 336
duma, 32, 144

economics, 40, 42, 45, 47–8, 55–6, 89;

postwar crises, xxiv, 207–8, 293–4,
    296; *see also* politics
education, 25, 62–3, 97, 99; and
    formation of revolutionary
    consciousness, x, xiv, xv–xvii, xix,
    xxvi, xxvii, 10–11, 99, 266–7;
    working-class, 105–6, 110, 123, 159;
    see also Cultural Association; Party
    School
Einaudi, Luigi, xvii
electoral systems, 98
emigrants, emigration, 293, 294, 323,
    332
Emilia Romagna, 228, 229, 263, 324
Engels, Friedrich, 43, 231, 270
engineers, *see* mechanical engineering;
    metal workers
England, *see* Britain
Enlightenment, 10–11
Eurocommunism, ix–x
Europe, 10–11, 293, 334; Eastern, 113
exports, 81, 293, 294

Fabian Society, 38
factory, workshop, xxii, 97–9, 113–14,
    170, 179; communist cells in, 160,
    271, 285; delegates' movement, 98,
    127, 129, 130, 156; factory-state,
    199–201; hierarchical relations, 164,
    185, 199; role and status of worker,
    151–4, 166–7, 183, 190–1, 252; *see
    also* Factory Councils; internal
    commissions; occupation of the
    factories
Factory Councils, xviii–xxiii, 117–20,
    156, 165, 168, 174, 299, 327; and
    Communist Party, xx–xxi, 161, 167,
    182–3; as model for proletarian state,
    xix, xx–xxi, 117, 118–20, 171–2; and
    trade unions, xviii, xix, xx–xxi,
    117–20, 167, 173–4, 182–3, 186,
    288n; *see also* Ordine Nuovo
Fancello (contributor to *Avanti!*), 324
Farinacci, Roberto, 292, 293
farmers, of Southern and Central Italy,
    80, 81–2, 83, 193, 227
Fasci, 227, 228, 229; Siciliani, 262
Fascism, x, xvii, xxii, 217, 231, 244, 274,
    308–9; associated with peripheral
    capitalist states, xxiv, xxvii, 298;
    bourgeois-agrarian bloc, xxv, 227–8,
    288, 291; and Catholic Action, 291;

Index

Index

Pacification Pact (between PSI and Fascists), 223–6, 228
Pagine rosse, 258
Pais Serra, Francesco, 81–2
Palazzeschi, Aldo, 244–5
Panunzio (contributor to *Avanti!*), 324
Papini, Giovanni, xii
Papini, Giuseppe, xlix, 244
Pareto, Vilfredo, xvii
Paris Commune, xviii, 180, 184, 272
Parliament, 104, 110, 112, 133, 228; English, 22–3; Italian, 63, 144, 237, 240, 241–2, 289–90
Partito Communista d'Italia, *see* Italian Communist Party
Partito Popolare Italiano, *see* Italian Popular Party
Partito Socialista Italiano, *see* Italian Socialist Party
party government, 60–1, 64, 149; *see also* political parties
Party School, xxvi, 265–7, 271
Pastore, Ottavio, 17n, 318
La Patria, 333
PCd'I, *see* Italian Communist Party
peasants, xviii, 134, 194, 310; and Fascism, 229; Northern, 324; organizations of, xxvi, 99, 113, 138, 228, 288n; parliamentary party (*see also* Italian Popular Party), 147, 192–3; proposed alliance of Northern proletariat with Southern, 211, 290–1, 311, 315, 323, 336–7; Russian, 301–4 *passim*; Southern, 253, 262, 263–4, 313–37 *passim*; *see also* banks; landownership
Pellegrino, Comrade, 35
Perseveranza, 83
pessimism, avoidance, 255–6, 259
petite bourgeoise, 84, 183, 193, 201, 289, 290, 294; and Fascism, xxv, 214, 292, 293; relations with proletariat, xxviii, 253; Southern, 262
Petri, Carlo, 102, 106
Piedmont, 63, 83, 84, 183, 331; economic system as model for proletarian revolution, xx, 137–8; Piedmontese hegemony, xxvii, 261
Pilsudski, Józef, 295
Pirandello, Luigi, xvii
Plekhanov, Georgi Valentinovich, xxvii
Po Valley, 250, 324

Poesia, 245
Poland, 295, 298, 299, 302
political parties, 132, 133; and the revolutionary process, 164, 167, 191, 192–6 *passim*, 216–17, 253; *see also* State
political science, proletarian, 270
politics, relationship between economics and, x, xv, xxvii, 47, 168–72, 217–18, 297–8
Popular Universities, xvi, 10, 36, 76, 79
Portugal, xxiv, 298, 299
positivism, xii, xv, 40, 43, 75–9 *passim*, 317
PPI, *see* Italian Popular Party
Prampolini, Camillo, 326
Prati, Marcello, 146
Prezzolini, Giuseppe, xi, xii, xlix, 62, 324
Il Principe, 244
Prison Notebooks, x, xxii, xxvii, xxviii
prison system, 141, 143
prisoners, release of, in Russia, 33
private property, 88, 108, 123, 124, 163; abolition of, 91, 105, 112, 113
production, xxii, 55–6, 156, 166–7, 217–18, 252; capitalist mode of, 112, 163, 178–9; in dictatorship of the proletariat, 15, 119, 124, 130–1, 161; ownership of means of, 91, 155; technical element, 16, 41, 115; workers as producers, 128–9, 134, 138, 182; *see also* capitalists
Proletkult, xvii, 245, 246
proletarian state, xiv, 93–5, 96–7, 99, 101–14 *passim*, 147, 175, 201–2; models for (*see also* Factory Councils), 138
proletariat, 30, 67, 206–8; anarchic tendencies, 142; arming of, xxi–xxii, 105, 170, 200–1, 234–5; and bourgeois state socialism, 21, 23, 24; British, 68; capacity to become 'true communist revolutionaries', 270–1; and culture, 8, 11–12, 36; and First World War, 4–5, 6–7, 65; historic mission of, 194, 210, 239, 253, 270, 334; international, 58, 165, 209; Russian, 32, 40–1, 45, 92, 93–5, 207; and Southern question, 210, 211; suffrage, 231; workers' democracy, 96–100; working-class institutions, 96–9, 108–9, 112–20

346

Index

Cambridge Texts in the History of Political Thought

Titles published in the series thus far

Aristotle *The Politics* (edited by Stephen Everson)

Arnold *Culture and Anarchy and Other Writings* (edited by Stefan Collini)

Bakunin *Statism and Anarchy* (edited by Marshall Shatz)

Bentham *A Fragment on Government* (introduction by Ross Harrison)

Bernstein *The Preconditions of Socialism* (edited by Henry Tudor)

Bodin *On Sovereignty* (edited by Julian H. Franklin)

Bossuet *Politics Drawn from the Very Words of Holy Scripture* (edited by Patrick Riley)

Burke *Pre-Revolutionary Writings* (edited by Ian Harris)

Cicero *On Duties* (edited by M. T. Griffin and E. M. Atkins)

Constant *Political Writings* (edited by Biancamaria Fontana)

Diderot *Political Writings* (edited by John Hope Mason and Robert Wokler)

The Dutch Revolt (edited by Martin van Gelderen)

Filmer *Patriarcha and Other Writings* (edited by Johann P. Sommerville)

Gramsci *Pre-Prison Writings* (edited by Richard Bellamy)

Harrington *A Commonwealth of Oceana* and *A System of Politics* (edited by J. G. A. Pocock)

Hegel *Elements of the Philosophy of Right* (edited by Allen W. Wood and H. B. Nisbet)

Hobbes *Leviathan* (edited by Richard Tuck)

Hooker *Of the Laws of Ecclesiastical Polity* (edited by A. S. McGrade)

John of Salisbury *Policraticus* (edited by Cary Nederman)

Kant *Political Writings* (edited by H. S. Reiss and H. B. Nisbet)

Lawson *Politica sacra et civilis* (edited by Conal Condren)

Leibniz *Political Writings* (edited by Patrick Riley)

Locke *Two Treatises of Government* (edited by Peter Laslett)

Luther and Calvin on Secular Authority (edited by Harro Höpfl)

Machiavelli *The Prince* (edited by Quentin Skinner and Russell Price)

Malthus *An Essay on the Principle of Population* (edited by Donald Winch)

Marsiglio of Padua *Defensor minor* and *De translatione Imperii* (edited by Cary Nederman)

James Mill *Political Writings* (edited by Terence Ball)

J. S. Mill *On Liberty*, with *The Subjection of Women* and *Chapters on Socialism* (edited by Stefan Collini)

Milton *Political Writings* (edited by Martin Dzelzainis)

Montesquieu *The Spirit of the Laws* (edited by Anne M. Cohler, Basia Carolyn Miller and Harold Samuel Stone)

More *Utopia* (edited by George M. Logan and Robert M. Adams)

Nicholas of Cusa *The Catholic Concordance* (edited by Paul E. Sigmund)

Paine *Political Writings* (edited by Bruce Kuklick)

Price *Political Writings* (edited by D. O. Thomas)

Priestley *Political Writings* (edited by Peter Miller)

Pufendorf *On the Duty of Man and Citizen according to Natural Law* (edited by James Tully)

The Radical Reformation (edited by Michael G. Baylor)

Herbert Spencer *The Man versus the State* and *The Proper Sphere of Government* (edited by John Offer)

Vitoria *Political Writings* (edited by Anthony Pagden and Jeremy Lawrance)

William of Ockham *A Short Discourse on Tyrannical Government* (edited by A. S. McGrade and John Kilcullen)